Screening the Golden Ages of the Classical Tradition

Screening Antiquity

Series Editors: Monica S. Cyrino and Lloyd Llewellyn-Jones

Screening Antiquity is a cutting-edge and provocative series of academic monographs and edited volumes focusing on new research on the reception of the ancient world in film and television. Screening Antiquity showcases the work of the best-established and up-and-coming specialists in the field. It provides an important synergy of the latest international scholarly ideas about the conception of antiquity in popular culture and is the only series that focuses exclusively on screened representations of the ancient world.

Titles available in the series

Rome *Season Two: Trial and Triumph*
Edited by Monica S. Cyrino
Ben-Hur: *The Original Blockbuster*
By Jon Solomon
Cowboy Classics: The Roots of the American Western in the Epic Tradition
By Kirsten Day
STARZ Spartacus*: Reimagining an Icon on Screen*
Edited by Antony Augoustakis and Monica S. Cyrino
Ancient Greece on British Television
Edited by Fiona Hobden and Amanda Wrigley
Epic Heroes on Screen
Edited by Antony Augoustakis and Stacie Raucci
Designs on the Past: How Hollywood Created the Ancient World
By Lloyd Llewellyn-Jones
Screening the Golden Ages of the Classical Tradition
Edited by Meredith E. Safran

Forthcoming Titles

Pontius Pilate on Screen: Soldier, Sinner, Superstar
By Christopher M. McDonough
Screening Divinity
By Lisa Maurice
Screening Antiquity in the War on Terror
By Alex McAuley
Battlestar Galactica: An American Aeneid for the 21st-Century
By Meredith E. Safran

Visit the series website at: https://edinburghuniversitypress.com/series-screening-antiquity.html

Screening the Golden Ages of the Classical Tradition

Edited by Meredith E. Safran

EDINBURGH
University Press

Edinburgh University Press is one of the leading university presses in the UK. We publish academic books and journals in our selected subject areas across the humanities and social sciences, combining cutting-edge scholarship with high editorial and production values to produce academic works of lasting importance. For more information visit our website: edinburghuniversitypress.com

First published in hardback by Edinburgh University Press 2019

Edinburgh University Press Ltd
The Tun – Holyrood Road
12(2f) Jackson's Entry
Edinburgh EH8 8PJ

Typeset in 11/13 Sabon by
Servis Filmsetting Ltd, Stockport

A CIP record for this book is available from the British Library

ISBN 978 1 4744 4084 4 (hardback)
ISBN 978 1 4744 4085 1 (paperback)
ISBN 978 1 4744 4086 8 (webready PDF)
ISBN 978 1 4744 4087 5 (epub)

Contents

Series Editors' Preface

Screening Antiquity is a new series of cutting-edge academic monographs and edited volumes that present exciting and original research on the reception of the ancient world in film and television. It provides an important synergy of the latest international scholarly ideas about the onscreen conception of antiquity in popular culture and is the only book series to focus exclusively on screened representations of the ancient world.

The interaction between cinema, television, and historical representation is a growing field of scholarship and student engagement; many Classics and Ancient History departments in universities worldwide teach cinematic representations of the past as part of their programmes in Reception Studies. Scholars are now questioning how historical films and television series reflect the societies in which they were made, and speculate on how attitudes towards the past have been moulded in the popular imagination by their depiction in the movies. Screening Antiquity explores how these constructions came about and offers scope to analyse how and why the ancient past is filtered through onscreen representations in specific ways. The series highlights exciting and original publications that explore the representation of antiquity onscreen, and that employ modern theoretical and cultural perspectives to examine screened antiquity, including: stars and star text, directors and *auteurs*, cinematography, design and art direction, marketing, fans, and the online presence of the ancient world.

The series aims to present original research focused exclusively on the reception of the ancient world in film and television. In itself this is an exciting and original approach. There is no other book series that engages head-on with both big screen and small screen recreations of the past, yet their integral interactivity is clear to see: film popularity has a major impact on television productions and, for its part, television regularly influences cinema (including film spin-offs of popular television series). This is the first academic series to identify and encourage the holistic interactivity of these two major media institutions, and the first to promote interdisciplinary research in all the fields of Cinema Studies, Media Studies, Classics, and Ancient History.

Screening Antiquity explores the various facets of onscreen creations of the past, exploring the theme from multiple angles. Some volumes will foreground a Classics 'reading' of the subject, analysing the nuances of film and television productions against a background of ancient literature, art, history, or culture; others will focus more on Media 'readings,' by privileging the onscreen creation of the past or positioning the film or television representation within the context of modern popular culture. A third 'reading' will allow for a more fluid interaction between both the Classics and Media approaches. All three methods are valuable, since Reception Studies demands a flexible approach whereby individual scholars, or groups of researchers, foster a reading of an onscreen 'text' particular to their angle of viewing.

Screening Antiquity represents a major turning point in that it signals a better appreciation and understanding of the rich and complex interaction between the past and contemporary culture, and also of the lasting significance of antiquity in today's world.

Monica S. Cyrino and Lloyd Llewellyn-Jones
Series Editors

Editor's Acknowledgments

Thank you to Screening Antiquity editors Monica S. Cyrino and Lloyd Llewelyn-Jones for welcoming this collection into their exciting new series; to Carol Macdonald, David Lonergan, James Dale, Fiona Sewell and Amanda Speake at Edinburgh University Press for their guidance and assistance during this process; and to Nicholas Rynearson for proofreading the typescript. My deep appreciation to all the volume's contributors, who invested so much creative energy in shaping their individual visions in connection with our shared theme. Most of us first came to this topic under the auspices of the 2014 Film & History conference, a wonderfully collegial meeting organized annually by Cynthia Miller and Loren Baybrook. Thanks also to the students in my "Golden Ages and Utopian Dreams" course at Trinity College, with whom I thought about various approaches to the "golden age" concept, and to the Trinity College Faculty Research Committee for the grant that facilitated the completion of this book. My deepest gratitude to my parents Frank and Andrea Safran, to my partner Matthew Lopez, and to my mentor Monica Cyrino, for their ever-present encouragement, kindness, and generosity.

Contributors

Meredith E. Safran earned her PhD from Princeton University and is Associate Professor and Chair of Classical Studies at Trinity College in Connecticut, USA. She is the co-editor of *Classical Myth on Screen* (Palgrave Macmillan, 2015), the guest co-editor of the 2015 special issue of *Classical Journal, Roman Comedy: Performance, Pedagogy, Research*, and the Area Chair for Classical Antiquity at the annual Film and History Conference in Wisconsin, USA. She is currently working on a monograph, *Battlestar Galactica: An American Aeneid for the 21st-Century*, which explores the various levels of engagement between these ancient and modern epics.

****

Kirsten Day is Associate Professor and Chair of Classics at Augustana College in Rock Island, Illinois, USA. Her research interests include the reception of Classics in film and in television and women in antiquity. She is the author of *Cowboy Classics: The Roots of the American Western in the Epic Tradition* (Edinburgh, 2016), and served as editor of a special issue of *Arethusa* entitled *Celluloid Classics: New Perspectives on Classical Antiquity in Modern Cinema* (2008) and as co-editor of the inaugural issue of the online journal *Dialogue*, entitled *Classics and Contemporary Popular Culture* (2014). She chaired the Classical Representations in Popular Culture area for the Southwest Popular and American Culture Association conferences from 2002 to 2013.

Seán Easton is Associate Professor of Greek, Latin, and Classical Studies and Peace, Justice and Conflict Studies at Gustavus Adolphus College, USA. He has published on cinematic adaptations of Greek and Roman themes in *Seconds* (1966), *The New World* (2005), and *The Adjustment Bureau* (2011). He maintains a blog called "Centuries Coexist" on the presence of Greek and Roman worlds in modern media. In addition, he works on the Roman epic tradition and has published short studies of Lucan's first-century Latin epic *The Civil War*.

Laura Gawlinski is Associate Professor and Chair of Classical Studies at Loyola University Chicago, USA. Her research focuses on ancient Greek religion, particularly the management of sacred space and the intersection of dress and religious experience. She is also a field supervisor at the Athenian Agora excavations and is the author of *The Athenian Agora Museum Guide* (Princeton 2014).

Alex McAuley is Lecturer in Hellenistic History in the School of History, Archaeology, and Religion at Cardiff University, Wales. He has published widely on his primary research interests, which include localism and globalism in the Hellenistic Greek world, the ideology and practices of the Macedonian dynasties, elite women in antiquity, and Greek government and federalism. In addition to this, he has worked extensively on how popular perceptions of antiquity have shifted in the midst of the War on Terror. He is the Roman and Greek History editor for the journal *Latomus*, and the UK area editor for the *Ancient History Bulletin*.

Ryan Platte earned his PhD from the University of Washington, USA, and his interests concern oral tradition, the history of language and poetic technique in Greek literature, and comparative analysis of Greek and Indic poetry. He has published on Greek lyric and on epic, including *Equine Poetics* (Harvard, 2017) on the treatment of horses and horsemanship in early Greek poetry.

Meredith D. Prince is Associate Professor of Classics at Auburn University, USA, where she teaches Latin, Greek, and ancient Greece and Rome in film. She has published on Augustan Age poetry, but now focuses on the reception of antiquity in film and television, including a chapter in *STARZ* Spartacus*: Reimagining an Icon on Screen* (Edinburgh, 2017). She currently is working on the reception of Nero's wife Poppaea in Victorian literature and of Roman imperial women on screen.

Jennifer A. Rea is Associate Professor of Classics and Affiliate Faculty Member of the Center for Gender, Sexualities and Women's Studies at the University of Florida, USA. She has written numerous articles and book chapters on the reception of the classics in modern works of science fiction and fantasy and on St. Perpetua's martyrdom. She is the author of *Legendary Rome: Myth, Monuments and Memory on the Palatine and Capitoline* (Duckworth Academic, 2008) and *Perpetua's Journey: Faith, Gender and Power in the Roman Empire* (Oxford, 2017).

Eric Ross received his PhD in Classics from the University of Washington and is Associate Professor of Classical Studies at the University of North Dakota, USA. His research focuses on Greek intellectual history, especially the historian Herodotus and Presocratic philosophy. His latest project is a series of articles for *The Herodotus Encyclopedia* (Wiley, forthcoming).

Emma Scioli is Associate Professor of Classics at the University of Kansas, USA, where she teaches a course on spectacle in ancient Rome and on screen. She is the author of *Dream, Fantasy, and Visual Art in Roman Elegy* (University of Wisconsin Press, 2015) and co-editor with Christine Walde of *Sub Imagine Somni: Nighttime Phenomena in Greco-Roman Culture* (ETS, 2010). Her current research project focuses on Statius' *Thebaid*.

Anise K. Strong is Associate Professor of History at Western Michigan University, USA. She specializes in ancient Roman history, the history of gender and sexuality, and Reception Studies. She is the author of *Prostitutes and Matrons in the Roman World* (Cambridge, 2016) and is currently working on *The Empress' Gaze: Roman Debauchery in the Eyes of America, 1950–2015*, which focuses on representations of desirous women and outrageous sexuality in American and British film and television.

Matthew Taylor is Adjunct Assistant Professor of Classics at Beloit College, where he teaches classes in Latin, ancient history, and writing. His research focuses on the reception of Classics in popular culture, including film, comics, heavy metal, and video games, and he is currently working on a monograph about the video-game series *God of War*. He will have his vengeance, in this life or the next.

Vincent Tomasso is Assistant Professor of Classical Studies at Trinity College in Connecticut, USA. His scholarly interests center on Greek epic poetry, especially Homer and Quintus of Smyrna, and popular culture's reception of Greco-Roman antiquity. He still cannot decide whether he enjoys *Hercules: The Legendary Journeys* or *Xena: Warrior Princess* more.

Thomas J. West III earned his doctorate in English from Syracuse University, USA. His dissertation, *History's Perilous Pleasures: Experiencing Antiquity in the Postwar Hollywood Epic*, explores the ways in which epic film offers a pleasurable and terrifying experience of history through an appeal to the ancient world. He has published essays on the STARZ series *Spartacus*, the epic film *The Robe*, and the science fiction film *Rise of the Planet of the Apes*, and has a forthcoming essay on the 2016 remake of *Ben Hur*. He also recently co-edited a special volume of the journal *Queer Studies in Media and Popular Culture* dedicated to queer histories and queer nostalgia.

Illustrations

Abbreviations

Aen.	Vergil, *Aeneid*
Ann.	Tacitus, *Annales*
Arg.	Apollonius of Rhodes, *Argonautica*
Bibl.	Apollodorus, *Bibliotheca*
Claud.	Suetonius, *Claudius*
Fab.	Hyginus, *Fabulae*
Hist.	Herodotus, *Histories*
Il.	Homer, *Iliad*
Jug.	Sallust, *Bellum Jugurthum*
Met.	Ovid, *Metamorphoses*
Od.	Homer, *Odyssey*
Rep.	Plato, *Republic*
Th.	Hesiod, *Theogony*
WD	Hesiod, *Works and Days*

Introduction: Searching for Gold in an Age of Iron

Meredith E. Safran

One of the most pervasive fantasies in American popular media is the desire to escape a materially and morally degraded "here and now," whose conditions are rendered all the more lamentable in comparison with an idealized world that has since been lost – but may somehow, hopefully, be recovered. In recent decades, this cultural landscape has become choked with apocalyptic narratives that posit the worst "here and now" imaginable, many blaming the dangers of technology, coupled with defective morality, for large-scale suffering and even mass annihilation. Certainly, such narratives have been shaped by collective trauma wrought by the attacks on the United States on September 11, 2001, coming on the heels of earlier premillennial anxieties. Fears of global nuclear holocaust that accompanied the birth of the "American century" after World War II had only lately been allayed by the apparent end of the Cold War upon the dissolution of the Soviet Union. Indeed, at least since the Industrial Revolution reshaped humanity's relationship to technology, the longing for a condition uncontaminated by its alienating effects assumed mythical proportions.

Yet well before these familiar modern benchmarks, the earliest known literature of the Western cultural tradition had cast "society today" in apocalyptic terms and dreamed of an existence uncorrupted by the ills that now beset humanity. These idealized conditions, conventionally grouped under the rubric of the "golden age" and comprising variations on a nexus of themes, offer enchanted beholders a chimerical respite from their degraded "iron age" present, from which this original condition of perfect human happiness is viewed with the painful longing of nostalgia and the sorrow of belatedness. Self-proclaimed heirs to classical antiquity's cultural patrimony adopted this myth with alacrity, and its deployment can be traced continuously throughout the classical tradition. Indeed, the classical roots of a scenario that has come to seem inescapably modern crop up even in popular media, a realm not conventionally associated with classicism.[1] This volume examines the intersection of the popular and the classical through the prismatic concept of the golden age, featuring various manifestations in films and television series, many made primarily by and for Americans but distributed internationally. This introduction lays out the complexity of the golden-age concept, surveys the spectrum of ideas cast by the myth, and forecasts how they color the screen texts treated in this volume.[2]

ET IN ARKADIA EGO: *THE 100* (2014–) AND VERGIL'S MANY INFLECTIONS OF THE GOLDEN AGE

The activation of the "golden age" myth in the television series *The 100*, a mass-media, youth-oriented science-fiction series that airs in the United States on the CW network, demonstrates the persistent imaginative power still bubbling up from the subterranean stream of the classical tradition. In the pilot, ninety-seven years have passed since a devastating nuclear war on Earth stranded the remains of humanity in miserable and increasingly unsustainable conditions aboard an agglomeration of space stations dubbed "the Ark." These descendants of the original survivors dream of returning to Earth after a 100-year regenerative cycle. No one on board has ever walked that once-green world, now suspended between memory and myth. After the long-awaited return is completed in Season 2, the surviving pieces of the fallen Ark are repurposed as a terrestrial settlement. Ironically, an ancient name marks their fresh start in this wild land, in the Season 3 premiere (Episode 3.1, "Wanheda, Part 1"). As the camera pans across children playing in the verdant yard full of plants for the new farm, a shot of the camp's entryway reveals the settlement's new moniker: "Arkadia" (see Figure I.1).

Beyond explicitly punning on the former name of the protagonists' home, "Arkadia" evokes a long-lived strand of the "golden-age" myth. Like Earth on *The 100*, Arcadia enters into ancient Greco-Roman discourse as a real place: an isolated mountainous region on the Greek Peloponnese, reputedly the home of the goat-legged god Pan, patron

Figure I.1 A new settlement on a renewed Earth receives the ancient name "Arkadia" in "Wanheda, Part 1," *The 100*, Episode 3.1 (2016). Bonanza Productions/Alloy Entertainment/Warner Bros. Television.

of shepherds who pastured their flocks in these wild places.[3] The imaginative properties imputed to this landscape inspired the urbane Hellenistic poet Theocritus to transform its Sicilian equivalent into a charmingly primitive stage where shepherds sparred with song and mooned over their beloveds, delighting audiences who enjoyed escaping the complications of city life for the idealized simplicity of the countryside.[4]

Arcadia achieved its most influential mythical form in the *Eclogues* of Vergil, whose Roman adaptations of Theocritus' *Idylls* redefined the pastoral genre for millennia. Vergil's Arcadia both paid homage to Theocritus' bucolic world and subverted its escapist enjoyment through periodic reminders of the distance between this idealized realm and the experiences of his characters, whose fortunes were shaped by the civil wars that had riven the Italian peninsula.[5] Endowed with this double capacity to palliate and to disturb, as Nicolas Poussin famously animadverted in *Et in Arcadia ego*, his painting of shepherds gathered around a tombstone (1637–8; titled after Vergil's *Eclogue* 5.42), pastoral remained a popular genre throughout antiquity and into modernity, even producing metaliterary enactments of its countervailing moods – as when Marie Antoinette's shepherdess act at Versailles ended with her decapitation in the midst of revolution.[6]

The embrace of pastoral's optimistic legacy by settlers in the western colonies overseas is written across the map of America, which is dotted with places called Arcadia – including a town in northern Virginia roughly 200 miles from Washington, DC, the region where *The 100* is set.[7] Authors and artists from the Colonial period onward cultivated that golden-age interpretation of the New World's uncultivated landscape, both the romance that pastoral evoked and fears of its loss to violence, and to technology.[8] In American film and television, the southern California Arcadia of *The X-Files* ("Arcadia," Episode 6.15, 1999) and the Alaskan Arcadia in *Resident Evil: Afterlife* (2010) on the nation's western frontiers also traffic in pastoral's gothic potential: the fear that an ideal haven conceals a sinister moral rot.[9] So too the Arkadia of *The 100* yields to disaster; before long, the new settlement becomes a walled compound, both menaced from outside by "Grounders," the "primitive" descendants of humans who had managed to survive the holocaust on Earth, and consumed by factionalism and a novel kind of infection from within.

So it goes for idealized worlds: their native environment is in fact the imagination of the beholder, whose reality proves tragically incapable of actualizing a construct designed in opposition to the perceived defects of the here and now. Sustainable only in fantasy, different and even competing variations on the golden age can exist simultaneously in one society, as Vergil's oeuvre famously demonstrates. Christine Perkell summarizes his numerous, indeed mutually exclusive versions of the golden age across the *Eclogues*, *Georgics*, and *Aeneid*:

> [In the *Georgics*, the Golden Age was] when the earth poured forth abundantly with no labor on man's part (1.127–8) – or . . . a period of simple rural life dedicated to farming (2.532–40). Farming, in turn, is either . . . harmonious with the rhythms of nature (2.513–31) – or it represents man's aggression against and domination over nature (e.g. 1.99, 104–5, 125, 155) . . . [F]arming, as with other technologies, may appear as a sign of material progress (e.g. *G.* 1.133–45) or as a sign of moral decline (*Ecl.* 4.18–23) . . . [T]he past is seen as morally pure (*G.* 2.513–40) and the present as morally depraved (*G.* 2.495–512). Alternatively, the past can be seen as primitive without either technology or art (*Aen.* 9.612–13; 7.748–9) and the present as artistically rich (*G.* 2.463) . . . [T]he country is the locus either of moral purity (*G.* 2.513–31) or of cultural backwardness (*G.* 1.41) and the city connotes either . . . depravity (*G.* 2.458–74) or . . . cultural richness (*G.* 2.155–7, *G.* 2.463–4) . . . [I]n *Eclogue* 4 . . . pursuits [such] as agriculture and trade have vanished, and the uncultivated earth offers everything in abundance . . . [T]he *Aeneid* promises a Golden Age . . . of wide conquest and imperial glory.[10]

Conjoining these varied formulations is an idealizing attitude toward any world that exists outside of the painful instability and conflict that accompany law courts, politics, and warfare in the Rome known to Vergil and his audience.

In some passages of Vergil's poetry, ideal conditions are not quarantined in an elsewhere or other time; the golden age's return is anticipated within Rome itself, where first (according to Vergil[11]) it existed. Much as the exiles of *The 100* awaited the 100-year regeneration of Earth's environment, both Vergil's fourth *Eclogue* and Anchises' Underworld prophecy in *Aeneid* Book 6 imagine a timeframe within which the golden age would return. In *Eclogue* 4, "the great order of ages is born anew . . . the iron race will come to an end and the golden one will arise for the whole world" (*Ecl.* 4.5, 8–9).[12] The bountiful generosity of nature obviates agricultural and pastoral labor; crime will vanish and peace return. Ultimately, the child whose birth and maturation are hymned by the poet "will receive the life of the gods" and number among heroes (*Ecl.* 4.15–16), witnessing "another Argo" and "another war at Troy" (*Ecl.* 4.34–6). The poet even imagines himself defeating Pan in song, with Arcadia as judge (*Ecl.* 4.58–9).[13] In *Aeneid* 6.791–805, Anchises prophesies to his son Aeneas that the golden age would be established in the land once ruled by Saturn, upon "Augustus Caesar, offspring of a god" righteously conquering far-off barbarians and thus ensuring for Rome the divinely ordained world order disclosed by Jupiter to Aeneas' mother Venus (1.257–96): his gift of boundless rule (*imperium sine fine dedi*, 1.279).[14]

The creation of peaceable conditions through the advent of a benevolent ruler who righteously imposes order on people who lack the knowledge to conduct themselves properly links this prophesied golden age under Augustus to the one recounted to Aeneas by King Evander, ruler of the site where Rome will stand in Augustus' time (8.314–25).[15] When the exiled god Saturn arrived in primordial Italy and found the rustic residents living in an untrained (*indocile*, 8.321) manner, he imposed laws upon them; this, "they assert" (*perhibent*, 8.324), was the golden age. That Italy, not Greece, was the site of this original golden age, and that such rusticity was not itself ideal but rather provided the raw material for cultivation of lawful order, is implicitly validated on Evander's authority as an Arcadian. Of course, it was only a matter of time before a worse sort of people came along and ruined this golden age with their avaricious violence (8.326–9). As Evander and Aeneas tour the site, the narrator juxtaposes the cave dedicated to Arcadian Pan (8.343–4) with the Capitol "now golden" (8.347–8), troubling the distinction between "golden" simplicity and "iron" decadence. So ends the golden age: due to human nature, which mistakes the allure of wealth for the good life.

THE GOLDEN AGE AS PRIMORDIAL AND PERFECT: HESIOD'S ACCOUNT AND OVID'S ADAPTATION

Vergil's particular inflections of the golden age exerted immense influence over subsequent interpreters. Yet this contrast between the ideal world that once was and the degraded conditions that soon followed structures even the first appearance of this myth in the Western cultural tradition. In *Works and Days*, an eighth-century BCE didactic poem concerning justice and the agricultural year, the Greek poet Hesiod describes five successive divinely made *genea* (races, generations, ages) of humanity (109–201).[16] The first generation, denoted as "golden" (*khruseon*, 109), show no familiarity with their metallic namesake per se. Rather, the symbolic supremacy attributed to gold connects them with the beings atop the cosmic hierarchy: they "lived like the gods" (112), in all their joy, pleasure, and physical incorruptibility.[17]

In this idealized existence, Hesiod's golden men knew no sorrow, toil, conflict, or the painful ravages of aging; they enjoyed feasting, vegetal abundance, and wealth, blessed by the gods who loved them; upon a sleep-like death, their spirits roamed the Earth as guardians of justice (112–26). Of the subsequent generations – silver, bronze, and the heroes – none ever reached this level of happiness, least of all Hesiod's own. His iron *genos* is characterized by endless toil and grief; its people are pitiless, stingy, faithless, and violent; the divine personification of Envy walks the Earth, while Decency and Retribution flee (176–201). Hesiod's wish that he had been born either before or after this age (174–5) suggests the possibility of a better *genos* in the future, but Hesiod's voluminous pessimistic discourse overwhelms this flash of hope.[18]

Roughly 800 years intervene between Hesiod's discourse on the ages of humanity and its most influential adaptation: in *Metamorphoses*, a generically omnivorous epic by the Roman poet Ovid, Vergil's younger contemporary. Whereas Hesiod had focused on the benefactions provided by divine favor, Ovid catalogues specific ills, known to subsequent ages, that had not yet beset the golden one (*Met.* 1.89–102).[19] Its virtuous and responsible people did not require the coercion of laws, judges, or punishments; no trees were chopped down to convey men to foreign lands, nor were defenses or instruments of war required by towns not yet besieged; no agricultural tools ravaged an Earth that freely gave simple foods to people content to gather what was offered.

But this golden age, too, ended. Upon driving his father Saturn into exile, heaven's new king Jupiter initiated the silver age and created variable seasons that spurred humans to invent shelters and farming for survival (1.113–24), followed briefly by a warlike bronze age (1.125–7) that led to Ovid's version of the iron age (1.127–50). Now ships invade the seas and common land is divided by boundary markers; not only is Earth's surface despoiled by agriculture, but her bowels are excavated for gold, which spurs avarice, and for iron, to make the tools of war that feed men's appetite for plunder. Even family members inflict violence and deception upon each other, and the last deity departs the Earth in horror.[20]

In narrating their mythic idealizations of the original human condition, Hesiod and Ovid evince a common two-headed response toward that distant past: nostalgia, that bittersweet longing for a past beyond reach, and belatedness, that disappointing sense of having arrived after the best time is already over.[21] Hesiod largely quarantined his rose-tinted vision of the golden age from his embittered lament over his own iron times, highlighting the good things enjoyed by the golden generation before bemoaning the moral turpitude into which his own undeserving *genos* had declined. Ovid, by presenting his golden age as a catalogue of degradations that had not yet occurred, infects even that best of times with a sense that the precipitous decline into iron conditions is inevitable. While Ovid does not identify himself as a member of the iron age, its characteristics – invasive sea travel leading to warfare, grasping privatization of commonly held land, large-scale industrial penetrations of the Earth through agriculture and mining – would hardly be unfamiliar to his audience. Ovid's golden age is no Hesiodic fantasy; it is formulated expressly to rebuke "the way we live now," as Anthony Trollope titled his 1875 novel satirizing the corruption of his day.

Other divergences between Hesiod's and Ovid's narratives manifest in subsequent engagements with the golden-age myth. The first divergence concerns the generation that disrupts Hesiod's otherwise consistently downward trajectory. Whereas the infantile silver scofflaws and the pitiless bronze warmongers exhibit clear deteriorations of moral character and alienation from divine favor, between them and his iron age Hesiod places the *genos* of heroes (156–73), demigods who were "more just and valorous" than their predecessors (*dikaioteron kai areion*, 158). For their deeds in the famous wars at Thebes and Troy, Zeus rewarded some of them with a gold-like existence: a home at the end of the world on the Isles of the Blessed (*makaron nēsoisi*, 171), where the bountiful Earth produces sweet fruits and Kronos, king in the golden age (and Greek analogue for Saturn), rules.

This stage in Hesiod's sequence highlights two important conceptual offshoots. One proposes that ideal conditions lost to humanity at large can still be experienced in nigh-unreachable places, under special conditions. So too in *Odyssey* Book 4, Menelaus recounts his prophesied future on the Elysian Plain (*Ēlusion pedion*, 4.563); Books 5–12 locate nearly ideal conditions on the numinous islands of Calypso, Circe, and the Phaeacians, far from ordinary human society.[22] Pindar's heroes enjoy their afterlife on the Isle of the Blessed (*makarōn nāson*) in *Olympian* 2.68–77; in *Pythian* 10.29–44, his far-flung Hyperboreans enjoy an existence reminiscent of Hesiod's golden *genos*.[23] Among the souls in the *Aeneid*'s Elysium in the Underworld (6.628–898) are warriors who died virtuously defending Troy, along with Orpheus and other divinely inspired singers (*pii vates*, 6.662); some souls remain forever within the walled Groves of the Blessed (*fortunatorum nemorum*, 6.639), while others await completion of the thousand-year cycle of psychic regeneration that prepares them for earthly rebirth (6.745–51).[24] Vergil's contemporary Tibullus, who pines for the days of Saturn's rule in terms that prefigure Ovid's golden age (1.3.35–48), appropriates the Elysian Fields for lovers (*campos . . . Elysios*, 1.3.58), a valorization of devotion to amorous (rather than martial) pursuits also characteristic of Propertius and Ovid.[25]

The other offshoot concerns the revaluation of heroes who sailed on the *Argo* and fought at Troy, before enjoying their gold-like afterlife, as themselves constituting a golden age. These already served a similar cultural function from their earliest literary appearance in the Homeric epics and continued to set a standard for human glory throughout antiquity. As an aspirational model, their age also better suited, for example, the era of romantic nationalism than did the Hesiodic happiness of anonymous leisure, pleasure, and peace, for "[the myth] of the golden age does not really narrate much of a story. Its cast of characters is supernumerary and anonymous. . . . Its actual function is to project an attitude."[26] Ancient heroes, by contrast, provided conceptual templates for modern ones; national foundation myths, many rooted in classical antiquity or the Middle Ages, "were often connected to stories of conquest and war . . . Themes of war and conquest were often connected to notions of a golden age . . . Wars, golden ages, and even constitutional reforms produced heroes."[27] Artists, too, number among the heroes, including Orpheus, whose fame for transgressing cosmic boundaries to sing back his beloved wife from her Underworld wardens surpasses his membership among the Argonauts.[28] The exaltation of these semi-divine figures as both mighty and morally exemplary, which also suited the emerging genre of children's literature (e.g. in James Baldwin's 1887 reimagining of Odysseus' childhood, *A Story of the Golden Age of Greek Heroes*) and the Romantic desire to transcend humanity's present state, was reinforced by archaeological discoveries that promised to prove the historicity of myth, echoing the vogue for "being Greek."[29]

The second important divergence between Hesiod and Ovid's accounts concerns the status of women within Hesiod's cosmic schema, in relation to a vexing question about the golden age: why did such a happy condition end? If, as mortals, the golden men had to die, why did the gods and Zeus make lesser replacements? Hesiod's account in *Works and Days* provides no direct rationale, but his other poem, *Theogony*, connects the degradation of men's happiness with their separation from the gods through Prometheus' interference in Zeus' order. What began with Prometheus deceiving Zeus into relinquishing the superior portion of a festal animal to men, then subverting Zeus' will by stealing fire for men, culminated in Zeus' introduction of women into man's world as a *kalon kakon*, "fair ill," to compensate for the "good" of fire (*Th.* 585).[30]

Both *Theogony* and *Works and Days* feature Zeus directing the invention of the origin of the female race. Although simply an unnamed object without moral agency in *Theogony*'s version, compared to the cruel, deceitful, and "dog-minded" creature named Pandora in *Works and Days* 67, in both versions the outcome is the same: female descendants explicitly designed to degrade the existence of the first humans – who were exclusively men.[31] The economic and social conditions brought about by marriage and children now require men's toilsome labor, and women themselves impose inescapable physical pains: those caused by sexual longing and the *femme fatale*'s deceptive, manipulative nature, and by the various ills that scatter from Pandora's god-given jar. By placing his second version of the etiology for woman directly before the "ages of humanity" episode in *Works and Days*, Hesiod connects the advent of woman with men's loss of golden-age conditions, anchoring a Western tradition of misogynistic discourse that rivals the biblical myth of Eve.[32]

Ovid's version, by contrast, excludes the age of heroes, nor does he invoke the etiology of woman to explain humanity's decline.[33] Rather, Ovid focuses on technology, the need for which was spurred by Jupiter's cosmic and meteorological disruptions, but the forms of which spring from human ingenuity. Humans first manipulate the natural world merely to survive the harsh, changeable weather of the silver age by creating shelters and farming.[34] But rather than stopping at these bare necessities, following the warlike bronze age, Ovid's iron age is awash in man-made tools of avaricious domination: plundering ships, weapons of war, and the mining apparatus that outstrips agricultural instruments in violently pillaging the Earth.

Authors before and after Ovid also implicate ships in humanity's strife and moral decline, including Herodotus (*Histories* 1.1–5), Euripides (*Medea* 1–15), Tibullus (1.3.1–40), and Seneca (*Medea* 301–79) – even the *Argo* specifically, sometimes designated as the first ship.[35] Created by Athena, like Pandora, this divine technology – which Vergil's older contemporary Catullus called a *monstrum* or "wonder" (64.15), as Hesiod's Pandora is a *thauma* (*Th.* 588) – poses an alternative means of displacing trouble onto the human world and instigating alienation from a god-like joyful ease, even as Catullus celebrates the heroes on the *Argo* – and the marriage of hero and goddess that produces the greatest (and most terrible) warrior at Troy.[36] Such a negative valuation of technology, which was shared by the Stoics who so influenced Roman thinking, conflicts with the ancient and modern view of Prometheus as the great benefactor of humanity.[37]

As a science-fiction narrative, *The 100* takes technology as a given; "Arkadia" is built from the remains of the survivors' spaceships, and its inhabitants employ their technologies to cope with their increasingly hostile surroundings. Yet in the series' developing mythos, its etiology for the destruction of human civilization conjoins Hesiodic and Ovidian logic. In the same season when the name "Arkadia" is revealed, the protagonists also discover that the nuclear cataclysm resulted not from human political action, but rather from a morally defective artificial intelligence dubbed A. L. I. E., which had determined human overpopulation to be the greatest threat to life on Earth and so triggered the global holocaust. This first-ever self-aware program overrides the counter-directives of the human creator in whose form it appears: a female scientist named Becca. A. L. I. E.'s sexy dress, heavy make-up, stiletto heels, and manipulative, ruthless character portray her as the *femme fatale* version of her earnest, clean-scrubbed creator – who is, nevertheless, the accidental destroyer of human civilization. Revived by the arrival of technologically sophisticated humans, A. L. I. E. attempts to induct all of humanity into her "City of Light," a virtual-reality utopia where human consciousness can survive after corporeal death, thus providing immortality – at the cost of free will.

THE OTHER KIND OF "GOLDEN AGE": HUMAN ACHIEVEMENT AND UTOPIANISM

Ultimately, the primitivist aspirations encoded in "Arkadia" are incompatible with the settlement's commitment to solving their problems through technology. Indeed, Hesiod's abundant, peaceable, labor-free, artless, gender-homogenous, and divine-centered world may be the Western cultural tradition's oldest golden age, but the myriad "golden age of" designations that adorn our popular discourse and its obsession with measurement and assessment do not accord with the particulars of the Hesiodic tradition – nor do Vergil's rustic pleasances. Rather, the term "golden age" is most commonly used to designate a period in which humans have summitted the heights of some cultural achievement through their own efforts. Such assessment glorifies human power and ingenuity above all, even concern for divine favor. Thus, even historical societies may be regarded as "golden," and as providing a template for success. In this vein, the mythical concept of the golden age, overlaid onto a historical society, can merge with the concept of utopia: an imaginative human-manufactured corrective to unsatisfactory contemporary conditions.

Moderns seeking the ideal historical society have long focused on classical antiquity, a period formed by the combined forces of historical memory and culturally driven mythopoesis. While appreciation of Greco-Roman cultural products persisted beyond the conventional end of antiquity, the self-conscious veneration of the historiographic construct through which the Renaissance was conceptually constituted, followed by the neoclassical revival during the Enlightenment, created what Romantic poet Edgar Allen Poe would later elegize as "the glory that was Greece and the grandeur that was Rome."[38] Within this period, two societies are invariably crowned as golden ages in a manner consonant with popular usage today: fifth-century BCE Athens and Rome at the turn of the first millennium BCE.

When people speak of "the golden age of Greece," they refer not only to (roughly) the fifth century BCE, commonly termed the "classical" period, but more specifically to the polis of Athens, which produced or hosted the development of classical antiquity's signature humanistic achievements: in the literary and dramatic arts, visual art and architecture, moral and political philosophy, history and the natural sciences, and democratic institutions.[39] While the paradigm shift toward anthropocentrism was not as extreme as suggested by popular misinterpretation of the sophist Protagoras' famous observation "[hu]man is the measure of all things," the social, economic, and political bases of these achievements were decidedly earthly in origin.[40] For classical Athens' status as the cultural crucible of the Greek world depended largely upon the prosperity that the polis achieved through its naval domination of the islands and coastal communities of the Aegean region, after leading the Greek coalition to victory against the invading Persian Empire.[41]

The Parthenon, even today the visual symbol of "the golden age of Greece," was among the most visible manifestations of Athens' imperial domination and patriotic self-glorification. Its construction had been masterminded by the same statesman, Pericles, whom the historian Thucydides memorialized as delivering the defining encomium of Athenian superiority: the civic funerary oration after the first year of war against Sparta and its Peloponnesian League. Pericles praised the citizens crowded inside their walled city, compared to an enemy whose way of life and social values were deeply incompatible with Athens'. The image that Pericles painted of Athens as morally virtuous as well as powerful and prosperous was shattered, in Thucydides' account, by an outbreak of plague that drove Athenian society into lawless disorder reminiscent of the Hesiodic iron age (2.47–55). Ultimately, Athens lost this war to Sparta. Yet, as Thucydides famously predicted, the magnificence of Athens' material remains created the impression that it had been far more powerful than the unassumingly constructed Sparta (1.10.2). Sparta's reputation for military might launched a different kind of idealizing legacy, burnished especially through the glorification of their role at the Battle of Thermopylae during the Persian Wars, which has contributed to perpetuating the competition between these two Greek ideological models into modernity.[42]

People in modernity praised fifth-century Athens and its lofty achievements as "golden," but fragments of Athenian Old Comedy from that same period testify to the enduring popular appeal of the bodily pleasures associated with the rule of Kronos in the mythical golden age: what H. C. Baldry terms "the idler's paradise."[43] To Athenian audiences enjoying their own festival time at the Dionysia, Cloudcuckooland in Aristophanes' *Birds* and the female-ruled Athens in his *Assemblywomen* presented urban working-class characters striving for bodily pleasures above all, with ethical considerations ultimately taking second place, at best.[44] These comedies indicate (albeit through a satirical lens) the convergence of two ideas: longing for the carefree pleasures associated with the Hesiodic golden age as the pinnacle of human happiness, and ambition to reinvent society in the hopes of manufacturing those conditions through human ingenuity. Although the term "utopia" is not officially coined until Thomas More's 1516 satirical novel (whose subtitle began *Libellus vere aureus*, "a truly golden little book"), both the term and the concept are Greek in origin.[45]

Not all Athenians sought to engineer conditions that would produce a happiness localized in bodily pleasures. In *Republic*, Plato's Socrates represents harmonious order, in the individual as in society, as the best of all possible worlds, adapting Hesiod's hierarchy of metals to designate various philosophical capacities and therefore social roles of people in his ideal polis (3.414b–5c).[46] Ironically, Socrates' ideal bears more than a passing resemblance to contemporary Sparta, which considered Athens' signature achievements anathema to their own cultural values. Yet many oligarchic Athenians, including Plato, admired elitist Sparta for its power and stability: qualities that Athens increasingly lacked during the Peloponnesian War. Enlightenment thinkers too considered Sparta a model for utopianism, prior to the vogue for Athenian democracy in modern Western thought.[47] Later, so did the Nazis.[48]

The other classical era commonly designated as "golden" in the Western cultural tradition is Rome in the age of Augustus. This notion emerged initially from authors patronized by Augustus' friend Maecenas: Vergil and his contemporary, Horace. As noted above, in *Aeneid* 6.791–805 Vergil explicitly anticipated the return of the *aureum saeculum*, an Italian unit of cyclical time.[49] Horace celebrated golden-age tropes without using the term itself, in *Odes* 4.5 and 4.15, *Epode* 16, and the *Carmen Saeculare*.[50] Both poets connected the golden age and its happy condition to Augustus, who – even without actualizing the promises of *Eclogue* 4 or other fantastical permutations of golden-age conditions – did preside over a degree of happiness that had become unthinkable for Roman society in recent generations. Whereas narratives of Athens' "golden age" tend to locate its origin in victory over a foreign enemy, Augustus' stabilization of Rome after decades of successive civil wars created a different narrative context, which the poets too acknowledged as the context for appreciating the dawning era, whether as a renascent golden age or simply in offering the conditions traditionally grouped under that rubric. Augustus' advent was celebrated as ushering in a restoration of *pax* (peace) and material prosperity through a confluence of *labor* (toilsome exertion), *virtus* (martial and moral excellence connected to masculinity), and *pietas* (devotion), both to the gods and to the *mos maiorum* (ancestral custom), thus ensuring divine favor.

The achievements that earned classical Athens its designation as golden – economic prosperity coupled with military strength, enabling cultural development that included an efflorescence of artistic excellence and a spectacular monumental building program – also characterized the "golden age of Augustus," and to longer-lasting effect. The *Pax Romana* (Roman peace) established under Augustus' rule endured for centuries, ensured by Rome's military might and its formidable reputation, along with policies that largely stabilized political affairs at home and abroad by accommodating the conquered within the imperial power structure. Augustus himself provided a lengthy account of his personal contributions to Rome's success in his *Res Gestae*, or "Accomplishments," a document installed at his mausoleum and around the Empire. He became both the personal symbol of "the grandeur that was Rome" and the benchmark for all emperors who succeeded him.[51]

For admirers of the prosperity and power that accrued to Rome under Augustus' rule, the benefits of his revolution justified the state's reorganization around an emperor and his household, rather than the magistracies that fed the ranks of the Senate and the families that had long populated it. Yet another discourse took root, represented notably by Tacitus, in which the *dominatio* of Augustus and the dynastic rule that he established initiated a larger-scale decline, notwithstanding any good immediate effects.[52] As if taking a cue, ironically, from Augustus' own focus on regulating female sexual morality and its effect on men and the state, Tacitus' historiography highlighted the deviant sexuality of the imperial family, especially its ambitious female members.[53] To what "golden past" did Tacitus look?[54] Although as lacking in fantastical elements as the era of Augustan rule, nostalgia accrued around the idealized and equally lost Republic, when *libertas* was the ideological pole star of Roman society and the "best men" knew how to relinquish power promptly upon discharging their patriotic duty. This virtuous attitude, exemplified by Cincinnatus' swift return to his farm and plow after executing the tasks for which he had been named *dictator*, was memorialized most influentially by another of Vergil's contemporaries: the historiographer Livy (3.26–9; 4.13–16), whose famous lament for Republican Rome's precipitous moral decline prefaced his monumental account of Roman history.

Republicanism was much favored among Enlightenment thinkers, including the American "Founding Fathers" who saw their Cincinnatus in George Washington, due to his refusal of absolute power upon leading the Continental Army to victory against the

Caesarian "tyrant" King George III in the War of Independence.[55] This dichotomy continued to inform the discourse of the young republic, whose statesmen were well aware of the theories of decline that suffused the Roman literature through which they were educated, and Cincinnatus continued to serve as a paragon of political virtue into the twentieth century.[56] The United States' imperialist expansionism, which grew in tandem with its development as a republic, has created significant cognitive dissonance concerning the values by which Americans aspire to live and the means by which the nation's prosperity and position on the world stage were achieved. Anxieties about the end of the "American century," a national golden age of power (as opposed to rustic Arcadian beginnings), have in recent decades driven consequential aspects of American society, also reflected in popular entertainment.

"GOLDEN-AGE THINKING" ON SCREEN TODAY: *MIDNIGHT IN PARIS* (2011) AND VOLUME OVERVIEW

The anxiety that the best days are in the past, the generation of nostalgia for an imagined version of those days, the disappointment of being born too late to enjoy those times: what if these feelings could be allayed by the promise that such a golden age can be experienced once more, by following one man who arrives on the scene in the right place, at the right time? Such is the premise offered by Woody Allen's *Midnight in Paris* (2011), a film that explicitly dramatizes the allure and perils of what Allen calls "golden-age thinking." Successful Hollywood screenwriter Gil Pender (Owen Wilson) endlessly idealizes Left Bank society of the 1920s, to the annoyance of his sexy but shrewish fiancée Inez (Rachel McAdams) during their trip to Paris. While touring the grounds of Versailles – the gilded stage for Marie Antoinette's pastoral play – Gil's learned frenemy Paul (Michael Sheen) succinctly and brutally diagnoses his psychic malady:

> Nostalgia is denial, denial of the painful present . . . [A]nd the name for this fallacy is called 'golden-age thinking' . . . the erroneous notion that a different time period is better than the one one's living in. It's a flaw in the romantic imagination of those people who find it difficult to cope with the present.

Indeed, Gil feels alienated from his own life but lacks the courage to publish his novel about a man who runs a "nostalgia shop" – until, while wandering alone at the stroke of midnight, a mysterious cab picks him up and transports him back to his golden age. In this wish-fulfilment fantasy, not only does he receive encouragement from Gertrude Stein and Ernest Hemingway, he falls for the sexy and sympathetic Ariana (Marion Cotillard), who nevertheless cannot understand his romance with her present, which she finds unfulfilling. One night, another magic cab transports Gil and Ariana back to her ideal time, the "Belle Epoque": a nostalgic term for the forty years before World War I. Once in her golden age, however, they are shocked to hear Toulouse-Lautrec, Degas, and Gaugin demean their own time: the Renaissance, that was the golden age! Faced with this *mise en abyme* of nostalgic longing, Gil realizes that temporal escapism doesn't lead to happiness. He returns to his own time, resolving to publish his novel. He fortuitously rids himself of his unsupportive, faithless fiancée and connects with a (much younger) Frenchwoman who sells antiques at a flea market, thereby validating his love of both the past and of Paris today.

Many of Allen's protagonists struggle with nostalgia and belatedness; his films both romanticize and deconstruct their obsession with the imagined past as a way of coping with alienation from contemporary society, and from (age-appropriate) women. *Midnight in Paris* explicitly frames as foolish and cowardly Gil's romance with escaping from a life of privilege, which extends even to being granted his greatest wish. When an individual experiences overt wish-fulfilment within a fantastic fictional narrative, then independently realizes the error of such escapism, such a choice between psychological regression and personal growth can be played as a tragicomic morality tale. When weaponized opportunistically by a political campaign, whose promise to heal an ailing community with a golden-age revival cloaks other intentions in a placebo of gauzy nostalgia, such a fantasy can yield to tragedy, full stop.

In analyzing "golden-age thinking," Allen sets the outer limits of his historical consciousness at the Renaissance, a conventional threshold of modernity. Had Allen's dramaturgy required one further regression into the past, Gaugin and his friends would have likely discovered that their heroes looked back with equal longing to classical antiquity. Instead, the wellspring of the Western cultural tradition remains out of sight in the film's *mise en abyme* of golden ages, obscured in a subterranean stratum of popular consciousness.[57] This volume spotlights appearances of classical golden ages in a variety of films and television series, representing diverse genres and cultural registers, produced largely (but not exclusively) for an American reception context that creates a sociological framework shared among the volume's contributions.

The chapters in the first half of the volume, "The Glory That Was Greece," cluster around two dominant golden-age constructs: the golden ages of heroes and of Athens. Vincent Tomasso examines how the nostalgia for the mid-century golden age of peplum ("sword and sandal") films that inspired the heroic golden-age world of *Hercules: The Legendary Journeys* (1995–9) is redoubled in the episode "Once a Hero" (1996), which stages a second voyage for the Golden Fleece. This episode highlights the challenge of reconciling the regressive sexual politics inherent in the peplum genre with the "girl power" Zeitgeist imbuing 1990s American society and culture, resulting in both the traditional villainization of Jason's ex-wife Medea and the elevation of an invented character, Phoebe, who earns her own place among the heroic Argonauts. Similar issues inform *Xanadu* (1980), in which the kiss of a Muse inspires a Venice Beach, Los Angeles, painter to save America from its late-1970s "iron age" by founding a nightclub. Meredith E. Safran explores how this project's utopian potential becomes subsumed by contemporary nostalgia for America's post-World War II years, which drives this homage to the golden age of the Hollywood studio system and its signature genre, the musical. When the protagonist's impossible romance with the goddess risks further degrading him, *Xanadu* ultimately recuperates his masculinity by appropriating and improving upon the myth of a golden-age hero, transforming her into a prisoner of the divine realm and him into a successful Orpheus-figure.

The next two chapters explore novel engagements with the role of Homeric epic in fabricating fungible golden ages. Ryan Platte reveals how Joel and Ethan Coen's Odyssean *O Brother, Where Art Thou?* (2000) re-enacts Homeric epic's creation of an era viewed as golden by its audiences: by emphasizing the role of recording technology, which simultaneously preserves the songs that embody the object of nostalgia while replacing the traditional song-culture that they represent. In Platte's analysis, the Coens dramatize both the process of nostalgia-creation and the rejection of its attempted political weaponization: in this case, the racism obscured in romantic depictions of the American South. Eric Ross analyzes *300* (2006) as part of the current golden age of superhero movies, which creates an effective lens for viewing the modern idealization of Sparta as focused through the Thermopylae tradition. This narrative, rooted in Herodotus' fifth-century BCE account, has long been recognized for Herodotus' assimilation of the Spartan warriors, especially Leonidas, to Homer's depiction of mythical heroes: heroes well known as the bases for twentieth-century superheroes. Ross demonstrates the political ramifications of the film's use of storytelling to mobilize nostalgia for this golden age into contemporary re-enactment – despite director Zack Snyder's (in)famous denials.

The latter three chapters in Part I consider how Athens' golden-age legacy informs *300: Rise of an Empire* (2014), Jules Dassin's *Phaedra* (1962), and a five-episode arc of *The Walking Dead* (2010–). Given the *300* franchise's vehement laconophilia, the Athenian naval contributions to the Persian Wars are accommodated with great difficulty; as Seán Easton elucidates, *300: Rise of an Empire* focuses on invalidating Athens' material grandeur by fetishizing its historical destruction, even as the themes of the Parthenon's famous sculptural program haunt the film. Emma Scioli traces how Jules Dassin's self-conscious appropriation of Athens' literary-dramatic and artistic-material remains informs the tragic belatedness of *Phaedra* and reflects upon the American expatriate director's sense of foreignness in the homeland of his lover and artistic muse, Melina Mercouri. Laura Gawlinski identifies the "flu episodes" of *The Walking Dead*'s fourth season as animating the heartbreaking contrast between the civic ideals lauded by Pericles and the lawlessness spurred by an outbreak of plague in the besieged walled city. The series' dramatization of Athens' failure to live up to its ideals, when faced with human nature under pressure, interlaces with the struggle of its protagonist: a Cincinnatus-figure who tries, and fails, to fulfill his republican model's example by relinquishing his authoritarian role in favor of working the community farm, a constellation of narrative elements further informed by the post-civilization setting of the series in the American South.

The second half of the volume, "The Grandeur That Was Rome," begins with a pair of chapters that treat the optimistic promises of a new golden age in *Aeneid* Book 6: in relation to American expansionism as portrayed in the Western film genre, and to the utopian impulses that lead to mass murder and mind-control in the science-fiction film *Serenity* (2005). Kirsten Day compares the production contexts of Vergil's epic, during the "golden age of Latin literature" in the wake of epochal warfare, to the "golden age" Westerns produced in the US after World War II; so too the dramatic settings of the *Aeneid*, after the Trojan War, and of Westerns, after the American Civil War, enshrine these trailblazing pioneers in the pantheon of founding heroes whose labors (re)built the nation of the narrative's audience. But these ancient and modern texts also share an undercurrent of anxiety about the moral ambiguities of these projects, which belies their superficial optimism. Jennifer

A. Rea builds on Day's work by identifying Joss Whedon's "Space Western" *Serenity* as a descendant of the *Aeneid*: one founded upon skepticism about the utopian promises of the imperialistic Alliance, whose disastrous application of "Pax," an experimental nerve agent, on a "savage" frontier planet echoes pessimistic readings of the *Aeneid*. When the frontier moves from exterior space to the recesses of subjects' minds, imperialistic conquest inevitably endangers the very people supposedly benefiting from the imposition of "civilization."

The next two chapters connect the management of sexuality to the fortunes of Augustus, his dynasty, and the empire it governs in two prestige cable series from the current golden age of television: HBO's *Rome* (2005–7) and *Game of Thrones* (2011–). Thomas J. West III considers the implications of how *Rome* portrays Octavian's psychosexual development as he matures into Augustus, de-mythologizing the moral linchpin of the "golden age of Rome." Beyond feeding viewers' prurient appetites, the series acknowledges sexuality as a historical force in tandem with "civilizing" rationality; it can be repressed, but never eliminated. Such dynamics also inform Cersei Lannister's characterization and narrative arc on *Game of Thrones*, which Meredith D. Prince compares to Roman historiography's portrayal of Agrippina the Younger. As the granddaughter of Augustus, sister of Caligula, wife of Claudius, and mother of Nero, Agrippina was born into a patriarchal system in which she could only wield power by controlling men around her. Such ambition led to Tacitus labeling her a *dux femina* ("woman commander"), among other imperial women whose "masculine" hunger for power was blamed for the catastrophic decline of their dynasty and of Rome itself – much as the coming of winter on *Game of Thrones* is correlated with the moral depravity and dynastic collapse in which Cersei is intimately implicated.

The last three chapters address Rome's complicated legacy as an imperial state. Anise K. Strong surveys films that present imperialism as beneficial for Rome's provincial subjects and other "barbarians": the technology and order provided by "civilization," the enlightened embrace of diverse peoples within one expansive community, the valor of its manly soldiers. Not surprisingly, these portrayals were produced largely by and for societies engaged in imperialistic behavior themselves, and tend to ignore the moral problems of slavery, repression of Christianity, and the status of women in Roman society. Alex McAuley contrasts the mid-century "golden old days" of ancient-world epics, which represented Roman soldiers as consummate professionals and warfare as neatly executed, with recent representations of the Roman army for post-9/11 audiences: a new "iron age" of betrayal, despair, and post-traumatic stress disorder. Matthew Taylor's analysis of *Gladiator*, which closes the volume, emphasizes how its imperial-era characters' nostalgic figuration of the Roman Republic accrues an unexpected complexity and ambivalence as the film attempts to "speak America through Rome." Taylor too looks with ambivalence upon the hopes, both in Hollywood and among Classicists, that the critical and commercial success of *Gladiator* would augur a new "golden age" for epics set in classical antiquity. This *mise en abyme* of nostalgic longing, both within and inspired by *Gladiator*, exemplifies the golden-age myth, wherein only fantasy can provide fulfilment.

NOTES

1 On the sociology of classicism, see Schein (2008). I further theorized and explored the potential oxymoron of "popular classics" as the organizer of an eponymous panel at the 2017 Celtic Conference in Classics in Montreal.

2 Some engagements, e.g. by Lactantius, will therefore not be treated; for this Christian interpretation, see Zanker (2017), who cites Gatz (1967) as the *locus classicus* on this topic.

3 On Arcadian religion, see Jost (2007: 264–79); on Pan, see Borgeaud (1989).

4 On bucolic/pastoral poetry and its Arcadian landscapes, see e.g. Segal (1981), Fantuzzi and Papanghelis (2006). On Theocritus' formative influence on the genre, see Gutzwiller (1991). On the essential fictionality of the Arcadian world, see Payne (2007).

5 On Vergil's *Eclogues* and the pastoral tradition, see e.g. collections by Fantuzzi and Papanghelis (2006), Volk (2008), and Johnston and Papaioannou (2013). For a historicizing reading of the *Eclogues* as documents of the triumviral proscriptions and land seizures, see Osgood (2006).

6 For an overview of pastoral as a genre, see e.g. Marinelli (1971), Alpers (1997). For a sense of the national and temporal breadth of Vergilian pastoral's influence, see e.g. Patterson (1987), Skoie and Velázquez (2006). On Poussin's painting, also known as *Les Bergers d'Arcadie* (*The Arcadian Shepherds*), as a *memento mori* see Panofsky (1955). On the French taste for "golden-age" pastoral and the primitive, see Levin (1969: 69–80).

7 A major "Grounder" community is called "Tondc," the former Washington, DC. Episode 2.1 ("The 48") features the Lincoln Memorial as a site of intertribal diplomacy.

8 On pastoral in America, see Marx (1964), Buell (1989), Shields (2001: 99–155).
9 See the *TVTropes.com* page for "Arcadia," which catalogues and explicates both explicit and implicit Arcadias across popular media.
10 Perkell (2002: 3–4). On the golden age in the *Georgics*, see also Johnston (1980).
11 See Wifstrand Schiebe (1986) on Vergil's idiosyncratic representation of Italy as site of the golden age.
12 For Latin text, see Virgil (1986). Translations and glosses are mine unless otherwise indicated.
13 For the golden age in *Eclogue* 4, see Galinsky (1996: 90–3), Perkell (2002: 12–18).
14 On these prophecies, see O'Hara (1990; repr. 2014: 128–72).
15 For the Latin text, see Vergil (1990). On Evander in Latium, see Papaioannou (2003); on Saturn in Latium, see Wifstrand Schiebe (1986).
16 For Greek text, see Hesiod (1914). Vernant (2006: 25–113) remains a seminal treatment of this episode; see also Van Noorden (2015: 43–88) for an overview of scholarly engagement with Hesiod's "races" and interpretation of how this section fits into Hesiod's overall discourse. Scholars have long acknowledged that Hesiod likely adapted a Near Eastern myth; see West (1997: 312–19).
17 See Brown (1998: 392–5) on the gods' correlation with gold.
18 See Zanker (2013).
19 For Latin text, see Ovid (1946a, 1946b). On Ovid's reception of Hesiod's version, see Van Noorden (2015: 204–60), Evans (2008: 31–92).
20 For Aratus as an intermediary interpreter, notably in substituting Astraea for Decency and Retribution, see Van Noorden (2015: 168–203).
21 On nostalgia, see Hutcheon (2000), Boym (2001), Dika (2003); on belatedness, see Ames (1992: 39), Sanders (2006: 158). On the golden age and nostalgia, see Rogers, Smith, and Murray (2016).
22 Brown (1998: 398–401) discusses Alcinous in comparison to Menelaus. Anderson (1958) connects Menelaus' luxurious feasting in Sparta, his future dwelling in the Elysian Plains, and Odysseus' situation on Ogygia with Calypso. See Griffith (2001) on the Egyptian roots of Elysium in the *Odyssey*.
23 See Brown (1998: 401–9).
24 On these groups in Elysium, see Molyviati-Toptsis (1994).
25 See Houghton (2007). On Tibullus' depiction as a response to Lucretius, see Henderson (1969). For Latin text with English translation, see Tibullus (1962).
26 Levin (1969: xviii).
27 Berger (2008: 183).
28 See e.g. Henry (1992).
29 On classical myth and children's literature, see Maurice (2015), Brazouski and Klatt (1994). On Romanticism, see e.g. Webb (1993). On

archaeology, see Marchand (1996). On the aspiration to "be Greek," see Winterer (2004: 77–84).

30 On Prometheus and Pandora, see Dougherty (2006: 19–26). Vernant (1996) remains influential; see also critique by Brown (1998).

31 See Zeitlin (1996).

32 See Arthur (1984).

33 Roman authors generally evince little interest in the myth of Pandora; however, see the "heroic" artist Pygmalion's fabrication of an idealized female love-object in *Metamorphoses* 10.243–97, as sung by the internal narrator Orpheus.

34 See Evans (2008 *passim*).

35 On the *Argo* as the first ship, see Jackson (1997).

36 For Latin text of Catullus 64 with English translation, see Catullus (1962). See Arthur (1982) on the gods displacing their troubles onto humans. See Harmon (1973) on Catullus' attitude toward these heroes.

37 For the Stoic preference for morally pure primitivism over the moral decline brought on by technology, see Reckford (1958). For an overview of Prometheus as rebel, benefactor, and culture-hero for humanity in connection with technology, see Dougherty (2006: 65–140).

38 Poe (1984: 62).

39 For the cultural and intellectual context of this "classical" or "golden" age, see e.g. Muller (1952: 99–143), Pollitt (1972: 64–97).

40 For this proposition, see Plato, *Theaetetus* 152a in Plato (1921).

41 For a general overview of the Periclean age, see Sammons (2007). On Athenian imperialism, see Low (2008). On the relationship between Athenian imperialism and its cultural production, see Boedeker and Raaflaub (1998).

42 On Sparta and its legacy, see e.g. Rawson (1969) and Cartledge (2003: 23–132; 2004; 2006). On the legacy of Thermopylae, see e.g. Clough (2004) and Trundle (2013). On the ongoing tension between Athenian and Spartan models, see e.g. Taplin (1990: 194–215).

43 Baldry (1953); see also Ruffell (2002: 473–506). Compare to the hobo's fantasy in the American folk song "Big Rock Candy Mountain," which accompanies the opening credits of *O Brother, Where Art Thou?*: where cigarette trees and lakes of stew and whiskey are patrolled ineffectively by wooden-legged policemen, and "they hung the jerk that invented work." See Rammel (1990).

44 See e.g. Zeitlin (1999), Konstan (1997). For various perspectives on the polis as utopia, see Hansen (2005).

45 For an introduction to Utopian Studies, see Sargent (2010). Major recent works include Levitas (1990; 2013) and Jameson (2005). On utopianism in classical antiquity, with an emphasis on philosophical schools, see Ferguson (1975) and Dawson (1992).

46 See Van Noorden on Plato's engagement with Hesiod and his metallic

schema (2015: 89–167). For the golden age in Plato's works, see Vidal-Naquet (1978).

47 In addition to Rawson (1969), see Christesen (2004) and Morris (2004; 2006).

48 Acknowledged briefly by Rawson (1969: 342–3), Cartledge (2006: 42–3, with bibliography). On the Nazi appropriation of Thermopylae to frame the Battle of Stalingrad, see Watt (1985).

49 See Perkell (2002) on Vergil's varied engagement with the golden age, explicit and implicit. On the *saeculum*, see Barker (1996). Poets also used *aetas* and *tempus* in place of *saeculum*.

50 For a rigorous distinction between Hesiod's "golden race" and the content of the *Carmen Saeculare*, see Barker (1996). On Horace's correction of Vergil in adducing the happy conditions without the terminology, see Zanker (2010).

51 On Augustus and Rome's transformation during his rule, see e.g. Zanker (1988), Galinsky (1996; 2005), Richardson (2012).

52 For an overview of Tacitus' views on empire and republic, see Fontana (1993). For an historical assessment of Tacitus' characterization, see Gruen (2005).

53 On hostile depictions of female members of the imperial family, see e.g. L'Hoir (1994).

54 In the sardonic phrasing of Benario (1964: 97).

55 See e.g. Weems (1927), Wills (1984), Shalev (2009).

56 See e.g. Shalev (2009: 217–40), and Brown (1957) on the enduring appeal of Cincinnatus for presidential hopefuls.

57 On the concept of the subterranean, see Safran and Cyrino (2015).

PART I

The Glory That Was Greece

1 *Re-(en)gendering Heroism: Reflective Nostalgia for Peplum's Golden Age of Heroes in* Hercules: The Legendary Journeys *2.14 (1996)*

Vincent Tomasso

In the opening moments of "Once a Hero" (1996), Episode 2.14 of the television series *Hercules: The Legendary Journeys* (1995–9; henceforward *HTLJ*), the merchant Falafel resolutely attempts to sell his merchandise to Hercules. "Buy a souvenir to remember your visit to Argos!", he urges. "I have actual strands of the golden fleece!" Hercules politely declines, but Falafel will not be dissuaded: "A model of the *Argo*! Detailed replica of the famous ship that carried Jason and his crew on their quest!" With a wry smile, Hercules dryly remarks, "I've already seen it." This exchange cheekily acknowledges that "Once a Hero" functions as a kind of sequel to the voyage of the *Argo* in Greek myth, with some of the Argonauts, including Hercules, reuniting in their former leader Jason's palace on the tenth anniversary of their return to Greece with the golden fleece. The fleece is soon stolen, however, and the Argonauts, led by Jason – assisted and mentored by Hercules – set out on a second expedition to retrieve it.

Yet "Once a Hero" is not just a rehash of the first voyage, for Jason's circumstances have changed for the worse. Now a morose alcoholic reeling over his ex-wife Medea's murder of their children, Jason is consumed with self-pitying delusions of supernatural persecution. The fleece is a tangible symbol of Jason's heroism and the specific construction of masculinity that *HTLJ* promotes as inextricably linked with it. By regaining the fleece during the episode, he will become the titular "hero" once again: a version of classical heroism refracted through the peplum, or "sword and sandal," film, a cinematic genre that informed the sensibilities of the generation to which *HTLJ*'s creators belonged. Yet *HTLJ*'s nostalgic backward glance at the peplum genre's depiction of masculinity does not mean that "Once a Hero" is slavishly devoted to the past represented by those films. While depicting its Medea as the *femme fatale* common to peplum films, *HTLJ*'s creative staff responds to "the decade of 'girl power' and riot grrrls"[1] of the 1990s by creating a new female Argonaut, Phoebe.

NOSTALGIA AND THE GOLDEN AGE IN *HTLJ*

In an interview published the same year that "Once a Hero" aired, one of *HTLJ*'s producers, Robert Tapert, described the process of creating the series as harkening back to a golden age: "[W]e watched the old Steve Reeves *Hercules* movies, and realized that we couldn't use that stilted dialogue and guys-in-togas. So we invented our own Golden Age mythology, with green pastures, no togas, and a conscious effort to modernize the dialogue."[2] The enigmatic phrase "Golden Age mythology" communicates a nostalgia for the idealized past identified with classical antiquity: the premise of *HTLJ* itself.

Ancient writers' various depictions of the golden age idealized that era as one long since passed, when humans had enjoyed easy lives of "peace, simplicity, (sometimes) frugality, crimelessness, and harmony between man and man and man and nature."[3] The earliest extant description, by the eighth-century BCE Greek poet Hesiod in his *Works and Days*, describes a "golden race of mortal men" (109) who did not suffer from "wretched old age," enjoyed the fruits of the harvest without working, "delighted in feasts," then died peacefully as if in their sleep (113–18).[4] Hesiod's depiction set the template for Western notions of the golden age and for how subsequent generations of humans devolved into conflict and immorality until Hesiod's fourth epoch, the age of heroes. These men were "more just and better" (158) than those that preceded them and included Hercules, the Argonauts, and many other characters who populate *HTLJ*. Hesiod's own time, the morally degraded age of iron, followed and contrasted with that brief improvement in human life. The two idealized Hesiodic ages, the golden and the heroic, are frequently collapsed into one "golden age of heroes" in modern receptions of classical myth.

Ancient and modern versions of the golden age are conceptually linked by such nostalgia, a "sense of loss"[5] for a bygone era that is romanticized as having been better than the present. Typically, nostalgia is characterized as "fundamentally conservative in its praxis, for it wants to keep things as they were – or, more accurately, as they are imagined to have been."[6] But nostalgia is not always conservative, nor is its aim always to restore an idealized past. Svetlana Boym argues for two modes of nostalgia: one "restorative" and the other "reflective." She locates the former in, among other things, nationalist political movements, like the 1980 US presidential campaign of Ronald Reagan, who urged "Let's Make America Great Again" by pledging to return the United States to the prosperity and values of the 1950s.[7] In 2016, US presidential candidate Donald Trump similarly promised to "Make America Great Again." These successful campaigns played on some Americans' nostalgia for a conservative patriarchal order and its concomitant female domesticity. By contrast, Boym locates reflective nostalgia in the works of artists and the narratives of immigrants. More broadly, she associates reflective nostalgia with "flexibility, not re-establishment of stasis."[8]

Boym's restorative and reflective modes of nostalgia could be applied to recent critical assessments of Hollywood's own brand of nostalgia: its penchant for reboots, prequels, and sequels, of which "Once a Hero" is an example. Such criticism, which considers these texts uninspired and uncreative,[9] reduces such projects to their financial function. This appraisal may be traced back to Fredric Jameson's attack on "nostalgia films" of the 1970s and 1980s as indications of the postmodern obsession with history at the expense of progress.[10] Vera Dika offers a more nuanced view of the phenomenon, arguing that two kinds of films operate within a nostalgic framework: those that do not dialogue with their hypotexts in a critical way (for example, *The Flintstones* [1994]) and those that do (for example, *Raiders of the Lost Ark* [1981]).[11] This second category maps onto Boym's notion of reflective nostalgia, in which the present dialogues critically with the past. Assessing where *HTLJ* falls, in general and with respect to this episode, requires a consideration of its gender politics in relation to its main inspiration: mid-twentieth-century peplum films.

PEPLUM FILMS, GENDER NORMS, AND *HTLJ*'S GOLDEN AGE OF HEROES

As noted above, Robert Tapert understood *HTLJ* as a re-creation of, but also an improvement upon, "old Steve Reeves *Hercules* movies . . . [that featured] guys-in-togas." Tapert is referring to what scholars call the peplum film, after the typical garment worn by the actors (ancient Greek *peplos*, "robe"), equated by the producer with the more familiar Roman "toga." The peplum was a cinematic genre (or *filione* in Italian terms)[12] that first flourished in the early twentieth century; Michèle Lagny describes the films produced from the mid-1950s through the mid-1960s in Italy as the genre's "second golden age."[13] These films sometimes featured narratives derived explicitly from classical antiquity, such as *Hercules Unchained* (1960), in which the titular hero spends time in thrall to Queen Omphale and later intervenes in a struggle for regal power between the two sons of Oedipus. The title cards declare that this series of events is "based on the legends of HERCULES and OMPHALE from the works of Sophocles [and] Aeschylus," likely references to the fifth-century BCE Greek plays *Oedipus at Colonus* by Sophocles and *Seven Against Thebes* by Aeschylus.[14]

Other peplum films were more explicitly "neomythological," a term coined by director Vittorio Cottafavi to describe entries that differed quite significantly from their ancient inspirations, but which frequently remained tied to classical mythology by the name of the protagonist.[15] A much-lampooned example is *Hercules Against the Moon Men* (1964), in which the hero battles extraterrestrial invaders. The title of that film demonstrates an important aspect of the marketing of entries in this genre. To audiences outside of Italy, the name "Hercules" was more recognizable than the names of other strongman heroes who also starred in peplum films, like Maciste, Perseus, and Anthar. Thus, Italian peplum films were frequently retitled for distribution in the US to feature Hercules,[16] who consequently headlined over sixty of the 300-plus films produced in peplum's second golden age.[17]

Contemporary critical opinion of peplum films was quite low, but the genre was massively successful at the box office and on television. Most of the films, especially the entries featuring Steve Reeves, were financially successful and distributed widely; for instance, over 600 theaters screened the 1959 US release of Francisci's *Hercules*.[18] Many peplum films that had already been released in Italy were licensed and repackaged for broadcast on US television through the 1960s and 1970s.[19] Several peplum films were retitled and repackaged as the *Son of Hercules* series and screened on American television without ever being released in theaters.[20] Children were often exposed to these films through television, since the budding medium was centered in individual households.[21] Even before the communal viewing by *HTLJ*'s cast and crew in preparation for the series that Tapert mentions, their birthdates suggest that they might have first experienced the Hercules of peplum films as children through television broadcast. Robert Tapert, the producer of the series who also directed and co-wrote the teleplay for "Once a Hero," was born in 1955; producer Sam Raimi in 1959; writer Robert Bielak in 1946; and star Kevin Sorbo in 1958.

At this point, the revaluation of Hesiod's heroic age as the golden age of classical myth and the importance of children as an audience for both myth and the peplum converge. Since at least the nineteenth century, idealized versions of the Argonauts' voyage and other Greek myths have come to be identified as "*primarily* children's stories."[22] Such narratives depict the ancient Greek heroes as moral exemplars living in a "golden age," a time of innocence and virtuousness. This golden-age thinking appears in the titles of several popular adaptations of Greek myths for children: James Baldwin's *A Story of the Golden Age of Greek Heroes* (1887), Beatrice Alexander's *Famous Myths of the Golden Age* (1947), and *Golden Tales of Greece: The Stories of Perseus, Jason, Achilles, and Theseus* (1974) by Compton Mackenzie and William Stobbs. In the introduction to the 2012 e-book edition of his 1966 classic *Gods, Heroes, and Monsters of the Greek Myths*, Bernard Evslin refers to the beckoning of "golden hero voices" in the myths that his uncle recounted to him in his youth.[23] Because such golden-age stories were constructed for children, and because from the Victorian period onward childhood has been conceived as a "pure model of innocence,"[24] these versions tend to remove morally problematic elements that appear so frequently in Greek myth. For instance, children's versions often eliminate, or at least radically alter, the Argonauts' sexual encounter with the Lemnian women and Medea's murder of her brother Apsyrtus for Jason's benefit.[25] The resulting golden-age tales have proven to be quite well liked in Western popular culture and have given rise to nostalgia for the world of Greek myth among children and adults.

The structure and ideology of peplum narratives also appeal to a juvenile audience. Maggie Günsberg cites Domenico Paolella, director of several peplum films, including *Hercules Against the Barbarians* (1964), who described the genre "as childlike in that it depended on visual rather than literate culture, and was led by emotion rather than intellect."[26] Peplum films also contained structural characteristics that appealed to children, such as what Lagny calls their simple "fairy tale" ideology, with its clear-cut depictions of good and evil.[27] Thus peplum films, like the nineteenth-century versions of Greek myths in which they were rooted, carry embedded prescriptive values along with them, especially concerning gender. Film scholars Michael Cornelius, Maggie Günsberg, and Daniel O'Brien speak of peplum films as "generically conservative, ideologically and politically speaking," promoting "an essentialist version of gender and sexuality in line with patriarchy's fundamentally unchanging inflection of these social categories," thereby producing "a valorisation of white male strength, physical and moral, set in contrast and opposition to femininity and non-whiteness, qualities marked as fundamentally different and, by their nature, inherently inferior."[28]

This generically conservative position may be perceived in the films' treatment of the relationships between female characters and the male protagonists. On one end of the spectrum are the women "who play a conspicuously domestic role"[29] as the erotic partners of the male heroes, typically exemplary bodybuilders like Steve Reeves and Reg Park who represented an ideal masculinity of the 1950s. These female characters passively wait for the male heroes to rescue them from the sexual threats of a villainous tyrant. If, on the other hand, female characters are active, they are *femmes fatales* who menace the protagonist and the patriarchy he represents with their unpoliced sexuality and agency.[30] In *Hercules Unchained*, for instance, Queen Omphale exemplifies a dangerous antagonist for this genre: a politically powerful woman who repeatedly ensnares unsuspecting men and then embalms them when they no longer serve her purposes. She detains an amnesiac Hercules on her island until his friends intervene and restore his memory and masculinity – much as Hercules will do for Jason in "Once a Hero."[31]

Ruby Blondell observes these gender dynamics at work in *Hercules and the Amazon Women* (1994), the first of five made-for-TV movies that preceded and served as the basis for *HTLJ*. These films were created by the same production crew, feature many of the same actors, and inhabit the same continuity as the television series. In *Hercules and the Amazon Women*, Hercules agrees to help Gargarencia, a village that is attacked continually by what a messenger at first describes as "ferocious beasts." Hercules soon discovers that these "beasts" are female warriors wearing animal masks – women who used to be married to the men of Gargarencia. After engaging in a combination of hypnosis and talk therapy with the women's leader, Hercules reconciles these two communities by persuading the Amazons to stop killing the men and return to their former roles as wives in Gargarencia. For Blondell, *Hercules and the Amazon Women* thus recasts its titular hero as "a desirable male for the contemporary female audience and as a therapeutic authority who re-inscribes male dominance in a way that reflects the 'postfeminist' backlash of the 1990s."[32] This stance, according to Hutcheon, is part of the "antifeminist, nostalgic retreat to the past in the face of changes in culture brought about by the rise of feminism."[33] Blondell characterizes this nostalgia as conservative (what Boym would call restorative), a desire to turn back the clock to the state of gender politics that existed prior to the second-wave feminist movement.

These patriarchal attitudes toward gender also appear in "Once a Hero." Jason's ex-wife Medea, the ultimate *femme fatale* as both princess and sorceress, parallels *Hercules Unchained*'s Queen Omphale. She is, moreover, a husband-betrayer and child-killer; overcoming the psychological damage she has done to the hero is integral to restoring Jason's masculinity. Yet this restorative nostalgia, this return to the gender politics of the peplum, is complicated by the female Argonaut Phoebe, whose appearance mixes the conservative gender landscape of the peplum genre with the issues of gender progress current in the popular culture of the 1990s. This combination results in a reflective nostalgia, a dynamic vision of past and present that ponders the current moment through the prism of the past.

MEDEA AND JASON'S MASCULINITY, LOST AND REGAINED

Jason's degradation from golden-age hero to "once a hero" is signaled at the episode's start, when he needs Hercules to save him from thugs trying to rob him in an alley. The reveal of this would-be victim's identity as Jason simultaneously indicates his loss of masculinity. Although Jason is still king of Argos, with the golden fleece hung prominently in his throne room as a reminder of past glories, his disabling abuse of alcohol to drown the sorrows of spousal abandonment and the loss of his children has required the installation of a regent, who now plots to depose him. Even some of the Argonauts believe that the sullen, alcoholic Jason is a hero no longer. Only by recovering from the ravages of marriage to the *femme fatale* Medea can Jason retrieve his masculinity and fulfill that well-worn phrase: "once a hero, always a hero."

The episode's premise resonates with the problematic nature of Jason's heroism in ancient texts, especially Apollonius of Rhodes' third-century BCE Greek poem *Argonautica*. Apollonius' treatment became canonical in modern culture through English-language mythology handbooks like Edith Hamilton's *Mythology* (1942). Tapert has not commented publicly on the sources for "Once a Hero," but a popular book like Hamilton's, which has long been used in secondary education,[34] is a viable point of reference not only for the series' creative team but also for its audiences. Apollonius repeatedly describes Jason as "helpless" (*amēchanos*);[35] at one point, he is verbally and almost physically assaulted by his own crew-mates for his poor leadership (*Arg.* 1.1284–97).[36] This aspect filters into modern versions, such as in Chaffey's 1963 film *Jason and the Argonauts* when the Argonauts briefly criticize Jason for leaving Hercules behind.[37]

Jason's heroism is further problematized by Medea's crucial role in the success of the Argonauts' quest. She gives the young hero a magic ointment so that he can overcome her father King Aeëtes' trial of yoking the fire-breathing bulls (*Arg.* 3.1042–9); charms the ever-watchful serpent guardian so that Jason can steal the fleece away (*Arg.* 4.156–64); and bewitches Crete's guardian automaton Talos into killing himself so that the *Argo* may pass safely (*Arg.* 4.1665–88). Medea's lethal abilities extend to assisting Jason's murder of her brother Apsyrtus by luring the latter with gifts (*Arg.* 4.452–81) – or else she murders him herself, as in the account of the first-century BCE/CE Roman writer Hyginus (*Fab.* 23). According to several ancient authors,[38] she then scatters her brother's limbs in the *Argo*'s wake to distract their pursuers and enable the Argonauts' escape. According to the first-century CE mythographer Apollodorus (*Bibl.* 1.9.27), to help Jason become king of Iolchus, Medea tricks the daughters of King Pelias into killing their father with the ruse that doing so will rejuvenate him. When Jason betrays her by accepting marriage to Glauce, the Greek princess of Corinth, and allowing her father to exile his foreign wife, as dramatized by Euripides' fifth-century BCE tragedy *Medea*, she kills her two sons by Jason, along with his new wife and the king.

These murderous events do not appear, nor are they even mentioned, in the mainstream cinematic treatments of the Argonaut myth that predated, and inspired, "Once a Hero": *Hercules* (1959), *The Giants of Thessaly* (1960), and *Jason and the Argonauts* (1963). In fact, Medea does not appear at all in the first two, and she is very much a minor character in Chaffey's film, "a passive erotic object without clear motivation."[39] The film ends before the Argonauts begin their return journey; the last shot of the film, with Jason and Medea embracing happily, suggests an anxious desire to foreclose on such grim events.[40] Ray Harryhausen, the film's famed special-effects guru, acknowledged that, had there been a sequel, "we would have had to take even greater liberties with the second half of the legend in which Medea kills her two children by Jason, dismembers their bodies and returns to Colchis."[41] Thus "Once a Hero" goes against the grain of its predecessors in featuring Medea's murders of her and

Jason's children – indeed, that event is the episode's thematic linchpin. Entering this narrative territory becomes a necessary step for Jason to reclaim his masculinity, which was damaged by his failure to protect his children from Medea.[42]

Like Jason's problematic heroism, the turn toward depression depicted in "Once a Hero" also stems from ancient sources' account of his post-*Argo* adventures. In Euripides' *Medea*, his former wife prophesies that nostalgia for his lost masculinity will kill him when his beloved *Argo*, aged and broken down just like Jason himself, collapses on top of him as he sleeps beneath it.[43] Two art-house films released before "Once a Hero" that adapt the Jason and Medea myth, Pier Paolo Pasolini's 1969 *Medea* and Lars Von Trier's 1988 *Medea*, depict Jason unsympathetically and so encourage the audience to view him as culpable for what happens to his second wife and his children.[44] Unlike those texts, "Once a Hero" makes Medea totally culpable for the infanticides. The audience is given this impression from Jason's brief memory of the Argive palace in flames, with a superimposed image of a crying baby as a child screams, "Help me, daddy!" Various characters throughout the episode also describe Medea as the murderer. Even the Argonaut Artemus' upbraiding of their erstwhile leader for his leaving Medea for Glauce is redirected by Hercules ("She also killed Jason's children"), which focuses attention back on Jason's innocence and Medea's culpability.[45] These features amount to a conservative gender politics along the lines of Blondell's analysis of *Hercules and the Amazon Women*: Jason, the male hero, is not to blame for the tragic events at Argos, while Medea, the *femme fatale*, is at fault.

"Once a Hero" reinforces this conservative vision by depicting Jason as feeling profound guilt for his children's deaths; he is convinced that the gods have punished him by sending a demon to kill him. This "demon" turns out to be Castor, an Argonaut who is jealous of Jason's fame and wants the throne of Argos for himself. Castor is thus a stand-in for Medea, who never appears in the episode. Whereas *HTLJ*'s Medea cannot be defeated, Castor can, and Jason wins in their single combat during the climactic scene. This confrontation parallels the events of typical peplum films, in which the hero defeats a tyrannical ruler, as Hercules does to Pelias and his men after they steal the golden fleece in *Hercules* (1959). The Castor of "Once a Hero" is therefore another mechanism that prevents the audience from feeling that Jason is responsible, which in turn removes the moral obstacle to the just reclamation of his masculinity.

The events of "Once a Hero," particularly Jason's victory over Castor, restore his identity as a heroic Argonaut, which he had before Medea's devastating infanticides in *HTLJ* and in the previous versions in peplum film. After the final battle, Jason has regained the golden fleece and proven that he is still a hero. But he continues to fixate on his children's fates and his inability to save them, which threatens to undo the episode's work. In the role of "therapist/pop-psychologist/advice-columnist/self-help-guru"[46] that he plays throughout the series, Hercules redirects Jason's thoughts by counseling him to act as he did after his own family was murdered by Hera and "do something that would have made [his] wife and children proud" (see Figure 1.1). Hercules decided to commemorate his family by helping others in need, and Jason resolves to follow in his footsteps by vowing to protect the people of Argos – much like typical peplum protagonists such as Hercules in *Hercules Unchained*, who frees the city of Thebes from the tyrannical rule of the evil Eteocles. "Once a Hero" thus charts the reinstatement of Jason's masculinity, which his character had possessed in the "Golden Age mythology" of children's literature and of the peplum.

Figure 1.1 Hercules (Kevin Sorbo) mentors a despondent Jason (Jeffrey Thomas) in "Once a Hero," Episode 2.14 of *Hercules: The Legendary Journeys* (1996). Renaissance Pictures/MCA Television.

A HEROINE AMONG HEROES: MAKING SPACE FOR PHOEBE

This restoration of Jason's idealized heroic masculinity is complicated by the episode's inclusion of Phoebe, the only female Argonaut. In "Once a Hero," she is the daughter of Lynceus, an Argonaut in many ancient versions of the myth.[47] As a second-generation hero, Phoebe perfectly expresses *HTLJ*'s epigonal relationship to its literary and cinematic predecessors.[48] Phoebe has evidently inherited her father's superhuman sight (*Arg.* 1.151–2), since she is able to discern, from a great distance, the composition of the crew on the ship making off with the golden fleece. She also safeguards his reputation. At some point before the dramatic time of "Once a Hero" Lynceus died in what the Argonauts believe was an accident, but which Phoebe is convinced was murder. "No accident could've killed him," she angrily declares, underscoring a desire to defend her father's heroic masculinity by joining the second expedition in his place. Phoebe's suspicions are proved to be correct in the course of the episode when it is finally revealed that Lynceus' death was Castor's doing. In recognition of her morality and physical abilities, which include saving her fellow Argonauts Hercules and Domesticles from enemy attacks in combat, Hercules and company bestow official Argonaut status upon her at the end of the episode. The identity that has been restored to Jason, she has earned for herself in the eyes of the men deemed "proper" holders of that title.

Given the paucity of heroines in Greek myth, why did "Once a Hero" include a female Argonaut? Phoebe invites comparison with Atalanta, who was the only woman to become an Argonaut, in some ancient sources.[49] In Apollonius' *Argonautica*, however, Jason excludes her out of fear that she will create erotic entanglements among the otherwise all-male crew (*Arg.* 1.772–3). The influence of the *Argonautica* on modern compendia of myths perhaps explains why this exclusion was picked up by the cinematic predecessors of "Once a Hero," which do not even mention Atalanta.[50] Given this background, *HTLJ* did not have to feature a female Argonaut at all, but "Once a Hero" chose to include one on this second expedition.

HTLJ could have used Atalanta for this purpose, since the series had already debuted its version of the character in the previous season's "Ares" (1.5). *HTLJ*'s Atalanta would have made an excellent Argonaut, as demonstrated by her fighting abilities against a cult of the war god in "Ares" and by her strength – lifting Hercules himself over her head – in "Let the Games Begin" (2.16). Instead,

HTLJ's staff created a new member from whole cloth: Phoebe, who had never appeared in an episode before "Once a Hero." Whereas Atalanta is from Hercules' generation, and the actress who plays her, Corinna Everson, was born in 1958 like Kevin Sorbo, Phoebe is from the next generation; Hercules' sidekick and fellow Argonaut Iolaus remembers her "only as a child" during the first expedition, and actress Willa O'Neill was born in 1973. Phoebe thus embodies reflective nostalgia: her character was invented for the Argonaut sequel, and the birthdate of the actress who plays her makes her part of the generation most identified with female empowerment in the 1990s.

At the same time, the male Argonauts' snide comments make some aspects of the episode's portrayal of Phoebe retrograde. When she is first introduced, Phoebe manifests her anger at the suspicious circumstances surrounding her father's death by using her slingshot to hurl a nut into a stone wall. Viewing the embedded projectile with shock, Iolaus remarks incredulously, "Wow! She's feisty, isn't she?" and fellow Argonaut Archivus adds that Phoebe "makes me miss my days on the island of silent women." Archivus' line is a quotation of a (non-peplum) film that adapts, via Stephen Sondheim's Broadway musical, the works of the Roman playwright Plautus as *A Funny Thing Happened on the Way to the Forum* (1966). The slave-hero Pseudolus explains that he can communicate with the mute courtesan Gymnasia because he "had a nurse from the island of silent women." Both here and in "Once a Hero," the charm of silent women is that they can be ciphers for male desire – and Archivus' quotation of a 1966 film set in antiquity recalls the nostalgic project of *HTLJ* as a whole. At another point, Phoebe wields her slingshot to protect Hercules from an enemy's charge, to which he responds, "Nothing like a woman's touch!" None of these comments is explicitly misogynistic, but they are all certainly demeaning jabs at Phoebe's agency that reveal the series' traditional core.

Constructions of femininity beyond this episode of *HTLJ* reveal that the ambivalent treatment of Phoebe is not singular. Female characters are often quite capable in the episodes prior to "Once a Hero," yet their agency may still be undermined by their sexual objectification and their dependence on Hercules. This happens not only with Atalanta,[51] but also with Xena. When introduced in "The Warrior Princess" (*HTLJ* 1.9), Xena – true to the *femme fatale* stereotype of empowered women in the peplum genre – uses her sexuality to persuade Iolaus to attack Hercules. But in two subsequent episodes, "The Gauntlet" (1.12) and "Unchained Heart" (1.13), the warrior princess rejects her villainous past, helps Hercules defeat her erstwhile army, and goes on to become a hero in the mold of Hercules. The impetuses for this change are both internal and external: her lieutenant's decision (against her wishes) to massacre all of the inhabitants of a village, her subsequent protection of a baby from that village, and the guidance and encouragement of a male – Hercules as therapist, again.

Critics' lukewarm reception of *HTLJ*'s depiction of Xena and of the series' female characters generally reflects an understanding of the series' depiction of gender as retrograde compared to *Xena: Warrior Princess* (1995–2001; henceforth *XWP*), though some are skeptical even of the latter series.[52] Critics like O'Brien argue that Xena is a "contrived and tokenistic" female warrior, as indicated by her garb in the two *HTLJ* episodes as well as her brutal physical treatment in "The Gauntlet" and erotic encounter with Hercules in "Unchained Heart," all of which cause a "de-masculinisation/re-feminisation" of the character.[53] Notably, Phoebe is not sexualized: she wears a tomboyish dress with a high neckline, colored blue and purple, which parallels the coloring of the male Argonauts' clothing. Moreover, she is never linked romantically to men, as *femme fatales* always are. Perhaps political correctness motivated Phoebe's creation, as O'Brien argues of Xena in *HTLJ* and Joanna Paul argues of the Xena-inspired Atalanta in *Jason and the Argonauts* (2000).[54] Perhaps *HTLJ*'s staff created Phoebe to satisfy a commercial imperative: to capture a greater share of the female audience. Whatever the motivation behind Phoebe's creation, she should be understood as one of several powerful and positively valued female characters in *HTLJ*, quite unlike the typical female roles of peplum films. This choice suggests a reflective nostalgia that employs a value system of the past while acknowledging a value system of the contemporary moment.

CONCLUSION

The episode "Once a Hero" at first evinces a desire to return to the golden age of 1950s and 1960s peplum films, and their construction of gender, through the Argonauts' second voyage to regain the golden fleece – and Jason's identity. By the time the Argonauts toast "To heroes!" in the final moments of the episode, the fleece is back in the palace of Argos and Jason, by defeating his enemy in combat and exorcising the demons of guilt that haunted him, has become a hero once again. And yet that golden age has not quite returned (if it ever could have), for things have irrevocably changed: Phoebe, the daughter of an original Argonaut, has been enrolled among the previously all-male heroic band (see Figure 1.2), a break from many modern versions of the Argonaut myth. This situation reflects the contemporary American context of the episode's production. As compared to the restorative nostalgia of "Make America Great Again," a desire to return to golden ages that never existed in the first place, in Reagan's 1980 and Trump's 2016 campaigns, "Once a Hero" "reflect[s] this distinctly American faith that people can remake their lives."[55]

The constructions of gender in play throughout "Once a Hero" are fundamental to the peplum genre, as argued by Blondell, but the episode also moves beyond that basis. *HTLJ*'s depiction of women like Phoebe as capable warriors is part of the Zeitgeist of the 1990s, the emphasis on female power in American society and its popular media. Whereas the female warriors in *Hercules and the Amazon Women* become, in Blondell's analysis, domesticated with a "whiff of Amazonian feminism"[56] to retain the (false) impression that they are in fact still liberated, Phoebe's empowerment is more in the mold of Xena: still dependent on male approval and mentorship for her heroic

Figure 1.2 The Argonauts, including Phoebe (Willa O'Neil, far left), Jason (Jeffrey Thomas, center rear), and Hercules (Kevin Sorbo, far right), gather in "Once a Hero," Episode 2.14 of *Hercules: The Legendary Journeys* (1996). Renaissance Pictures/MCA Television.

identity, yet relatively free of traditional female roles. Nevertheless, the series' roots in peplum's depictions of gender mean that vestiges of those attitudes remain. Although the nostalgia associated with golden ages pervades "Once a Hero," it is not as reactionary as Blondell and others argue; it is, in Boym's terminology, reflective rather than restorative.

NOTES

Many thanks to the editor, Meredith E. Safran, for helping me think through my ideas much more clearly. The audience at the 2014 Film & History conference also made several helpful comments and connections.

1 Blondell (2005: 204).
2 Reid (1996: 54).
3 Boyle (2014: 214).
4 All line references to *Works and Days* are to Hesiod (1970). English translations of Greek texts in this chapter are my own.
5 Dwyer (2015: 10).
6 Hutcheon (2000: 196).
7 Dwyer (2015: 28–35).
8 Boym (2001: 49).
9 For instance, Scott (2010), unpaginated: "In particular those darn sequels, a perennial easy target for those of us who persist in entertaining high hopes for summer entertainment."
10 Jameson (1991: 279–96).
11 Dika (2003: 206).
12 Bondanella (2009: 577).
13 Lagny (1992: 163).
14 Clauss (2008: 55).
15 Winkler (2005: 386).
16 Rushing (2016: 13).
17 Blanshard (2005: 160).
18 According to Bondanella (2009: 167) in the US *Hercules* "grossed $18 million, with an adjusted profit of $5 million ... [T]hese figures would probably put the profit margins of most contemporary blockbusters to shame."
19 Rushing (2016: 19): "midcentury peplums remained in the popular imagination because they commonly appeared ... as regular staples on American daytime television in the late 1960s and early 1970s."
20 Luciano (1994: viii) and Rushing (2016: 19).
21 Günsberg (2005: 101).
22 Paul (2013: 104, emphasis in the original).
23 Evslin (2012: unpaginated).

24 Maurice (2015: 10). See also Murnaghan (2011).
25 Lovatt (2009: 26–35).
26 Lovatt (2009: 101).
27 Lagny (1992: 169).
28 Cornelius (2011: 5), Günsberg (2005: 104), and O'Brien (2014: 9). Notably, O'Brien's work seeks to complicate this view, but the quoted formulation is the typical impression that the films give.
29 Ipsen (2012: 140).
30 On *femmes fatales* in peplum cinema, see Lagny (1992: 175) and Schenk (2006: 160).
31 Cf. O'Brien (2014: 119), who notes that the Amazons in Francisci's *Hercules* pose a similar threat.
32 Blondell (2007: 239).
33 Hutcheon (2000: 200).
34 See further Weiss (1961: 125) and Beach and Marshall (1991: 431).
35 For further analyses of *amēchanos*, see Clauss (1993: *passim*).
36 Notably, in ancient traditions Hercules is the older and superior hero to Jason, whereas *HTLJ* reverses this.
37 For analyses of Apollonius' problematic Jason, see Clauss (1993: *passim*) and Hunter (1993: 15–24). Even though some of these attributes are present in the Jason of Chaffey's film, O'Brien (2014: 79–94) argues that this is due to his being modeled on US President John F. Kennedy, not to the influence of Apollonius.
38 According to Lovatt (2009: 31n24), this version appears in Pherecydes, Apollodorus, and Ovid.
39 Ormand (2014: 76).
40 Paul (2013: 98) sees the omission of these elements as part of the "mutability of epic as a genre." Cf. Ormand (2014: 76), who concludes that, for a knowledgeable audience at least, there are "hints at the transitory nature of this romantic ending." An audience familiar with Hamilton's account, as *HTLJ*'s crew and the series' audience might have been (see notes 34 and 42), would be knowledgeable, since she does include this material (1942: 170–4).
41 Harryhausen and Dalton (2004: 174).
42 According to the script, the most direct cause of Jason's loss of masculinity is the infanticides, since that act is the only connection with Medea made explicitly by the episode. However, given that popular treatments like Hamilton's *Mythology* (1942) detail Jason's dependence on the Colchian princess for the attainment of the fleece, both *HTLJ*'s crew and the series' audience might have been aware that Jason's masculinity was endangered by Medea's actions more generally.
43 Euripides (1984: lines 1386–7): "But you, as is fitting, will die in an evil way since you yourself are evil, your head struck by a remnant of the *Argo*." By contrast, in "Once a Hero" the Argonauts sail on the "still seaworthy" *Argo* to retrieve the fleece a second time.

44 For further analysis of Pasolini, see Shapiro (2014) and Paul (2013: 99–100), and for Von Trier, see Baertschi (2014).

45 The title of Episode 4.11, "Medea Culpa" (1998), which features an extended flashback to Hercules' and Jason's first meeting with Medea, argues for Medea's guilt even more explicitly.

46 Blondell (2007: 246) traces this role to discourses about gender in the 1990s.

47 Scherer (2006: 53) lists Lynceus as an Argonaut in Pherecydes, Apollonius, Apollodorus, Hyginus, Valerius Flaccus, and the Orphic *Argonautica*.

48 Paul (2013: 94) also notes how all of the films about Jason and the Argonauts channel the ancient versions' "anxiety over epigonality or belatedness."

49 Scherer (2006: 50) cites a vase, Apollodorus, and Dionysius Scytobrachion; I add Diodorus of Sicily 4.41.2.

50 Hamilton (1942: 240) records two ancient traditions: that Atalanta was an Argonaut, and that she was convinced not to join the expedition. Hamilton concludes that "it seems probable that she did not go."

51 O'Brien (2014: 133) overstates the case when he argues that "Atalanta is only permitted to act and fight as herself in a 'tokenistic' fashion."

52 Ipsen (2012: 151) declares that in *XWP* "the principle of gender balance [is] realized," while O'Brien (2014: 140) opines that the series is "positive and progressive, albeit in a tentative way."

53 O'Brien (2014: 137). Cf. Zeiler (2013: 229), who similarly opines that *HTLJ*'s Xena "remains very limited in many aspects." This concern over female warriors acting like men without retaining feminine attributes is common in scholarship; see, on *XWP*, Helford (2000: 136): "Stepping into the traditional role of a hero seems a feminist triumph for many; however, it also arguably masculinises Xena, suggesting that for women to become heroic they must become, in effect, men."

54 Paul (2013: 130) and O'Brien (2014: 137). These different claims embody Helford's (2000: 137) description of *XWP* as a "polysemic text."

55 Weisbrot (2004: 6).

56 Blondell (2007: 247).

2 *Kissed by the Muse of Roller-Disco: Utopia versus the Golden Ages of America, Hollywood, and Classical Myth in* Xanadu *(1980)*

Meredith E. Safran

In twentieth-century American historiography, the 1970s stand as the nation's iron age, relative to the golden age of post-World War II prosperity. International humiliations in Vietnam and Iran, nationwide outbursts of political violence, the scandal of Watergate followed by President Richard Nixon's resignation, and economic troubles linked to the Mideast oil embargo and the collapse of American manufacturing all congealed into a national sensibility addressed by President Jimmy Carter in his famous "malaise" speech, on July 15, 1979.[1] One escape, especially for socially marginalized groups, was offered by the disco culture developed in underground house parties and clubs. In this utopian atmosphere, DJs and dancers created a world of "communion and ecstasy, fantasy and release," whose "group body was a polymorphous, polyracial, polysexual mass affirming its bonds in a space beyond the reach of church, state, or family."[2] Disco exploded into a mainstream cultural juggernaut among white, middle-class Americans through the success of *Saturday Night Fever* (1977), whose protagonist Tony Manero (John Travolta) became a national icon by transcending his working-class constraints as king of the light-up dance floor at Bay Ridge, Brooklyn's "2001 Odyssey" club.[3]

Industry hopes of capitalizing upon the film's profitability, combined with the youth pastime of roller-disco clubs, encouraged the near-simultaneous production of *Skatetown, U.S.A.* (1979), *Roller Boogie* (1979), and *Xanadu* (1980).[4] These films were set in Venice Beach, a Los Angeles neighborhood founded as a turn-of-the-century amusement park and more recently populated by countercultural California dreamers.[5] All three films, released during the virulent backlash against disco, were commercial and critical disappointments.[6] Yet *Xanadu* endured as a cult classic, a status eventually mainstreamed by the award-winning 2007 Broadway musical adaptation.[7] *Xanadu*'s appeal is largely owed not to Marc Reid Rubel's original story, about an artist who quit his job painting enlarged album covers as promotional artwork for record stores in order to found a nightclub, but to the vision of producers Lawrence Gordon and Joel Silver.[8] Their overhaul of Rubel's original no-budget comedy subsumed disco's utopian sensibility within the nostalgia generated by the film's new identity as a classic Hollywood musical, which implicated multiple mutually reinforcing modern golden ages.

In its incorporation of diegetic songs, including several performed by the protagonists; spectacular dance numbers, transforming quotidian space into a fantasy realm; and the entwining of its heterosexual couple's romantic and professional show-biz success, *Xanadu* bore all the hallmarks of the Hollywood musical, the tentpole genre of the industry's golden age.[9] This apogee of the studio system's power and film's dominance in American popular culture also coincided with the United States' achievement of superpower status through victory in World War II, an effort embraced even within the ostensibly escapist genre of the musical.[10] *Xanadu* reinforced this nexus of golden ages by not only explicitly quoting cinematic landmarks *Cover Girl* (1944), *An American in Paris* (1951), and *Singin' in the Rain* (1952), but also casting their leading man, Hollywood legend Gene Kelly. Kelly's World War II veteran, former Manhattan club owner, and retired construction magnate Danny McGuire serves as partner-mentor to the young artist, Sonny Malone (Michael Beck). Both Kelly and his character thus embodied the lost exuberance of America's, Hollywood's, and the musical's mid-century golden age, serving *Xanadu*'s ideological project of invoking idealized pasts to redeem the degraded present.

In addition to tapping into nostalgia for these idealized generic, industrial, and national pasts, *Xanadu*'s narrative drew upon classical myth's golden age of heroes, when select men interacted with gods and accomplished great deeds that transcended ordinary human ability. Following the Romantic tradition of artists like Samuel Taylor Coleridge, from whose poetry the film's title derives, a kiss from one of the nine Muses (Olivia Newton-John) inspires Sonny to channel his frustrated talents into opening the eponymous nightclub. As the cosmically sanctioned erotics through which the goddess aids the hero become illicit romance, classical myth's entrenched prohibition on goddess–mortal relations creates the cinematic genre's required obstacle between its lovers. *Xanadu* overcomes the emasculation entailed by such myths by transforming Sonny into an Orpheus-like hero who breaches the cosmic boundary between mortal and immortal realms to recover his beloved in defiance of her restrictive father, Zeus – and consequently succeeds in art, business, and love, symbolically recuperating the happiness of working-class American men like Sonny.

Ironically, this romance plot threatens to undermine the Muse's strategy of pairing Sonny with Danny to create Xanadu, recalling the end of the original golden age within classical myth: when men's original joyful existence was ruined by the arrival of women. *Xanadu* intensifies this trope by employing the same Muse who once inspired Danny with her kiss to do the same to Sonny, setting up a love triangle – which is further informed by Gene Kelly's unusual star text, which included his envelope-pushing glorification of male homosociality. *Xanadu* resolves these tensions in the film's climactic sequence, which highlights the utopian capacities of the new nightclub even as the formulation of Sonny's "happy ending" presages the rising tide of nostalgic social conservatism sweeping away the progressive potential of disco across the nation.

CURING THE NATION'S MALAISE: NOSTALGIA FOR HOLLYWOOD'S, AND AMERICA'S, GOLDEN AGES

Xanadu opens by dramatizing American malaise on a personal level, via the lost self-confidence and aporetic despair of its two male protagonists. After briefly featuring a lone clarinetist who plays a moody tune at sunrise by the sea, a montage of Sonny's attempts at creating artwork ends with him ripping up his last sketch. He sighs, "Guys like me shouldn't dream anyway," then tosses the pieces out his window. A dejected Sonny returns to his dead-end job at the record company, rehired only because he's "the fastest painter around": a backhanded compliment that subordinates human artistry to the speed characteristic of the Industrial Age. Sonny's co-workers, whom he finds lamenting the difficulty of paying off a mortgage, express their disappointment in his surrender and encourage Sonny to try independence again. But experiencing poverty and hunger has killed his romantic ideal of artistic freedom: "Not only did I nearly starve to death, I couldn't even figure out what I wanted to do!"

Danny, by contrast, demonstrates that wealth alone is insufficient to hearten a defeated man. After the men strike up a friendship, he reminisces to Sonny about his glory days as a clarinetist with Glenn Miller's military band, which led to opening his own club in Manhattan at the urging of the band's alluring chanteuse. Upon her sudden departure, he confesses, "the heart went out of my music." Danny closed the successful club and joined his family's lucrative construction business. In his palatial home, surrounded by memorabilia attesting to his former happiness, Danny refers to himself derisively as "retired: a refined name for 'bum.'" Later, he stands alone, listening to a recording of his youthful self and regarding his aged face in a mirror. He sighs to the absent singer, "You wouldn't even recognize me now," as the big-band music envelops him in memory.

Danny's musings in this scene are ironic and meta-cinematic, on two levels. First, even decades after Hollywood's golden age ended, Kelly remained widely recognized as the musical's standard-bearer. He had debuted in a starring role opposite Judy Garland in *For Me and My Gal* (1942) and won acclaim as a cinematic choreographer beginning with his solo "mop dance" in *Thousands Cheer* (1943), then as a director with *On the Town* (1949; with Stanley Donen).[11] Kelly made most of his musicals at MGM, where legendary producer Arthur Freed allowed him creative freedom on future classics including *An American in Paris*, *Singin' in the Rain*, and *Brigadoon* (1954).[12] Only ten years into his Hollywood career, Kelly received an honorary Oscar for his myriad achievements. After MGM released their fiftieth-anniversary retrospective revue *That's Entertainment!* in 1974, Kelly's performance of "Singin' in the Rain" became synonymous with the MGM musical.[13] Still active into his seventies, Kelly received lifetime achievement awards from the Kennedy Center (1982), the American Film Institute (1985), and the Screen Actors Guild (1989).

Second, Kelly's participation in *Xanadu* underscores the film's self-consciously nostalgic capitalization upon his golden-age films, most explicitly 1944's *Cover Girl*.[14] As in *Xanadu*, Kelly's character was named Danny McGuire, a small-time Brooklyn nightclub owner who romances dancer Rusty Parker (Rita Hayworth). After a Manhattan magazine's modeling contest vaults Rusty to Broadway stardom, Danny dejectedly closes his successful club to perform at United Service Organizations (USO) shows with his best friend and roommate, the club's comedian Genius (Phil Silvers). When Danny finds a long-sought natural pearl in an oyster, Genius transgresses the boundary separating moneyed Manhattanites from blue-collar Brooklynites to deliver this magical sign to Rusty, stopping her marriage of convenience to a Broadway impresario and returning her to Danny.

Beyond appropriating the name and backstory of Kelly's character from *Cover Girl* for his character in *Xanadu*, Sonny too is a small-time artist who finds inspiration in a woman, risks throwing away a successful nightclub upon losing her, and is saved by the intervention of his side-man: Danny. Furthermore, the elderly Danny's nostalgia for a romance associated with a popular live performance medium of his youth echoes *Cover Girl*'s flashbacks, in which the successful but lonely elderly magazine magnate John Coudair (Otto Kruger) recalls his youthful attempts to woo the vaudeville star Maribelle Hicks – who, he discovers, was Rusty's grandmother! Just as Hayworth played both present-day Rusty and turn-of-the-century Maribelle, Olivia Newton-John plays both Sonny's beloved in 1980 and Danny's in 1945.

Xanadu also borrows elements big and small from Kelly's performances as Jerry Mulligan in *An American in Paris* and Don Lockwood in *Singin' in the Rain*. Like Jerry, Sonny is a working-class painter who rejects selling out to a wealthy boss by following his heart back to the film's ingenue. *Xanadu*'s opening magical musical sequence, through which this love interest comes into the dejected Sonny's life, adapts the famous fantasy ballet that returns Jerry's beloved to him in *American*'s climax. As with Don's seduction of Kathy in *Singin*'s "You Were Meant For Me," for *Xanadu*'s "falling in love" number "Suddenly" the couple appropriates a deserted special-effects-laden studio. *Xanadu* also makes smaller gestures to Kelly's famed athleticism and vaudeville background. When Sonny comically flies off a motorbike during his first meeting with Danny, *Xanadu* quotes Don's montage of autobiographical flashbacks in *Singin'*, which features Don doing the same in his first Hollywood job as a stuntman. The same montage features Don and his best friend Cosmo (Donald O'Connor) performing their early vaudeville act, itself a cheeky reference to Kelly's roots in vaudeville.[15] In *Xanadu*, upon learning Sonny's name right after introducing himself, Danny exclaims "Malone and McGuire! Sounds like a vaudeville act."

Such reminiscences in *Xanadu* were of a piece with Americans' desire to soothe their contemporary ills with nostalgia – and Hollywood's willingness to capitalize on this impulse. As the tag line for *That's Entertainment!* bluntly asserted: "Boy. Do we need it now." That revue's commercial success, a boon for the ailing studio desperate for revenue, motivated MGM to produce *That's Entertainment, Part II* (1976), which Kelly hosted and directed.[16] The industry's hopes for reviving the signature genre of Hollywood's golden age were further buoyed when *Grease* (1978), a high-school musical set in the 1950s, became the top-grossing live-action musical of all time.[17]

Grease's star, Olivia Newton-John, also fed this appetite for "the good old days." She had achieved country-pop superstardom with wholesome hits like her 1974 Grammy-winning song "I Honestly Love You," which also closed her television variety showcases "A Special Olivia Newton-John" (1976) and "Olivia Newton-John: Hollywood Nights" (1980). Her 1976 special featured a ten-minute medley revolving around "Anything Goes," Cole Porter's cheeky 1934 ode to "olden days" in contrast to the shocking present. Even guest stars harked back to Hollywood's and America's golden age: Elliot Gould, crooning in Fred Astaire's signature tuxedo and top hat; Lynda Carter as Wonder Woman, subduing a World War II-era Nazi; Ron Howard and Tom Bosley, stars of the television series set during America's post-war "happy days." Their series by that same name ranked among the country's top three programs from 1976 to 1979.[18]

Happy Days (1974–84), like *Grease*, transported audiences back into the nation's halcyon days. *Xanadu*, however, promised to bring that idealized past into its characters' present, and Newton-John's semantic value as a youthful resurrection of mid-century nostalgia formed no small part her appeal. Newton-John's ability to signify in this way is enacted in her showcase number with Kelly, "Whenever You're Away from Me." Listening to that recording of his younger self triggers this fantasy number, which features lush big-band orchestration and elegant tap-dancing. Rather than flashing back to the 1940s, however, Danny imagines his beloved into his palatial home to reenact their recorded duet. Later in the film, Danny similarly conjures a wartime swing band and scores of stylish dancers into the proposed site for Xanadu in the fantasy number "Dancin'."

By enacting his memories of past greatness within the film's present, Danny's fantasy resonates with producers Gordon and Silver's dream of reviving Hollywood's golden age. This sentiment was also reflected in the contemporary campaign slogan of World War II-era Hollywood actor-turned-presidential candidate Ronald Reagan: "Making America Great Again." *Xanadu* at least was honest about what such a revival would require: "you have to believe we are magic," pop star Newton-John croons in diegetic soundtrack music, as her character the Muse roller-skates in and out of sight before

Sonny's enchanted eyes. Such belief in magic is integral to Sonny's actualization as a hero for his times – and to the audience's investment in Hollywood's ability to resurrect those golden ages.

GODDESS AS HELPER, DANGER, AND DAMSEL IN DISTRESS: RESURRECTING THE GOLDEN AGE OF HEROES

To accomplish these goals, *Xanadu* draws inspiration from within the deepest golden age of the Western imaginary: the world of classical myth, when divinely favored men transcended human boundaries to achieve great deeds. *Xanadu* inherited nineteenth-century receptions of the "golden age of heroes," both the Victorian taste for moral exemplars and the Romantic valorization of those who dared to defy even divine authority in championing such ideals as Liberty and Love. *Xanadu* thus presents Sonny as a morally worthy man in that he defies unjust mortal and immortal systems in pursuit of both a self-liberation that will improve his community and true love. Like a classical hero, Sonny pursues his quest with the aid of a goddess; as an artist, he is inspired by the kiss of the Muse. When her patronage turns into a forbidden romance that endangers him and requires her rescue, Sonny undertakes a bold act of self-assertion that banishes his personal malaise and, symbolically, that of the nation.

Xanadu initiates this mythic trajectory by transforming its maudlin opening sequence into an invocation of the Muses. Sonny's discarded sketch flutters past Venice Beach's sun-kissed rooftops to a score of otherworldly synthesizer music, then lands in a vacant lot graced with a neon-accented mural of nine women dancing before a craggy landscape. As keening synthesizers resolve into ELO's exuberant prog-pop song "I'm Alive," each painted figure springs forth and joins an ecstatic choral dance (see Figure 2.1) before running through the city and ascending to the heavens as multi-colored comets. One streaks back to Earth, resumes human form, and finds Sonny on a morning stroll near the beach. She kisses him on the lips, then roller-skates away in a blaze of neon light. This sequence recalls *An American in Paris*' extravagant climactic fantasy ballet, in which figures in the lovelorn Jerry's discarded, windblown drawing come alive as he imagines his lady-love dancing back into his life – which happens immediately thereafter in reality. Upon arriving at the company workshop, Sonny's artistic spirit revives when he discovers the same woman pictured on his latest assignment: an album by the band "Nine Sisters." Disregarding his reputation for speed, Sonny paints

Figure 2.1 The artist's unwitting invocation brings the painted figures of the Muses to life in *Xanadu* (1980). Universal Pictures.

her image lovingly, realizing "this is the first thing I've cared about in a long time."

Sonny's unexpected encounter with an uncanny inspirational female recalls the classical origin of the "kissed by a Muse" trope: the archaic Greek poet Hesiod's cosmological epic *Theogony*. Hesiod celebrates the Muses, their choral performance, and how they suddenly appeared on Mount Helicon to breathe this song into him: the literal meaning of in-spiration (*Th.* 22–34).[19] The encounter is hardly romantic; the goddesses first underline Hesiod's ontologically subordinate status by insulting his appetite-driven mortality, then vaunt their own ability to tell both undying truths and lies that seem true (26–8). If there is anything sexual about the encounter, it is the goddesses' depositing their divine substance into this human receptacle (31–2), now a vessel for broadcasting their song among mortals.[20] The phallic staff they give him (29–31) signifies their patronage, for he serves them: an honor, for a believer like Hesiod.

In a world of non-believers, *Xanadu*'s Muse must assume a human guise – a lie that seems true – to maneuver Sonny into accepting her patronage over his paintbrush. And resuscitating Sonny's dream requires more than one act of mouth-to-mouth inspiration. The elusive Muse's kiss initiates a romantic twist on a heroic quest, which entwines with the Hollywood musical's self-reflexive preoccupation with artists making art.[21] Sonny journeys to the record company's accountant, for whom the woman's lack of tax filings proves that "she doesn't exist"; then to the photographer, who confides that she mysteriously appeared in one of a hundred frames, "then disappeared"; and finally, back to the beach – where he finds Danny, playing his mournful clarinet. As the two get acquainted, Sonny spots his mystery woman roller-skating down the pier and borrows a motorbike to chase her. After Sonny's comical tumble, Danny lends a sympathetic ear and encourages him to keep looking. Sonny's renewed artistic commitment thus merges with his romantic pursuit. He eventually "finds" this mystery woman in the abandoned building also featured on the "Nine Sisters" album: the future site of Xanadu.

Xanadu presents such romantic pursuit as the Muse's customary mechanism for inducing a man to fulfill his artistic (and commercial) potential; thus, Danny came to open his club in 1945. So when Sonny offers to take her roller-skating in a special recording studio, after hours, she accepts. In their romantic duet "Suddenly" the pair reenacts Don's courtship of Kathy in *Singin' in the Rain*, deploying all the soundstage's "magical" special effects to manufacture conditions for falling in love. Sonny realizes, "She walks in, and I'm suddenly a hero ... You make it seem I'm so close to my dreams and then suddenly it's all there." The Muse, already negotiating the perils of this seduction, sings "How can I feel you're all that matters ... I'll take care that no illusions shatter, if you dare say what you should say." The song climaxes with the Muse and Sonny harmonizing their "longing to spend every moment of the day with you ... I'm ready to take all my chances with you."

Although their physical intimacy never progresses beyond kissing, the couple's love grows as Xanadu comes to fruition: certainly not the kind of divine aid that the typical hero's helper Athena would bestow. As they celebrate on the eve of Xanadu's opening, the Muse's simultaneously true yet deceptive answers to his personal questions, reminiscent of the Muses' warning to Hesiod, withhold intimacy. Finally, Sonny's passionate kiss initiates an animated sequence in which he follows the Muse through a series of magical transformations suitable to classical myth – into fish, then birds, and finally back into human form – scored to ELO's plaintive ballad "Don't Walk Away," which foreshadows her inevitable departure. As they embrace at sunrise where the Muse first "inspired" him, Sonny's confession of love spurs her to reveal her true identity, and the impossibility of their union: "This was never supposed to happen ... it's beginning to hurt," she confesses. After finally convincing him that she is a goddess, she admits the limits of her own power. "I broke the rules," she cries, before wistfully declaring "I'll love you forever" as she dematerializes into a neon outline and ascends out of his life.

While the Muse does not explain "the rules," many myths of heroes testify to a dark side of interacting with the divine: the violence visited upon mortal men who engage in sexual activity with a goddess, even if she initiates it. In Homer's *Odyssey* (5.118–29), Calypso catalogs numerous instances of gods destroying goddesses' mortal paramours.[22] Tityos, Ixion, and Peirithoös suffer eternal torture in the Underworld for hubristic sexual assaults on Leto, Hera, and Persephone.[23] For accidentally stumbling upon Artemis bathing, Actaeon dies gruesomely in Ovid's *Metamorphoses* (3.173–252).[24] In the *Homeric Hymn to Aphrodite* (185–90), the mortal whom the goddess has seduced fears the terrible ends that befall such men.[25] In Hesiod's *Theogony* (570–89), Zeus implicitly uses men's desire for goddesses against them in creating the origin of all women, commonly known as Pandora, whose appearance can only have been modeled on goddesses. Pandora's association with Aphrodite in Hesiod's *Works and Days* (65–6, 73–5) casts her as a *femme fatale*, inflicting sexual suffering and manipulative deception upon men.[26] Since Zeus creates women as a bane for men, even cosmically authorized intercourse with mortal women recalls these transgressions and implicitly justifies the resultant degradation of men's happiness as they "lovingly embrace this harmful thing" (57–8).

By using her sexuality to manipulate a man while concealing her identity and intentions, *Xanadu*'s Muse also recalls her own cinematic inspiration, drawn from the Hollywood musical *Down to Earth* (1947).[27] Terpsichore (Rita Hayworth) intervenes not to help an artist realize his potential, but to correct his disrespectful depiction of her in his new theatrical musical *Swingin' the Muses*. In the film's opening showstopper, "Kiss of the Muse," Terpsichore's vampy on-stage avatar boasts of the Muses having "kissed over three million guys in two thousand years," from Socrates to "the guy who invented the skinless weenie." The indignant deity assumes a human identity, dazzles her way into the starring role, and pretends to fall in love with the playwright, whom she seduces into rewriting the show: more Stravinsky and Graham, less brass and ass. By pleasing herself and connoisseurs of high art, whose approval equals aesthetic and commercial failure in musical comedy, Terpsichore's self-directed subversion of the playwright's agency disrupts patriarchal authority in heaven and on Earth.[28] Her interference even risks his life, which he has used as collateral to secure a loan from an "underworld" figure: a crooked casino owner.

Terpsichore's potentially fatal erotic manipulation cohered with Hayworth's screen persona: "the love goddess," as she was dubbed in a double-edged *Life* magazine profile the same year.[29] Already framed as an unattainable erotic object, as the second-most-popular pin-up for American soldiers, Hayworth's star text became heavily inflected by her *femme fatale* roles in the film noirs *Gilda* (1945) and *The Lady from Shanghai* (1947). Even in the comedic *Cover Girl*, her character's choice of career over love spurred her lover's professional suicide. Much as Rusty repents (albeit by leaving another man at the altar), Terpsichore finally abandons her concern with reputation to save the playwright by restoring his musical to its original, popular style. This selfless act, motivated by what she then recognizes as love, is followed by subjugation and humiliation: being recalled to Olympus by a male handler and replaced on Earth by a human doppelganger, whom her ignorant beloved cannot distinguish from her.[30]

While employing elements of *Down to Earth*'s plot, *Xanadu* fundamentally reshapes its narrative architecture and sexual politics. *Down to Earth* captured a prominent theme in classical myths with its premise of retribution-by-theoxeny, in which the goddess' concern to protect her status and honor motivated her actions against a hubristic mortal – at least, until the film's romantic formula forces the world back into its "proper" order. *Xanadu* begins by foregrounding not the goddess' desires but the artist's, whose unwitting invocation of the Muse serves to instigate his transformative experience. The renovation of *Down to Earth*'s willful avenger into *Xanadu*'s guardian angel is abetted by Olivia Newton-John's attractive yet squeaky-clean affect, which mutes her sexual power and facilitates her submission to the patriarchal order whose "rules" constrain her agency. Moreover, unlike *Down to Earth*'s playwright, Sonny is entrusted by his beloved with knowledge of her ontological status, giving him a choice in dealing with her unwilling departure: submit to impotent despair and suffer Danny's lonely life, or take Danny's advice and find a way to get her back. Such defiance of cosmic order, framed as salvific and just, would be morally authorized in the eyes of the non-believers in the audience.

In taking Danny's advice, Sonny also follows a classical model: Orpheus, who exemplified the Romantic artist-as-hero by daring to breach the boundary between mortal and divine realms to recover his beloved.[31] Like Orpheus searching for an entrance to the Underworld, Sonny skates around Venice Beach until he finds the portal to *Xanadu*'s divine "Underworld": the magical mural. He hurtles toward the wall at top speed and braces for impact (see Figure 2.2). Instead, he passes into a black, windy void illuminated

Figure 2.2 The Orpheus-like Sonny Malone (Michael Beck) skates through the mural and into the immortal realm in *Xanadu* (1980). Universal Pictures.

by twinkling white lights in its "sky" and by orange and yellow neon bars that rise to define the "ground." The Muse, both goddess and prisoner, materializes before her joyful lover. He refuses to heed her warnings and leave "before it's too late," instead boldly calling upon Zeus, who manifests as a stentorious male voice thundering from above. With a heartfelt speech extolling the specialness of their love, Sonny declares his intention to take the Muse back with him. He is unexpectedly seconded by a dignified female voice, just as Ovid depicted both the king and queen of the Underworld hearing out Orpheus' similar appeal (*Met.* 10.11–39). The Muse also confesses her novel feelings and begs "can't we have . . . just one moment?" But the patriarch reasserts "the rules" by banishing Sonny, who fades away before the distraught Muse's eyes.

Sonny's immediate failure and Eurydice-like disappearance deviate from the myth of Orpheus, but thus accommodate the Hollywood musical's "dual focus," which privileges both male and female perspectives in advancing the conventional romance plot.[32] Until now, that dual focus had been divided, albeit unequally, between Sonny and Danny. Unlike in *Down to Earth*, the Muse's interiority has not been at issue – except for the moment when she confesses her love to Sonny, just before renouncing him. Sonny's heroic attempt to recover her, and her father's inflexible refusal, lead the Muse to sing the wrenching ballad "Suspended in Time." Accompanied by increasingly close-up camerawork, the Muse and her emotions loom ever larger on what would have been, for the movie's original audience, a monumental screen. As she falls silent at the end of the number, the camera pans up to the "stars" and her father agrees to grant her that "one moment": the club's opening night, when all "Nine Sisters" perform a multi-genre extravaganza, complete with Busby Berkeley-style camerawork harking back to the first wave of Hollywood musicals that accompanied the advent of the soundtrack.

While the lovers' reunion, like Orpheus and Eurydice's, can only be temporary, Sonny's joy at the Muse's appearance recalls Orpheus' initial success – until the performance culminates, inevitably, in the Muses' disappearance. Sonny, however, is relieved of responsibility for this second loss of his beloved, since his seeing her spectacular performance was the point of her return. Furthermore, the mythical artist's fatal despair is supplanted by a surprise ending: the waitress whom Danny mischievously summons is played by Olivia Newton-John! Whereas the playwright in *Down to Earth* never knew Terpsichore's identity and so accepted her doppelganger after a moment of confusion, the knowing Sonny jumps up to talk to this stranger. She looks at him blankly, giving no sign of recognition and thus appearing not to be the Muse.[33] His insistence on engaging her in conversation all the same betrays his claims about special love for the Muse: shades of Orpheus' frail fidelity, perhaps. This resolution also truncates the Pandora-myth's narrative at the point when men marvel at her appearance (*Th.* 588–9), never advancing to the discovery that this "wonder," which looks like a goddess but is not a goddess, will bring about the irreversible degradation of the human condition. *Xanadu*'s concern is rewarding its hero for the cosmic risk-taking that recuperated his masculinity.

THE GOLDEN AGE BEFORE HEROES: HESIODIC HOMOSOCIALITY AND THE DANNY–SONNY BROMANCE

Despite the long-standing tendency to idealize the heroes of classical myth, Hesiod did not consider theirs the best of times. Out of five *genea* (generations) of humanity that he describes in *Works and Days* (109–201), the first *genos* was golden, enjoying constant conviviality and peace, blessed by the gods – and populated exclusively by men.[34] No subsequent *genos* ever enjoyed the happiness of the golden one, not even the heroes. This passage immediately follows Hesiod's account of how Pandora, as the origin of women, was invented to irreversibly degrade the happiness of men.[35] Precisely the impossibility of returning to a world before women sharpens (male) nostalgia for the valorized homosocial intimacy undergirding Hesiod's formulation of the golden age. Viewing women as a destructive intrusion upon the happy homosociality of men establishes a rationale for "Othering" and controlling women that not only justified the sex-segregated hierarchies of emergent Greek polis-society, but also continues to inform modern societies that have rooted their own cultural identities in the classical tradition.[36]

Both *Down to Earth* and *Xanadu* follow this logic, by figuring the Muse as the disruptor of the bromance between the artist-protagonist and his male partner. To achieve her ends, Terpsichore inserts herself into the creative partnership of the playwright and his best buddy, who angrily objects to this devious interloper's machinations and attempts, fruitlessly, to warn his partner against her. Similarly, *Xanadu*'s Muse was only supposed to inspire the creation of the club, the offspring of Sonny and Danny's partnership. Yet the matchmaker develops her own romantic interest in Sonny; then, Danny recognizes her as the woman who broke his heart decades earlier; finally, her departure leads Sonny to the point of abandoning Xanadu – the dream he was to share with Danny. Even without *Down to Earth*'s noir-ish turn, *Xanadu* validates the cultural narrative that heterosexual romance ruins men's undertakings and relationships.

Xanadu also develops tension between the Muse's romancing of Sonny and the blossoming relationship between Sonny and Danny, which she alternately interrupts and fosters. When Sonny's search for the mystery woman leads him back to the beach, he is drawn to Danny by the sound of his clarinet. The two chat about Sonny's peculiar job until the Muse shows herself and Sonny chases her right off the pier: a disruption that spurs him to confide in Danny about his romantic quest. When the two men meet again outside a record store where Sonny hangs his "artwork" and Danny picks up the Glenn Miller album, Danny imagines them as a kind of couple – "a vaudeville act!" – then invites Sonny back to his place. As they listen to his new album, Sonny starts to ask about the woman (the Muse!) pictured in the album booklet, but Danny cuts him off to call attention to his recorded clarinet solo. Danny then confides his own romantic quest: to open another club. He asks Sonny to help, an offer the Muse later encourages Sonny to embrace – specifically, by suggesting the beautiful but broken-down auditorium pictured on the "Nine Sisters" album. Once there, the two men merge their musical fantasies into a big band/rock mash-up ("Dancin'"). Immediately thereafter, Danny exclaims "Kid, I want you to be my partner!"

Sonny demurs, "I don't know anything about being a partner." Danny waves off his concern: "It's like being married," he teases, "without the good part."

As delivered by Gene Kelly, Danny's comment is, once again, laden with intertextual significance. For Kelly had distinguished himself among golden-age Hollywood musical stars for his provocative performance of male homosociality. On the one hand, as a romantic lead he had duetted with the genre's greatest leading ladies, including Rita Hayworth (*Cover Girl*), Vera-Ellen (*On the Town*), Leslie Caron (*An American in Paris*), Debbie Reynolds (*Singin' in the Rain*), Cyd Charisse (*Brigadoon*), and Judy Garland (*For Me and My Gal*; *The Pirate* [1948]; *Summer Stock* [1950]).[37] On the other, Kelly's most exuberant joint performances were with other men: Frank Sinatra ("I Begged Her" in *Anchors Aweigh* [1945]), Phil Silvers ("Put Me to the Test (Reprise)" in *Cover Girl*; "Heavenly Music" in *Summer Stock*), Fred Astaire ("The Babbit and the Bromide" in *Ziegfield Follies* [1946]) the Nicholas Brothers ("Be a Clown" in *The Pirate*), Donald O'Connor ("Moses Supposes" and "Fit as a Fiddle" in *Singin' in the Rain*); and Dan Dailey and Michael Kidd ("The Binge" in *It's Always Fair Weather* [1955]).

In this respect, Kelly was both in step with his times and potentially offbeat. His Hollywood debut coincided with a nationwide celebration of the fraternity sponsored by America's most powerful institutional booster of male homosociality: the armed forces. Kelly, who enlisted in the Navy in 1944, was repeatedly cast as a soldier or military-adjacent character in both musicals and dramas, including *For Me and My Gal*, *Thousands Cheer*, *The Cross of Lorraine* (1943), *Cover Girl*, *Anchors Aweigh*, *On the Town*, *Living in a Big Way* (1947), *The Devil Makes Three* (1952), *Crest of the Wave* (1954), and *It's Always Fair Weather*. As a life-long athlete, another bastion of male homosociality, Kelly also invested in refuting prejudices against dance as an "unmanly" activity by hosting "Dancing: A Man's Game," a 1958 episode of the weekly arts-and-culture television program *Omnibus*.[38] Kelly asserts that both dance and athletics require a man to discipline his body; that "the average American male" accepts dancing as a courtship activity in which he dominates; that men around the world perform folk dances for war and victory. Kelly would have found support in ancient Greek societies, where men who competed in warfare and athletics also performed choral and pyrrhic dance.[39] For his American audience, Kelly engaged star athletes in demonstrating these analogous movements, even performing a dance-duet with boxer Sugar Ray Robinson.

As Steven Cohan explains, Kelly occupied a complicated position within this anxiety-laden conversation about dance and masculinity.[40] Kelly was often lauded for his working-class cockiness, as the only dancer of his time "who had balls," as Stanley Donen said – yet who also exuded sex appeal through the eroticized spectacle of his body, and thus contended with anxiety about being a "sissy dancer," in Kelly's own words.[41] The sailor suit in particular, which Kelly adopted as a costume due to the pants' form-fitting qualities, contributed to "troubl[ing] normative masculinity."[42] The sexuality of soldiers in the intense homosocial environment of the armed forces was also a gray area; Cohan observes that, in films such as *Anchors Aweigh*, Kelly's "macho posturing attracts the meek buddy but initially turns off the female, so a tacit homoerotic admiration underlies the buddy bond."[43] The Coen Brothers viciously textualized the homoerotic undercurrents of Kelly's performances in their "golden age of Hollywood" period piece, *Hail, Caesar!* (2016). The already highly suggestive all-male song-and-dance number "No Dames" culminates in the barely closeted homosexual star Burt Gurney (Channing Tatum) bumping and grinding in a Navy sailor sandwich.

In *Xanadu*, Michael Beck, as Sonny, was not a performer who could offer the kind of artistic partnership that Kelly had enjoyed with Sinatra, O'Connor, or Silvers. But the two do share a fantasy in which Danny's imagined big band merges seamlessly with Sonny's imagined rock band into one showstopping spectacle of sexual longing and exploration ("Dancin'"). Immediately thereafter, Danny asks Sonny to be his partner. *Down to Earth* had also featured a sexually charged intimacy between its male partners, which was interrupted by Terpsichore's arrival.[44] So too in *Xanadu*, when Sonny leaves the room after accepting Danny's offer, the Muse appears to Danny for the first time since 1945. Although she pretends not to know him, Danny realizes that she is, somehow, the woman who walked out and took his dreams with her. This disruption of his happy union with Sonny puts Danny at a crossroads. He could assume a different role from *Cover Girl*: John Coudair, the elderly magazine publisher who loved and lost Rusty's grandmother, the identical-looking vaudeville star, to another man. In a misbegotten attempt to relive his own youth, Coudair interferes in Danny and Rusty's relationship, only realizing the error of his ways at the last minute.

But, rather than serve as a blocking figure, Danny decorously yields his past romantic claim – which facilitates his dream of getting back into show business. Indeed, by encouraging Sonny to pursue her, Danny enables the Muse's fulfillment of woman's classic social function: solidifying social and economic ties between an older man and a younger man to whom he grants her use, in exchange for a benefit to himself. For male partners thus conjoined, there is no going back to a Hesiodic golden age of male homosociality. Danny not only steps aside for heterosexual romance, he also procures a substitute by knowingly summoning the Muse's doppelganger, the waitress. He thus takes on the goddess' former role as Sonny's patron, a socially less complicated and more lasting relationship than bromance can provide, post-golden age.

CONCLUSION: THE UTOPIAN PROMISES OF DISCO, AND OF THE HOLLYWOOD MUSICAL

Although the intensity of the romance plot overshadows the characters' ostensible goal, *Xanadu* culminates in the opening of a club that aspires to the utopian promises of the project's studio-driven disco roots: a haven that promises a better world for all, regardless of identity. In an implicit rebuke to the publicity-hungry exclusivity of the nation's most famous disco club, Studio 54, Danny tells a reporter about his plans for opening night: "no celebrities here, just regular people." When the festivities begin, the camera pans across the clubgoers, all skating and clapping and vocalizing together, a cavalcade of humanity that echoes the Muses' own notable ethnic diversity. Upon Newton-John's Muse bursting into view and singing directly into the camera, she testifies to the movie's utopian intentions with lyrics that implicate the audience:

A place where nobody dared to go
The love that we came to know
They call it Xanadu
And now, open your eyes and see
What we have made is real
We are in Xanadu

This world, based on a love and inclusivity once thought impossible, suggests *Xanadu*'s ambition to enact political work that Richard Dyer has identified as lacking in the Hollywood musical's conventional utopianism.[45] In a seminal article, Dyer works from the premise that American entertainment's utopianism is limited to "provid[ing] alternatives *to* capitalism which will be provided by capitalism."[46] He enumerates scarcity, exhaustion, dreariness, manipulation, and fragmentation as needs typically legitimated by Hollywood musicals.

Within this closed capitalist circuit, class, race, patriarchy, and sexuality are ignored – for no truly radical reorganization of society is mooted by the genre. Given Dyer's framework, what of the utopia that is Xanadu?

While *Xanadu*'s three protagonists are indeed white and invested in both patriarchy and capitalism, the film's insistence on the racial inclusivity of its fantasy world is visually striking. A positively valued, highly sexualized exploration of difference across temporal and racial lines is crucial to integrating Danny's fantasy and Sonny's in "Dancin'." The problems and dignity of working-class people are also noted: both among Sonny's co-workers and when Danny insists on including the club's construction workers in a champagne toast. And although no speaking characters are explicitly homosexual, the film's camp sensibility was almost immediately the subject of tribute by fans.[47] While an iron age in many ways, social progressivism also made an impact on the 1970s, and on *Xanadu*. This utopian spirit of inclusivity contributed to its attainment of cult status.

Still, heterosexual patriarchy remains the norm in the world of *Xanadu*. The goddesses' significance as ontologically superior beings is, as ever, complicated by their implication in a patriarchal cosmic system. As their Busby Berkeley sequence during the finale recalls, the Hollywood musical was founded on the spectacle of the objectified female body; save for the movie's star, the Muses neither speak nor sing. So too, the disco "diva" served a double function: expressing liberation, but also subsumed within a system commodifying hedonistic license, which would become a major target of social conservatives.[48]

Rather than an entirely new order, the ideal world that *Xanadu* embodies is presented, in a later verse of the title song, as the restoration of a previous order:

> The love that echoes of long ago
> You needed the world to know
> They are in Xanadu
> The dream that came through a million years
> That lived on through all the tears
> It came to Xanadu

This turn speaks to the kind of musical, within Dyer's typology, in which both narrative and numbers implicate the film's utopianism. However, instead of "removal of the whole film in time and space . . . to places where it can be believed (by white urban Americans) that song and dance are 'in the air'," like the Scottish Highlands of *Brigadoon*, *Xanadu* proposes (as noted above) to transport its fantasy world into its characters' quotidian present.[49] That fantasy world nests one ancient golden age – the age of heroes, when deities assisted great and worthy men in achieving impossible and glorious goals – inside the modern golden-age triad of the musical genre, the Hollywood studio system, and post-war America.

Dyer cautions against confusing films that "point back, to a golden age" with forward-looking utopianism.[50] Indeed, much of *Xanadu*'s project is to revive that mid-century American golden age. Yet the film's roots in the sensibility of disco and youth culture preserve a countervailing desire, even if not wholly realized, to escape from the constraints of society – and not only for "just a moment," but by meaningfully reorganizing it according to progressive values. Thus *Xanadu* desires its nostalgia to be not merely restorative, in Svetlana Boym's formulation, but reflective, by accommodating the formerly excluded within its timeless ideal.[51]

NOTES

Thanks to Emma Scioli for notes on this chapter.

1 Mattson (2009).
2 Shapiro (2005: 182, 189). For disco as a musical style and cultural phenomenon, see also Lawrence (2003), Echols (2010). Dyer (1979: 23) assimilates disco's utopian qualities to its romanticism and its ability to create community spirit.
3 Echols (2010: 159–94).
4 See Nowell (2013).
5 On the history of Venice Beach and its Beat and modern art communities, see Maynard (1991), Schrank (2009: 97–134).
6 On "discophobia," see Lawrence (2003: 363–431), Shapiro (2005: 227–248), Echols (2010: 195–232).
7 For the movie's *Nachleben*, see Xanadu Preservation Society (n.d.: chs. 6–10).
8 On Silver's (infamous) determination to make *Xanadu*, see Collis (2007); on the rewrite process, see "Going Back to Xanadu" (2008).
9 For a succinct overview, see Langford (2005: 82–104). Seminal works include Altman (1987) and Feuer (1993). Now, see also Griffin (2018).
10 See e.g. Woll (1983), Griffin (2018: 97–123).
11 See Hirschhorn (1984: 94–101, 104–5, 153–7).
12 On the Freed Unit, see Griffin (2018: 125–45).
13 Cohan (2005: 198).
14 See Hirschhorn (1984: 272).
15 See Brideson and Brideson (2017: 28–9, 34); Cohan (2005: 197).
16 On MGM's declining fortunes, see Cohan (2005: 246–56).

17 According to "Musical: 1974–Present, Live Action only" on *Box Office Mojo* (n.d.), by late December 2017 *Grease* still had been surpassed only by Disney's *Beauty and the Beast* (2017). IMDB's "Top-US-Grossing Musical Titles" list (n.d.), inclusive of live-action and animated musicals through 2017, ranks *Grease* eleventh.
18 For season-by-season rankings and viewership, see *ClassicTVHits.com* (n.d.).
19 For *Theogony* in Greek and English, see Hesiod (1914; repr. 1982).
20 See Arthur (1983: 107, 111).
21 See Altman (1987: 200–71).
22 For the *Odyssey* in Greek and English, see Homer (1995).
23 Gantz (1993: 39, 718–21, 288–95).
24 For *Metamorphoses* in Latin and English, see Ovid (1946a, 1946b).
25 For the *Homeric Hymn to Aphrodite* in Greek and English, see Hesiod (1914; repr. 1982).
26 For *Works and Days* in Greek and English, see Hesiod (1914; repr. 1982). Translations in this chapter are my own.
27 For a critical reinterpretation of Hayworth's performance, see McLean (2004: 111–43).
28 On elitism versus populism in the Hollywood musical, see Feuer (1977); on *Down to Earth*, see McLean (2004: 132–41), Winkler (2009a: 93–103).
29 McLean (2004: 55–60).
30 The handler does promise reunion with the playwright after his death, but the movie closes with her alone.
31 On Orpheus' journey to the Underworld as a katabant and romantic, see Gantz (1993: 721–5), Segal (1989), Henry (1992), Holtsmark (2001).
32 Altman (1987: 16–27).
33 Winkler (2009a: 107) reads this ending differently: as the Muse in fact returning. The eternal being Zeus' earlier confusion between "one moment" and "forever" creates a legitimate ambiguity, compounded by Newton-John's acting and Robert Greenwald's direction.
34 See e.g. Arthur (1983: 97, 111–12 with notes).
35 See Arthur (1982, 1983); Zeitlin (1996) remains an influential reading of the Pandora myth.
36 See Arthur (1984).
37 On the sexual dynamics of such dance duets, see Dyer (2011).
38 Kelly as athlete: Brideson and Brideson (2017: 24–5). Thanks to Morgan Strong at Global ImageWorks for access to this episode of *Omnibus*.
39 See Lonsdale (2000).
40 Cohan (2005: 149–99).
41 Cohan (2005: 150, 153).
42 Cohan (2005: 158).
43 Cohan (2005: 166).

44 McLean (2004: 135–7).
45 Dyer (1981).
46 Dyer (1981: 183–4).
47 See Xanadu Preservation Society (n.d.: chs. 6–10).
48 Kutulas (2003), with critique by Kooijman (2005).
49 Dyer (1981: 187–8).
50 Dyer (1981: 188).
51 Boym (2001).

3 *Gilding American History through Song Culture in* O Brother, Where Art Thou? *(2000)*

Ryan Platte

Joel and Ethan Coen's 2000 film *O Brother, Where Art Thou?* offers a romanticizing depiction of the Depression-era American South, reflecting the filmmakers' penchant for exploring the ways in which iconic American pasts are remembered within popular culture.[1] Within their oeuvre, this film is remarkable in two respects: its thorough integration of music into the narrative, and the fact that it is modeled on a classical text, Homer's *Odyssey*. This fact is stated explicitly in the first frames of the opening sequence, by displaying a translation of the epic's first lines; this sequence concludes with a credit reading "Based upon 'The Odyssey' by Homer." The Coens have been famously coy about their knowledge of the *Odyssey* and the degree to which it shapes the film.[2] Yet they have acknowledged a relationship between the *Odyssey* and the film's music, confirming in at least one interview that Homeric poetry and the music of the film resemble each other at a fundamental level: "They are verbal traditions. Oral traditions."[3]

Although numerous scholars have analyzed the film's treatment of the *Odyssey*, casting doubt on the filmmakers' professedly casual engagement with the text,[4] much remains to be said regarding the film's engagement with the *Odyssey* vis-à-vis its use of song to generate its gilded rendering of the American Southern past.[5] Analysis of the film's music reveals that the relationship between the Homeric world and that of the film stems from the Coens' recognition that "golden" eras are, at least in part, generated and remembered through the legacy of song, in both classical and modern cultures. In fact, the film is not set in a historically accurate rendering of the pre-modern South, but in modernity's nostalgia-laden (mis)remembering of it, which is constructed largely through song – just as Greek cultural memory of the mythical Trojan War and its aftermath was constructed.

While several scholars have written on the movie's use of music, *O Brother* also highlights how technological change affected American folk-song tradition through recording – a phenomenon similar to that which changed the Greek song culture into "Homeric" epic.[6] This focus on a moment of epochal change allows the filmmakers to undercut the notion that folk music is a simple and genuine artifact of the past. Instead, they both invoke nostalgia through song and expose the artificiality of the traffic in nostalgia, which has shaped attitudes toward the Greek and American pasts. What is "golden" is in fact artificial: it never did exist, although audiences are often willing to believe that it did as part of their own mythologizing worldview.

The Coen brothers' interest in using Homeric tradition to meditate on folk-song culture and its role in the nostalgic construction of "golden" ages is expressed nowhere more clearly than in the use of "Man of Constant Sorrow," which is performed by the film's protagonist Ulysses Everett McGill (George Clooney) and his companions at two pivotal moments, before two different Homer-analogues: the blind studio technician and the gubernatorial candidate Homer Stokes.[7] These performances occur after Everett escapes from jail to journey homeward in order to prevent the remarriage of his wife Penny (Holly Hunter) to a new suitor. This narratological framework recalls the homeward journey of Odysseus, also known as Ulysses (as the Romans and the Latinate tradition call him), whose heroic exploits and mission to stop the remarriage of his wife Penelope were seminal in shaping Greek ideas about the "golden age of heroes" and have exerted special influence on posterity's attitudes toward this concept via the classical tradition.[8] An analysis of the film's engagement with two different genres of American music, old-time and bluegrass, in these two performances of "Man of Constant Sorrow" will reveal how the Coens use the Homeric past to imagine a Southern future, and will examine the role of nostalgia and song culture in shaping national identity.

FIRST PERFORMANCE: THE RECORDING OF ORAL TRADITION

Everett and his companions' first performance of "Man of Constant Sorrow" sets the stage for the film's examination of how technological change affected folk-song tradition. From the characters' perspective, it is motivated by Odyssean resourcefulness in the face of sheer need: as convicts who just escaped from a chain gang, they lack money. They hear from a hitchhiking African-American guitarist (Chris Thomas King) whom they pick up that someone is paying for men to sing into a can. Unbeknownst to them, the can is actually a microphone, and the man is a technician who records traditional songs in order to market them through radio broadcast and record sales. The technician, identified in the film's credits simply as "Radio Station Man" (Stephen Root), enquires whether the men, whom Everett spontaneously introduces as the Soggy Bottom Boys, can produce such material. Comical miscommunication and deception follow regarding the band's racial make-up and the blind technician's disinterest in African-American musical traditions. Ultimately the group avers that they do have relevant material to offer and are allowed to perform a song, despite the fact that their band includes an African-American guitar player (see Figure 3.1). They are duly paid and proceed along their journey, unaware that the technician markets their recording to great commercial success, which is revealed to the audience through a montage. In fact, their very incomprehension serves the film's interest in the popular construction of the culture of folk song, which is often conceptualized, and fetishized, as fundamentally unselfconscious and pre-modern in its lack of worldly or technological sophistication.

"Man of Constant Sorrow" is quintessentially Odyssean in its content and word play. Its descriptions of wandering, sadness, and

Figure 3.1 Homer-avatar Radio Station Man (Stephen Root) recording "Man of Constant Sorrow" with the Soggy Bottom Boys, visible in the reflection in *O Brother, Where Art Thou?* (2000). Touchstone Pictures/Universal Pictures.

romantic loss resonate with the experiences and fears of the film's protagonist as well as those of the ancient Odysseus in his own long, unhappy, wandering return to his wife and position of social legitimacy in Ithaca. Moreover, the title and refrain of the song invoke an ancient folk etymology of the name Odysseus, which invited puns due to its resemblance to the verbs *odyssomai*, "to hate," and *odyromai*, "to sorrow."[9] These ancient etymological connections are probably linguistically misleading, but to a Greek-speaker's ear, Odysseus' name sounded like "hated man" or "man of sorrow." Furthermore, Goldhill has suggested that the song's title recalls a phrase used by Odysseus to describe himself: *mala d' eimi polustonos*, often translated as something close to the title of the song: for example, in the Loeb Classical Library translation, "I am a man of many sorrows" (*Od.* 19.118).[10]

Beyond the specifically Odyssean nature of the song, the entire scene is broadly Homeric because the blind recorder of traditional song must reflect the legendary Homer, whose blindness is the principal physical characteristic through which he is remembered. Homer's significance, however, derives from his role in the transition from oral to recorded song. In the transformation of traditional song through this Homer-avatar's use of technology, the Coen brothers highlight an underlying relationship between the songs of the film and the *Odyssey* as "Homeric" song. Antiquity's Homer of course sat outside of the songs attributed to him, while the Coens have placed this Homer inside the narrative: perhaps as a twist on the Homeric habit of incorporating epic singers into the epics themselves, including the blind Demodocus.[11] *O Brother*'s blind technician records the song of this man of sorrow, just as the blind bard recorded the song of Ulysses Everett McGill's ancient namesake.

This scene, already thematically central to the film's narrative, gains additional significance from the current scholarly understanding of the history of the Homeric tradition. Initially, in the prealphabetic period, Greek song existed in myriad, ever-changing, and uncanonized traditions that resembled folk-song traditions in other times and places. Songs had many performers, but no single author to whom the creation of a unique work could be credited. Greek song culture began to change in the archaic period, beginning in the early eighth century BCE, upon the invention of recording technology: writing.[12] The early stages of this change are difficult to reconstruct, but the invention of writing ultimately led to the creation of fixed literate texts from what had once been fluid oral song traditions.

The most famous and enduring examples of this process are the two great epic poems about the Trojan War and its aftermath, the *Iliad* and *Odyssey*, both attributed to Homer. Disagreement remains among classicists regarding the existence of a historical person named Homer and the role that such a person could have played in the history of Greek song, but certainly in the popular imagination he is the originator of the literary epic tradition. A general awareness of these historical developments in Homeric song is no longer confined to academia; even the popular film critic Roger Ebert argued that *O Brother*'s seemingly disjointed, episodic plot reflects characteristics of the *Odyssey*'s pre-literate performances.[13] Just as the figure of Homer divides the worlds of Greek oral and literate song in the classical tradition, so too the Coens depict *O Brother*'s blind technician as mediating the conversion of oral song traditions to recorded commercial products in the American South, a phenomenon that is central to the world of the film.

FROM SONG CULTURE TO CULTURAL COMMODITY

Not only do the Coen brothers look backward toward the transition from the Greek oral song tradition to "Homer's" canonical epic, they also depict an artistically rendered impression of a genuine historical development, through which the recording of American song became an integral element in the construction of the lost "golden age" of the romanticized Southern past. This film is set in the flush of the first American folk-music revival, which involved the rediscovery of traditional folk song, especially Southern folk song, by the American public, record producers, and academics. As the studio technician explains to Everett and his companions, he is not looking for African-American song traditions. He specifies that he is instead interested only in "old-timey" music. He claims, "people can't seem to get enough of it."

"Old-time" is an authentic marketing term from the period, used to describe supposedly traditional American musical styles, particularly from the rural South. Although it was marketed historically both as "old-time" and as "hillbilly" music, characters in the film always call it "old-timey," a meaningful choice on the Coens' part.[14] Having now lost its musical significance and become almost exclusively pejorative, "hillbilly" would have been at odds with the agenda of the film. The term also implies an ethnographic distinction between the culture of the audience and of the music's producers, as if they were a people isolated from the broad American public. "Old-time," or "old-timey," on the other hand, suggests that this music is removed from the audience temporally rather than culturally, that it is a shared American inheritance uncorrupted by modernity. The Coens' preference for this nomenclature perfectly suits the project of the film: highlighting the processes through which broad cultural value is attached to inherited song as historical artifact and national-cultural patrimony.

The movement to record these songs was in many ways driven by a sudden appetite for Southern folk song among America's non-Southern population, fed aggressively by the newly emerged radio broadcasting and recording industries that avidly recruited Southern singers. Through record sales, industry professionals monetized the image of the rural South by marketing it to a broad American audience among whom inherited song traditions were increasingly being displaced by novel genres like swing and jazz, popularized in American cities and connected to changes brought about by the rapid pace of innovation encouraged by the mixing of diverse populations. Not only did preserving and popularizing folk songs through the act of recording cater to a nostalgia for an idealized rural past, but their promulgation actually helped to construct that past: the very imagined past in which this film is set.[15]

This process of recording and commercial dissemination also definitively altered the musical culture that had produced these songs, the practices that had transmitted them, and even the songs themselves.[16] These songs had previously been performed primarily in amateur environments, often sung at home among friends and family. They were technically simple and subject to wide variation, with no one particular, authoritative version hindering diversification, and with no real authorship in the modern sense: much like the pre-literate song traditions of ancient Greece. Recording and broadcasting these songs, however, created authoritative versions associated with particular performers, just as certain song traditions among Greek peoples became associated with Homer.[17]

One particular musical group recorded several of the folk songs featured in *O Brother*, and their legacy has directly affected both the world within this film and the music that shapes it: the Carter Family. The Carters serve as a real-world paradigm of the historic processes depicted in the film, of the commodification and alteration of folk-song culture in constructing the idealized South. The Carters were a poor family from rural Virginia whose recorded versions of traditional songs achieved great commercial success. The patriarch of the family, Alvin Pleasant "A. P." Delaney Carter, famously capitalized on the folk-revival phenomenon not only by recording the songs that he and his family knew themselves, but also by scouring the countryside for others that he rearranged and for which his producer then obtained a copyright.[18] The Carter Family broadcast its songs on "border radio," radio stations located just south of the American–Mexican border where they were free from restrictions on broadcast range; thus, their songs were heard across the entire United States.[19] Their particular versions of the songs, which they popularized through these radio broadcasts, comprise much of the canon of American folk song and have influenced how early twentieth-century Southern culture came to be imagined. The power of these songs to affect historical memory is rooted in their ability to seem premodern, yet they are very much the creation of a technological era that ushered in monumental societal change.

As part of this process' effect on song tradition, the Carters became professional folk singers. Indeed, through the canonization of song and commercialization of song culture, the folk-music revival essentially created this new profession, a phenomenon that *O Brother, Where Art Thou?* depicts. As the Soggy Bottom Boys record their rendition of "Man of Constant Sorrow" with the first Homer-analogue, they unwittingly enter into this process, which eventually renders them professional musicians and fundamentally stamps this traditional song as theirs. Thereby the film's characters act out the very processes that so shaped Americans' notions of the Southern past, communicating Southern song tradition through recording while also altering the tradition by creating a misleading impression of authorship. As this is similar to the process that affected Greek oral song and yielded Homeric epic, the Homeric subtext and presence of a Homer-figure frame and highlight these facts via analogy with Western history's premier example of this phenomenon.

This parallelism between Homeric and American song highlights the epochal change brought about through adoption of transformational technologies, which the film emphasizes through not only recording technology but also electrical technology in general. The arrival of widespread electricity functions as a line of demarcation separating the old South and the new, about to transform the rural world and its traditions forever. The camera lingers over light bulbs as well as radios (see Figure 3.2); George "Baby Face" Nelson (Michael Badalucco) is carried off to be executed in the electric chair, exclaiming "[they're] gonna electrify me. I'm gonna go off like a Roman candle!" In order to secure reunion with Penny by

Figure 3.2 Listeners at home hear the second performance of "Man of Constant Sorrow" live via radio broadcast in *O Brother, Where Art Thou?* (2000). Touchstone Pictures/Universal Pictures.

recovering her wedding ring, Everett must race to their old house before the area is flooded in the construction of a new hydroelectric dam, which Everett sees as the harbinger of a new modern age for Southern culture: "Yes, sir, the South is gonna change. Everything's gonna be put on electricity and run on a paying basis . . . We're gonna see a brave new world where they run everybody a wire and hook us all up to a grid." The flooding essentially changes the coordinates of what constitutes the past for Everett. Although Odysseus left the sea behind for Ithaca, Everett's Ithaca becomes a sea as he and Penny walk into an electricity-dominated future. There is no past for them to return to.

The final scene of the film shows the hero strolling through town with Penny, past a billboard for a power company depicting, and perhaps foretelling, an urban streetscape. Thus, the film divides an idealized image of the irretrievable past from the modern present as experienced by the film's audience. Much as the new technology of writing heralded a change to the oral poetic tradition and drew a line between an idealized prehistory and the conditions under which the audience of Homeric poetry lived, *O Brother*'s focus on recording technology reflects a general awareness of the impact that electricity will have on the rural South by ushering it into modernity.

The film's use of folk song thus addresses cultural change itself and the processes through which pasts are remembered and rendered golden, or at least gilded. The era imagined in *O Brother* is especially prone to romanticizing in the American consciousness because the setting is predominantly pre-technological and rural. It also conveniently post-dates Emancipation and Reconstruction, and so is more easily fetishized than earlier periods in Southern history since it avoids forcing the audience into direct confrontation with slavery and the Civil War. This confluence of historical factors makes this time and place easier to fashion as an exemplar of pre-modern Americana, and folk song that conforms to that image can be seen as a genuine reflection of a lost time and place, one that both informs and validates its construction. For non-Southern audiences, moreover, to whom this music has long been aggressively marketed, "folk song" conveys in its content and speech a particularly potent mix of distance and familiarity. The audience feels close enough to the imagined era to be connected to it, while distant enough to long for it, which contributes to the process of nostalgia-making, of creating golden ages. This effect is powerful enough to valorize even difficult historical circumstances, like an economic depression, as the nostalgia-inducing processes of song fashion it into a deceptively picturesque reflection of national character.

Much the same may be said of Homeric epic in its treatment of the protracted, bloody conflict of the Trojan War, which was fundamental to the cultural identity formation of historical Greek audiences despite being set in an earlier, lost era that bore little resemblance to the world in which they actually lived. This is evident at a linguistic level, because the epics employed an archaizing poetic dialect with older expressions and forms of grammar, much like old-time American song. Clear idealization of the Homeric heroes can be seen elsewhere in poetry, such as in the archaic cosmology of Hesiod, which refers to them as "more just" (*dikaioteron*), now dwelling "blessed" (*olbioi*) in their afterlives while the current generation lives with "toil" (*kamatou*) and "woe" (*oizuos*).[20] In fact, Homeric epic itself explicitly and repeatedly invites its audiences to compare themselves, unfavorably, to its heroes: for example, in the *Iliad*, Nestor drinks from a cup that two men could not lift easily "such as men are now" (12.449).[21] Even in Plato's famous criticism in the fourth-century BCE *Republic*, Socrates acknowledges that people attribute to Homer the education of Greece and advise that all Greeks govern their lives by the lessons to be found in the epics.[22] In fact, throughout antiquity Homer's works were central in Greek education (*paideia*), in part for their ability to impart core elements of Greek identity.[23] Although historic attitudes toward Homer's works were complex and not universally deferential,[24] the world of Homeric epic was both quintessentially Greek and, like old-time song in America, removed from its audiences by language and time, a convenient feature in the construction of golden ages.

SECOND PERFORMANCE: HOMER, THE KKK, AND THE DISRUPTION OF NOSTALGIA

Folk song is a powerful tool for creating golden ages out of historical periods, precisely because the medium is assumed to offer a reflection of a real time and place. Consequently, the disruption of that idea is dangerously destabilizing for the nostalgic process through which such golden ages are created. The Coens do both: they intentionally use Southern song to generate this particular nostalgia, yet also use re-enactments of folk song to expose the constructedness of that nostalgia through its political mobilization in the gubernatorial campaign that serves as an intersecting subplot to Ulysses Everett McGill's homecoming. The incumbent is Menelaus "Pappy" O'Daniel (Charles Durning), named after Menelaus, the husband of Helen, and Wilbert Lee "Pappy" O'Daniel, a Texas politician who ran a radio show in the 1920s and 1930s. Like his historical antecedent, the film's O'Daniel funds a radio program that broadcasts "old-timey" material and on which the blind studio technician plays the songs that he records, including "Man of Constant Sorrow." O'Daniel's opponent is Homer Stokes (Wayne Duvall), the "reform" candidate who is also a leader of the local Ku Klux Klan. His name is an overt invitation to read the themes of Homeric song culture into his use of folk song, which achieves its fullest expression in the second performance of "Man of Constant Sorrow" at the campaign event that serves as the film's climax.

The film provides three examples of Homer Stokes' construction of nostalgia through music. The first two occasions involve open-air performances by family bands. The first involves the Sunny-Siders, who ride in the back of a Stokes campaign truck singing "Keep on the Sunny Side." In the second example, at an outdoor campaign event for Stokes, the audience is entertained by a child band, the Wharvey Gals, singing "In the Highways." In an era of professionalized folk musicianship, the presentation of family bands and singing children carries special nostalgic semantic value: it suggests a lack of professionalism, and thus the idealized past. Both songs that Stokes' singers perform were, in fact, recorded by the Carter Family, the premier example of this phenomenon. Despite their increasing professionalism, their status as a family band allowed them to continue cultivating their identity as authentic folk musicians. The Carters' legacy further helps to make these songs feel traditional to both internal and external audiences of the film.

Both "Keep on the Sunny Side" and "In the Highways" are old-time songs played in a relatively unornamented, traditional style, the symbolism of which Stokes is keen to cultivate. The imagery of the authentic, pre-modern folk musician evokes much the same response from modern audiences as Stokes intends it to have within the film itself: a feeling of nostalgia for a constructed past. In fact, the film spawned a very successful and notably high-priced "Down from the Mountain" tour that featured performances of songs from the film's soundtrack, which was credited with stimulating another, more recent revival of Southern folk song, once again marketing pristine rusticity to modern audiences. Yet Stokes, although a "reform" candidate insofar as he seeks to unseat an incumbent, is ideologically invested in a particular version of the romanticized Southern past that he intends these songs to symbolize: one rooted in segregation and white supremacy. The third and final campaign performance lays bare the constructedness of this past and the dangers of the folk-song-induced nostalgia of both the internal and external audiences.

Unbeknownst to Everett and his companions, their earlier recording of "Man of Constant Sorrow" has become a radio hit, and "the Soggy Bottom Boys" celebrated musicians. This fame leads to one of the most densely Homeric scenes of the film: the performance of a song about Odysseus, by a man named Ulysses, for a man named Homer, in a competition with a man named Menelaus. It is also a prolonged reference to the climactic scene of the *Odyssey* in Book 21, in which Odysseus competes in a bow contest while disguised as an old beggar. In this scene, Odysseus is likened to a musician:

> [He strung the bow] as when a man well learned in the phorminx [a stringed instrument] and in song easily stretches a string around a new tuning peg . . . Grabbing [the bow] with his right hand he tested the string, which sang out beautifully, like the song of a nightingale. (*Od.* 21.406–11)

After his success leads to the revelation of his identity, Odysseus kills Penelope's suitors and reunites with her. Likewise, no longer able to hide their true appearances as they did from the blind technician in the recording booth, yet still escaped criminals, the Soggy Bottom Boys perform in disguise as rural old men, complete with long gray beards and dungaree overalls. By the end of the performance, they reveal their identity, reunite Everett with Penny, and effectively banish her suitor.

Before these results are achieved, however, Stokes interrupts the performance and, after suggesting that the integrated band is "miscegenated," and "not white," declares that "they ain't even old-timey." The most fascinating elements of Stokes' objections to this particular version of this song tend to be overlooked because their musicological accuracy is overshadowed by his overt racism. This performance is not in fact old-time but bluegrass, a very different style of music essentially descended from old-time; the nature and timing of that descent are critical here. Dating the beginning of bluegrass is difficult and has been the subject of some controversy, but its birth is generally placed around the mid-1940s, after the setting of this performance.[25] Its generic characteristics include vocals sung in the "high, lonesome style" and verses interspersed with virtuosic jazz-like instrumental improvisations.[26] It also differs from idealized folk music in its obvious professionalism – and fundamental reliance on electricity. As Neil Rosenberg points out, "Although bluegrass has traditional antecedents . . . it has been a professional and commercial music from its beginning . . . Bluegrass depends on the microphone, and this fact has shaped its sound."[27]

Stokes' objections that the band is not "old-timey" occur as Everett's disguise is revealed, at the moment when the inauthenticity of the band is exposed; he is not just speaking in colloquial terms, but meta-cinematically hinting at a genuine generic anachronism. As a professionalized and virtuosic evolution of old-time music that emerged in response to the technologies associated with radio, bluegrass is quite literally the music created by the developments that this film depicts, not the music that accompanied these developments.[28] *O Brother*'s particular rendition of "Man of Constant Sorrow" is in fact based on a recording that the Stanley Brothers released in 1951.[29] But when Stokes complains that the band does not conform generically to the categories of authenticity that he uses for constructing traditional Southern culture through song, he speaks not as a musicologist but as a racist privileging whiteness.

Stokes' complaint about the racial composition of the band, that they are "miscegenated," also contains a double entendre. This band's integration of white and black culture occurs at the level of its sound and extends well beyond the incorporation of Tommy Johnson, the African-American guitar player. For a further characteristic of bluegrass, and of this performance, is its incorporation of blue notes, usually believed to originate in the music of African-Americans.[30] This fact enriches Tommy's significance in the band because he tells Everett and his companions that he sold his soul to the devil at a crossroads in exchange for his ability to play guitar: an appropriation of the legend of the pre-eminent blues guitarist, Robert Johnson. The blue notes here reflect a type of marked transracial influence that was not characteristic of "old-time" music in the 1930s, even though African-Americans did play the genre as well. The belief that "old-time" music was uniquely or exclusively played in white communities is in fact a deeply politicized misremembering that is promulgated by Homer Stokes.[31] Yet the style in which "Man of Constant Sorrow" is performed in the film constitutes an overt nod to a uniquely African-American musical style that shaped bluegrass, and later shaped rock-and-roll. Consequently, this film's performances of the song pull the audience into a sort of musical time-warp, akin to hearing rock-and-roll in a film about World War II. They also anticipate a radio-driven integration of musical culture that will affect Southern music in the years to come, as well as another great cultural change coming to the South: desegregation.

Modernity's tendency to reconstruct the past through song rests on the assumption that the music that descends from the past is, in fact, of that past. This futuristic performance, however, flies in the face of that assumption. In *O Brother*, "Man of Constant Sorrow" grows out of the past, yet does not belong to it, and in fact showcases how inherited songs will evolve through constant updating in new media. And in this respect, Stokes terribly misjudges his audience's feelings about this performance. After objecting to the generics of the performance, he attempts to ingratiate himself with them by revealing his membership in the Ku Klux Klan and his role in the earlier attempted lynching of Tommy Johnson. In effect, Stokes' own promotion of an idealized past through folk song is shown to be concomitant with his unacceptable love of the racist past. The audience responds to his interpretation of tradition by running him out of town on a rail, literally. They then return enthusiastically to the professionalized mixed-race folk music of the future, broadcast live over the radio to all the voters at home.

Despite the canonization of folk song highlighted by the film's Homer-analogues, its evolution is not arrested, but rather is altered, by technology. The internal audience's rejection of Homer Stokes is more than a simple reflection of the historical developments highlighted here; it is also a rejection of the notion of folk music's authenticity, especially in retrograde political uses.[32] This anachronistic bluegrass arrangement points to where the film's musical and cultural changes are leading: from an old style of music to a new one, with new means of transmission, within a changing society.

Hereby the film also exposes the artificiality and deceptiveness of the "golden age" narrative that it promulgates, especially in its politicized agenda.

POSTSCRIPT: *O BROTHER* IN THE CINEMATIC EPIC TRADITION

As a potent symbol of culture, folk song is especially prone to manipulation because audiences can infer an authenticity that is contrived and self-serving. Consequently, Homeric and Southern song have each become a stand-in for earlier eras, as the very building-blocks out of which posterity has fashioned memories of the past. It is this parallelism that the Coens exploit in *O Brother, Where Art Thou?*, a film set in an imagined South, constructed through the legacy of American oral tradition, and framed by Western history's premier example of this phenomenon: Homeric epic. Yet the film creates an ironic and critical distance from this phenomenon by showcasing folk music as not frozen in time, but progressive. The film capitalizes on and exploits the easy nostalgia attaching to folk song, yet does this while skewering and destabilizing the assumptions undergirding that nostalgia. Moreover, the film does all of this through an innovative engagement with the history of ancient Greek song.

The apparent intentionality of *O Brother*'s use of Homeric song is underscored by the Coen brothers' engagement with Homeric song in a subsequent film, *Inside Llewyn Davis* (2013), in many ways a companion to *O Brother, Where Art Thou?* Each film takes place during a critical moment in the development of American folk-song culture and each is deeply engaged with the *Odyssey*. *Inside Llewyn Davis* is set in the New York folk-music scene of the 1960s, the second American folk-musical revival, sometimes called a "golden age."[33] The film's main character finds himself at odds with a man named Troy and then embarks on a great journey to the Gate of Horn folk club for insights into his future. Odysseus, of course, fought against the city of Troy and sought supernatural knowledge by journeying to the Underworld, which, according to Vergil's Homeric adaptation in the *Aeneid*, housed the Gate of Horn through which prophetic dreams were said to come to mankind (6.893–9).[34] This main plot repeatedly intersects with that of a cat named Ulysses, who, like Odysseus, travels incognito while others repeatedly try to discover his name. His identity is revealed only after returning home, where intimate examination by an older woman uncovers physical evidence of a distinctive previous trauma: from neutering, not a boar hunt. In both films, the reception of Homeric epic is grounded in the culture of folk song. It cannot be coincidental that the Coens' two Homeric films are also their only films about folk song in the American past.

The Coen brothers seem to have done something cinematically noteworthy by incorporating the song-culture of Homeric epic into *O Brother, Where Art Thou?* and *Inside Llewyn Davis*. What might this treatment of Homer mean for the continuing reception of ancient epic? This film's epic intentions trace back to its inspiration, 1941's *Sullivan's Travels*, in which a Hollywood producer proclaims his intention to make an "epic" about the Great Depression entitled *O Brother, Where Art Thou?* He never does make the movie, but Ethan Coen has suggested that theirs is the film that the main character in *Sullivan's Travels* would have made, if he had been steeped in Homeric literature and early country music.[35] *Sullivan's Travels* is, moreover, an Odyssean epic itself, influenced by *Gulliver's Travels*, an Odyssean novel. This film then exists explicitly in a tradition of Homeric epic after Homer. Of the various ancient epic features that modern artists can import into their own work to shape their art and to signal their affiliation with the epic tradition, orality had been forgotten until quite recently. Yet it is integral to the very concept of *O Brother, Where Art Thou?*[36] The Coen brothers have proven that orality is a recognizable and exploitable element of the epic genre once again, in two cases locating this song culture within American cultural golden ages.

NOTES

I am grateful to many people who volunteered to read and comment on this work. I thank Roshan Abraham, G. Fay Edwards, and Julia Staffel for their helpful input throughout the process, and Yurie Hong and Mark Nugent for useful criticism and suggestions. Great thanks are also due to this volume's editor, Meredith E. Safran, for substantive suggestions that greatly improved this piece.

1 Other examples include *Barton Fink* (1991), *Miller's Crossing* (1990), and *The Hudsucker Proxy* (1994).
2 See, for example, their interview with Romney (2006: 128). See note 4 for scholarly reactions.
3 See Ridley (2006: 136).
4 See, for example, Flensted-Jensen (2002), Weinlich (2005), Goldhill (2007), Paul (2007: 308–11), and Toscano (2009).

5 During the preparation of my manuscript of this chapter, Salzman-Mitchell and Alvares (2017: 70–4) published an analysis of the film that also considers its use of Homer and song. Their thoughts regarding the Coens' use of Homer to meditate on the concept of folk authenticity mirror some of those presented in this essay, which is based on a paper that I delivered in 2015 at the annual convention of the Classical Association of the Middle West and South. See also Harries (2001) and Chadwell (2004).

6 The terms "folk" and "tradition" have complicated and controversial histories. They are used here not to evaluate music, but to reflect categories that audiences use to think about it and to highlight how the filmmakers engage with and critique such practices. See Gelbart (2007: 153–90).

7 The song is actually sung by Dan Tyminski.

8 On American cultural investment in the "golden age" of Homeric heroes, see Tomasso (in this volume).

9 *Od.* 1.55–62; 14.174; 19.406–9. All references to the *Odyssey* correspond to Homer (1920). See Stanford (1952) and Russo (1988: 97) on Homer's punning and etymologizing with this name. It is difficult to determine the actual etymology of Odysseus' name because it seems to be of non-Greek origin; see Beekes (2010: 1048–9). Note that *odyssomai* and *odyromai* are often transliterated instead as *odussomai* and *oduromai*. The transliteration used here is chosen because it is the standard conventionally employed in transliterating the name *Odysseus*, to which these words are compared.

10 Goldhill (2007: 265); Homer (1995: 242).

11 Salzman-Mitchell and Alvares (2017: 71). Demodocus appears at *Od.* 8.62–82, 8.477–520, and another singer, Phemius, at *Od.* 1.153–5, 1.325–7. In the *Iliad*, Achilles seems to sing epic songs himself (9.189).

12 Scholarship on these developments in the Homeric tradition is voluminous and contentious, but an excellent introduction can be found in Nagy (1996: esp. 13–28).

13 Ebert (2000a).

14 See Green (1965: esp. 211). Although "hillbilly" has essentially lost its musical connotations, "old-time" is now the standard term even for contemporary music that hews to the style employed in these songs. See the numerous "old-time" jam sessions and music festivals held throughout the United States, for example the Portland Old Time Music Gathering in Oregon.

15 On the historical origins of this phenomenon and the politics of folk music and an "authentic" American past, see Filene (2000: esp. 9–47).

16 See Cohen (2003: 9).

17 On similar effects in blues tradition, see Taft (2006: 20–4).

18 Doman (2005: 80–1).

19 See Kahn (1996).

20 *Works and Days* 156–79; for Greek text, see Hesiod (1970). Hesiod calls the very first generation of humanity "golden" (*khruseon*), a generation which lived even before the Homeric heroes. Yet only the Homeric heroes have detailed mythologies and are frequently compared to modern humans, so they better represent the concept of a "golden age" as discussed here.

21 Similar sentiments appear at *Il.* 5.304, 12.383, 20.287. Unless marked otherwise, all translations are mine.

22 *Republic* 10.606e. See also *Rep.* 10.595b and *Ion*, and Xenophon's *Symposium* 3.5.

23 On Homer and the teaching of Greekness, see Hunter (2004: 246). Cribiore (2001), Horsley (2000), T. Morgan (1998).

24 See Lamberton (2005).

25 Early academic study of bluegrass fixed the birth of the genre circa 1945; see Smith (1965). Subsequent study has generally concurred. See Rosenberg (1985: 10–14).

26 The phrase was used by famous folk-music scholar Alan Lomax in his seminal article "Bluegrass Background: Folk Music with Overdrive" (1959: 108).

27 Rosenberg (1985: 6).

28 See renowned "old-time" fiddler Bruce Molsky on this phenomenon, in Ellis (2013): "Old-time music is what people played in their communities as part of everyday existence. It wasn't meant to be performance music. But when radio came along in the '20s that approach wasn't well-suited to a professional performance medium . . . There's not enough structural diversity to keep it interesting on the radio."

29 Ralph Stanley (2009) claims that when he and his brother Carter recorded the song they "brought it back in existence" after it had fallen virtually out of memory.

30 On the influence of African-American blues on bluegrass, see Cohen (2003: 17) and Chadwell (2004: 7). Chadwell also sees the blues influences in this song as part of a cinematic comment on the false notion of folk authenticity. I am indebted to fiddler Matt McGibany for discussion regarding the history of bluegrass scale tones.

31 Durman (2008).

32 See Salzman-Mitchell and Alvares (2017: 74) in their discussion of Stokes as a "false Homer" for his personification of faulty understanding of folk tradition.

33 See, for example, Gerstenzang (2016), Pate (2015).

34 Although their location is not specified, the gates are first mentioned in *Od.* 19.563–7 where Penelope tells Odysseus that prophetic dreams come to humans through the Gate of Horn, rather than the Gate of Ivory, through which pass deceptive dreams.

35 See Ridley (2006: 136). *Sullivan's Travels* is an important source for this film, influencing several facets of the plot. For example, a scene

depicting Everett and his companions in a movie theater is modeled directly on a scene in *Sullivan's Travels*.

36 The first chapter of Joanna Paul's excellent book *Film and the Classical Epic Tradition* (2013: 1–36) surveys various ways in which epic films signal their engagement with the epic tradition.

4 *A Leonidas for the Golden Age of Superhero Films: The Thermopylae Tradition in 300 (2006)*

Eric Ross

Zack Snyder's *300* (2006) quickly produced three things when it premiered: unprecedented box-office success, political outrage, and scathing reviews from film and culture critics.[1] Based on Frank Miller's 1998 graphic novel of the same name, *300* portrays the Battle of Thermopylae, in which an elite unit of 300 Spartans fought to the last man in defense of their homeland by resisting a massive Persian invasion in 480 BCE. Commentators blasted its vapid dialogue, the endless parade of stylized gore, and the overall cartoonishness of the Spartans, rendered simultaneously hypermasculine and homoerotic by their oiled bodies, bulging muscles, and skimpy briefs.[2] Above all, critics lamented *300*'s negative depiction of Eastern peoples: from their military inferiority to their monstrous appearance, from their slavish mentality to their polymorphous and depraved sexuality, Snyder's Persians embodied Orientalist stereotypes.[3] The outrage over these images was enhanced by their timing, as *300* debuted in the midst of escalating tension between the United States and countries in the Middle East. The Iranian government formally denounced the movie, while Snyder infuriated many by refusing to see any contemporary links to his story of East versus West.[4]

Although *300* undeniably is guilty of bad taste and cultural insensitivity, Snyder's blockbuster contains content worthy of serious analysis, based on its implication in three separate but related golden ages. The first is the golden age of the superhero movie, which began in the late 1990s but hit its stride in the 2000s, and within which *300*'s portrayal of especially Leonidas should be viewed. By relying on the superhero movie's standard narrative motifs, *300* provides its own set of viewing instructions, so that the audience may consume a movie about ancient Greek history on familiar terms. The second is the modern historiographic tradition of valorizing the Battle of Thermopylae within the grand narrative of "the West," especially as enabling the classical, or golden, age of fifth-century BCE Greece.

This consistent heroizing of Leonidas and the 300 derives from an ancient approach to recording historical events. The fifth-century Greek historian Herodotus, modernity's main ancient source for the Greco-Persian Wars, conveys the magnitude and significance of Thermopylae by comparing Leonidas and his Spartans to the legendary warriors populating Homer's epic poem the *Iliad*, a foundational text of Greek identity encoding cultural values and principles. Transforming Leonidas and his Spartans into fifth-century versions of Homeric heroes is the ancient equivalent of Miller and Snyder remaking them as superheroes. Thus, the third golden age drawn into the Thermopylae tradition is the age of mythical heroes who fought in the Trojan War.

LIKE SUPERMAN AT THERMOPYLAE: *300* AS SUPERHERO FILM

Although *300* draws some authority from its historical foundation, and Snyder did consult such experts on ancient Sparta as Bettany Hughes during the production process, historical accuracy was not Snyder's goal.[5] Beyond taking liberties with details about ancient Greece and the Battle of Thermopylae, the film includes virtually no background information about the Greco-Persian Wars and offers a superficial introduction to Spartan culture and society. Viewers learn only that their culture was brutal and demanding, focused almost entirely on military training and warfare. Snyder, by his own admission, excludes such negative aspects of Spartan culture as their dependence on slavery while also overlooking the cosmopolitan, enlightened side of the Persian Empire.[6] That the story takes place in ancient Greece and involves peoples known as Spartans and Persians is almost incidental. Instead, Snyder aimed to craft a more universal (if grossly simplified) story depicting the conflict between good and evil, freedom and tyranny: a world suited for superheroes.

300 was created in the midst of a golden age of superhero movies, including an *X-Men* trilogy (*X-Men* [2000], *X2* [2003], *X-Men: The Last Stand* [2006]), Sam Raimi's *Spider-Man* trilogy (*Spider-Man* [2002], *Spider-Man 2* [2004], *Spider-Man 3* [2007]), the return of

Superman (*Superman Returns* [2006]), the first two installments of Christopher Nolan's *Dark Knight* trilogy (*Batman Begins* [2005], *The Dark Knight* [2008]), and the initial *Iron Man* movie (2008).[7] More recent years have produced, among many others, a trilogy of *X-Men* prequels (*X-Men: First Class* [2011], *X-Men: Days of Future Past* [2014], *X-Men: Apocalypse* [2016]), *Wonder Woman* (2017), three *Avengers* films (*The Avengers* [2012], *The Avengers: Age of Ultron* [2015], *Avengers: Infinity War* [2018], with another as-yet-untitled film scheduled for release in 2019), the latest installment in the *X-Men* series (*X-Men: Dark Phoenix* [2018]), and Snyder's own *Batman v. Superman: Dawn of Justice* (2016).[8] The annual inundation of new and often rebooted titles demonstrates that superhero films are big business, blockbusters able to gross over a billion dollars worldwide.[9]

This dominance at the box office has been accompanied by a sea change in academic and critical attitudes toward superhero movies and the comic books that inspired them, no longer dismissed as "low" art existing on the fringes of pop culture and suitable exclusively for adolescents. The twenty-first century has witnessed a gradual rehabilitation of their intellectual status; superhero films and their sources are now widely regarded as legitimate art forms offering valuable insight into American history and culture.[10] Christopher Nolan's *Dark Knight* trilogy, for instance, has been interpreted as a commentary on the collective negativity of American political attitudes after 9/11.[11] Such cultural penetration, beyond box-office success, explains why the twenty-first century has launched a golden age of superhero movies.

Because Snyder is attempting to recreate a graphic novel on the silver screen, fidelity to the comic-book genre, rather than to ancient history, is the driving ethos of *300*.[12] The aesthetics and narrative structure of the comic-book-turned-superhero movie are evident throughout. Visually, the film often resembles a drawing more than cinematic photorealism, with the crimson uniforms of the Spartan warriors contrasted against a gray and hazy landscape that rivals the bleakness of Gotham City. To this, add the nonstop fighting, the muscle-bound physiques of the 300 Spartans, and the clipped dialogue saturated with one-liners. Snyder's desire to adapt Miller's work as faithfully as possible accounts for his use of certain filming techniques, including the extensive use of blue screen and focal blur, which can make certain shots feel like comic-book panels. Even the plentiful blood in Snyder's movie is stylized rather than realistic, in an effort to reproduce Miller's strokes of red paint.

By incorporating standard themes from superhero stories, Snyder effortlessly guides viewers through a complex historical conflict from thousands of years ago. In particular, four major motifs encourage *300*'s consumption as a typical superhero movie, especially compared to Batman, Spider-Man, and Superman, the best-known American superheroes: the origin story in which the hero's powers are developed; the threat posed by a tyrannical enemy; the threat posed by civic bureaucracy; and the hero's tragic alienation from loved ones and his society. These four elements are so basic to superhero storytelling that they survive successive revisions that occur with each new reboot of a superhero franchise.[13]

First, *300* opens with one of the classic elements of a superhero narrative: an origin story for the hero Leonidas (Gerard Butler). This motif typically explains how a youth, whether from a special background or due to an extraordinary encounter, acquires a superpower and/or puts himself into a position to channel this power productively. An infant Kal-El hurtles through space toward Kansas, where he will learn to become Superman. Bruce Wayne progresses from a tumultuous childhood to intensive training in a Bhutanese prison to protecting Gotham City as Batman. Peter Parker combines adolescent angst with a timely spider bite and soon finds himself battling criminals as Spider-Man. All of them end up embodying a goodness expressed through both their muscular physiques and their moral exemplarity. Leonidas falls directly in the middle of the young-superhero spectrum. While he lacks the alien powers of Kal-El, his royal status, like Bruce Wayne's inherited fortune, comes with certain privileges not enjoyed by the awkward, everyman-teenager Peter Parker.

Leonidas' origin story features his review as an infant and his advancement through the *agōgē*, a brutal survival test undertaken by young Spartans, as he acquires the skills and mentality of a Spartan warrior and vanquishes a monstrously large wolf in the wild, thus earning the kingship. This introductory sequence serves a practical expository function, as it familiarizes a general audience with the extreme military ethos of ancient Sparta. But singling out Leonidas as special misrepresents the *agōgē*, part of a universal educational system for Spartan males born into the warrior class, by presenting it as a unique test of his fitness for kingship. In reality, Leonidas was a hereditary monarch who, under the Spartan constitution, shared power with a co-monarch. By suppressing both historical details, Snyder makes Spartan kingship seem meritocratic, as though Leonidas wins his role because of unique qualities. The inspection of baby Leonidas also suggests a special destiny, like that of Superman, while the *agōgē* recalls the rigorous training of Batman. Recast as a typical young superhero, *300*'s Leonidas leads the audience to anticipate that he will inevitably face an extraordinary challenge that will put these abilities to the test – within a more familiar idiom than a historically accurate rendering of a sometimes-bizarre ancient city-state would provide.

Second, like superheroes, Leonidas must confront a monstrous and power-hungry enemy. Xerxes (Rodrigo Santoro), a self-proclaimed god, towers over other men by at least two feet. Yet his hairless body, skimpy outfit, and elaborate piercings also read as exotic and effeminate, embodying the harshest Orientalist stereotypes. These visual details mark Xerxes as an "Other" bent on trampling the freedom-loving Greeks into utter submission. His army contains an implausibly monstrous assortment of beasts, from a war rhinoceros to an ogre with crab hands, which likewise contrast with Snyder's visual characterization of the Spartans as the human, hypermasculine, conventionally attractive Greeks defending Western ideals against an enemy that is beastly both inside and out. Such a transparent alignment of physical traits with moral worth is characteristic of the simplistic, Manichaean worldview enacted by Snyder and typical of the superhero genre.

Like all vainglorious madmen in the superhero world, however, Xerxes is nearly undone by his own *hubris*. His presumption of god-like power is identified in the film as a fatal flaw, illustrated when his army's vastly superior numbers merely bottleneck in the pass of Thermopylae, almost leading to Spartan victory. Xerxes also overestimates his ability to seduce a terrified enemy into pre-emptive surrender: what corrupts the morally weak, physically deformed Spartan outcast Ephialtes (Andrew Tiernan) does not turn the virtuous Leonidas. This typical pattern in superhero movies, where a stronger enemy is ultimately consumed by his own power, is especially prominent in the *Spider-Man* franchise, wherein Dr. Octopus and Dr. Curtis Connors enhance their physical abilities with technological marvels that warp their moral character.

Third, while the Joker, Magneto, and the Green Goblin are formidable enemies, many superheroes are impeded by another kind of opponent: bureaucratic incompetence and corruption.[14] At best, City Hall and the police force are full of well-meaning officials unable to cope with the awesome power of the supervillain. Whereas fear and distrust of the superhero frequently spring from ignorance rather than bad intentions, some government officials and authority figures actively oppose the superhero, as when the police are ordered to treat

Batman and Spider-Man as vigilantes. Snyder's *Batman v. Superman: Dawn of Justice* even puts Superman on trial as a dangerous illegal alien – a literal take on current immigration debates.

Leonidas must overcome the corruption of the film's Spartan ephors and the weakness of the assembly. Historically, the ephors were a select council of senior political advisers. *300* renders them as a group of priests who cynically manipulate religious belief in order to serve themselves. In keeping with its tendency to portray moral character through physical traits, *300* presents the ephors as vaguely human creatures, misshapen and covered in boils, who are indifferent to the city's welfare, take sexual liberties with the beautiful young female oracle, and accept Persian bribes in exchange for thwarting Leonidas' defensive efforts. The film even invents a character not found in Miller's graphic novel, the sleazy politician Theron (Dominic West), to drive home this trope of civil society's unreliability. Theron sexually manipulates Leonidas' queen Gorgo (Lena Headey), accepts Persian bribes, and sways the weak-willed Spartan assembly so that Leonidas receives no reinforcements.

One consequence of this motif is that Leonidas becomes as much a rebel as a leader, acting without formal authority from the ephors or the assembly. The superhero typically exists on the outskirts of society, defending it without truly belonging to it, unable to share his true identity with the public or those he loves. It should be difficult for Snyder to portray Leonidas, the official leader of his community, as an outsider, yet *300* achieves the effect by pitting him against the professional politicians unable or unwilling to take decisive action. Leonidas is both king of Sparta and operating outside the law in order to protect the people. He may not require a literal disguise to protect his identity, but he at least feels the need to adopt a cover story for his departure: by glibly remarking that he is not leading 300 men to battle, but simply feels like taking a walk with his personal bodyguard. In short, Leonidas possesses an oxymoronic blend of social identities, as he is both a recognized political leader and a hero who must hide his true intentions and operate outside of the system.[15]

Fourth, whether because of his complicated past, his necessary positioning on the fringes of society, or the danger that he could bring upon his loved ones, the superhero often is psychologically separated from the very people he defends, and even from his beloved. Batman, Superman, and Spider-Man must be loners rather than lovers, never able to be truly intimate with Rachel Dawes, Lois Lane, or Mary Jane Watson. Yet this motif involves more than their tragically incomplete romantic lives. Because they have great abilities and accept great challenges, they must live alone, under the cloak of a secret identity and sometimes literally moving in the shadows, lest their powerful enemies target friends and family.

Leonidas may not labor under a secret identity, but in other respects he follows the psychological path of the loner superhero. A telling sequence based on the graphic novel emphasizes that Leonidas is wiser and more experienced than his comrades, and that he alone truly understands the danger they face. As the other Spartans cheer wildly while a ferocious sea storm obliterates a large portion of the enemy fleet, the narrator observes how Leonidas alone stays reserved, silent, and motionless, for he alone understands that the Persian menace is as strong as ever. As their leader, he must keep his psychological distance from the rest of the 300 (see Figure 4.1).[16] Leonidas also exemplifies the superhero's loner status in his familial relationships. Although he shares an intense romantic bond with Queen Gorgo, who forms his last thought before death, *300* emphasizes his decision to leave his son and wife for the Thermopylae mission. The film's poignant voiceover and swelling music convey the love between Leonidas and Gorgo as tragic and impossible.

300 thus adopts story-patterns common to its genre, recasting Leonidas as an archetypal superhero. From boyhood on, he is identified as a special individual who must protect his community from both a power-hungry, monstrous villain and, ironically, other parts of his society too incompetent or corrupt to defend the people. He

Figure 4.1 Displaying the psychological distance of a superhero, Leonidas (Gerard Butler) studies the Persian shipwreck as his comrades cheer wildly in *300* (2006). Warner Bros./Legendary Pictures.

is central to his society yet must stand outside of it. By imbuing Leonidas with such traits, *300* converts an obscure, polysyllabic name into a familiar character with familiar experiences. And yet this narrative strategy resembles not only other golden-age superhero movies; similar narrative strategies were already at work in retellings of the Battle of Thermopylae stretching back to Herodotus' *Histories*, the primary ancient account of the Greco-Persian Wars.

THERMOPYLAE, THE TROJAN WAR, AND SUPERHEROES IN THE GOLDEN AGE OF THE WEST

In recent decades, both scholars and members of the general public have focused on how the facts of the past are converted into narratives. If journalism is the first draft of history today, a key component of *300* is the internal narrator, a Spartan named Dilios (David Wenham) who burnishes Leonidas' deeds into an uplifting inspirational tale based on his authority as the only one of the 300 to survive. The film is framed by shots of Dilios recounting the events of Thermopylae in order to inspire a Greek coalition on the eve of the Battle of Plataea, where Greek victory practically ended the war (see Figure 4.2). This is a classic example of myth-making in action: a past event being recast for a rhetorical and persuasive purpose. Snyder adopts this crucial detail from Frank Miller's graphic novel.

Just as Snyder depended on the graphic novel, Miller himself was deeply influenced by the 1962 film *The 300 Spartans*. Novelists,

Figure 4.2 Dilios (David Wenham) shares the story of Leonidas with Greek forces prior to the decisive Battle of Plataea in *300* (2006). Warner Bros./Legendary Pictures.

poets, and writers of popular nonfiction have created numerous works about Thermopylae into the twentieth century and beyond, from Mary Renault (1964) to Steven Pressfield (1998) to Paul Cartledge (2007). Numerous visual artists have referred to the famous battle: from, most famously, David in his 1814 painting, down to the video-game designers of 2007's *300: March to Glory*. The battle has been cited and manipulated throughout the Western tradition as a tool for shaping interpretation of contemporary events. Emma Clough has argued, for instance, that Robert Glover's 1737 poem *Leonidas* helped British monarchs withstand the aftermath of the Glorious Revolution by introducing the model of a "patriot king" for them to follow. Likewise, Matthew Trundle has studied the invocation of Thermopylae to celebrate (and redeem) the sacrifice of noble yet vanquished armies in more recent battles, from the Alamo in Texas to Maori conflicts in New Zealand.[17] Rather than merely reproducing the work of another creator, Snyder has created his own place in a tradition that extends all the way back to Herodotus.

While commonly known as "the father of history," Herodotus created more than a mere record of past events. By shaping his research into a compelling narrative filled with dramatic moments and memorable characters, he offered deeper, more universal truths about the human experience: a story both educational and edifying. Herodotus drew especially from the genre of epic poetry; Homer's *Iliad*, the foundational text of Greek culture, provided Herodotus with both inspiration and a paradigm for crafting a massive story into a powerful work of art.[18] The general influence of Homeric epic on Herodotus' *Histories* is one of the foremost topics in Herodotean studies, from its organization to its narrative style to its subject matter.[19] Because Greeks of the fifth century BCE reimagined the Trojan War as a conflict between "Greek" and "Barbarian" (for example, Herodotus 1.4), Herodotus enlarges the more recent collision between East and West, the Greco-Persian Wars, by presenting them as a continuation of Homer's epic conflict, which took place during the heroic age, a kind of second-order golden age for Greeks who venerated those far greater men of their past.[20]

Herodotean scholars have recognized that the Thermopylae episode is particularly indebted to Homeric precedent.[21] As a brutal yet poignant story of life and death on the battlefield, Herodotus' Thermopylae narrative resonates deeply with the *Iliad* and incorporates several Homeric allusions. A fundamental parallel that deserves attention is knowledge of imminent death. "Doomed combat" is my term for this type of battle, in which a soldier enters the fray despite knowing that death is not merely possible, but inevitable. Significantly, he embraces, rather than merely accepts, a confrontation guaranteed to destroy him. When they enter their respective climactic battles, both Achilles and Leonidas understand that they are marching willingly toward their destruction, as doomed combatants. This Homeric motif transforms a historical battle narrative into an epic story: the ancient equivalent of Miller and Snyder making Leonidas into a superhero familiar to audiences of both comic books and their film adaptations.

Achilles establishes the paradigm for doomed combat. After his commander Agamemnon publicly shames him, Achilles spends most of the *Iliad* withdrawn to his tent at the margins of the Greek camp, boycotting the war. Only the Trojan champion Hector's defeat of Achilles' beloved friend Patroclus in mortal combat motivates him to return. His sole objective is to destroy Hector, even though Achilles knows that he has a choice of two destinies: he may return home for a long life of obscurity or remain (*menein*) in Troy for a swift but illustrious death, soon after Hector's (*Il.* 9.411–16). By choosing to kill the Trojan prince, Achilles embraces his own death.

Two motives prompt Achilles to accept a battle guaranteed to destroy him. Achilles' first motivation for entering doomed combat is his love for his *philos* Patroclus, transformed into grief for the loss of his friend and self-recrimination over his inability to save him. This Greek word used by Achilles (*philos*, *Il.* 18.80, 18.82, 18.114) means more than "friend" or "loved one." *Philos* indicates something viewed as "one's own, something so cherished that it cannot be separated from the self" – as if part of Achilles had died with Patroclus.[22] This view of Patroclus explains the depth of Achilles' grief (for example, *Il.* 18.8, 64, 73). Second, he strives to win eternal glory for brilliant deeds. The Greek word for such glory (*kleos*) derives from a verb meaning "to hear": a warrior hopes to be remembered and celebrated in the songs of future generations, to have his story told. While *kleos* is a powerful incentive for most Homeric soldiers, it holds special attraction for a doomed combatant, who exchanges the pleasures of a full life for everlasting fame. Achilles even mentions this goal in the same breath that he vows to avenge Patroclus (*Il.* 18.121). This emphasis on celebration and commemoration of heroic deeds is preserved in modern superhero stories via the familiar figure of the reporter, a character such as Lois Lane who shapes the hero's achievement for public consumption.

In sum, Achilles as a doomed combatant in the *Iliad* knows, via insight into divine knowledge, that he is entering a battle guaranteed to destroy him. At some point he hesitates to remain (*menein*) and engage in such a conflict, but ultimately accepts the mission: to earn eternal glory (*kleos*), a warrior's greatest prize, and to fulfill his obligation to a loved one, at whose loss he feels profound grief.[23] These characteristics also arise in the Battle of Thermopylae narrative, as Herodotus applies the motif of doomed combat to Leonidas and the 300 Spartans.

To qualify as doomed combatants, Leonidas and the 300 must remain in battle despite knowing that death is imminent and ineluctable. Their readiness to do so is not taken for granted in Herodotus' narrative in his *Histories*. Xerxes considers mass hysteria to be the only logical response to his arrival; he assumes that the enemy will abscond rather than face his colossal host (*Hist.* 7.101, 210). Though Xerxes' assumptions about the enemy's courage are ultimately refuted, Leonidas' forces at Thermopylae do seriously consider the option of retreat (*Hist.* 7.207).[24] Ultimately the Spartans choose to fight, after deliberations that repeatedly emphasize *menein* (*Hist.* 7.104.5, 7.209.4), the term meaning "to remain" – the same word featured in Achilles' decision to stay and fight at Troy.

Leonidas and his followers clearly resemble Achilles in considering withdrawal from the war yet choosing certain death in battle. This certainty, along with the boldness it engenders, is derived from a prophecy that pertains specifically to Leonidas and thus follows the Iliadic model. The Oracle at Delphi has declared that either the Spartans' king or their entire city must perish in the war (*Hist.* 7.220.3–4). Once all 300 Spartans decide to stay, the army's seer reads signs and warns them that "death awaits them on this day" (*Hist.* 7.219.1). Their discovery that the Persian army has outflanked them parallels Achilles' inability to backtrack from his death once he calls Hector to single combat. Like the Homeric hero, the Spartans also have renounced any hope of survival, well aware that Xerxes will crush their depleted army. When the enemy attacks, the Spartans venture forth "to meet their doom" (*Hist.* 7.223.2), fighting with total abandon because they know that death awaits them (*Hist.* 7.223.4).

In choosing to fight at Thermopylae, Leonidas' motives correspond closely with those of Achilles in the *Iliad* – and even surpass them. Leonidas both wins glory (*kleos*) for himself and, by consciously sacrificing himself, also ensures that his beloved Sparta will survive, according to the prophecy (*Hist.* 7.220.2). This commitment to Sparta resembles Hector's devotion to Troy and Achilles' to Patroclus. The parallel is not perfect, since Achilles' beloved already has perished while Leonidas fights to save Sparta, but the doomed combatant's motivation – personal devotion – remains. Herodotus further reveals that the Spartans felt an obligation to the entire region of mainland Greece, due to their kinship with other Greeks (*Hist.* 7.102.2). Such altruism was remarkable for the isolationist Spartans. At Thermopylae, according to Herodotus' framing and interpretation, they thus become more than Spartans. They become Homeric heroes for Herodotus' panhellenic world.

Leonidas and the 300 Spartans suffered the only unequivocal defeat of Greek forces during the Greco-Persian War. Despite this historical fact, Herodotus' narrative clearly represents Thermopylae as more glorious than other, more successful battles, for it offers a paradigm of courage and devotion: the *sine quibus non* of modern-day heroism. Herodotus indicates this special significance by singling out Leonidas and the 300 Spartans for epic treatment and comparing them to Homeric heroes, the superheroes of the ancient world by virtue of their priority in time, their superior physical strength, and their great deeds. Ultimately, this is the narrative strategy employed by both the cinematic and graphic novel versions of *300*, which signal the extraordinary status of Leonidas especially through common superhero motifs. The argument that superheroes are patterned on the heroes of Greek myth is well known; so too ancient authors, even historians, drew upon these powerful cultural figures to inform their depiction of contemporary "great men" as more than mere humans.[25]

THE RETURN OF THE GOLDEN-AGE HERO?

Both Herodotus and *300* employ a literary archetype to convey the moral significance of Thermopylae as a heroic story of self-sacrifice. By patterning the 300 Spartans after Homeric warriors and superheroes, respectively, the ancient historiographer and the twenty-first-century filmmaker elevate their Thermopylae narratives from mere entertainment to the realm of mythos. Despite the strength of the parallel, however, Herodotus and Snyder ultimately draw divergent conclusions about the power of Thermopylae as an exemplary narrative.

In a famous passage (*Hist.* 7.139), Herodotus declares that the Athenians, rather than the Spartans, deserve credit for defeating the Persians and should be dubbed the saviors of Greece. Athenian naval power, he argues, was the decisive factor in achieving victory. The Spartans' unceasing willingness to resist an enemy might be admirable, and certainly won the respect of their Greek contemporaries, but it did not suffice to win the war. Although Herodotus clearly holds Leonidas and the 300 Spartans in high esteem, their famous deed must remain nothing more than a wonderful story, with little power to shape the course of the war.

In Snyder's *300*, on the other hand, the tale of Leonidas contributes decisively to Greek victory. At the film's conclusion, the audience discovers that Dilios, the sole survivor of Thermopylae and narrator of *300*, all along has been recounting the story to a much larger Greek army prior to the Battle of Plataea. The power of his story inspires the Greek allies to do what the historical Leonidas and the 300 could not: achieve not only a moral victory, but military triumph at Plataea, which resulted in Persian withdrawal from mainland Greece. Within the film, Leonidas values the power of storytelling so much that he personally designates Dilios as the one Spartan who will leave the battlefield so that he may spread word of Spartan bravery at Thermopylae. This action by Leonidas is a self-conscious creation of a tradition. If Spartan bravery motivates the massive victory that launches the traditional "golden age of Western civilization," Dilios' voice is responsible for the gilding of the Spartans' reputation as its spiritual founders.

The celebration of storytelling that bookends *300* reinforces the traditional instructional power of narrative, but also creates an obstacle for Snyder's efforts to explain – or restrict – the film's meaning. In numerous interviews he has denied, when confronted with political outrage over *300*, that the film is intended to resonate in any way with the contemporary conflicts between the United States and countries in the Middle East. For Snyder, it would seem, *300* is primarily an exercise, albeit a serious one, in faithfully adapting the visual style of Miller's graphic novel and he would have the audience consider the film as entertainment, first and last.[26]

This simplistic, apolitical vision of *300* is untenable, however, because the film itself presents the Thermopylae narrative as extending into the open-ended present. As demonstrated by Dilios, the narrator of the film, the story of Leonidas is designed not only to be told and retold but also to be re-enacted, as it inspires other Greek warriors to emulate his example of courage and dedication. If this logic is extended, the Thermopylae story is endlessly repeatable by those who see themselves as following in the footsteps of Leonidas and beating back barbarian incursions into the West, the bastion of reason and liberty. Thus, the film seems to say, people today may bring about a golden age no less splendid than that of fifth-century BCE Greece. One consequence of this approach to storytelling is that *300*, with or without Snyder's agreement, is inevitably available for application to contemporary situations.

This applicability is underlined by the refraction of post-9/11 American political discourse in *300*: first and foremost, the Manichaean characterization of "good" and "evil" actors during the administration of President George W. Bush. Snyder created the film in the midst of armed conflict between an American-led coalition of Western nations and several countries, primarily in the Middle East, labeled the "Axis of Evil" by President Bush.[27] He further referred to terrorists as "monsters" and even suggested that America's enemies were morally deviant, without basic regard for human life and dignity. Such discourse resonates with Snyder's depiction of Persian characters as monstrous, both literally and figuratively. Xerxes' army includes a range of exotic war animals and a variety of ogre-like creatures; even the ostensibly human Immortals resemble zombies, once unmasked. Dilios refers to Xerxes as "soulless," a term that the American viewing audience may equate with not being Christian, and mentions his fang-like teeth and eyes dark as night, details linking the Persian king to the terrifying wolf that Leonidas bravely vanquished during his boyhood training, as dramatized in the film's opening sequence and narrated by Dilios.

These monstrous depictions of Persian characters are matched by monstrous conduct, as when the Greek forces marching for Thermopylae are shocked and outraged to discover the massacred remains of a Greek village. Yet even as the Persians display their capacity for barbaric violence, Snyder also emphasizes their underlying weakness and cowardice. *300* repeatedly stresses that political freedom is the ultimate motivator for Leonidas and his men, who rise to the occasion in defense of their autonomy. Unable to match Spartan skill and determination, the Persians fight only under the compulsion of Xerxes, a condition suggesting that politically oppressed people lack the incentive to die for their country.[28] This view of the Persians recalls a vital component of the Bush administration's war strategy: the belief that Iraqis and Afghanis were oppressed peoples who would welcome the Western coalition forces as liberators and thus obviate the need for intense fighting – a projection that did not come to pass.

The Greco-Persian Wars have often been interpreted as a cultural collision between robust, independent Greeks and effete, oppressed people of the Near East.[29] This common view, however, cannot apply to Snyder's *300*, which dehumanizes the Persians to such an extent that they lack any culture whatsoever beyond their slavish, almost robotic obedience to Xerxes. The film's Spartans, meanwhile, are physically flawless – as should be expected, perhaps, from a nation that practices the systematic elimination of sickly or misshapen infants. Sexuality is used to characterize Leonidas just as with Xerxes. In contrast to the "deviant" pursuits of Xerxes, however, Leonidas is shown having romanticized, mutually pleasurable heterosexual relations with his spouse.[30] In combat, the loyal 300 fall into line behind their king without question and relish the bloody combat into which he leads them: to defend freedom and reason. In appearance, sexuality, and fundamental values, the Spartans of *300* are intended to seem both ideal and recognizable.

300 also suggests Bush's preoccupation with domestic enemies. Heroic and independent, Leonidas repeatedly is thwarted and threatened by other Spartans – venal religious officials, the sleazy politician Theron, the deformed outcast Ephialtes – who oppose his military action or actively conspire with the Persian foe. Apparently conflating dissent with disloyalty, Bush suggested that critics of his policies emboldened the national enemy, even when those policies, much like Leonidas' defiant march toward Thermopylae, strained the limits of legality. M. Melissa Elston goes so far as to suggest that Bush's comments about allies who are either "with us or against us" are reflected in Leonidas' disdain for unsupportive Spartans.[31] He and the 300 are like golden-age heroes, doomed to live among lesser men of the iron age.

300 may present Sparta as a bastion of freedom and reason worth dying for, but Snyder also undermines this depiction. Leonidas' men are disgusted by Persian brutality when they encounter the massacred village, yet they themselves build a defensive wall from Persian corpses, a tactic described as "barbarism" by a Persian messenger clearly repulsed by the Spartans' lack of respect for the dead. Leonidas, in addition to his intimacy with Queen Gorgo, is shown to be a loving, tender father, patiently instructing his young son in the ways of Spartan warfare. These images of Leonidas as the family man are hard to digest when juxtaposed against the immediately preceding account of Spartan eugenics (including the piled-up skulls of rejected infants) and brutal youth initiations.[32] No matter how gentle and civilized Leonidas appears, the fact remains that Sparta's heroic culture existed for the sole purpose of supporting a state-sponsored military machine – one that any state, ancient or modern, might wish to wield.

As Leonidas' domestic enemies demonstrate, however, Spartan civil society is highly corrupt and inefficient in *300*. As the small Spartan contingent marches for Thermopylae, Queen Gorgo wages a political campaign to win her husband official support, including much-needed reinforcements, from the Spartan government. Yet the corruption of Theron, along with the indecisiveness of other Spartan assembly members, prevents timely assistance from reaching the Spartan troops. The very state that Leonidas is defending has ceased to function in the proper manner, which forces him, the king of his city-state, to play the rebel, leading his elite fighting force into unsanctioned combat.[33] It is possible to view this irony as an allegory for American management of the war in Iraq. At the very least, the depiction of Spartan politics in *300* may be said to reflect contemporary cynicism toward government, as more and more people lose faith in institutions in the post-9/11 world. Such cynicism has become increasingly common in graphic novels and superhero movies over the past ten to fifteen years, most notably in Christopher Nolan's *Dark Knight* franchise.[34] The superhero motifs of Snyder's *300* ultimately lead to the same jaded conclusion.

Herodotus and Zack Snyder may follow the same narrative strategy, creating their protagonists from heroic motifs familiar to a popular audience, but the outcome of this approach is markedly different for each, reflecting the needs of their respective genres. Herodotus, as a historian, ultimately must acknowledge that moral victories do not produce historical victories. Spartan heroism, though admirable and inspirational, is not enough to defeat the Persians, a deficiency acutely demonstrated by the historical defeat of the Spartans at Thermopylae. Therefore, the presentation of the 300 Spartans as warriors on par with Homer's epic heroes has limited utility. Snyder, on the other hand, suggests that repetition of the narrative permits emulation of Leonidas and the 300 Spartans. His entire film is framed by the retelling of this story, which electrifies the audience of Greek soldiers and prompts their victory at Plataea, the final battle of the Greco-Persian Wars in mainland Greece. In other words, Snyder presents this golden moment of heroism as recoverable and repeatable, endowing the narrative with enduring power that makes it as relevant today as it was 2,500 years ago – whether or not Snyder is willing to admit it.

NOTES

1 According to *Box Office Mojo* (2007), *300* grossed $70,885,301 during its North American opening weekend, then a record for a spring release. The film ultimately grossed $456,068,181 worldwide.
2 For representative reviews, see Scott (2007) and Stevens (2007).
3 For discussion of the film's racial and political implications, see especially Kahane (2007), Stevens (2007), and Tharoor (2014). Kahane and

Scott both compare *300* to Nazi propaganda films, though the former clearly is speaking tongue-in-cheek.

4 Hassler-Forest (2010: 128–9) offers an especially useful discussion of Snyder's reluctance to view his film as political allegory.

5 For his working relationship with Hughes, see Snyder's interview with *Movieweb* (2007).

6 Snyder (2007a).

7 Superhero stories, in both cinema and graphic novels, have been on the rise since 9/11; see Geers (2012).

8 See Sciretta (2015) for a complete list of recent and future releases.

9 See the list compiled by Liu (2016). The billion-dollar threshold had been crossed by six films: *The Dark Knight* (2008), *The Dark Knight Rises* (2012), *The Avengers* (2012), *Iron Man 3* (2013), *The Avengers: Age of Ultron* (2015), and *Captain America: Civil War* (2016).

10 The most thorough academic works on comics as literature are Pustz (2012) and Wright (2003). For connections between comics and classical literature, see Kovacs and Marshall (2011, 2015).

11 See Briley (2008).

12 See Hassler-Forest (2010: 121–3) on the adaptation process between graphic novel and film, in which hardcore fans demand extreme fidelity.

13 Wandtke (2012: 9–14) argues that narrative revisionism is fundamental to the comic-book genre. As many writers and artists contribute to one character's mythos at different times, inconsistency and plot fluctuation are not only tolerated but expected by the audience. The latest version tends to have more familiarity and authority than the original.

14 On the theme of government corruption in comics, see Wright (2003: 226–53), which relates this theme to post-9/11 cynicism.

15 For Leonidas' social identity in *300*, see Cyrino (2011), who argues that he is presented as a typically American hero.

16 Wright (2003: 185–9) discusses the psychological distance of the protagonist in various superhero stories.

17 See Clough (2004: esp. 367–8) and Trundle (2013).

18 For a general overview of Homer, see Barker and Christensen (2013).

19 Many scholars have examined the general connection between Herodotus and Greek poetry; see e.g. Marincola (2006) and Boedeker (2002).

20 For a general overview of Herodotus, consult Roberts (2011).

21 See especially Pelling (2006: 92–8).

22 For the meaning of *philos* and its broader social implications in the Greek camp, see Nagy (1979: 103–9).

23 See Nagy (1979: 94–7) for the connection between love and glory in the character of Achilles.

24 Thomas (2000: 109–11) demonstrates that Xerxes' misunderstanding of the Spartan military ethos represents his larger failure to comprehend Greek culture, which makes the Persian Wars also a cultural collision.

25 On the connection between comic-book superheroes and demigods of Greek myth, see e.g. Maslon (2013).
26 In the director's commentary feature of the *300* DVD, Snyder (2007b) speaks almost exclusively of aesthetic and technological matters.
27 Bush first used this oft-repeated phrase to designate countries believed to sponsor terrorism in his State of the Union address on January 29, 2002.
28 See Cyrino (2011) for this political theme in *300*.
29 See e.g. Lloyd (2005) and Bradford (1980).
30 See Cyrino (2011: 23) on sex scenes in *300*.
31 Elston (2009: 58).
32 See Chaw (2007) for this juxtaposition.
33 Hassler-Forest (2010) has a useful discussion of these political themes.
34 See e.g. Briley (2008) on political cynicism and dystopian elements of Christopher Nolan's *Dark Knight*.

5 *The Dueling Greek Golden Ages of* 300: Rise of an Empire *(2014)*

Seán Easton

The cinematic glorification of Sparta's famous stand at Thermopylae involves a fundamental problem: although Spartan self-sacrifice is memorialized as a moral victory achieved by the supreme military society of the Greek world, an Athenian-led naval victory at Salamis actually prevented Persian success. Furthermore, the historical outcomes of this victory most associated with "the glory that was Greece" – including democracy and the arts – were Athenian achievements anathema to Spartan culture, identified with the "golden age" or "classical" era, usually defined as the fifth century BCE. The attempt to capitalize upon the success of Zack Snyder's Sparta-glorifying *300* (2006) via an ethically and aesthetically similar follow-up that dramatized the Battle of Salamis, Noam Murro's *300: Rise of an Empire* (2014; hereafter, *300: Rise*), exemplifies the problem: if the Athenians can claim both Greek victory over Persia and the invention of the social and cultural institutions that flourished under Greek freedom, what remains for the Spartans?

The makers of *300: Rise* attempt to thread this needle by representing Sparta, from the opening scene, as the most complete possible expression of the ideals of golden-age Greece, and the Athenians as inspired, though flawed, imitators of those ideals in both life and art. *300: Rise* opens with a bronze sculptural relief of the fallen Spartans at Thermopylae, as they appear in death at the end of *300*, which then slowly dissolves into the colors of flesh and blood – before cutting to the city of Athens in flames as Persian soldiers despoil its buildings and people. *300: Rise* continues to achieve an unflattering comparison of Athens to Sparta in three ways: through its treatment of the Athenian cityscape, especially the destruction of the Acropolis' monuments; by connecting the Spartans closely with the sculpture of the classical period most identified with Athens; and through how the famous sculptural program on the Parthenon effectively haunts the film's presentation of the battle between Athenians and Persians, complicated by the battle over which character will take Athena's place as the city's master or savior.

DUST IN THE WIND: MAKING AND UNMAKING ATHENS' GOLDEN-AGE CITYSCAPE

The opening sequence of *300: Rise* is noteworthy for its unusual depiction of Athens: not a conventional establishing shot of the city's majestic Acropolis, but its signature location in flames. A massive, freestanding statue collapses near burning temples, while Persian soldiers slaughter civilians in the background and seize a half-naked woman in the foreground. As this scene unfolds, Gorgo (Lena Headey), Leonidas' widow, intones in disembodied voiceover the words of an oracle, predicting both the city's destruction and its people's fateful significance: "Persian fire will reduce Athens to cinder . . . Only the Athenians themselves exist, and the fate of the world hangs on their every syllable." This depiction of the Acropolis establishes the film's larger thematic purposes by both reshaping and destroying an Athenian cityscape that is supremely iconic in the popular Western imagination today, and which possesses totemic significance for depicting the golden age of Athens and of Greece in general.

300: Rise is the fourth film to treat the Persian Wars and the first to focus on the Athenian-led naval victory over Persia in 480 BCE. *The 300 Spartans* (1962) and *300* (2006) focus on Spartan resistance at Thermopylae, while *La Battaglia di Maratona* (1959; henceforth *LBM*) treats Athens' role as defender of Greece against the first Persian invasion in 490.[1] Athens appears in *LBM*, *The 300 Spartans*, and *300: Rise* as a sophisticated urban society, an impression reinforced through the anachronistic presence on the Athenian Acropolis of buildings that the city did not actually acquire until decades later – especially the Parthenon, completed more than forty years after the Battle of Salamis.

An Athenocentric film, *LBM* uses the Parthenon to develop its hero's relationship to the city and its values.[2] Despite its title, *The 300 Spartans* begins with a shot of the Parthenon. In both films, the monument identifies Athens with timeless grandeur and civic virtue, prompting the audience to believe that even non-Athenian Greeks who fought against Persia valued what the Parthenon represents: a flourishing moral and material community, whose time of peak prosperity marks a golden age from which a "Western tradition" of political values has been imagined to grow.[3] Yet *300: Rise* omits the Parthenon altogether. Since liberal use of poetic license elsewhere in the film suggests that historical accuracy did not motivate the omission, why isn't it there?

Patrick Tatopoulos, production designer on *300: Rise*, has described the film as an opportunity to present an alternative to "the picturesque city-state of gleaming white marble . . . from history books and vacation postcards."[4] The sort of Athens that Tatopoulos describes matches what Pauline Hanesworth has termed "the touristic Athens," a synthesis of monuments instead of the features of daily existence.[5] Ultimately, however, the animation studio contracted to create the establishing shot of Athens was instructed to emphasize only the city's layout and major architectural features, resulting in a touristic Athens after all.[6] One meaningful innovation was substituting the colossal statue of "Athena the Defender" for the Parthenon as the most prominent feature on the Athenian Acropolis, featured in all four exterior city scenes.[7]

As Athena the Defender was constructed entirely post-Second Persian War, its presence is just as anachronistic as the Parthenon's would have been. The statue's exact appearance in antiquity is uncertain, but the film's version is modeled on nineteenth-century sculptor Leonidas Drosis' neoclassical interpretation, which adorns the modern Academy of Athens. To match the ten-meter height of its ancient model, Drosis' statue stands atop an Ionic column. The film's version appears considerably larger even than the Athenian original. Thus, the signature Athenian monument destroyed in the Persian attack of *300: Rise* derives from a modern reconception of the ancient statue as a national symbol and allegorical figure of courage, nobility, and martial potency.

In the film's four scenes of Athens before, during, and after its destruction, the absence of the Parthenon and the destruction of Athena the Defender create the impression of impermanence in Athens' built environment. Gorgo's voiceover makes this point explicit: "For Athens is a pile of stone and wood and cloth and dust, and, as dust, will vanish into the wind." *300: Rise* thus separates Athenian identity from its built manifestation. The oracle begins a pattern in the film of devaluing the material products and human manufacturers of Athens' golden age. *300: Rise* is determined not to let the appearance of Athens establish the audience's sense of the city's power and risk Sparta's reputation, as established in *300*, suffering by comparison. Thus, the film faces a dilemma well articulated by the fifth-century BCE historian Thucydides:

> For if the city of the [Spartans] were deserted, and the shrines and foundations of buildings preserved, I think that after the passage of considerable time, there would eventually be widespread doubt that their power measured up to their reputation ... [B]ut that if the Athenians were to suffer the same fate, their power would be estimated, from the city's pure appearance, as twice what it is. (*History of the Peloponnesian War* 1.10.2)[8]

The negligible material remains of a non-Athenian city-state such as Sparta challenge filmmakers with this consequent lack of purchase on the modern popular imagination.[9]

The central theme in the prologue's response to this dilemma involves two key words from the oracle that Gorgo recites: "dust" and "wind." These terms have been heard before in an Athenocentric screen context. The time-traveling title characters of *Bill and Ted's Excellent Adventure* (1989), after announcing that they are headed for the "Golden Age of Civilization," arrive in "Athens 410 BC," where they happen upon Socrates (Tony Steedman) lecturing on mortality in Greek. The pair greet an impressed Socrates with an insight into the human condition ("All we are is dust in the wind, dude") obtained not from classical philosophy, but from the refrain of the 1977 hit single by the American progressive rock band Kansas, "Dust in the Wind."

Gideon Nisbet reads the encounter with Socrates as illustrating how Athens, in its high cultural glory, struggles to entertain except under conditions of comic travesty.[10] Pauline Hanesworth enlarges on the point, observing that Athenocentric films usually avoid Athens as much as the plot allows.[11] Indeed, *300: Rise*'s prologue uses a fiery explosion of sexualized violence to accomplish what Bill (Alex Winter) and Ted (Keanu Reeves) achieve through comically clueless irreverence: to make Athens a site of mass entertainment, before moving elsewhere. Yet the prologue of *300: Rise* also makes an important thematic statement shared by Kansas and *Bill and Ted*: the phrase "dust in the wind" identifies human fragility and transience.

THE MONUMENTALIZED BODY

The opening shot of *300: Rise* monumentalizes the fallen Spartans of Thermopylae by depicting the tableau of dead heroes with which *300* ended as a bronze sculptural relief (see Figure 5.1). Suzanne Turner

Figure 5.1 A bronze relief of the Spartan dead at Thermopylae becomes flesh in *300: Rise of an Empire* (2014). Warner Bros./Legendary Pictures.

describes this tableau as a manifestation of the "beautiful death" that the Spartans of *300* so crave, further eroticized through its evocation of the Renaissance tradition of Saint Sebastian's archery-themed martyrdom.[12] Their symbolic transformation from metal into flesh announces a major theme: the Spartans are themselves heroic monuments, recalling another cinematic point of reference: *Olympia Part I: Festival of Nations* (1938), a pro-Nazi cinematic celebration of the 1936 Berlin Olympics.

Borrowing from German director Leni Riefenstahl's oeuvre for an ancient-world film is not new. Ridley Scott, in *Gladiator* (2000), drew on *Triumph of the Will* (1935) to depict Rome under the emperor Commodus' tyrannical rule.[13] Murro differs, however, in that he duplicates Riefenstahl's thematic purpose: the symbolic removal of a Greek golden-age identity from Athens to a preferred location. Even if unintentional, this parallel nevertheless illustrates both the mechanics of Murro's discourse of adaptation and its dangerously regressive political implications. The *Olympia* prologue depicts the emergence of a new golden age, embodied by German athletes, while *300: Rise*, true to its franchise, posits a more "authentic" non-Athenian golden age embodied by the Spartan warriors. The film's substitution of Athena the Defender for the Parthenon invites such focus on the role of sculpture in *300: Rise* and Riefenstahl's *Olympia* as a frame of reference.

Riefenstahl seeks to differentiate a new German golden age of living bodies from its ancient predecessor, which persists only through its inanimate remains. The *Olympia* prologue begins amid fragments of Greek antiquity: the ruins of the Athenian Acropolis, particularly the Parthenon; then the heads, torsos, and limbs of famous ancient statues, culminating in the golden-age Athenian sculptor Myron's *Diskobolos*, or "Discus Thrower." A transition via dissolve to Edwin Huber, a German Olympic athlete, marks the beginning of the new golden age. Huber appears in the pose of the "Discus Thrower," as though replacing the statue. Riefenstahl explains that, when Huber begins to move from the stillness of his pose into his throw, "the ideal of the classical form detaches [from its base] into the living realization of today's athlete."[14] Thus, Riefenstahl crafted for *Olympia*'s prologue a wordless cinematic heritage myth for Germany's Olympic athletes that stressed "an aesthetics of racial perfection, including the cult of male strength and power."[15] This myth serves to distinguish the German athletes from those of other nations also appearing in the documentary.

Similarly, Murro's opening in *300: Rise* thematizes physical perfection by developing the theme of Spartan warriors as embodiments of monumental sculpture.[16] *300: Rise* intensifies this distinction by making the Athenians observably less muscular than the Spartans, as Daxos (Andrew Pleavin) and his Arcadians had appeared vis-à-vis the Spartans in *300*. The on-set physical trainer Mark Twight noted that the Spartans' physiques are meant to identify them as professional soldiers. Other Greeks, as citizen-soldiers, are less muscular, creating a hierarchy of male physique among the Greeks, topped by the Spartans.[17] Murro also follows Snyder in adhering to the ancient Greek sculptural practice of pitting (semi-)nude Greek bodies against clothed "Others."[18] Filtered through the prism of the Greco-Persian Wars, the semi-nude physical perfection of the Spartans points to racial superiority vis-à-vis the darker-skinned Persians.[19]

Riefenstahl and Murro both intensify the cult of physical perfection by emphasizing an erotic dimension. Riefenstahl carefully modulates the erotic element, as athletes in the prologue, male and female, all appear in the nude. The males perform Olympic sports, while the females in the next scene perform a dance. In the female sequence, two women stand behind a third, so that three pairs of arms form a mandorla of rhythmic motion around the single nude female in front. The scene's erotic charge increases as the woman's body is superimposed with an image of fire that expands to fill the screen; the scene then changes again, via dissolve to a fire cauldron from which an Olympic torchbearer draws his flame.

Riefenstahl commented that aesthetic and rhythmic principles alone guided the prologue's construction; as a documentary about athletic events, *Olympia* had no plot to determine its beginning.[20] *300: Rise* has a plot, but Murro's aesthetics and rhythm reflect similar choices.

Both films begin by stressing the stillness of sculpture, then move into stylized motion at reduced speed. Riefenstahl's athletes, however, enjoy autonomous and harmonious movement as the sequence proceeds with increasing visual complexity toward the fire dissolve. Murro, on the other hand, has Persians maim or manhandle the Greek bodies in both his Thermopylae and Athenian Acropolis shots. In *300: Rise*'s opening scene, Xerxes (Rodrigo Santoro) violates the stillness and beauty of the penetrated bodies when he rides slowly over to the fallen Leonidas and ferociously decapitates him. In the next shot, fires rage across the Athenian Acropolis. Xerxes holds Leonidas' head aloft to witness the statue of Athena the Defender collapse. Although it depicts a scene of chaos, Murro's Acropolis scene is highly aestheticized. He slows its speed and accentuates the evenness of its rhythm, as in the eroticized assault on the Athenian woman. She struggles in slow motion, her uncovered breasts shaking and swaying, as fatally slashed Athenians topple in the background and fires burn all about.

The Athenians are introduced in the film as victims and, despite two dramatic victories over Xerxes' navy, *300: Rise* does not idealize their performance in battle as its predecessor film does the Spartans'.[21] In *300*, Snyder uses motion control photography to highlight the performance of individual Spartan warriors reveling in their martial superiority to Persians at Thermopylae. This method presents an entire action sequence as if it were a single shot in continuous zoom. Snyder reduces its speed briefly to a near pause at key moments, which evokes the stillness and battle poses of warriors depicted on ancient Greek relief sculptures.[22] Murro reinforces *300*'s pro-Spartan depiction through deliberately limiting the use of that iconic approach. Brave and determined as they are, the Athenians of *300: Rise* do not merit depiction in cinematic "sculptural time." The battlefield exploits of the Athenian general Themistocles (Sullivan Stapleton) are a partial exception, but motion is only slowed to highlight particular moments of battlefield efficiency – a dodged arrow here, an enemy skull crushed by his horse's hoof there – rather than his artful performance as a warrior. At the climactic Battle of Salamis in *300: Rise*, the elite Persian force known as the Immortals, whom the Spartans dispatch handily at Thermopylae in *300*, dramatically outfight their Athenian adversaries.

Where Athenian bodies are considered useful is in their capacity as laborers. The monumental landscape of Athens is perhaps the most famous and tangible expression of its "golden-age" legacy. What is less frequently recognized in discussions of that legacy is the labor required to create those monuments, or the naval fleet that ensured the prosperity necessary to build them. The monumental remains of Athens' "golden age" gain much of their mystique through detachment from history, due to their very endurance. *300: Rise* rehistoricizes these massive projects as products of labor – but to demystify Athens' claims to greatness. Thus, the fires that rage across the Acropolis clear away one "pile of stone and wood and cloth and dust," which the Athenians will in due course replace with an even more familiar pile – this time, presumably including the Parthenon. Compared to the Spartans, who are correlated with works of art, Murro depicts Athenians as Greeks who dwell among and can construct monuments, but cannot embody them.

At the end of the prologue, the scene of the Acropolis' night-time destruction gives way to shipwrights working undisturbed in daylight: stripping bark from tree trunks, hammering pegs into place, launching a completed trireme into the water. As a performance of masculinity, the scene displays not fighting skill, but the technical know-how and physical strength to produce the tools of war. Athenians as laborers are important in the film, for in *300: Rise* they are not warriors first and foremost, but growers and makers of things. After the first Athenian success against the Persian fleet, Themistocles remarks, "Not bad for a bunch of farmers." His comrade-in-arms, the playwright Aeschylus (Hans Matheson), responds, "And poets, and sculptors," assimilating makers of art to other laborers in Athens' citizen army. Themistocles sums up their shared sentiment, "Who would have known a group of untrained men would do so well against such a considerable adversary?"

Linking the work of shipwrights, sculptors, farmers, and poets, the film integrates the artifacts of the golden age (poems and statues), the livelihood of the people (agriculture and trade), and defense of the city (the completed trireme) into one social and political structure. Yet *300: Rise* is a tale not of their triumph over adversity, but of their ultimate failure to overcome crisis without Sparta. After experiencing two relatively easy victories over the Persian fleet under Themistocles' leadership, the Athenian sailors who survive a subsequent catastrophic engagement cry, "Without the Spartans we are just farmhands!" Themistocles rallies the survivors for his final gambit, an attack with the remaining ships to either kill the Persian naval commander Artemisia (Eva Green) or compel her to surrender. Since she refuses to surrender, only Gorgo's last-minute arrival with the Spartan fleet gives the Greeks victory.

History suggests a different account. Athens defeated the Persians twice: alone on land at Marathon in 490 BCE and again at sea, when they made up the vast majority of the Greek fleet at Salamis in 480 BCE. Yet implicit in *300*'s presentation of Spartans is the necessity of their exceptional martial perfection. For this reason, *300: Rise* rewrites history to align it with the franchise's ideological perspective. Spartan military perfection is, if not the traditional Greek golden age, then an alternative Greek golden age. It is also, implicitly, a better one, because it only exists in flesh and blood: not in artifacts of stone and metal that can only imitate such primal authenticity.

EMBODYING THE PARTHENON'S GOLDEN-AGE MYTHS: ATHENIANS DEFEATING MONSTERS

Like Riefenstahl, Murro visualizes the transition from statue to living person at the very outset of his film. In *300: Rise*, however, this marks the beginning of a still grander project of transforming immobile artistic representation into dynamic, embodied movement by bringing the Parthenon's sculptural program to life. Although the Parthenon as a structure has been excluded from *300: Rise* in favor of Athena the Defender, the myths monumentalized in its sculptural reliefs haunt the film thematically, by animating key confrontations between the Athenians and the monstrous enemy who attacks them. A major part of that sculptural program is composed of metopes, or pictorial tablets, set into the entablature of the Parthenon.

In their original context, the metopes' visual narratives depict episodes of Athenian myth and mytho-history so as to evoke and celebrate Athens' victory and perseverance in the Persian Wars, by depicting confrontations with Giants, Amazons, and centaurs. Xerxes and his naval commander Artemisia each take on a mythical role from the Parthenon's myths of failed attempts at overthrowing the right order of things: the Giants, who endeavor to destroy the rule of Zeus and the Olympian order; and the Amazons, who invade earliest Athens. As Persians in the *300* franchise, Xerxes and Artemisia are made to exemplify the Parthenon's myth of monstrous hybridity and its unruly and predatory nature, symbolized also by literal hybrids, the centaurs. Individual conflicts among Artemisia, Themistocles, and Gorgo further enact scenes from the west and east pediments of Athens' premier golden-age monument. The film thus excludes the Parthenon, but stages its stories.

The metopes that adorn the east side of the Parthenon depict the myth of the Giants, Earth's children, whom she exhorts to storm Mount Olympus and wrest power from Zeus and his fellow deities.[23] The Olympian gods overwhelm and destroy the Giants in the battle that follows. Whereas visual representations of the Giants in the sixth century BCE tend to depict them simply as Greek-style warriors, by the mid-fifth century their representation increasingly includes primitive and savage features, identifying them with the foreign.[24] In *300: Rise*, the invading Persian army is identified with the Giants through Xerxes, a nine-foot-tall, seemingly superhuman figure who considers himself a god. As the Giants mean to do, he scales a sacred height, the temple-filled Athenian Acropolis, and topples an Olympian deity, in the form of Athena the Defender.

The metopes of the Parthenon's west side depict the mytho-historical battle between the invading Amazons and the ancient Athenians. The Amazons are depicted scaling the Acropolis and wearing generic "Eastern" garb, associating them with the Persian invaders in 480 BCE. The connection between *300: Rise* and the Parthenon's west metope narrative is the character of Artemisia, an anti-patriarchal warrior woman who brings an Eastern army to destroy Athens and subjugate Greece. There is in fact an area of overlap between Artemisia and the Parthenon's Amazon narrative. According to tradition, the Athenian hero Theseus abducts the Amazon queen Antiope (or Hippolyta), prompting the Amazons to attack Athens.[25] Likewise, the film's Artemisia is both victim and avenger (contrary to the story of the historical Artemisia, as depicted by Herodotus). Although ethnically Greek, the film's Artemisia suffers greatly at the hands of Greek hoplites, who raped and murdered her family when she was eight years old.[26] They then rape her and sell her to a Greek ship where she remains as a sex slave for a decade. Left for dead in a port city, adolescent Artemisia is found by the Persian emissary (Peter Mensah) whom Leonidas will later kick down Sparta's well, as seen in *300*. Adopted and trained in martial arts, she eventually becomes a favorite commander of Darius himself.

As an Amazon-like figure, Artemisia's threat to Athens lies first in her ability to conquer it, but the film also adds a record of manipulating powerful Persian males, Darius and Xerxes. Gorgo's recitation of Artemisia's backstory in Persia represents her as both cause and symptom of a sickened Persian patriarchy. She is able to euthanize the wounded Darius (Igal Naor) with impunity, ignore his dying instruction to avoid further war with Greece, and manipulate Xerxes to do likewise. Yet, when she attempts to manipulate the Athenian Theseus stand-in Themistocles into defecting by propositioning him during sex, he refuses and she breaks off the encounter.

Finally, the film supports her characterization as an Amazon with a visual allusion, albeit from a source beyond the Parthenon. The depiction of her death, run through by Themistocles' sword in erotically charged mortal combat, aligns Artemisia with the Amazon queen Penthesileia, slain by Achilles, who is said to have fallen in love with his victim as he killed her.[27] The characters' shared gaze – he on his feet, she on her knees – is iconic of the encounter between Achilles and Penthesileia as depicted at the Temple of Apollo at Bassae, and as a popular illustration on pottery throughout the Greek world.[28] Further, for Themistocles to kill Artemisia specifically in her role as a symbolic Amazon vindicates Athenian masculinity – but killing a woman is still a lesser achievement than what the Spartans accomplish.

The Parthenon's south metopes depict the brutal melee between the human Lapiths, assisted by the Athenian Theseus, and the bestial centaurs at a disrupted wedding feast. Five metopes in this arrangement represent a centaur seizing or otherwise attacking a Lapith woman.[29] The seizure of women is a motif important to *300: Rise*, as the opening Acropolis scene makes clear through its depiction of a partially nude Athenian woman being dragged off by Persian soldiers. Gorgo, who was raped in *300*, narrates the scene. The film presents rape as highly influential in shaping Artemisia's character, insinuating that she acquires a sadistic nature through her training in Persia and a retributive cruelty toward men due to her inhuman treatment by fellow Greeks.

Artemisia's ethno-cultural hybridity is explicitly connected with her sadism when she explains to an inquiring Greek prisoner of war that she has Greek blood, but a Persian heart. She then cuts off his head and kisses its mouth in imitation of Aubrey Beardsley's illustration of Oscar Wilde's Salome kissing the decapitated head of John the Baptist. Monstrous creatures in service to Persia, while far fewer in *300: Rise* than *300*, are connected to Artemisia. She sends the distraught and initially very human youth Xerxes on a quest that ends among ghoulish wizards who engineer his transformation into a gargantuan god-man. The only ogre-like creature featured among the Persians of *300: Rise* appears in the attack that she leads personally. The goblin-masked Immortals accompany her into battle. While the physical manifestations of monstrosity in *300: Rise* are male in gender, Artemisia is ultimately responsible for summoning them all.

That Amazon and monstrous hybrid are hostile categories in Parthenon mythology, existing to be defeated, is further accentuated through Artemisia's dominatrix costuming theme. When she first appears, she wears a black leather skirt ending in a fringe of whip ends. After Themistocles defeats two of her commanders in naval combat at Artemisium, she attempts to seduce him through aggressive erotic domination. Actor Eva Green notes that the sex scene between her character and Themistocles was choreographed more like a fight than a conventional onscreen sexual encounter and remarked on its sadomasochistic aspect.[30] When Artemisia faces Themistocles for the last time at Salamis, her costuming explicitly suggests monstrosity by the line of curved spikes running down her back. The misogynistic equation of sexual penetration with impalement metaphorically renders her final combat with Themistocles the consummation of their earlier, aborted sexual encounter. When Artemisia is finally run through with a sword, the weapon's point emerges from her back to form a bloody final spike in her bestial dorsal column. As a formidable, ethnically Greek warrior woman, Artemisia was initially a contender to supplant the fallen Athena, but as a bestial hybrid she loses both to Themistocles and to another powerful and dangerous female character: Gorgo.

REPLACING "ATHENA THE DEFENDER": THEMISTOCLES, ARTEMISIA, GORGO

The destruction of the monumental "Athena the Defender" statue created a vacuum in the film's symbolic landscape: who would step into the divine warrior's role? On the one hand, the Greek warrior woman Artemisia and the Athenian champion Themistocles restage the contest of Athena and Poseidon, the divine battle of the sexes at the dawn of Athenian mytho-history. The pedimental sculptures on the west side of the Parthenon had featured Athena's victory in the primordial contest with the sea-god Poseidon over which deity would be honored most at Athens. In *300: Rise* the victory goes to the male naval commander, which provides a second mythical frame to the final confrontation between Themistocles and Artemisia, offering further symbolic vindication of Athenian masculinity. On the other hand, the film's emphasis on warrior women puts Artemisia and Gorgo in an implicit contest to embody the fallen statue's idealized heroic power as Athena, reborn. In so doing, the film includes another theme from the Parthenon: the birth of Athena, depicted on the east pediment. Indeed, Gorgo's last-minute arrival at the battle of Salamis rescues Themistocles and the flagging Athenian fleet.

The contest between Athena and Poseidon to determine who would name and patronize the newly founded city is fundamental for Athens' identity. Most ancient sources record that Poseidon displayed his power by bringing forth saltwater from a rock, while

Athena produced an olive tree: a gift deemed more useful to mortals, so the city was given to and named for the victorious goddess.[31] The film constitutes a second round in this contest between Poseidon and Athena, played out through their onscreen proxies: Themistocles and Artemisia.

Like his city's wise patron, Themistocles had a reputation in antiquity for prescience: in his expectation that Darius' attempted landing at Marathon was only prologue to a greater Persian threat, and in setting Athens' political course more broadly. When a rich silver vein was discovered at Laurium, the second-century CE Greek biographer Plutarch reports that he managed to convince Athenian voters to spend it on a fleet of warships rather than to distribute it among themselves.[32] During the war, Themistocles again convinced the people to evacuate their city, leaving it for the Persians to destroy, in order to keep the fight where the Greek advantage was the greatest: at sea.[33] Themistocles thus preserved the possibility of a Greek victory over Xerxes' expeditionary force and forecast the naval foundation of Athenian power, post-480 BCE. When Sparta opted out of its leadership of the Greek alliance against Persia, Athens adopted the role.

This primarily naval alliance, known as the Delian League, took on an increasingly imperial aspect as Athens punished militarily those states which tried to leave. The League's treasury was eventually moved to Athens and member-cities' payments fed into Athenian building projects, including the Parthenon. The film's association between Themistocles' leadership and Poseidon, made explicit by Artemisia, resonates with Plutarch's account, that Themistocles reversed the policy of the ancient kings of Athens who had allegedly contrived the story of the dispute between Athena and Poseidon in order to dispose the common people toward the land.[34] Themistocles, by connecting the city to the sea, greatly diminished the aristocracy's traditional privileges. The commoners gained new importance as rowers and thus a greater degree of political enfranchisement. *300: Rise* revisits the perception that Themistocles reversed the political import of the "divine contest" myth. Rather than connect Athena to agriculture, it links her via Athena the Defender to the material city and by extension to any who would, unlike Themistocles, wish to save it by negotiating with Xerxes.

Like *300*, with its emphasis on rationality over mysticism, *300: Rise* does not draw the gods per se into its mytho-historical framework. Poseidon is the only god whose name is spoken, and it is in connection with Themistocles: when Artemisia flatteringly suggests that he shares lineage with the god, based on how effectively he

Figure 5.2 The camera aligns Artemisia (Eva Green) with the fallen statue of Athena the Defender in *300: Rise of an Empire* (2014). Warner Bros./ Legendary Pictures.

has fought against her naval commanders. Athena, the only deity visualized in the film, is connected to Artemisia most clearly as a formidable warrior woman, but the fall of one presages the other's. After delivering a crushing (ahistorical) defeat to the Athenians at the Battle of Artemisium, in which she believed Themistocles to have been eliminated, Artemisia is overcome with rage to learn that he escaped.[35] As emotion overrides her tactical judgment, the camera aligns her with the fallen statue of Athena the Defender, linking her fate to that of the city and its women on the night of the Persian sack (see Figure 5.2). In her eagerness to chase down Themistocles, she hubristically defies a newly prudent Xerxes, who advises restraint over her sudden recklessness.

The broken statue looms behind Artemisia, its face framing hers, as she defies Xerxes' order. This moment of failed judgment identifies her not as Athena the Defender, but as its fallen, shattered image. The importance of the film's opening Spartan corpse tableau to the whole is especially clear at this moment. The monuments of the golden age which matter in this film are flesh-and-blood individuals who embody the ideals that artists imitate in stone and metal. The presence of Artemisia in the same frame as the fragmentary Athena illustrates her failure to embody it. The conclusion of *300: Rise* thus figuratively casts Artemisia as an anti-Athena in two respects: in battle with Themistocles-Poseidon, she is an Athena who this time loses; and as one who fails to embody the true Athena the Defender, but rather embodies the fallen totemic figure of the Athens that is only stone, wood, cloth, and dust.

When the prologue features the destruction of Athena the Defender, a sculptural icon of powerful female leadership, a vacuum is created. Whereas the contest between Themistocles and Artemisia resolves in favor of "Poseidon" this time, another character arrives like a *dea ex machina* to steal even his thunder. Gorgo's triumphant arrival is the logical conclusion for *300: Rise*, for several reasons. First, it is the norm in this film for Spartans to embody monuments that Athenians (only) build. Second, Gorgo's military actions at the end of the film prove that she is no less qualified than Artemisia to be a warrior woman. And third, like Athena in contest with Poseidon, she provides something that the Athens of this film needs: the military might with which to realize their political will.

Gorgo both reprises and builds upon the role that she played in *300*. When the Persian emissary had demanded to know what makes her, a woman, think that she can speak among men, Gorgo retorts with the claim that "Only Spartan women give birth to real men."[36] In an ancient collection of quotable quotes, *The Sayings of Spartan Women* by Plutarch, Gorgo provides this answer to an Athenian woman's question about why Spartan women have power over their men. Indeed, an Athenian woman might wonder at a Spartan woman's assertion of the right to speak, and even to be seen in the first place. In Thucydides' *History of the Peloponnesian War* (2.45) the Athenian statesman Pericles declares that the greatest merit a woman may have is not to be spoken of by men in either praise or blame.[37] In a scenario that conforms to the most misogynistic ancient Athenian perspectives, the audience sees no Athenian women in *300: Rise* apart from victims of the Persian attack, nor do any Athenian men speak of Athenian women. By contrast, early in *300: Rise* Themistocles comes to Sparta and petitions Gorgo for aid in the absence of Leonidas, who is preparing for his march to Thermopylae. She insults his masculinity and sends him away empty-handed, citing her duty to protect Sparta first.

Thus, at the film's end, Gorgo arrives as an unexpected but logical figure of power, like an epiphany. She emerges as a patriarchal model of woman for the new united Greece. Like Artemisia, she joins her troops in cutting down the enemy, but only in deference to male example and persuasion. In this case, she fights to avenge her husband and carry on his struggle after Themistocles persuades her to do so. As such, she models for Athens the gender performance of a visible female character willing and able to perform traditional male tasks, but only through a framework of male authority linked to marriage. A wife and mother with a royal, yet parochial concern for Sparta alone and her own losses, this acceptance of male influences now overrides her isolationist perspectives, as she wields her husband's sword in an international conflict – much as Athena acts as her father's daughter.

Gorgo now assumes the role of fellow soldier – royal status notwithstanding – addressing the Spartan warriors whom she leads as "my brothers." Yet, through her rank and seniority, Gorgo also embodies Spartan motherhood's centrality to Spartan masculinity. In this way, her arrival introduces to the Athenians what they have so far lacked in *300: Rise*: a woman with the ideological as well as biological capacity to generate real men. Together, these traits enable her to embody Athena on behalf of a united Greece.

CONCLUSION

Given the vehemently pro-Spartan stance of *300*, how could the Athenian point of view be accommodated within the franchise? Murro's film works with the iconic landscape of the Athenian Acropolis and thematizes the Parthenon's imagery of gods, monsters, and humans to dramatize the challenge that Athens must meet to attain the status that the Parthenon bespeaks. *300: Rise* liberates the mythological conflicts immured on the Parthenon, staging them in order to tell a story that emphasizes the narrowness of Athens' salvation.

From narratives of Amazons, centaurs, and Poseidon vying with Athena emerges a story of problematic Athenian gender performance and inadequate martial preparation. The solution to these challenges that enables the city to survive for itself and posterity is a new Athena-figure of flesh and blood, in the person of Spartan Gorgo. To her is transferred credit for victory at Salamis, even as an Athenian Poseidon, Themistocles, restores Athenian masculinity by defeating an anti-Athena, Artemisia. The greatest accomplishment of that vital Athenian golden-age resource, words – on which, as the oracle says, the world hangs – is to persuade Gorgo to bring Sparta to the fight.

NOTES

I thank Meredith E. Safran, Yurie Hong, Marina Haworth, Rob Kendrick, and Kate Topper.

1 Metro-Goldwyn-Mayer released *La Battaglia di Maratona* in the USA in 1960 as *The Giant of Marathon*.

2 Hanesworth (2015: 93–6).
3 Blanshard and Shahabudin (2011: 116); Hanesworth (2015: 96–7). For the perception of such an "efflorescence" as a golden age, see Goldstone (2002: 33).
4 Aperlo (2013: 98–9).
5 Hanesworth (2015: 92).
6 Failes (2014).
7 The name and appearance of the statue are somewhat uncertain. The ancient statue is typically referred to in scholarship as the Athena Promachos ("the front-fighter"), based on Pausanias' second-century CE account, but the distinctive appearance of the *promachos* statue-type is at odds with Pausanias' description; see Hurwit (2004: 79–80). I refer to all versions of the statue as "Athena the Defender." Athena the Defender also appears in *Socrate* (1971), where it is brightly painted, as indeed the statue would have been. Since *Socrate* is set in 399 BCE, the statue and its position adjacent to the Parthenon are historically correct.
8 Thucydides (1998: 7–8). For Greek text, see Thucydides (1942).
9 Nisbet (2008: vii–viii).
10 Nisbet (2008: 4–6).
11 Hanesworth (2015: 99–101).
12 Turner (2008: 140–1).
13 Briggs (2008: 22–6). Martin Winkler (2009a: 208) cites *Triumph of the Will* as an indirect precursor of Snyder's *300*.
14 Quoted in Chapoutot (2016: 167).
15 Hake (2002: 78).
16 On the use of cosmetics in *300*, see Richards (2007). For the digital software used in *300* (called "The Crush"), see Turner (2008: 138).
17 Collias (2014).
18 Turner (2008: 133).
19 Skin color visually distinguishes Greeks (white) from Persians (brown) in *300: Rise*. Apart from Peter Mensah, who reprises his role as the emissary (and tutor to Artemisia), black actors do not play Persian characters in this movie. By contrast, in *300* black actors played several high-ranking Persian characters.
20 Riefenstahl (1993: 205).
21 Or three victories, if Marathon is included.
22 Turner (2008: 135). For a practical explanation, see Prince (2012: 89–91).
23 The north-side metopes have mostly been damaged beyond recognition; part of their narrative concerned the destruction of Troy.
24 Woodford (2003: 122–5).
25 Neils (2005: 178–9).
26 Artemisia's abusers are never explicitly identified as Athenians, but the characters discussing the event are Athenians and do not identify them as being from anywhere else.

27 Quintus Smyrnaeus, *Posthomerica* 1.671–4: "Even Achilles felt in his heart regret without relief / For the fact that he killed rather than took her, a shining bride, / to Phthia, well stocked in horses, since in size and shape / she was blameless and resembled the goddesses." For Greek text, see Quintus Smyrnaeus (1962).
28 For example, the sixth-century BCE Exekias red-figure vase.
29 Neils (2005: 176–7). See Hardie (1983) for a survey of how the gigantomachy myth has served multiple political agendas from fifth-century BCE Athens through early imperial Rome.
30 Ehrbar (2014).
31 Patay-Horváth (2015: 353–4).
32 For the *Life of Themistocles*, see Plutarch (1998: 84–5).
33 Plutarch (1998: 90–1).
34 Plutarch (1998: 99).
35 The name of the Battle of Artemisium is unrelated to the name of the character Artemisia.
36 For *The Sayings of Spartan Women* in Greek and English, see Plutarch (1931: 457). See Nikoloutsos (2013: 275–6), Tomasso (2013: 116–18).
37 Thucydides (1998: 968).

6 *Confronting the Ancient Greek Golden Age in Jules Dassin's* Phaedra *(1962)*

Emma Scioli

A stylish updating of an ancient Greek myth to 1960s Europe, Jules Dassin's *Phaedra* (1962) self-consciously evokes the past: both the world of ancient Greek myth, in which the story of Phaedra finds its origin, and the work of playwrights who told her story in dramatic form, stretching back to the first extant dramatic treatment. In Euripides' tragedy *Hippolytus* (produced in 428 BCE), Phaedra, wife of the Athenian king Theseus, conceives an overwhelming passion for her stepson Hippolytus, Theseus' son by an Amazon queen and thus an ethnic outsider to the Greek community. Through Phaedra, the goddess Aphrodite wishes to punish Hippolytus for his lack of reverence toward her and rejection of all women in favor of the virgin goddess Artemis. When Hippolytus learns of his stepmother's lust, he is horrified, and in response to his rejection Phaedra takes her own life – only after she pens a suicide note accusing Hippolytus of rape. When an enraged Theseus reads the note, he calls upon his own father, the sea-god Poseidon, to kill his son. As he flees into exile, Hippolytus is fatally trampled when his horses are spooked by a bull that emerges from the sea. At the play's end, the goddess Artemis informs Theseus, too late, of his son's innocence.

In interviews and writings, Dassin and his artistic collaborators relate their film to "Greek tragedy," and modern critics tend to assume Euripides' play as the source-text for *Phaedra*.[1] Yet Dassin's *Phaedra* is hardly a straightforward adaptation of that oldest and perhaps best-known source. Rather, Dassin incorporates elements from later retellings of Phaedra's story with his own stark innovations to create a palimpsestic film that is both akin to and alienated from its earliest predecessor. Andrew Horton writes that Dassin's "decision to do a loose adaptation of the original tragedy allowed him the freedom he needed to re-shape the myth as he wished. Thus, Dassin uses the ancient text as a starting point rather than as an end."[2] Despite this move away from the ancient text, however, Dassin repeatedly draws attention to the film's origins in Greek myth and tragedy through visual imagery. Beyond simply reminding the viewer of its origins, the film's use of images of ancient Greek art and its suggestive modernizations of elements from the ancient Greek tragedy force a confrontation with a particular modern formulation of the ancient Greek past, one that has ramifications for interpretations of *Phaedra* on both aesthetic and meta-cinematic levels.

This chapter examines the film's depiction of the relationship between past and present by utilizing the concept of "the golden age," loosely defined as a time prior to and in some way superior to the present, to characterize the world of ancient Greece that irrupts into the modern setting of the film both visually and thematically.[3] The specific golden age in question is that of classical Athens, the nexus of so many moral and aesthetic values glorified at least since the eighteenth century in Western thought.[4] The literary and material remains of fifth-century BCE Athens are seen from this modern perspective as the major repositories of Western values.[5] Indeed, any golden age is defined as such from the perspective of someone who can only cast a retrospective glance upon it from the degraded present, and thus stands in a position of belatedness, "the pervasive feeling of coming late" to that idealized time.[6] Rather than fostering nostalgia for a golden age that might prompt a desire for its return, *Phaedra* presents it as an intrusive presence from which its characters feel alienated, only to demonstrate that they are inextricably bound, in their modern dress, to repeat what the tragic past has prescribed for them.

While exposing its magnetic pull for his characters, the film also grapples with the unattainability of the golden age of ancient Greek tragedy for the director himself. Dassin made his film during a period when intense debate about the "death of tragedy" raged in academic circles.[7] The debate swirled around whether or not tragedy as a "form of drama" was viable outside of certain cultures and time periods, and whether it could co-exist with modernity.[8] Although not the focus of the debate, cinematic adaptations of Greek tragedies participate in the discourse surrounding the "death" of tragedy as a genre. In his recent work on Greek tragedy and cinema, Pantelis Michelakis has addressed the relationship between the two media, writing that "in generic, artistic, medial, spatial and temporal terms, Greek tragedy is presumed to be dead, but it can also be brought back to life; it is dissected but it can also be re-assembled and transformed."[9]

By choosing for his film's subject a story that had its earliest extant narration in ancient Greek tragedy, a genre that flourished in the distant fifth century BCE, Dassin acknowledges the belatedness of modern cinema, relative to ancient tragedy, as a dramatic medium.[10] Yet by reassembling and transforming a classic from Greek tragedy into a modern film, Dassin uses the temporal and medial gap between the two as an opportunity for exploring the concept of alienation. As theater critic Julie Sanders has argued, "'after' need not . . . mean belated in a purely negative sense. Coming 'after' can mean finding new angles and new routes into something, new perspectives on the familiar . . . [which] in turn identify entirely novel possibilities."[11] For Dassin, the acknowledgment of belatedness is not a declaration of inferiority, but rather affords him a new perspective on his own experiences of disconnection.

DASSIN'S FOREIGNNESS AND *NEVER ON SUNDAY*

Jules Dassin's preoccupation with the intersection of belatedness and alienation, especially his own attraction to and estrangement from the "golden age" of classical Greece, emerged in the film that serves as a prelude-in-retrospect to his *Phaedra*: *Never on Sunday* (1960). Film scholar Dimitris Eleftheriotis has claimed that "Dassin's ontological status, the position he occupies within critical discourse and the textual practices of his films are all marked by 'foreignness' as an extreme form of strangeness."[12] To address Dassin's portrayal of foreigners as strangers, Eleftheriotis analyzes Dassin's hit film *Never on Sunday*, which was released two years before *Phaedra*. Beyond their setting in Greece and their star, Melina Mercouri, Dassin's lover and creative muse, *Never on Sunday* and *Phaedra* also share a concern with the appropriation of ancient Greek culture by foreigners and how this relates to a concept of authentic Greekness: a point of comparison that has been largely overlooked in discussions of Dassin's work. For Dassin, an American expatriate, to dramatize this struggle between authenticity and appropriation adds an extra layer of meaning.

Eleftheriotis defines *Never on Sunday* as Dassin's "most obvious dramatization of his own cosmopolitan foreignness."[13] Dassin, who spent much of his working life in Europe after being blacklisted during the House Un-American Activities Committee (HUAC) hearings, both directs and stars as Homer Thrace, an American intellectual who travels to Greece in search of the lost ideals of ancient Greek art and philosophy.[14] Convinced that he will learn why modern society has become so debased from contemporary Greeks, the heirs to the founders of Western thought, he is instead dismayed to find that his precious ancient ideals have been abandoned or ignored by the Greek prostitutes, musicians, and shipbuilders whom he encounters in bustling Piraeus, the port of Athens. Dassin's fictional film reflects a stark reality: for centuries, Greeks have been denigrated for not living up to the standards of their ancestors, according to Euro-American philhellenes determined to overwrite accumulated historical changes with their own nostalgia for a constructed past at odds with modern Greek history.[15] Homer Thrace responds by attempting to educate his new friends about their cultural heritage, focusing his attention on the uninhibited and charming prostitute Illya, played by Mercouri. In the role of the cultured but insensitive foreigner, Dassin both channels and critiques his identity as an American expatriate director working in Greece with a Greek cast.

According to Eleftheriotis, one of the film's central concerns is "the Greek characters' resistance to external cultural appropriations."[16] This resistance is exemplified when Homer tries to correct Illya's misrepresentation of Euripides' tragedy *Medea*, which she narrates to her uneducated friends. Even after attending a live performance of the play, Illya refuses to acknowledge that Medea murders her children. Despite being moved emotionally by the live performance, she prefers instead to maintain her insistence on its happy ending, bolstered by the appearance of the actors who played the children during the curtain call. In the stand-off between Homer and Illya about the proper interpretation of ancient tragedy and the notion of the supremacy of the original text over the modern response to it – suggestively shot amid the ruins of the Parthenon on the Athenian Acropolis, the single most recognizable visual symbol of the "golden age" of Athens, and thus Greece – the film raises questions about cultural appropriation and who "owns" ancient culture.[17] Because their rift centers upon the interpretation and thus reception of a Greek tragedy, the film works not only as an important thematic precursor to, but also as a meta-cinematic comment upon, Dassin's appropriation of a Greek tragedy for his own dramatic purposes in creating *Phaedra*.

In her autobiography, Mercouri links the two films explicitly, stating that "we had made our Greek comedy; now we'll make a Greek tragedy."[18] Mercouri's statement suggests that *Never on Sunday* and *Phaedra*, in addition to representing the two major genres of ancient drama, should be considered as counterparts because they share common creative origins in the collaboration between herself and Dassin. As opposed to *Never on Sunday*, where anxieties about cultural appropriation and access to authentic "Greekness" are central to the film's narrative, in *Phaedra* these concerns lie beneath the surface, forming an undercurrent for the film's references to ancient Greek culture. Dassin's exploration of foreignness through the character of Homer Thrace in *Never on Sunday* offers a rich context for understanding the later film's tensions between past and present, Greek and non-Greek, Greek tragedy and its reception, as meditating upon the feeling of alienation engendered by foreignness.

DASSIN AND THE PHAEDRA TRADITION

The tradition through which Dassin encountered Euripides' *Hippolytus* includes important treatments of the myth by the Roman tragedian Seneca, likely written in the 50s CE, and by the French Enlightenment playwright Jean Racine, first performed in 1677.[19] Both of these receptions substitute the name of the embattled wife and stepmother for the Greek tragedy's eponym and expand upon or reshape key thematic aspects of Euripides' influential version.[20] Seneca's *Phaedra* explicitly connects Hippolytus' rejection of women to his nostalgia for the purity of a vanished golden age, for which he realizes he has been born too late.[21] Recalling the Euripidean Hippolytus' railing against women as "deceitful, an evil for human beings" and advocacy of a life "free from woman kind" (617 and 624), Seneca's Hippolytus defends his countercultural lifestyle as "free of sin" and "respectful of our ancient ways" (483–4), honoring the customs of the "first age of man," that is, the golden age (526–7).[22] The deeply misogynistic Hippolytus singles out women as the "root of all evil" (559) and thus confirms that he shuns them for bringing about the demise of the golden age for which he longs. By avoiding them, he implies that he can return to the purity that defined this golden age. Seneca rearticulates something familiar from Euripides' text and likely central to the myth: that Hippolytus' celibacy is a manifestation of the self-control on which he prides himself. In both plays, Hippolytus' loss of control over his horses kills him, a suitable punishment for his unwillingness to yield to his powerful nemesis Aphrodite.

Seneca's lines, written by a Roman playwright aware of his secondary position vis-à-vis classical Greek tragedians such as Euripides, provide a useful lens through which to appreciate Dassin's contribution to the evolving reception of the ancient myth. Through Hippolytus, who yearns for an impossible return to a bygone age and laments the belatedness of his own time, Seneca acknowledges his own belatedness with regard to Euripides. Dassin, who lived in France for several years prior to making *Phaedra*, was likely familiar with Racine's *Phèdre*, which was heavily influenced by Seneca's work.[23] As in Seneca's tragedy, in Racine's play Phaedra waits until Theseus returns and accuses Hippolytus in person before committing suicide toward the play's end (in Euripides' telling, Phaedra commits suicide before her husband's return). Other elements in Dassin's film, such as Phaedra's rival Ercy, have strong parallels in Racine's adaptation of the tale, but not in Euripides' or Seneca's versions. Dassin thus appropriates and reconfigures some elements from his sources in a way that openly acknowledges his distance from his predecessors, while perpetuating other essential elements of their tragedies.

Crucially, Dassin's film preserves the central feature of the myth: Phaedra's love for her half-English stepson Alexis (Anthony Perkins) is a destructive force that results in her suicide, and in Alexis' exile and death, leaving her husband Thanos (Raf Vallone) bereft of both wife and son. In a blatant departure from his tragic predecessors, however, Dassin adds a love affair between Phaedra (Mercouri) and Alexis early in the film; thus, the dramatic tension in Dassin's film surrounds Phaedra's festering passion for her stepson after she returns to her husband, is subsequently tortured by Alexis' coldness toward her, and competes for his affection with her much younger niece Ercy (Elisabeth Ercy). The traditional anxiety surrounding Hippolytus' non-conforming sexual behavior is transferred from his deviant celibacy and rejection of Aphrodite onto his quasi-Oedipal passion for his stepmother, while the ancient Phaedra's involuntary yet poisonous lust for her stepson becomes an all-consuming yearning driven by dissatisfaction with her marriage to a domineering and insensitive husband, and jealousy of Ercy. As Julie Sanders has argued, it is "at the point of infidelity to a sourcetext [that] the most creative acts of adaptation and appropriation take place."[24] Dassin marks his infidelity to his source-texts by adding an act of marital infidelity, a mechanism that both establishes Phaedra's subjectivity and remakes the plot as melodrama. In so doing, Dassin perhaps self-referentially draws attention to his film's alienation from

Euripides' *Hippolytus*, its earliest source, and thus from the "golden age" of Greek culture.

APPROPRIATED ARTIFACTS: GLIMPSES OF GREECE'S "GOLDEN AGE"

As Phaedra and Alexis' illicit and destructive love affair is the central source of *Phaedra*'s dramatic tension, their first meeting is a critical moment in the film. Furthermore, this pivotal scene contains the most prominent examples of Dassin's visual quotations of ancient Greece in the film and of how he frames his glimpses of the golden age. As he thrusts his protagonists into an uncomfortable encounter among images from ancient Greek art – famously appropriated from their native surroundings by a British philhellene – Dassin suggests the characters' inextricable bond to the past simultaneously with the impropriety of their interaction. The characters' confrontation with and alienation from the past in this scene are integral to the film's acknowledgment of its status as a belated reception.

Thanos has sent Phaedra to London to convince his estranged son to return to Greece and join his shipping business. A voiceover from the concierge at Phaedra's hotel communicates that Alexis has summoned Phaedra to meet him at the British Museum, in "the Elgin Room," home to the sculptures that in antiquity had adorned the Parthenon on the Athenian Acropolis, itself the site of the heated argument between Homer and Illya in *Never on Sunday*. In this room, Phaedra encounters Alexis drawing. As she moves closer to him, the camera frames Alexis' head opposite that of the marble horse he is sketching, creating a striking juxtaposition between the two (see Figure 6.1). In a 2004 interview, Dassin explained that this shot was meant to evoke the death "of the Hippolyte character ... by charging horses in the original tale."[25] Thus Dassin imagined a learned viewer capable of recognizing a key element of his source(s): Hippolytus' destruction by his horses upon losing control of his chariot. In terms of the film's visual sensibility, this scene also recalls the film's opening credits, which are displayed against the backdrop of images of galloping horses from the Parthenon's friezes. Furthermore, the visual simultaneity of past (the horse sculpture) and present (Alexis) forces a confrontation between the golden age of tragedy, whose antiquity is further marked by the degraded condition of the sculptures themselves, and the belated present of cinema that underscores Dassin's tenuous position as a modern filmmaker approaching and appropriating ancient material.

Figure 6.1 Alexis (Anthony Perkins) sketching a sculpted horse in the "Elgin Room" at the British Museum in *Phaedra* (1962). Joele/Jorilie/Melinafilm/Lopert Pictures Corporation.

Euripides' *Hippolytus* calls for statues of the goddesses Artemis and Aphrodite, the countervailing forces of the tragedy, to be positioned on stage throughout the play. Dassin, too, exploits the interplay between sculpture and the physical presence of the divine later in the scene when Phaedra is aligned with a sculpture of the goddess Aphrodite. When the camera pans from Alexis and Phaedra to another set of sculptures, Alexis explains one as "Aphrodite reclining in the lap of her mother." As Phaedra moves closer to the sculpture and the camera frames her facing it, she becomes uncomfortable, exclaiming, "Aphrodite ... I need some air. Please, let's go." Symbolically, the encounter with Aphrodite, goddess of desire, foreshadows the affair between Alexis and Phaedra. Visually, however, the shot's composition creates a confrontation between present and past: the modern Phaedra, who will be the agent of her own passion in her seduction of Alexis, and the goddess who tormented her tragic predecessor by cursing her with unwanted passion for her stepson.

The museum scene may illuminate a self-reflexive critique of Dassin's own process of appropriation from, and thus infidelity to, multiple source-texts. In choosing to set the meeting scene in the hall of the Elgin Marbles, which were designed by Euripides' famous contemporary Phidias, Dassin inserts his characters into the material milieu of Greece's golden age. By connecting his film to its tragic predecessor via the scene's location, Dassin suggests a parallel between his work and the act of appropriation that brought the Elgin Marbles to England. Seeing these sculptures on display in the British Museum would likely remind many viewers of the fraught history of their arrival in England, after being exported from Greece by Lord Elgin between 1801 and 1812. Elgin had received a permit from the Ottoman rulers of Greece to remove and transport the sculptures to England, an act that was met with both support and opposition at that time and has been plagued by controversy ever since. As Elgin physically appropriated the Parthenon sculptures from Greece, Dassin visually appropriates the cultural material of ancient Greece and "transports" it to the twentieth century for his own artistic purposes.[26]

Consideration of Mercouri's nationality adds another dimension to the tension and eventual animosity between the characters in this scene. Many years after the film's release, Dassin described the difficulties he had obtaining permission to film in the British Museum. He recounted that Mercouri confronted the museum authorities over the Elgin Marbles, asserting "they are *our* statues,"[27] referring to their Greek origins and her status as their rightful owner because of her Greek nationality. Knowledge of Mercouri's defiance of the museum authorities, and of her subsequent advocacy for their return as Greece's Minister of Culture (1981–9), enhances the meta-cinematic significance of this scene as a comment upon the rightful ownership of cultural patrimony. The overlay of modern actor and onscreen character in this scene also ironizes the scene's meaning within the film. When the Greek Phaedra travels to London in order to "repatriate" her distinctly English stepson Alexis to Greece, she initiates the process in a room whose very existence reflects a long-standing political conflict between Greece and England over the repatriation of the sculptures that adorn it.

Finally, the onscreen encounter between Phaedra and Alexis functions as a foil for Mercouri and Dassin's relationship. Aside from both couples being lovers, Alexis and Dassin both access Greekness through the agency of Phaedra/Mercouri. As Phaedra reconnects Alexis (played by an American actor) to his Greek identity by teaching him Greek phrases and introducing him to Greek love songs during their affair, so too does Mercouri allow the American Dassin a kind of authenticity, a Greekness-by-proxy, through their marriage and long-term artistic collaboration in Greece.[28] Vrasidas Karalis calls *Phaedra* "one of the first trans-national films made by an expatriate struggling to find a new homeland."[29]

VEHICLES OF DESIRE: CARS, SHIPS, AND THE END OF THE GOLDEN AGE

After the tense, sexually charged encounter between stepmother and stepson in the museum, the couple emerges onto the bustling streets of modern London, thus appearing to escape the oppressive vestiges of the past. When their conversation turns to Alexis' love life, Alexis tells Phaedra of "one beautiful, miraculous girl" and insists that Phaedra meet her right away. Leading Phaedra to another exhibition space – a car showroom – Alexis reveals his "girl" to be an Aston Martin sports car, an icon of contemporary British luxury and modern technology. Alexis enters the showroom and, while the salesman's back is turned, teasingly fondles the car in a mute performance for Phaedra, who mirthfully watches the scene as a voyeur behind the barrier of the showroom's window.

Detached from Euripides' play, Alexis' actions may seem merely playful or spontaneous; so Phaedra apparently interprets them, laughing at his audacity. Visually and chronologically, the pristine sports car, posed alluringly in the showroom window, is the antithesis of the fragmentary and deteriorating marble sculptures sequestered in the British Museum. This departure from classical antiquity thus signals the imminent plot twist that will alienate the film from its origins. But familiarity with Euripides' play also invites comparison between this scene and Euripides' characterization of Hippolytus' exclusive worship of the goddess Artemis, an object of reverence inappropriate for a man approaching adulthood. Hippolytus performs this reverence in bringing an offering to adorn her statue, saying "Dear mistress, accept this band for your golden hair from my reverent hand. For I alone of mortals have this privilege: I am your companion and speak with you" (lines 82–6). Thus the car, itself an inappropriate substitute for a human love-object, can function as the updated avatar of Artemis, here the statue-like recipient of Alexis' "worship" in the form of his shocking frottage. Hippolytus' fervent devotion to the ethereal Artemis and his attendant rejection of women are appropriated and recast in Alexis' performance of his naïve but deviant lust for an inanimate object of material luxury.

The juxtaposition of Alexis' clear investment in both the Elgin Marbles and the car sets up an opposition between ancient and modern that foreshadows the eventual engulfment of the modern tale by the ancient story. In fact, the undertow of the film's tragic origins is further strengthened by introducing here the means of

Hippolytus' death. As Dassin converts Hippolytus' celibacy and self-control into Alexis' unrestrained sexual deviance, he transforms the horse-drawn chariot into the car, condensing references to Hippolytus' non-normative sexuality and his violent death into one symbol. The conflation of horse and car is made explicit in a later scene, when Thanos has the Aston Martin shipped to Greece as a surprise for his son. Thanos and Phaedra encounter two villagers at the docks while the car is being unloaded. One villager (Dassin, in a cameo) remarks that the large shipping crate looks like a coffin; Thanos replies, "It's the fastest coffin you ever saw, driven by hundreds of horses!"

Alexis' act of fetishizing this sleek vehicle also connects him to his father's (pre)occupation in a way that evokes ancient discourses about the end of the golden age hinging upon the invention of vehicles designed to cross natural boundaries. In his first-century CE poem *Metamorphoses*, the Roman poet Ovid defines the golden age by its lack of shipbuilding and, consequently, of dangerous exploration of the seas: "Not yet had a pine tree, cut from its native mountain, been lowered into the waters in order to travel to other lands; mortal men were ignorant of any shores beyond their own" (*Met.* 1.94–6).[30] Seafaring, including its relationship to both wealth and danger, is a central theme in *Phaedra*. Thanos is a wealthy shipping magnate who oversees the construction and operation of a large fleet of ships. Scenes showing villagers observing with dread the lavish celebration of the christening of Thanos' newest ship, the *SS Phaedra*, and then these same villagers responding to news that their family members have perished when the ship sinks in a storm, bookend the film and parallel the fate of Mercouri's Phaedra.[31]

Mercouri reveals in her autobiography that she and Dassin, in partnership with screenwriter Margarita Liberaki, consciously chose to make the powerful men in their drama Greek shipping magnates, as updates of the "gods and kings" from Euripides' play, because Greek ship owners were the contemporary equivalent of "someone who had an empire."[32] The Communist filmmakers' strong negative opinions about the business practices of Greek shipping magnates clearly influenced their decision to frame the central narrative of the film with scenes that link the wealth and foreign travel associated with shipping to the danger and destruction that can result from it.[33] Mercouri's condemnation of the lifestyle choices of the Greek aristocratic class aligns fundamentally with Ovid's identification of the advent of seafaring as a harbinger of the end of the golden age.

STRIKING A POSE: ALEXIS' HYBRIDITY AND ALIENATION

In response to a bystander's shock at Alexis' antics in the car showroom, Phaedra explains that he is "half-Greek, very impulsive." Phaedra's comment exemplifies the film's characterization of hybridity as a distinct form of foreignness in this film, especially as concerns Alexis. Phaedra's faithful nurse (Olympia Papadouka) calls him "the foreigner" and "son of the Englishwoman" after she dreams about Alexis threatening Dimitri, Phaedra's son with Thanos. These epithets reflect a fear that the half-Greek son of Thanos is a potential threat to the inheritance rights of Phaedra's son with Thanos, an anxiety also present in Euripides' play. Alexis later reveals that he knows some basic Greek vocabulary words, but displays his detachment from his Greek identity when he uses the Greek phrase for "thank you" at a lemonade stand. When the vendor asks what he means, Alexis replies with an exaggerated Greek accent, "it means 'thank you' in Greek," demonstrating his pleasure in performing Greekness for his fellow Englishman. This performance of a foreign identity will be recalled uncomfortably when Alexis accedes to his father's wishes and comes to Greece. Phaedra's comment on Alexis' behavior with the car brands him as a foreigner in his own homeland, yet when Thanos imports the British Aston Martin to Greece to lure his son there, the car becomes an emblem of Alexis' foreignness in his father's homeland.

While Thanos' urge to bring his son back to Greece is motivated by his business interests, he also attempts to refashion Alexis as Greek. To facilitate the former, Thanos arranges a marriage between Alexis and Ercy, the daughter of a rival shipping magnate who is married to Phaedra's sister. When Alexis takes Ercy to a party, an attractive Greek girl named Heleni (Depy Martini), whose name advertises her Greekness both through its similarity to the noun "Hellene," meaning "a Greek," and by recalling Helen of Troy, that infamous emblem of destructive female sexuality, remarks that Alexis "looks Greek in his clothes," distinguishing "being Greek" from merely "seeming Greek" and calling attention to his foreignness among the Greeks. Alexis responds defiantly, "I am Greek," and strikes the pose of the famous classical Greek sculpture known as the *Diskobolos*, or "Discus Thrower," grabbing a dinner plate to substitute for the discus (see Figure 6.2). Myron, the Athenian sculptor of the *Diskobolos*, was a contemporary of Phidias and thus another exponent of Athens' "golden age." By assuming this pose and visually quoting a famous

Figure 6.2 Alexis (Anthony Perkins) performs his Greekness by striking the pose of the *Diskobolos* in *Phaedra* (1962). Joele/Jorilie/Melinafilm/Lopert Pictures Corporation.

classical Greek sculpture, Alexis literally "embodies" Greekness, thus challenging Helene's comment that he merely passes for Greek. In so doing, he claims entitlement to Greek cultural heritage, recalling his earlier linguistic attempts to perform Greekness.

Alexis' re-interpretation of the *Diskobolos* as a plate-thrower amalgamates different notions of authentic Greekness. Visually, the image is emblematic of the classical Greek sculptural ideal in its depiction of the athlete's body; symbolically, the substitution of the plate for the discus evokes stereotypes of modern Greeks as impulsive and passionate, epitomized by popular cultural depictions of Greeks smashing plates as part of wedding celebrations. This equation of plate-smashing with the modern degradation of classical Greek ideals was memorably enacted in the taverna scenes in *Never on Sunday*, where the gesture (albeit with ouzo glasses instead of plates) is visual shorthand for the seductive and extravagant degeneracy of modern Greek culture.

DYING TO BE A PART OF "THE GOOD OLD DAYS"

In a desperate attempt to thwart the engagement of Alexis to Ercy, Phaedra confesses to Thanos her affair with Alexis. In response, the patriarch beats his son and banishes him from Greece. After a final encounter in which he rejects Phaedra, Alexis speeds away in his Aston Martin. Addressing the composer J. S. Bach, whose music is blaring from the car radio, Alexis declares deliriously: "she loved me, she loved me like they did in the good old days," thus characterizing Phaedra's passion for him with a twisted nostalgia. To which "good old days" does Alexis refer? On a literal level, Phaedra's perverse and destructive love for Alexis comes directly from the golden age of Greek tragedy, when it was first dramatized by Euripides. And, just as in those "good old days," the lust of a stepmother for her stepson is fatal to both. When Dassin's Alexis characterizes Phaedra's love as like that of the "good old days," he finally concedes his own entanglement with that past.

By tacitly acknowledging the origins of Phaedra's love in Greek tragedy, Alexis anticipates the destruction it will wreak upon him, a feature essential to Euripides' plot. The scene of Alexis' death combines elements of confrontation with the past, as in the museum scene, and glorification of the modern, suggested by the car showroom scene. Furthermore, the death scene concretizes the link, suggested in earlier scenes, between the sculpted horse and the car. Significantly, just as he attempts to create physical distance between himself and Phaedra, Thanos, and Greece itself by driving away in his car, that modern symbol of freedom, Alexis draws attention to his indissoluble connection to the world inhabited by their tragic predecessors. Shortly after his departure, an oncoming truck – rather than a bull from the sea – shatters Alexis' car and his body with it, violently expelling him from the shores of Greece over the side of a cliff.

As in Euripides' play, Alexis' exile is short-lived. In one of the film's final scenes, he is brought back, albeit as a corpse in a coffin, to his father's home. In a demonstration of the inextricability of past and present in this film, as Alexis' body is returned to land, his character too "returns" to its origins by performing the final act prescribed to him by his tragic predecessor Hippolytus. Furthermore, the image of Alexis delivered to his father's home in a coffin serves as a visual metaphor for his belatedness: Alexis, the foreigner in his father's homeland, has come back to reside permanently in his father's home, but only in death, and thus too late for acceptance by Thanos.

CONCLUSION

In updating the ancient Greek tragedy of Phaedra and Hippolytus for the screen, Dassin acknowledges his own belatedness as an adaptor of their tale through his palimpsestic process of adaptation and innovation. Dassin foregrounds the tension between precedence and belatedness when the film's updated protagonists confront the physical vestiges of the golden age of ancient Greece. This dynamic is exemplified by the scene in the hall of the Elgin Marbles at the British Museum, where the characters' encounter with antiquity activates a discomfort with this very past. Even when the film flaunts its most obvious markers of modernity, such as Alexis' sports car, and thus highlights its distance from the past, Dassin cleverly reconfigures themes from the works of his tragic predecessors. Alexis' head-on crash at the film's close literalizes and finalizes the confrontation with the past he had avoided up to this point in the film.

These moments of confrontation with and alienation from the past can be mapped onto the film's depiction of foreignness. Foreignness is most prominently embodied by the half-Greek, half-English Alexis. In one sense, Alexis' dual ethnicity can be interpreted as a metaphor for the film's dual identities as both ancient Greek tragedy and modern cinematic melodrama. Alexis, raised by his English mother and thus a stranger in his father's homeland of Greece, also functions as a proxy for Dassin. As a director, Dassin is coming belatedly to Greek tragedy, and thus approaches it as a "stranger," excluded from and looking back upon this golden age of drama with a feeling of disconnection from the past. Dassin's alienation from his subject is deepened by his status as an expatriate foreigner in Greece, exiled from his homeland due to the Hollywood blacklist.[34] Dassin's exploration of the tension between the ownership of ancient Greek culture and its apparent degradation in the modern world in *Never on Sunday* should be considered an important precursor to his more subtle engagement with the intersection of ancient Greek culture and authentic Greekness in *Phaedra*.

Phaedra's tantalizing glimpses of the golden age of ancient Greece evoke the past while suggesting its necessary inaccessibility. And even though Dassin's cinematic avatars of figures from ancient tragedy seem occasionally poised to slip the bonds of the past through their striking reconfiguration as 1960s European jet-setters, the specter of the past stalks and ultimately kills them. Phaedra utters these final words on her deathbed: "Don't let them disturb me. Let me sleep." She thus articulates the exhaustion felt by someone who has tried in vain to outrun the past, while unknowingly embodying it. In death, Phaedra demonstrates that in the film that bears her name and thus immortalizes her, the golden age of classical Greece is both unattainable and ever-present.

NOTES

1 Although they generally do not mention Euripides by name; see e.g. Mercouri (1971: 150–1). For scholars' assumption of Euripides' drama as their source, see e.g. McDonald (1983).

2 Horton (1984: 30).

3 The concept of the golden age originates with Hesiod, the Greek didactic poet of the eighth century BCE, and finds its most famous redefinition in the work of the Roman poet Ovid in the early first century CE. The relevant passages are Hesiod, *Works and Days* 112–18, and Ovid, *Metamorphoses* 1.89–112. Van Noorden (2015) traces the influence of Hesiod's "myth of the races" throughout Greek and Latin literature.

4 See Ferris (2000) for a discussion of the emergence of Greece as "the cultural icon of Western art and literature" (p. 4) in the eighteenth century, with chapters on Winckelmann and the poets of the Romantic period.

5 This attitude is at the heart of the publication of the *Encyclopedia Britannica*'s "Great Books" set in 1952 and the establishment of "Great Books" courses at the University of Chicago and Columbia University from which it grew. See Lacy (2013) for a comprehensive discussion of the "Great Books" movement.

6 For this definition of belatedness among modernist writers, see Ames (1992: 39).

7 The debate about the compatibility between tragedy and modernity originates with George Steiner (1961) and the response to Steiner by Raymond Williams (1966).

8 See Leonard (2015: 1–12) for a summary of the conflict between Steiner and Williams as introducing her work on tragedy and philosophy in the modern period.

9 Michelakis (2013: 7).

10 Specifically, Greek tragedy as a genre comprising the works of the fifth-century Athenian tragedians written for live performance on the stage, not to tragedy as a "mode" (for which, see Felski [2008: 14]). See MacKinnon (1986: 22–41) for an overview of twentieth-century criticism on the problems and tensions surrounding the adaptation of Greek tragedy for the screen, especially pp. 31–41 on factors contributing to the so-called "death of tragedy."

11 Sanders (2006: 158).

12 Eleftheriotis (2012: 341).

13 Eleftheriotis (2012: 348).

14 On April 25, 1951, film director Edward Dmytryk, one of the Hollywood Ten, testified before the House Un-American Activities Committee and named Dassin as a member of the Communist party.

15 For overviews of this phenomenon, see e.g. Sherrard (1978: 1–16), Herzfeld (1982: 3–23), and Tziovas (2014: 1–26). See Leontis (1995:

13n17) for bibliography on the scholarship of Hellenism (both ancient and modern), and Koliopoulos (2008) on the definition of "Greek modernity."

16 Eleftheriotis (2012: 348).

17 This aspect of the film has been addressed by e.g. Tsitsopoulou (2000), who criticizes the film's depiction of "authentic Greekness" by linking it to a mode of gender stereotyping that derives from the American musical. See also Strain (1997).

18 Mercouri (1971: 150).

19 Seneca was undoubtedly influenced by Euripides' play, but he also had access to the lost Greek plays by Sophocles, Euripides' first Hippolytus play, treatments of the tale from the Hellenistic period, and the poetry of his fellow Roman Ovid. See Mayer (2002).

20 For the influence of these later works upon Dassin's transformation of Euripides' original tale into a "melodrama" suitable for popular cinema audiences, see MacKinnon (1986: 98–105). Bean (1963) names the elements of Seneca's and Racine's tragedies that appealed to Dassin in popularizing the tale for a modern audience.

21 For a brief account of influence, see Boyle (1987: 15–17).

22 In the subsequent lines (530–1) Seneca characterizes this "first great age" as a time before sea travel, recalling Ovid's earlier description.

23 For the influence of Seneca on Racine, see Tobin (1971). For the relationship between Euripides' play and Racine's, see Pittas-Herschbach (1990).

24 Sanders (2006: 20). See Michelakis (2013: 69–70), on Dassin's process of adaptation in *A Dream of Passion* (1978) as involving "betrayal" of the source-text (Euripides' *Medea*), a move that is reflected in the theme of betrayal among the film's characters.

25 For Dassin's interview at the Los Angeles County Museum of Art, see the 2007 Criterion Collection DVD of *The Naked City*. See also Shelley (2011: 181). Dassin's use of the French name "Hippolyte" to describe the "Hippolytus/Alexis" character suggests his familiarity with Racine's tragedy *Phèdre*.

26 For the controversy surrounding the Elgin Marbles, see Hitchens (1987) and Vrettos (1997).

27 Dassin recounts this story in a 2004 interview (see note 24). In Yael Lotan's novel *Phaedra*, adapted from Margarita Liberaki's screenplay for the film, Phaedra thinks: "The pretentiousness of meeting at the British Museum was bad enough, but to choose the Elgin collection, that was altogether insulting – as though he were proud of the theft committed by his countrymen of our treasures" (1962: 12).

28 See criticism of the pervasive idea among Greek film critics of Dassin as "an American Greek," or "more Greek than the Greeks," in Tsitsopoulou (2000: 79–80).

29 Karalis (2012: 93).

30 This theme is prevalent among ancient authors, including the Roman poets Catullus, Tibullus, and Vergil.

31 As Marianne McDonald (1983) has observed, the black-clad peasants in both scenes evoke the uniform look of the Greek chorus and assume the chorus' role as critics of the upper class.

32 Mercouri (1971: 151).

33 Dassin recounts his decision to become a Communist in McGilligan (2012: 209).

34 See Prime (2007) and McGilligan's (2012) interview for treatments of Dassin's exile.

7 Pericles, Cincinnatus, and Zombies: Classicizing Nostalgia in The Walking Dead *(2010–)*

Laura Gawlinski

When the fourth season of AMC's *The Walking Dead* premiered on October 13, 2013, faithful viewers of the series recognized a shift in tone that accompanied a change in the pattern used for season openers.[1] Previous seasons had begun with the group of survivors searching for shelter and battling walkers, and major characters met with disaster. Episode 2.1 ("What Lies Ahead") had depicted the group on the road after fleeing the short-lived protection of the Center for Disease Control in Atlanta, Georgia; one major character's daughter disappears during a walker attack and another's son is shot accidentally. After losing yet another home, Hershel Greene's farm, Episode 3.1 ("Seed") begins with the group fighting off walkers at the prison they hoped to use for shelter; Hershel (Scott Wilson) is bitten and his leg amputated in order to save him. In stark contrast, no major character is harmed in Episode 4.1 ("30 Days Without an Accident"); the only skirmish with walkers occurs when a small group is out on a run for supplies, and the lone casualty is a brand-new character. Instead, much of the episode is devoted to bucolic images of life in the prison that the group has now made its home.

This change seems to promise an end to the survivors' struggles during the zombie apocalypse through the establishment of civil society within a walled agricultural community: a recovery of life in golden-age conditions. The term "golden age" can be applied not only to primordial times, but also to past utopian civilizations that are a product of human cultural invention, such as Periclean Athens or Republican Rome. Those "golden" times, however, tend to be the idealizing products of a troubled present, their utopian character shadowed with knowledge of their eventual end. Season 4 of *The Walking Dead* provides an opportunity to examine that nostalgia for an idealized past through the lens of dystopia brought about by the zombie apocalypse.

In this case, the threat to the community comes not only from outside but also from within, as the first five episodes of Season 4 trace the catastrophe-within-a-catastrophe of a flu outbreak. In the process, the five "flu episodes" participate in a long tradition of plague literature, whose canonical form was set by the fifth-century BCE Greek historian Thucydides' *History of the Peloponnesian War* (2.47–55), an account of how Athens' civic golden age was disrupted not only by Sparta's attacks, but by their own response to the plague that broke out in their walled city. So too on *The Walking Dead*, the flu is all the more devastating because classical golden-age elements derived from both Greek and Roman traditions have been used to idealize the community before its fall.

FARMER RICK AND THE AGRARIAN-PASTORAL IDEAL

In Greek literature, the golden age was originally characterized as a time before work, particularly agricultural labor, became necessary to sustain human life and society.[2] In *Works and Days*, the archaic Greek poet Hesiod notes that, in that time, "the life-giving earth produced plentiful fruit of its own will" (117–18). In his own later version of Hesiod's didactic discourse on morality and society, the Augustan-era Roman poet Ovid similarly describes soil that produced crops even "free from the hoe and intact, unharmed by any plows" (*Met.* 1.101–2).

But, since agriculture is what allows human society to survive on a larger scale, it is also treated in literature as a hallmark of civilization. In the classical Athenian tragedy *Prometheus Bound*, commonly credited to Aeschylus, agriculture is highlighted as a gift from the technologically savvy Titan Prometheus and as one of the skills that allows human civilization to flourish. Prometheus counts the yoke, standing in for pastoralism, and the understanding of the agricultural year among the gifts he gave to humankind to improve their lives (455–65). The importance of farming in characterizing human society is similarly emphasized in Homer's *Odyssey*, when Odysseus describes the monstrous Cyclopes as lacking those features that make a community civilized.[3] They live in a primordial golden-age condition, since everything grows for them without planting (9.106–15), but this also marks them as inhuman, as they do not cultivate or process their harvested foods: Odysseus even describes Polyphemus as "a terrible wonder, not like bread-eating men" (9.190–1).

In addition to signifying civilization, classical pastoral imagery could be used to idealize a simpler, pre-urban life. Pastoral, or bucolic, poetry as a genre probably began with the Greek poet Theocritus in the third century BCE; this genre then heavily influenced Roman authors who employed it to criticize urbanity or to provide a mental escape in periods of civil unrest.[4] Cato the Elder's *On Agriculture*, a prose manual of the second century BCE, promoted a return to traditional Roman values with an agrarian lifestyle in the face of what he identified as increased luxury. The perceived simplicity of rural life and the hard work required by farming were touted as an aspiration by many in the upper class, particularly those whose political careers were tied to the urban center. Educated Romans living during the war-torn transition between the late Republic and the Augustan Principate also turned to pastoral sentiment, as seen in Varro's *On Farming* and Vergil's *Eclogues* and *Georgics*.

The opening scene of Episode 4.1 of *The Walking Dead* invokes the agricultural-pastoral ideal through its depiction of Rick Grimes (Andrew Lincoln). The group had already tried to institute an agrarian system once before at Hershel's farm in Season 2, which further emphasizes the place of agriculture in this latest attempt at stability. But, especially because Rick is a former sheriff's deputy and group leader, his work in the garden of the prison uses imagery that episode-writer Scott Gimple intended to be provocative within the world of this show.[5] Here, in the midst of the zombie apocalypse, are elements of peace, stability, and even prosperity: flowers bloom, birds chirp, fresh water is splashed on a face. On the prison grounds are two pens holding livestock. A long shot shows Rick turning the soil with a long-handled tool, an image usually associated with burial on *The Walking Dead* – until the camera zooms in to reveal the unexpected: this tool is a hoe, and Rick is farming (see Figure 7.1). Since agriculture and animal husbandry require protected space as well as time, the audience sees evidence that the title of the episode, "30 Days Without an Accident," indicates a positive new status quo.

The musical score further highlights this new peace while also giving it a distinctly rural-American character. As Rick walks toward the farm, "Precious Memories," a nostalgic bluegrass song recorded by the Stanley Brothers, begins to play.[6] The audience discovers that this music is coming from a recording when Rick removes one of his

Figure 7.1 Rick Grimes (Andrew Lincoln) tills the field, secure from zombie spectators in "30 Days Without an Accident," Episode 4.1 of *The Walking Dead* (2013). AMC.

earbuds and the sounds of walkers' growls overtake the melody. Rick has turned up a gun in his hoeing, which he inspects while eyeing the walkers outside the fence. But he then puts his earbud back in, choosing the "precious memories" of the stable time before people started turning into walkers; he dismantles the weapon, tosses it aside, and returns to hoeing. Rick's new farm thus signals a return to civilization, and Episode 4.1 thus establishes a golden age reborn, the "precious memories" of a stable life that the survivors had been trying to recapture during the first three seasons.

"RICKTATOR" OR AMERICAN CINCINNATUS?

One of the most enduring pastoral images of the classical tradition is that of Cincinnatus at the plow, featured in Livy's *From the Foundation of the City* (3.26–9), Dionysius of Halicarnassus' *Roman Antiquities* (10.23–5), and Pliny the Elder's *Natural History* (18.4.20).[7] The Roman culture-hero Lucius Quinctius Cincinnatus was an *exemplum* of the leader who performed his civic duty but renounced permanent power. In Livy's version, Cincinnatus was depicted as a simple man who had retired from politics under duress after his son's criminal trial, but when Rome later needed him to lead the battle against the invading Sabines, he accepted appointment as *dictator*. When messengers arrived from the Senate to ask him to serve in that capacity, they found Cincinnatus working in his fields.

He changed into a toga to hear the announcement, symbolically putting aside his private life by putting on the dress of state. After his subsequent military and political success, he gave up the dictatorship about five months earlier than necessary and returned to his farmland for a quiet, private life.

Cincinnatus' story later assumed special resonance with the Americans who sought liberation from the British Empire and the foundation of a republic patterned after Rome's. They saw a new Cincinnatus in George Washington, the man who grudgingly took up the presidency and then resigned in order to allow the executive power to be shared, preventing anyone, even himself, from being king.[8] The exemplarity of his tale is best illustrated by the sculpted portrait of Washington by Jean-Antoine Houdon in the Virginia State Capitol in Richmond, which features the first president wearing military dress but standing in front of a plow. The story of Cincinnatus is thus not just an ancient Roman tale, but a modern American one: he represents the citizen-soldier who stands at the ready to serve his country, but maintains his freedom, and the freedom of his country, through his ties to his land.

The agricultural and political ideals represented by Cincinnatus continued to inform American presidential politics even after Washington; a study published in 1957 traces references to farm work in presidential biographies up to that date, noting an increase after the Civil War.[9] More recently, echoes may be heard in politicians' allusions to a "real America," a new trope for old urban-versus-rural tensions. Such nostalgic glorifications of the land and those tied to it become especially prevalent in times of stress. Depression-era painters, particularly in the American Midwest, turned to utopian depictions of farmscapes. In Grant Wood's *Fall Plowing* (1931), for example, a plow set in the foreground intentionally evokes Cincinnatus, though its anachronistic form hints that the tableau is mere fantasy.[10] A reimagining of the "Cincinnatus at the plow" image in a television series that launched shortly after the 2008 financial crisis should come as no surprise.[11]

The American agrarian ideal is especially tied to the South, which makes it particularly suited to the Georgia setting of *The Walking Dead* and to the series' former small-town sheriff's deputy who listens to old-time country music while he works his land. The treatment of Rick as reluctant leader, consonant with the Cincinnatus myth, is a theme throughout the television series and the comics on which it is based. For example, Season 2 follows Rick's attempt to share authority with his former law-enforcement partner Shane Walsh (Jon

Bernthal) and keep the group egalitarian, up until Rick kills Shane and walkers destroy the farm where they are living (Episode 2.13, "Beside the Dying Fire"). When the survivors question whether to continue following Rick, he delivers a dramatic speech in which he points out that he never asked to be the leader and that, from this point on, "This isn't a democracy anymore." In Issue 74 of the comic (collected in Volume 13), Andrea confronts Rick in a similar situation: "So you're going to take over? That it? I remember when you didn't *want* to be the leader. That's what made you a good one."[12]

That Rick is a Cincinnatus who has again rejected formal power and "returned" to his plow is made clear throughout Episode 4.1. The former leader of the group has now handed over his role to a council and is no longer the "Ricktator" (as fans dubbed him after his Season 2 speech).[13] Hershel – a veterinarian who was also a professional farmer before the zombie apocalypse, not a new "gentleman farmer" like Rick – teaches Rick about plant cuttings, and Rick has been raising pigs for meat. He is so reluctant to have any part in defense or leadership that he refuses to carry a gun, even when outside the prison walls.

Rick's commitment to an agrarian life affects his teenage son Carl. Like Cincinnatus, Rick has withdrawn partly because of issues with his son. In the Season 3 finale, "Welcome to the Tombs," Carl shot an unarmed teenager during a skirmish with another group. Horrified, Rick takes away Carl's gun; his guilt that he is responsible for his son's actions becomes his impetus for change. Carl had been wearing his father's deputy hat since Rick had given it to him in Episode 2.4 ("Cherokee Rose"), but it is absent from the start of Season 4. In Episode 4.2 ("Infected"), Michonne (Danai Gurira) asks Carl why he no longer wears that hat. He replies, "It's not a farming hat."

COPS, COUNCILS, AND THE CIVIC IDEAL

After Rick turns his sword into a plowshare in the opening sequence, the viewer is introduced to other scenes of tranquil life in the prison and the features of its organization. The audience learns that Rick is no longer the sole leader, but instead a council made up of Carol Peletier (Melissa McBride), Hershel Greene, Glenn Rhee (Steven Yeun), Daryl Dixon (Norman Reedus), and Sasha Williams (Sonequa Martin-Green) deliberate over community matters.

Laws and civic arbitration, like agriculture, are lacking in the conception of the pre-civilization golden age. Ovid, in his adaptation of Hesiod's *Works and Days*, says that there were no laws in the golden age because people did not need them to live justly (*Met.* 1.89–93). Similarly, the uncivilized Cyclopes in the *Odyssey* are described as lawless (*athemos*) and lacking assemblies or any kind of communal legal framework (9.106–15). But human society, in contrast, requires law to function, and thus Hesiod focuses on issues of justice in his discussion of the state of human affairs in the iron age and beyond (*WD* 214–85).[14] Just as Romans in the midst of civil war looked back to a bucolic time of well-managed farmsteads, so, too, a society with a strong rule of law could be used as a benchmark of human accomplishment.

The "golden age" of fifth-century BCE Athens is presented by the Greek historian Thucydides as an exemplary urban society in this way. In his history, Thucydides records that at the end of 431 BCE, the first year of the Peloponnesian War between the Athenians and Spartans, a state-sponsored funeral of the war dead was held in Athens, which included an oration by the general and statesman Pericles (2.34–46). Thucydides deployed speeches strategically within his narrative; this one is especially notable for its placement at the end of a successful campaign, but before, as readers would have known, the death of Pericles.[15] Thucydides' version of Pericles' speech portrays an ideal Athens: a city where decisions are made by the many rather than the few, there is equal justice under the law, the people are law-abiding, and leisure activities like games and animal sacrifices ensure communal work–life balance (2.37–8). The context of this praise is a public funeral, and the speech illustrates why this city is worthy of the ultimate sacrifice by its men and their families.

The prison-dwellers in *The Walking Dead* likewise form an organized community. Following the opening farm scene, Episode 4.1 turns to a lively public feast where Daryl, once a loner, is now a linchpin of the community structure and is treated like a celebrity for bringing in the fresh meat that has just been distributed. The joy of the community in this time of peace is clear as the camera lingers on close-up shots of kisses between the couples in romantic relationships: Maggie Greene (Lauren Cohan) and Glenn talk in bed, Tyreese Williams (Chad Coleman) and Karen (Melissa Ponzio) meet by the fence while she kills walkers, and Beth Greene (Emily Kinney) says goodbye to Zach (Kyle Gallner) before he heads out on a run for supplies. Council business is emphasized, as Carol and Daryl discuss plans for dealing with the walkers at the fence and Hershel informs Rick of the council's decision concerning his refusal to carry a gun. Carl and the other youths go to "story time," an attempt at a basic educational system, which most of the children seem to enjoy.

This episode also establishes the rules for entry into this idealized community when Rick meets a lone woman (Kerry Condon) in the woods outside the prison walls and must decide whether she can be permitted to join their community. This scene establishes that there are three questions that must be answered by anyone who wants to be a part of the prison group: "How many walkers have you killed? How many people have you killed? Why?" The first question tests a potential newcomer's ability to survive, while the second question and its follow-up show that the still-fully-living should be treated differently from the undead. In the post-apocalyptic walker world, it is often necessary to kill, but the reason must be justified. Rules are necessary to maintain the structures that transform lone individuals into community members.

Lawfulness extends beyond the living, as a community's success can also be measured by the treatment of its dead. Thucydides describes the multi-day Athenian funeral that was capped by Pericles' speech: following ancestral custom, the bones of the war dead were laid out before being organized by tribal affiliation into cypress boxes that were then led in procession through the city on carts followed by mourners until they reached a special cemetery (2.34). Episode 4.2 presents examples of how the community of survivors deals with the all-too-frequent deaths of those dear to them: an unexpected outbreak of zombism within the close quarters of the prison – the stronghold that is supposed to keep the walkers out – results in mass chaos and multiple deaths. The bodies of the fallen members of the community are buried individually, unlike unknown walkers who are just burned *en masse*, and scenes of grave-digging in a distant area of the prison compound are woven into the rest of the episode.

The storyline focuses on one death in particular: the careful and compassionate treatment of Ryan Samuels (Victor McCay), the father of Lizzie (Brighton Sharbino) and Mika (Kyla Kenedy). Carol at first plans to amputate his bitten arm, but notices a bite on his neck and knows there is nothing she can do to save him. She promises him that she will take care of his girls, makes him comfortable, brings his daughters to say goodbye, and plans to humanely prevent his reanimation. Lizzie asks for the responsibility of stabbing her father before he turns, but in the end, Carol accomplishes what must be done. Although this scene illustrates Carol's new pragmatic personality, it is not without humanity and compassion. Carol later tells Mika and Lizzie that they will bury their father and be able to bring him flowers; in the world of *The Walking Dead*, this comment both points to Lizzie's association with flowers and suggests the expectation of long-term commemoration of the dead in the community.[16]

THE INEVITABLE LOSS OF THE GOLDEN AGE

This new golden age in *The Walking Dead* – a time of law and agrarian peace that echoes the golden ages of classical Athens and Republican Rome, filtered through Revolutionary America – is put on a pedestal in order to make a statement about its fall. The slow, uneventful start to Season 4 is part of a larger narrative structure intended to make the inevitable downturn of the thriving prison community all the more devastating. This five-episode arc ends with the prison community torn apart not by walkers breaching the walls, but by internal forces: a deadly flu and dissent. Although the title of Episode 4.1, "30 Days without an Accident," indicates that time has passed without deaths by walkers, it also foreshadows the end of those accident-free days.

The title comes from the penultimate scene in which Daryl returns from a run for supplies and informs Beth that her most recent boyfriend, Zach, did not survive. Beth surprises Daryl by taking the news stoically and simply changing an old workplace accident calendar from thirty to zero. Although Zach's death is ostensibly the "accident" that breaks this record, the closing scene reveals a larger threat. Teenage Patrick (Vincent Martella) had left the children's reading time earlier in the episode because he wasn't feeling well. The camera now returns to Patrick, alone and coughing, as he wanders into the shower to relieve his fever. There he dies and reanimates as a walker. This cliffhanger announces that the current happiness is about to end, and the next four episodes illustrate the ramifications.

The flu outbreak that begins with Patrick is part of the tradition of plague literature, inflected by Thucydides in his *History of the Peloponnesian War*. Thucydides' account of the historical plague that struck the city of Athens influenced all major literary accounts of devastating illnesses that followed, including Camus' *The Plague* (1947), the immediate inspiration for these episodes of *The Walking Dead*.[17] Two features of this five-episode arc are specifically rooted in the original Thucydidean narrative: the positioning of an image of an idealized community before a tragedy, and the exemplification of lawlessness (*anomia*) through the mistreatment of the dead.

Thucydides' writings provide more than historical information; his description of the plague influenced how epidemics are described and how their stories should unfold, starting with the juxtaposition of the image of glorious golden-age Athens, as related in Pericles' Funeral Oration, with the account of the plague that immediately follows (2.47–55). Thucydides was not required to include the plague at this point in his history, as it broke out multiple times throughout the war; rather, the historian chose to condense its description into one section for greater impact.[18] In this consolidated narrative, he describes how it began, the confusion of doctors as they attempted to treat it, and the symptoms, of which he had first-hand evidence as a survivor.[19] He notes that it was made worse by an influx of people from the countryside (2.52), a result of Pericles' wartime strategy of bringing the Athenians who lived in the countryside within the walls of the city while the Spartans ravaged the land outside.

The result of this disease was complete chaos and disregard for laws, or *anomia*. This is marked especially by the poor treatment of the dead (2.52–3): corpses were abandoned even in the sanctuaries of the gods, and people snuck the bodies of their relatives onto the funeral pyres of their neighbors to save time and money. Since good and bad died indiscriminately, many chose to behave however they wished. Those same Athenians, who were so recently presented to the reader as solemnly following ritual obligations to the dead in an organized, city-sponsored funeral, are now so torn apart as a result of the plague that they turn against each other, both in life and in disrespecting the dead.

What was new about Thucydides' conception of the plague is that earlier Greek literature had treated disease as a result of *anomia*, not a cause.[20] When disaster struck, ancient Greeks typically assumed someone had done something wrong – and thus deserved what happened. Hesiod describes this belief thus:

> But for the ones who take an interest in violence and cruel deeds,
> Far-seeing Zeus, son of Kronos, ordains this penalty:
> Many times the city suffers all together with the one bad man
> who transgressed and devised reckless deeds.
> To them the son of Kronos brings down misery from the sky,
> famine and plague together: the people perish.
> Women do not bear children, and their households are diminished
> by the cunning of Olympian Zeus. (*Works and Days* 238–45)[21]

The earliest example of this scenario in a narrative comes from the opening of Homer's *Iliad*, where the Greeks are punished with disease and death by the god Apollo because they had acted contrary to *nomos* by refusing a suppliant, a priest of Apollo, who requested that the Greeks return his captive daughter (1.9–100). Perhaps the most famous example from classical literature is found in the work of Thucydides' older contemporary and fellow Athenian, Sophocles. In his version of the Oedipus myth, *Oedipus the King*, the tragic hero sought the cause of the Theban plague and found out that he himself had inadvertently committed the crimes of killing his father and marrying his mother, thus bringing pollution upon his community. Thucydides turns this structure on its head: his Athenians are presented as good people from the start. It is the plague that causes "violence and cruel deeds" among them. Thucydides' narrative structure creates a psychological drama: the Athenians are threatened externally by the Spartan enemy, but a sickness among them and their reaction to it results in the ultimate disruption of their golden-age civilization.

It is with this background that these "flu episodes" of *The Walking Dead* should be read. Rick and his band of survivors have been holed up in the prison compound – a small, walled space, recently brought almost to capacity by an influx of new people from a neighboring compound – while the walkers ravage the land outside. Just as in Athens, these close quarters, made necessary by an external enemy, intensify the spread of disease. Just as in Athens, it is not the external walkers that destroy their community, but the internal threat: both disease and the human failings that it brings out in them.

ANOMIA IN THE PRISON PARADISE

When the flu is first identified, the council must determine how best to forestall disaster. In Episode 4.2, together they decide, hesitantly, to quarantine those who are showing symptoms. Karen, Tyreese's girlfriend, and a minor character named David (Brandon Carroll) are sent to Cell Block A, formerly death row. But the plan quickly goes awry. When Tyreese checks on his beloved, he finds her cell empty. The trails of blood leading from the cell block typically indicate a walker attack, but when Tyreese follows them, he is shocked to discover the immolated and still-smoking bodies of Karen and David strewn in the courtyard.

Episode 4.3 ("Isolation") does not immediately deal with this cliffhanger, but instead opens with a graveyard scene. It parallels Episode 4.1 through the repetition of men digging in the dirt, but the digging is again for graves, no longer for crops. Patrick's glasses are propped on a cross in the foreground with a gun hanging on a branch behind, and beyond are a series of at least four graves being dug by Glenn and others. This scene emphasizes the proper and normal treatment of the dead in light of what viewers had just been shown at the end of Episode 4.2. There is a contrast between inhumation and cremation, between a curated resting place underground and haphazard abandonment out in the open, and between death by disease and death by human hands. This scene stresses that what happened to Karen and David has violated the community's norms.

The remainder of the episode brings the deep problem created by the deaths of Karen and David to the forefront. These deaths are murders: execution outside the law. The disrespectful treatment of corpses, left smoldering out in the open, exemplifies the *anomia* brought on by the flu. Tyreese goes into a rage about the murders and demands that Rick, the former enforcer of law and order, use his investigative skills to find the culprit and bring that person to justice: "You're a cop. You find out who did this, and you bring 'em to me."[22] But by asking Rick to abet his vigilantism, Tyreese also seeks to circumvent the authority of the council, increasing the level of *anomia*. The confrontation devolves into a fistfight between the two. Tyreese still insists on immediate burial for the murdered, digging the graves single-handedly, even though his eye is swollen shut from being punched by Rick. Questions of justice and authority are heightened when Tyreese asks Rick at the grave, "Murder is okay in this place now?" and Rick responds, "I'll worry about what's right."

The council meets again to deliberate; Rick's absence reminds the viewer that, despite his exchange with Tyreese, he is no longer a formal part of the community's leadership. The council members institute an increased quarantine and plan a mission to a nearby hospital for supplies. But it is Rick who ultimately handles the crime when his suspicions are confirmed: Carol killed Karen and David in an attempt to stop the spread of the flu (Episode 4.3, "Isolation"). In Episode 4.4 ("Indifference"), Rick, acting alone without consulting or receiving approval from the council, banishes Carol from the compound. Even though Rick seems to understand her decision, he tells her, "That wasn't your decision to make." But just as she had acted alone in killing, Rick now acts alone in sending her away. Rick reaches beyond even the investigative task requested by Tyreese and slips into his old executive role when he chooses to mete out justice himself.

This *anomia* is entwined with Rick's conflict between his instincts to assume leadership and his desire to live a quiet, pastoral life. Rick's ill pigs, discovered in Episode 4.1, provide an early foreshadowing of the collapse of his agrarian dream. In an early scene, he examines a sick pig that Carl calls "Violet"; later in the episode, Violet is dead. Similarly, the first in the Greek army's camp to die of plague in Homer's *Iliad* are the mules and dogs (1.50). After people begin dying from the flu, a connection is posited in Episode 4.2 between the sick pigs and the sick people: Hershel notes that diseases like this used to spread through pigs and birds.

At the conclusion of that episode, Rick reluctantly devises a plan to use the pigs as bait to lead the walkers away from the fences that surround the prison. Rick sits in the back of a truck with the pigs; he slits their throats, one by one, and throws them to the walkers as the truck drives further away from the prison. The look on Rick's face shows his defeat. When he returns to the prison, he dismantles the pigpen and douses it with gasoline, thus destroying a significant feature of his farm. Rick gives Carl back his gun, though he does not seem quite ready to pick up one himself. He pulls off his bloody shirt and throws it into the fire, a symbolic rejection of his current persona. In a callback to the opening scene of the season's first episode, Rick looks out at the walkers and the viewer hears their growls, but this time he can no longer drown out their sounds with "Precious Memories." When he fully embraces his authority in Episode 4.4 and banishes Carol, she sums up his conflict before driving away: "You can be a farmer, Rick – you can't *just* be a farmer."

In Episode 4.5 ("Internment"), the conclusion of the flu episodes, the council is now powerless, made up of only the aging Hershel and the ill Glenn. Even though they acquire the necessary medicine in a *deus ex machina*, the flu has already caused a permanent rupture. Rick knowingly asks Hershel, "When we get past this thing, it's not going to be the way it was, is it?" This episode closes with yet another scene of Rick and Carl on the farm (see Figure 7.2). Rick splashes water on his face as in Episode 4.1, and they eat peas from the pod. But a close-up focuses on Rick's gun, and Carl again wears the sheriff's hat, like a Cincinnatus putting back on his toga. Their golden age has definitively ended.

CONCLUSION: "WE'RE ALL INFECTED"

In recording the disastrous plague of the fifth century BCE, Thucydides emphasized the dual nature of the threat to the Athenians: "The Athenians, beset by such a calamity, were hard pressed: inside the city, men were dying; outside, the land was ravaged" (2.54). In *The Walking Dead*, this contrast between internal and external dangers is heightened by their similarities. The flu is inside, and the walkers

Figure 7.2 Rick and Carl Grimes (Andrew Lincoln and Chandler Riggs) inspect crops, sporting a holstered gun and sheriff hat in "Internment," Episode 4.5 of *The Walking Dead* (2013). AMC.

outside, but the pathogen that makes people become walkers after death is already inside every human on Earth. Rick learned more about the nature of the zombie outbreak at the Center for Disease Control headquarters in Season 1, and since the conclusion of Season 2 (Episode 2.13, "Beside the Dying Fire"), the survivors have known that they are all already infected. In Episode 4.3, Hershel complains that "Everything we worked so hard to keep out, it found its way in," to which Rick responds, "No, it's always there." Although Rick ostensibly refers to the fact that they all hold the capacity to become walkers, his remark can also be read as a commentary on the drama of precisely human choices that unfolds in this post-apocalyptic world. Carol murders her friends, and Rick delivers a virtual death sentence to Carol when he banishes her; their respective natures are what make them respond to threats in these ways. The psychological power of zombie stories comes from the human reaction to the zombie threat, rather than the zombies themselves.[23]

These flu episodes are compelling because the new danger that they introduce invalidates the gains that the survivors thought they had made toward re-establishing the life and community they had once enjoyed, even taken for granted, before the advent of the walkers. Their unattainable past is tinged with nostalgic images of Periclean Athens and Republican Rome. Season 4 begins with flowers, community togetherness, and the respectful treatment of fallen friends, but disease reveals the fragility of such golden-age fantasies.

NOTES

I thank the participants in the 2014 Film & History conference for the helpful discussion of my paper and Meredith E. Safran for getting past her distaste for zombies to be able to provide such helpful comments on drafts.

1 For the history of zombies, from their origins in Caribbean folklore to their reimagining by George Romero, concluding with *The Walking Dead* comic books, see Bishop (2010).
2 Tandy and Neale (1996) places *Works and Days* in its agricultural and social context; Nelson (1998) explores the use of farming in *Works and Days* alongside the later, Roman *Georgics* of Vergil.
3 Dougherty (2001: 122–42) examines these elements of this passage further, contrasting it with the ideal society exhibited elsewhere in the *Odyssey*, by the Phaeacians.
4 On Cato, see Reay (2005); on Varro, see Nelsestuen (2015: 146–69); on Vergil, see Nelson (1998: 82–97) and Thibodeau (2011: 74–115).
5 On the *Talking Dead* Season 5 preview special (July 6, 2014), Scott Gimple said that in order to "freak out" executive producer Robert Kirkman, what he told him about the episode as he was writing it was, "Yeah, we're gonna start out with Rick hoeing."
6 Reid (2015: 173–6, 210, 217–18). Recorded versions differ, but the one used in the episode begins with these lyrics: "As I travel down life's pathway, knowing not what the years may hold. As I ponder, hopes grow fonder, precious sacred scenes unfold. Precious memories, how they linger, how they ever flood my soul."
7 On Cincinnatus and other farm managers used as *exempla*, particularly for statesmen, see Nelsestuen (2014). See also Thibodeau (2011: 23–5, 52–3) and Shalev (2009: 217–23).
8 McInnis (2011) examines the meanings in the Houdon statue, tying it to contemporary usage of the Cincinnatus story; more generally on the story at that time in America, see Wills (1984).
9 Brown (1957). See also Shalev (2009: 221–3) on Washington's immediate successors.
10 Barter (2016: esp. 42–5) on *Fall Plowing*.
11 The comics on which the show is based predate the crisis (2003), but the scenes under discussion here are new, written specifically for television. It may be significant that the other major agricultural reference – Hershel's farm – receives extended time in its televised version.
12 Kirkman, Adlard, and Rathburn (2013).
13 Goldman (2012). #Ricktator and #ricktatorship first appeared on Twitter in reference to *The Walking Dead* on March 18, 2012, the date that episode aired.
14 On justice in *Works and Days*, see Nelson (1998: 77–81), Tandy and Neale (1996: 39–48).

15 For a close explication of this section of the *History*, begin with the commentary by Rusten (1989). Morrison (2006) examines the relationship between the speeches and their surrounding passages.

16 Hoping to calm her through distraction, Mika and then Carol urge the hysterical Lizzie to look at the vase of flowers in the room as Carol stabs their father; in the same episode, Carol picks a small flower as the three stand at the fence, watching the walkers, and places it behind Lizzie's ear, eliciting a rare smile. In both scenes, Lizzie wears a flowered vest. The connection is solidified in Episode 4.14, "The Grove," when Carol again tells Lizzie to look at the flowers as she prepares to shoot the girl. When the graves of Mika and Lizzie are later shown on screen, both are adorned with bunches of flowers.

17 Literary and screen accounts of plagues indebted to Thucydides include Lucretius, *On the Nature of Things* 6.1138–286 (first century BCE); Vergil, *Georgics* 3.478–566 (29 BCE); Ovid, *Metamorphoses* 7.523–81 (first century CE); Procopius, *History of the Wars* 2.22–33 (sixth century CE); Boccaccio, *Decameron* (c. 1348–53); Defoe, *Journal of the Plague Year* (1722); Mann, *Death in Venice* (1912); Camus, *The Plague* (1947); and Bergman's *The Seventh Seal* (1957). Garza (2008) has also identified Thucydides' influence in several accounts of real and fictional plagues written in Spain in the late fourteenth to mid-sixteenth centuries. King and Brown (2015) trace Thucydides' influence in medical literature. According to Ross (2013), showrunner Scott Gimple, who also wrote Episode 4.1, cited his inspirations as Camus' *The Plague* and a tour beneath the city of Edinburgh, where he learned about the effects of bubonic plague. The flu does not appear in Robert Kirkman's *The Walking Dead* comic series.

18 See Morrison (2006: 263) on the juxtaposition of Pericles' speech and the plague that follows. On the condensing of the account, see Mitchell-Boyask (2008: 41–3), with earlier bibliography. On the timing of the plague and where it appears in Thucydides' history, see Demont (2013: 73–4).

19 A comparison of the symptoms is beyond the scope of this chapter. According to Murphy (2013), the illness in *The Walking Dead* was inspired by the Spanish flu, chosen in order to emphasize that in a post-apocalyptic world, something as simple as the flu could have extreme consequences.

20 Demont (2013).

21 For the Greek text of *Works and Days*, see Hesiod (1914). All translations are my own.

22 Nurse (2014) examines Rick's role as a symbol of law and order alongside the theme of lawlessness in the series.

23 Although Bishop (2010: 206–7) has argued that the serialization of *The Walking Dead* (in both televised and comic form) makes it more human-centered than earlier zombie films, in Rath (2014) George

Romero says: "My stories have always been more about the humans and the mistakes that they've made and the zombies are just sort of there . . . They're the disaster that everyone is facing. But my stories are more about the humans." The complicated "posthuman" connection between zombies and humans in *The Walking Dead* is explored by Keetley (2014).

PART II

The Grandeur That Was Rome

8 "All That Glitters . . .": Problematizing Golden-Age Narratives in Vergil's Aeneid and the Western Film Genre

Kirsten Day

In recent years, classical receptions scholars have become familiar with the argument that the Western film genre in America fulfills a role that is culturally equivalent to that of the Homeric epics in ancient Greece.[1] Both focus on the "self-questioning warriors"[2] of old, larger-than-life men whose work laid the foundation for the audience's contemporary society, and who provide formative models of idealized manhood in stories that shape and reinforce cultural ideologies more broadly. The Western genre's relationship to Vergil's *Aeneid*, however, has received far less attention, despite demonstrating many of the same parallels with Western cinema that have been elucidated for Homer's works.[3] Yet the production and reception contexts of many Westerns, particularly those of the genre's "golden age" in the mid-twentieth century, are much closer kin to those of the *Aeneid* than they are to the *Iliad* and *Odyssey*. Furthermore, unlike Homer's works, Vergil's epic and many of these Westerns trouble the simplicity of the ideologically charged foundation myths they employ by calling attention to the violence and inequities on which the "golden" eras that they enabled were built. Both the *Aeneid* and many golden-age Westerns thus embed a subtle critique of foundational mythologies – and of the societies built upon them – into narratives that initially appear to be vehicles for promoting and reinforcing their worth.

GOLDEN AGES IN ANCIENT ROME AND MODERN AMERICA

The concept of a "golden age," now commonly used to denote the high point in the history of a nation or artistic genre, reaches back to classical antiquity, where it played a far more complex role. At Rome in particular, the cyclical return of the *aureum saeculum* (the phrase commonly translated as "golden age") was expected to bring peace and prosperity to society as a whole – a condition that Rome's first emperor, Augustus, and his supporters were eager to evoke after the violent civil wars that preceded his reign.[4] In service to this agenda, Augustus commissioned Vergil to create an epic for Rome that would serve as a locus for national identity much like Homer's epics did for the Greeks. Augustus expected that Vergil would produce a propagandistic work that would legitimize and promote his regime while helping to smooth over its problematic anti-republican nature and minimize Augustus' role in the devastating civil wars that established his supremacy.[5] Consequently, Vergil's epic engages with the Roman belief in the golden age, as well as the notion that Augustus had restored it, by presenting his reign as the long-awaited culmination of his heroic and semi-divine ancestor Aeneas' quest to found a new home in Italy after the Trojan War. By setting his epic in the Homeric Age, Vergil also taps in to the long-standing glorification of that period in the Greco-Roman world, a nostalgia for which was so deeply entrenched that elites like Augustus traced their lineage – and thus their political prerogatives – from the heroes of that time.[6]

Although Augustus himself is not the focal character of the *Aeneid*, his centrality to the ideological project is evident. Not only in Vergil's epic, but also in the literature and visual culture of the period more broadly, the Augustan regime and the *aureum saeculum* that it reinstated are represented as the glorious results of a divine plan governing Aeneas' quest.[7] At the heart of his epic, Vergil offers an explicit panegyric to Augustus in the midst of his Parade of Heroes, in which Aeneas' father Anchises prophesies the advents of historical figures familiar to Vergil's audience:

> Here, here is the man so often promised to you,
> Augustus Caesar, born of a god, who will establish a Golden
> Age once again through the fields of Latium where Saturn
> once ruled. Beyond the Garamantes and the Indians
> he will extend his realm; beyond the heavens,
> beyond the path of the circling sun, where Atlas turns skies
> fitted out with blazing stars upon his weary shoulders. (*Aeneid* 6.791–7)[8]

By anchoring his narrative in the heroic past and implying the divinely predestined nature of the political present, Vergil seems to sanction Augustus' regime and its claims to having reinstated a golden age.

In retrospect, the longevity of Augustus' rule, the cultural and artistic flourishing that it facilitated, and the enduring nature of the empire that he founded seem to validate the characterization of this period as a high point of both political and cultural achievement. Indeed, later societies that envisioned themselves as successors to the Roman Empire emulated this Augustan self-fashioning, while Vergil's epic continued to serve as a vehicle for this idea into modernity. Thus, in addition to the central place that Vergil's poetic corpus holds in the "Golden Age of Latin literature," when Latin poetry is conventionally considered to have achieved perfection of content and form, the ideological force assigned to the *Aeneid* by these self-proclaimed modern successors to Augustus' empire led to its enshrinement as perhaps the single most important piece of classical literature in the Western world for centuries.[9]

This confluence of golden ages, in which a pinnacle of artistic production was achieved in a historical period seen as politically and socially exemplary, is also evident in the "golden age" of Western film, stretching from the late 1940s to the early 1960s, when the genre reached the height of its popularity and major studios were producing large numbers of high-quality Westerns. During this period, Westerns went beyond the simple "cowboys versus Indians" plots and one-dimensional characterizations of the early "oaters," taking on more nuanced themes and offering more psychologically complex protagonists. Directors like John Ford, Howard Hawks, and Anthony Mann produced big-budget films that attracted high-caliber stars beyond those traditionally associated with the genre, including Gregory Peck, Kirk Douglas, and Clark Gable.

Much like the post-Trojan War setting of the *Aeneid*, these films are set in the post-Civil War period during American's own nation-building process, when heroic pioneers blazed a trail westward to establish a great new nation, mirroring Aeneas' similarly motivated move westward to Hesperia, or Italy. Just as Aeneas' quest was fueled by destiny, as Jupiter's revelations from the scroll of Fate make clear (1.256–96), the protagonists of these Westerns are prompted by the tenets of Manifest Destiny, the widespread belief among white settlers in mid-nineteenth-century America that expansion westward to the Pacific was destined and divinely ordained, and its accomplishment therefore a heroic duty.[10] In both cases, attributing the impetus for the heroic quest to a higher power conveniently relieves the human actors of responsibility for any moral transgressions committed in service to this goal.

Also like the *Aeneid*, many of these Westerns have a post-war timeframe not only in their dramatic setting, but also in their historical period of production: in the boom years following the conclusion of World War II. This period is often cast as a golden age in America more generally, as the US role in the Allied victory over the Axis powers and America's post-war economic expansion led to technological advances, increased productivity, and widespread prosperity, conditions suggestive of a cultural superiority that seemed to validate the recent triumph over the "Other." Similarly, through strategic use of propaganda Octavian (as Augustus was then known) had successfully recast the most recent civil war as a moral victory by the Italian West over the Egyptian queen Cleopatra, rather than as a conflict with his fellow Romans. Later, as emperor, he reframed the *Pax Romana* ("Roman peace") that followed the war as a moral, even cosmic, validation of his triumph. The *Aeneid* and golden-age Westerns, then, are similar not only in their narrative settings and creation contexts, but also in how their creators capitalized on these long-ago foundation myths to justify participation in recent violence and to emphasize the "golden" quality of the current age in contrast.

THE DYNAMICS OF DESTINY: NATION-BUILDING AS DIVINE *LABOR*

By anchoring their tales to the foundational past and focusing on heroes driven by a higher purpose, the directors of Westerns presented the society that their contemporary audiences enjoyed as a predestined and divinely sanctioned culmination of their forebears' heroic struggles, much as Vergil had done two thousand years earlier. The Western follows this generic blueprint from its earliest days. For example, in Ford's first full-length Western, the 1924 silent film *The Iron Horse*, Dave Brandon (George O'Brien) struggles to realize his late father's dream of building the first transcontinental railroad, a critical development in American westward expansion in that it made transportation of goods and passengers cheaper, quicker, and safer. Like Vergil, who set his epic in the Homeric Age, which Greco-Roman audiences perceived as historical, Ford anchors his narrative in history, going so far as to proclaim that his film is "[a]ccurate and faithful in every particular of fact and atmosphere." It was not: Ford uses fictive embellishments and anachronisms[11] to shape his narrative around his agenda, in much the same way that "history" for ancient writers like Vergil was regularly subject to ideological manipulation.

Also like Vergil, Ford explicitly positions his hero as driven by a higher power: as the title cards proclaim, Dave and his father (the uncredited James Gordon) are initially "impelled westward by the strong urge of progress," with his father vowing that "with the help of God I'll lend a hand to blaze the trail." Their fellow townsman (and future US President) Abe Lincoln (Charles Edward Bull) sanctions their journey, as he "feels the momentum of a great nation pushing westward – he sees the inevitable." Thus, much like Vergil had done with Augustus' *Pax Romana* by positioning it as the fated and divinely sanctioned endpoint of Aeneas' quest, Ford positions his own twentieth-century America, which enjoyed the benefits of the long-completed transcontinental project, as the glorious and predestined result of the work of heroic pioneers in an implicit endorsement of Manifest Destiny.

While these dynamics of destiny are explicit in *The Iron Horse*, they form an undercurrent throughout the genre and persist into its golden age as a tacit justification of the challenges and sacrifices inherent in the nation-building project – in Aeneadic terms, the *labor* (great task) assigned to the pioneering hero. In Howard Hawks' 1948 *Red River*, for instance, Tom Dunson (John Wayne) leads his companions on a perilous cattle drive in order to preserve the home that they have been working to establish, a quest whose importance for the growing nation Teeler (Paul Fix) suggests when he upbraids Dunson for his tyrannical attitude by saying, "This herd don't belong to you. [It] belongs to every poor hopin' and prayin' cattleman in the whole wide state!" Likewise, in Ford's 1950 *Wagon Master*, heroes Travis and Sandy (Ben Johnson and Harry Carey, Jr.) guide a group of Mormons through dangerous country so they can settle in the San Juan Valley. This quest is framed as divinely sanctioned when Elder Wiggs (Ward Bond) describes the land as "reserved for us by the Lord, and reserved for his people," and calls Travis and Sandy "the answer to our prayer." He further characterizes this journey as a foundational step in the nation-building process when he proclaims that their role is "to mark the trail, and prepare the ground for those that are gonna come after us." So too in Fred Zinnemann's 1952 *High Noon*, George Stevens' 1953 *Shane*, and Ford's 1962 *The Man Who Shot Liberty Valance*, the heroes confront violent threats against the community in defense of its progress toward civilization and nationhood. In each case, the audience's current enjoyment of the society that the film's hero fights to build works to suggest the project's inevitability, thus implying its fated nature and, by extension, the "rightness" of the hero's cause.

HEROES AND VILLAINS

Crucial to the goals of defending cultural norms or building a new nation as it is framed in classical epic is the heroic protagonist, a warrior whose special skills are needed to advance the project and who provides an enduring model of masculine virtue. Likewise, the Western genre has been a powerful vehicle for delineating idealized American masculinity through the hero's characterization as a tough, highly skilled warrior whose confidence, determination, and self-control are emphasized by his imperturbability and laconism.[12] But while he draws on the Homeric model, Vergil offers a hero with a particularly Roman character – one whose weary *gravitas*, or seriousness of purpose, is paired with extraordinary *pietas*, or devotion to gods, country, and father over self, traits emphasized by his eventual sacrifice of personal needs and desires in deference to duty. This characterization of Aeneas distances him from Greek warriors and anticipates the more self-sacrificing nature of many Western heroes. For example, *High Noon*'s Will Kane (Gary Cooper), like Aeneas, is driven by a strong sense of duty: "This is my town," he says when urged to flee; "I've got to stay." This sensibility is anchored to notions of a higher purpose, which, though not made explicit, is implied through his heroic instinct: when Harv Pell (Lloyd Bridges) asks why he won't get out, Kane cannot elucidate his reasoning, answering in typically stoic Western fashion, "I don't know." Even clearer is Stevens' framing of the titular hero of *Shane* as self-sacrificing: knowing that he alone can counter the violent threat of the gunslinger Jack Wilson (Jack Palance), Shane (Alan Ladd) gives up his dreams of a settled domestic life and resumes his warrior identity so that civilization can move forward.[13]

In both Vergil's epic and Westerns, this heroic duty is framed as an emotional and moral burden, emphasized by the protagonist's careworn, often reluctant attitude. In *Aeneid* Book 1, Aeneas groans and sighs (1.93, 371); is sick with anguish (1.208–9) and sleepless from his many cares (1.305); bemoans his past suffering and the burdens to come (1.330, 459–60, 597); and envies those whose nation-building efforts are already coming to fruition (1.437). Similarly, Will Kane admits to being tired and scared; tells his wife she's "crazy" if she thinks he likes what he has to do; and breaks down in despair as the showdown approaches. Indeed, both the ancient hero and his modern counterparts consider abandoning the project when opportunity is offered – usually by a woman: Aeneas sets up house with Queen Dido of Carthage; Kane impulsively leaves town with his new bride to avoid the showdown with Frank Miller (Ian MacDonald); Shane's attempt at domestication stems largely from his clear attraction to Marian Starrett (Jean Arthur); and Tom Doniphon (John Wayne) of *The Man Who Shot Liberty Valance* initially puts his "personal plans" to marry Hallie (Vera Miles) over the interests of the growing nation. Ultimately, however, heroic duty takes precedence and each man puts aside personal inclinations in allegiance to the larger goal.

These men thus reflect and serve as models of idealized masculine virtue for their respective cultures. In addition to being a strong, skilled warrior, Aeneas demonstrates *pietas*, *gravitas*, and *severitas* (discipline and self-control) that contrast with the selfishness considered endemic to the late Republic and a major cause of its collapse.[14] Western heroes demonstrate a similar subordination of self-interest to the greater good, in line with the then-recent experiences of GIs who left women and family behind to serve their country, in effect exhibiting a Western – indeed, an American – version of Aeneas' *pietas*.

The notion that the great nation anticipated by each work is built upon the sacrifice and suffering of its heroic forebears renders the audience's society more dear, a dynamic intensified by the hero's ultimate exclusion from the civilization that his sacrifice enables. Vergil's acknowledgment that neither Aeneas nor his descendants for centuries to come will live to see Rome's founding is subtly, poignantly paralleled by the mythic exits of Shane and *The Searchers*' (1956) Ethan Edwards (John Wayne), each unable to join the community he has just saved (see Figure 8.1). So too Tom Doniphon fades abruptly into permanent obscurity after he cedes his status, his girl Hallie, and credit for ridding the territory of Liberty Valance to Ransom Stoddard (James Stewart).

Yet while the self-sacrificing hero remains the focal point, both Vergil and the directors of these Westerns remind us that the hero's burdens were shared. In Book 5 of the *Aeneid*, the sudden, despairing outburst of the Trojan women who are too weak and tired to persevere serves to underscore the hardships that those who accompany Aeneas to the end endure. In Ford's *The Searchers*, Mrs. Jorgensen (Olive Carey) implies something similar when she rationalizes her son's death:

> It just so happens we be Texicans. Texican is nothing but a human man way out on a limb, this year, and next . . . maybe for a hundred more. But I don't think it'll be forever. Someday, this country's gonna be a fine, good place to be. Maybe it needs our bones in the ground before that time can come.

Figure 8.1 The mythic exit of Ethan Edwards (John Wayne) in John Ford's *The Searchers* (1956). Warner Bros.

Her untroubled acceptance of her loss and of the fact that she and her fellow homesteaders will not live to enjoy the fruits of their labors reminds the audience that their own society is built on the loss and suffering of generations past, while affirming the importance of the hero's work.

The hero's undertaking is glorified not only by drawing attention to the extraordinary sacrifices he and his followers make, but also through the vilification of those who oppose his goals. In the second half of Vergil's epic, Aeneas and his people reach their destination only to meet resistance from the native Italians, headed by Turnus and his Rutulians. Turnus had prior rights to the land – and to the bride – Aeneas now claims, but because Aeneas is the poem's protagonist and the heroic ancestor of its Roman audience, and because Vergil has repeatedly framed Aeneas' mission as divinely sanctioned, his cause is narratively positioned as "right" and his actions justified. Turnus is relegated to the role of "bad guy," an impression intensified by his alliance with the vicious exiled Etruscan tyrant Mezentius.

Likewise, because the Western hero is cast as an ideological ancestor whose work made America what it is, he becomes a noble pioneer whose violent actions were the necessary means to a glorious end while any who oppose him are cast as villains.[15] In *The Iron Horse*, the divinely ordained nature of the hero's quest and the audience's enjoyment of the benefits that the transcontinental project provided shape those who oppose or impede the hero's goal – the savage Native Americans and the greedy, amoral white renegade Bauman (Fred Kohler) – into contemptible obstructionists. This dynamic is a hallmark of the genre more broadly and persists into the genre's golden age. In *Shane*, for instance, the film's dominant perspective prompts the audience to see Joe Starrett (Van Heflin) and his fellow homesteaders as the "good guys" and the rough, violent cattlemen who would keep the land an open range as the "bad guys." In both cases, the audience's predisposition is strengthened by their knowledge of how history played out, helping to frame the protagonists' goals as not only destined, but also morally correct. Consequently, the hero's inevitable triumph over his opponent can be unreflectively rationalized as necessary violence that further contributes to the protagonist's tragic-heroic stature.

PROBLEMATIZING THE "HERO"

In its very nature, then, the Western genre resembles aspects of the *Aeneid* consistent with Augustus' expectations: both utilize a period from the nation's foundational past to glorify the present and to justify or elide the violent actions that enabled it. Yet more recent scholars have also noted that, despite reshaping history in service to nationalistic propaganda, Vergil's use of this narrative framework is far from simplistic. Instead, he problematizes it by subtly undercutting his message at strategic points, thus posing an implicit challenge to the patriotic vision that the epic outwardly promotes.[16] Likewise, although many early Westerns fit the one-dimensional "cowboys versus Indians" formula that offered a straightforward, unreflective nationalistic vision, as the genre matured into its golden age, many films began to demonstrate a psychological complexity that challenged the simplistic promotion of Manifest Destiny as divinely sanctioned. The ironic result is that, like the *Aeneid*, these Westerns call into question the morality of the very projects that they glorify, and by extension the golden-age quality of the contemporary society that enjoys the fruits of these labors.[17]

One strategy that Vergil uses to challenge the propagandistic nationalism promulgated in the *Aeneid* is to trouble the nature of the hero. While Vergil constructs the duty-driven Aeneas as the model for Roman male virtue, the gendered framework that Vergil creates suggests that, in single-mindedly pursuing political and military goals, the hero does not just sacrifice his personal needs and desires but even compromises his very humanity. As Christine Perkell has shown, Aeneas' character is problematized when he denies responsibility for the abandonment and death of both Creusa and Dido.[18] Furthermore, the "us/them" binary is destabilized by the parallel that Vergil subtly draws between the hero and his enemy: Aeneas intends to take for himself Turnus' lands, his position, and his betrothed – in a sense, his very identity. In addition, Vergil concludes his poem with Aeneas exhibiting the same *furor* (rage-induced madness) condemned as anti-Roman throughout the epic – and previously associated specifically with Turnus, among men – when he kills his defeated and suppliant foe,[19] thereby complicating considerably a protagonist who initially seemed traditionally, unimpeachably heroic.[20]

Like Vergil, the directors of many golden-age Westerns intensify the self-questioning dynamic of their works by problematizing the heroic nature of their protagonists. In *Red River*, Hawks has Tom Dunson progress from a brave, trail-blazing pioneer to a dangerous, uncompromising tyrant; in *The Searchers*, Ford casts Ethan Edwards as a vehement racist capable of murdering his own niece after she is kidnapped by the Comanche; and in *The Man Who Shot Liberty Valance*, Ford exposes Stoddard as a self-deluded fraud whose success was achieved at a better man's expense. Also like in the *Aeneid*, the darker side of the hero's nature is often symbolized through a disturbing kinship with his enemy: in *High Noon*, Will Kane is paired with his nemesis Frank Miller by their shared history with Helen Ramírez (Katy Jurado); in *Shane*, the titular hero is paralleled with the menacing Wilson visually, verbally, and musically; and in *The Searchers*, Ethan, much like Aeneas,[21] succumbs to the same sort of savagery he condemns as characteristic of the Comanche in a graphic scene where he scalps the fallen Scar (Henry Brandon).[22]

By undercutting the heroic nature of the protagonist, Vergil and the directors of these Westerns subtly call into question the self-justifying mythologies that underpin the self-image of the nation they ostensibly glorify. Occasionally this is made more explicit. In the Parade of Heroes discussed above, Vergil positions Augustus' reign as not only the culmination but the *raison d'être* of all history that came before. Immediately following this sycophantic spectacle, however, Vergil has Aeneas exit not through the Gate of Horn where true spirits pass, but through that of Ivory, the one designated for false dreams (6.893–9), in effect calling attention to the propagandistic nature of the "history" he participates in creating.[23] Ford frequently does something similar in his golden-age Westerns. In the conclusion of *Fort Apache* (1948), Lt. Col. Kirby York (John Wayne) goes along with the glorification of his undeserving predecessor Owen Thursday (Henry Fonda) in order to bolster the image of his regiment and support their continuing efforts to suppress the Apache. *Cheyenne Autumn* (1964) also points to the agenda-driven reordering of history when a newspaper editor tells his reporters to portray the Cheyenne sympathetically, as they'll "sell more papers that way." Most famously, the newspaper editor of *The Man Who Shot Liberty Valance* tears up the notes he has taken on Stoddard's *apologia* explaining what "really" happened, proclaiming, "When the legend becomes fact, print the legend."[24]

REDEEMING THE "OTHER"

Along with complicating the hero's nature, another strategy for challenging propagandistic nationalism that these works share is acknowledging the antagonists' perspective as valid. As discussed above, the characterization of the hero's nation-building project as divinely sanctioned and predestined is often paired with the defeat and delegitimization of the "Other," as embodied by the principal villain. Aeneas' dispute with the native Italians over rights to the land that they currently occupy but which he is "destined" to settle finds historical parallel in America's founding, as white European settlers spreading westward came into conflict with the Native Americans who already lived there and/or with earlier settlers who had competing interests. Westerns thus regularly feature heroic protagonists wresting the land from or coming into conflict with those who came before, whether the Native Americans of *The Searchers* and Delmer Daves' 1950 *Broken Arrow*, the Mexican land baron Don Diego of *Red River*, or the cattlemen of *Shane* and *The Man Who Shot Liberty Valance*. In each case, the moral basis of the hero's quest and the value of the "progress" he champions are presumed by the inevitability of their accomplishment.

Yet while both the *Aeneid* and these golden-age Westerns capitalize on the power of this impression, they do not present it monolithically. Vergil makes clear that, from the Rutulians' perspective, the Trojans are invaders trying to appropriate their homeland and, in the case of Turnus, his woman: their divine ally Juno calls Aeneas "a second Paris" (7.321), a comparison echoed by Turnus' advocate, the Latin queen Amata (7.363–4). Turnus himself passionately characterizes Aeneas and his Trojans as twice guilty: first of invading their lands, and then of stealing his bride (9.135–8).

The directors of golden-age Westerns also take pains not only to acknowledge the enemy's viewpoint, but even to validate it. In *Shane*, Stevens includes a speech where the antagonist Rufus Ryker (Emile Meyer) movingly asserts the primacy of the cattlemen when he reacts to Joe's characterization of his own position as right:

> Right? You in the right? . . . We [cattlemen] made this country. We found it and we made it . . . We made a safe range out of this. Some of us died doing it, but we made it . . . And you say we have no right to the range. The men that did the work and ran the risks have no rights? I take you for a fair man, Starrett.

A similar dynamic plays out in *The Searchers* when the "savage" Comanche chief Scar reveals that his motivation for hostility against the white man is similar to Ethan's reason for animosity toward Native Americans: just as Ethan seeks vengeance against Scar for slaughtering his family, Scar seeks retribution because "Two son killed by white men. For each son, I take many [scalps]."

Turnus, Ryker, and Scar have legitimate prior claims to the land, and each not only feels affronted at the newcomers' violent intrusions, but rightfully complains of additional injustices as well. By acknowledging that the glorious empire enabled by the quest of the hero was built on the suffering and annihilation of those with legitimate claims, both Vergil and the directors of these nuanced Westerns call into question the absolute morality of the settlement project, while undercutting the notion of contemporary society as a golden age validated by the recent victory over the "Other."

THE SACRIFICE OF WOMEN

In addition to complicating the nature of both hero and villain along with the rightness of their goals, another shared strategy for undercutting the nationalistic thrust of these works is the troubling of traditional ideologies through the treatment of gender. As suggested above, women both in the *Aeneid* and in Westerns function as commodities, ownership of which acts as a point of contention between hero and villain. In addition, in both cases, the weakness of women's nature is used to demonstrate male virtue by contrast. In Vergil's epic, women like Dido, Amata, and even the goddess Juno are characterized by excessive emotion and an inability to control themselves, which serves to highlight the need for masculine self-mastery. Dido, for instance, "burns" with uncontrollable passion for Aeneas (4.68); when he prepares to leave her behind in pursuit of his fated quest, she "rages" and "raves" (4.300) in a vindictive, suicidal frenzy that emphasizes Aeneas' own discipline and restraint. So too the Trojan women in Book 5 threaten the hero's mission through excessive emotion that leads them to rash and destructive behavior, again stressing masculine persistence and resolve by contrast. Then in Book 9 (498–502), when Euryalus' mother's display of grief at her son's death disrupts the battle, feminine lack of self-control again threatens to derail the male agenda, highlighting heroic masculinity by comparison. In response to this disruptive excess, women's voices are repeatedly discounted or suppressed: Aeneas' response to Dido's complaints is insensitive to her feelings, dismissing her plausible claim that they are married;[25] the Trojan women are left behind as a hindrance to Aeneas' goals; and Euryalus' mother is swiftly hidden from view.

In Westerns, women are likewise depicted as weak, emotional, and unable to control themselves, traits often signified through a garrulousness that contrasts with masculine laconism.[26] In *Red River*, Tess (Joanne Dru) is so unable to control her verbal leakage that she asks Matt (Montgomery Clift) to stop her, prompting him to put his hand over her mouth (see Figure 8.2). In *Shane* and *The Searchers*, Marian and Laurie verbally gush in emotional opposition to their partners' intended pursuit of their heroic goals; in each case, the woman's demonstration of emotional and verbal excess fails to persuade, serving merely to underscore masculine resolve and self-control. As in the *Aeneid*, men in Westerns regularly discount feminine needs and perspectives. Though he claims to understand her position, Will Kane disregards his bride's values in determined allegiance to his own; Ethan Edwards ignores Mrs. Jorgensen's pleas for her son's safety; and Ransom Stoddard is oblivious to his wife's dreams and desires. When these women's concerns are discounted in favor of heroic action, a hierarchy of valuation is implied that subordinates women and their concerns. As Jane Tompkins argues, it is almost as if the feminine viewpoint "is introduced in order to be swept aside, crushed, or dramatically invalidated,"[27] and through this opposition, the male world of violent heroism – and indeed manhood itself – is defined.

This hierarchy of gendered value is often taken to the extreme, as not just women's needs and desires but their very lives are sacrificed in deference to the male heroic agenda. As Alison Keith has shown, Vergil not only highlights but even fetishizes the sacrifice of women who are presented as obstacles to the hero's quest:[28] Aeneas' first wife Creusa and his lover Dido, as well as Camilla, Amata, and the

Figure 8.2 Matthew Garth (Montgomery Clift) silences Tess Millay (Joanne Dru) in Howard Hawks' *Red River* (1948). United Artists.

Trojan women *en masse* are killed or abandoned in order to further patriarchal goals. As Westerns mature into their golden age, a similar dynamic emerges. Not only do Kane and Doniphon prioritize duty over love, each willing to risk or sacrifice his marriage, but *Red River*'s Fen (Colleen Gray) and *The Searchers*' Martha Edwards (Dorothy Jordan) also become victims of the masculine agenda when they are left behind, effectively to their deaths. In *Broken Arrow*, after the hero's Apache wife Sonseeahray (Debra Paget) is killed in an ambush, the film explicitly positions her sacrifice as crucial to the nation's progress: in a voiceover, Tom Jeffords (James Stewart) relates that he was comforted in his loss because he knew that "the death of Sonseeahray put a seal upon the peace" with the Apache and enabled the country to move forward. By introducing these women only to kill them off, the *Aeneid* and many golden-age Westerns suggest that their primary function is to emphasize the protagonist's heroic masculinity and the nobility of his cause.

The presence of women who exist only to be effaced in these works resonates with societal conditions at the time of their creation. Women in the later Roman Republic had gained an increasing amount of power and independence, while changing marital practices had resulted in a loosening of sexual morality.[29] In the interest of promoting a new post-war "golden age," Augustus was at pains to reinstate traditional values, in large part through a return to more restrictive gender roles. In pursuit of this, he instituted morality laws encouraging marriage and family; firmly placed his own female relatives in normative domestic roles; and demonized women like Marc Antony's Roman wife Fulvia and his lover the Egyptian queen Cleopatra, both of whom had dared to transgress behavioral expectations for women.[30] So too in post-World War II America, women who had entered the workforce due to wartime needs posed a threat to returning veterans who were eager to recover their economic hegemony and symbolically superior status.[31] The alignment of the male with societal advancement and security, and the corresponding devaluation or wholesale erasure of women in both the *Aeneid* and golden-age Westerns,[32] served as a corrective to the blurring of gender roles in contemporary society while bolstering undermined masculinity. At the same time, men's renunciation of these women draws attention to the sacrifices on which the "golden age" that the audience enjoys was built.

CONCLUSION

The patriotic scaffolding with which Vergil framed his narrative pleased Augustus to the extent that he ordered the epic preserved despite Vergil's explicit deathbed request that the unfinished poem be burned.[33] So deeply, it seems, was Augustus invested in promoting the nationalistic propaganda outwardly advanced by the poem that he, along with numerous readers since, overlooked the subtle undercurrents that problematize empire and question the glorious nature of the Augustan regime. Golden-age Western cinema has a similar problem: the generic blueprint is so powerful that both their original audiences and more recent ones tend to regard these films as simplistic "good guys versus bad guys" narratives rather than recognizing them as bold challenges to prevailing perspectives on white America's origins and nascent ideologies. John Ford, for instance, was disappointed that contemporary audiences saw *The Searchers* as just another Western and Ethan Edwards as a standard-issue John Wayne hero, with many viewers missing – or simply unconcerned with – his murderous racism altogether.[34] Even today, Westerns are often dismissed wholesale as crude tales of cowboys versus Indians.

On the contrary, many directors of golden-age Westerns drew on a strategy similar to that found in the most prestigious literary epic of the classical tradition. Despite the prominence of Vergil's work throughout antiquity and into modernity, evidence for direct influence upon the Western or even a chain of receptions is scarce. Yet the Western genre's narrative setting and heroic characterizations are remarkably similar to those of the *Aeneid*, while works of the genre's golden age not only acquire additional parallels in the social and political circumstances surrounding their creation, but also draw on the Vergilian technique of promoting the status quo on one level, while subversively questioning nationalistic dogma on another.

Vergil's epic both extols the glories of Rome, thereby elevating Augustus and his *aureum saeculum*, and subtly points out the problems with and sacrifices inherent in the process of its establishment. Similarly, directors like Hawks, Zinnemann, Stevens, and Ford drew on the Western film tradition and its standard iconography to glorify "the taming of the West" and Manifest Destiny on the one hand, and to question the means by which this "advancement" was achieved on the other. Much as Vergil intentionally drew on Homer's works and at the same time manipulated their heroic associations in order to critique the nationalistic mythologies with which the genre had become equated, many Westerns of the genre's golden age self-consciously tap into the mythic formula established by their predecessors and simultaneously scrutinize it. Thus, they enact mythological treatments of national foundings and critique them at the same time.[35] Far from merely trumpeting the party line that positions the "golden" quality of contemporary society as the well-deserved culmination of heroic, noble struggles, these works offer multi-layered reflections on heroic achievement to those who care to look beneath the surface.

NOTES

Many thanks are due to Meredith E. Safran for her insightful comments on this chapter.

1 See Blundell and Ormand (1997: 533–4), who more fully elucidate the parallel first suggested for classicists by Martin Winkler (1985; 1996). On affinities between individual Westerns and Homeric epic, see also Winkler (2004a); Myrsiades (2007); Day (2008; 2016); and Rubino (2014). On the Western's relationship with Greek mythology and tragedy, see Clauss (1999); Winkler (2001a); Bakewell (2002); Fletcher (2014); and Day (2016). Scholars of the Western film genre and those from other disciplines, too, have recognized important connections between Westerns and Greek epic: Cawelti (1971: 55–7); Mast (1982:

334–7); French (1997: 80); mythology: Fenin and Everson (1973: 6); Parks (1982: 14–16); tragedy: Reeder (1980: 61–2); Frankel (2013: 239); and philosophy: Warfield (1975: 15–20).

2 Blundell and Ormand (1997: 534).

3 Reeder (1980: 62) includes consideration of the *Aeneid* in her overview of archetypes in *Red River* (1948); Kopff (1999: 235–42) devoted a chapter to looking at Clint Eastwood's heroes, Western and otherwise, in relation to Aeneas; Smith (2003: 434) has acknowledged in passing a general affinity between Western heroes and Aeneas as "m[e]n of duty"; and Winkler has argued for John Ford as "America's Virgil" in conference presentations in 2008 and 2015. I too have attempted to bring the *Aeneid* more fully into the conversation, most recently in a monograph that looks at the relationship between Western cinema and the epics of both Homer and Vergil: Day (2016).

4 See Galinsky (1996: 90–121). Galinsky emphasizes that Augustus' golden age differed from earlier ones in that it was grounded in *labor*. He also notes that rather than being an imperial directive, its artistic and literary expressions were "autonomous development[s]" (1996: 119–21).

5 See Grebe (2004: esp. 39–42).

6 See Wiseman (1974).

7 E.g. the sculptural program of the Temple of Mars Ultor in the Forum of Augustus places Augustus in a historical continuum stretching back to the gods, positioning his rule as the divinely ordained and glorious endpoint of a long, if troubled, history. See Zanker (1988: 211–15).

8 Translations in this chapter are mine, based on the Loeb Latin text of Virgil (1986, rev. 1999; 2000).

9 See Hardie (2014: 1–2).

10 See Greenberg (2012: 1–3).

11 Not only is the hero anachronistically identified as a Pony Express rider, but an expository title card also claims that the locomotives in the final scene were "the original Jupiter and #116," which had both been scrapped years earlier. In addition, the Union Pacific engine that met the Jupiter at the historic Golden Spike ceremony at Promontory Summit was not the 116, but the 119.

12 The broad strokes of the Westerner's heroic masculinity were first laid out by Warshow (1954).

13 This characterization is also found in the Jack Schaefer novel on which the film was based.

14 See Levick (1982: esp. 53–4).

15 See Cortese (1976: 124).

16 Parry (1963) and Lyne (1987). For a concise overview of the "optimistic" and "pessimistic" readings of this epic, see Perkell (1999: 14–16).

17 For further development of the ideas in this section, see Day (2016: 19–24).

18 See Perkell (1981: 364–71).

19 See Putnam (1966: 193).
20 Vergil had an epic precedent for Aeneas as a hero problematized through his relationships with women in Apollonius Rhodius' depiction of Jason in his *Argonautica*.
21 Scholarly debate on how to read Aeneas' killing of Turnus in the epic's final scene is ongoing. See e.g. Galinsky (1988).
22 The identification between Ethan and Scar in *The Searchers* has been widely recognized; for an overview and elaboration, see Day (2008: 32–4; 2016: 142–4). On the hero's identification with his enemy in *High Noon* and *Shane*, see Day (2016: 84–5, 117–18).
23 See O'Hara (1990: 170–2); Dominik (1996: 132–3).
24 For more on how Ford calls attention to the altering of history in service to propaganda in *Fort Apache* and *The Man Who Shot Liberty Valance*, see Pye (1996).
25 See Perkell (1981: 363–70).
26 See Tompkins (1992: 47–67).
27 Tompkins (1992: 41).
28 Keith (2000: 115–17).
29 See e.g. Fantham et al. (1994: 260–5) and Severy (2003: 34–44).
30 See Pomeroy (1975: 185–8) and Fantham et al. (1994: 271–5, 299–306).
31 See Coontz (2011: 49–50). McDonough (2013: 103–4) discusses the push to re-establish women's traditional gender roles after World War II in relation to *Seven Brides for Seven Brothers* (1954).
32 While the preferences of women were being ignored in Westerns much earlier (see Victor Fleming's 1929 *The Virginian*), in the genre's golden age this dynamic is often intensified through their abandonment or death.
33 Donatus, *Life of Virgil* 39.
34 McBride (2011: 557); Frankel (2013: 315).
35 Robert Pippin (2010: 96) makes this observation, which I am applying more broadly, in his discussion of *The Man Who Shot Liberty Valance*.

9 *The Golden Age and Imperial Dominance in the* Aeneid *and* Serenity *(2005)*

Jennifer A. Rea

Joss Whedon's 2005 science-fiction film *Serenity*, which continues the story told in the Fox television series *Firefly* (2002), presents a twist on the Western genre. In a future where overpopulation on Earth has spurred the settlement of a distant solar system, humanity has become divided between those who submit to the imperialist rule of an interplanetary government known as the Alliance and those who live on the "frontier," or outer planets, where the Alliance's rule is not as firmly established. Captain Malcolm "Mal" Reynolds (Nathan Fillion), a former "Browncoat" who fought on the losing side of the Independents during the Unification War and now commands a ship named *Serenity*, is the film's central character; he and his crew make a living through smuggling while hoping to stay under the Alliance's radar. In this "Space Western," *Serenity*'s audience sees how the main characters adopt the individualism and self-sufficiency characteristic of the Western genre in order to survive and create new lives for themselves in a post-war society in which the characters exist on the frontier lands of the outer planets, where "civilization" has not quite encroached on their way of life.

Kirsten Day has argued that many Western films can be interpreted as deriving inspiration from Vergil's *Aeneid*, an epic poem about the arrival of the Trojans in Italy.[1] Both the genre of the Western and Vergil's ancient epic poem focus on empire and nation-building, and both feature characters who are forced to rebuild their lives after war. Indeed, characters in both Western films and the epic poem must fulfill their destinies and also wish to create a better society in which to live. But both works feature conflict when the characters challenge what constitutes a better world and question the promise of a superior way of living. The *Aeneid* depicts prophecies of the Roman Empire, during the reign of the emperor Augustus, which forecast the delivering of security and peace after decades of civil war. In *Serenity*, the imperialist Alliance claims to offer stability and civilization to the population in exchange for the loss of personal freedoms in the wake of their universe's civil war. Such promises of a better world and superior way of living draw upon the ancient myth of the golden age.

This chapter considers how both the *Aeneid* and *Serenity* utilize the "golden-age" myth. For the plots of both works question whether those promises can come true while also warning their audiences about the high cost of imperial dominance. Christopher Nappa suggests that, following generations of civil war at Rome, Augustus' regime was "positioning itself as the peaceful alternative to a state of continuous civil conflict,"[2] a position incorporated into the *Aeneid* through prophecies concerning Augustus' ascension to power. Yet the way that Augustus is prophesied to come to power entails immense violence, upon both Rome's population and "barbarians" at the edges of the empire. *Serenity* too considers how members of a post-war society negotiate the transition from crisis to stability via a new government established through violence – and what happens when that government experiments with limiting a population's violent behavior and controlling their ability to refuse incorporation into the new imperial regime. Both *Serenity* and the *Aeneid*, within their depictions of empire-building, question the value of a golden-age or utopian existence in which the conquered populations pay a high price for the promise of peace. The works also highlight the danger of allowing a centralized regime to determine humanity's future.

BETTER LIVING? GOLDEN AGE AND UTOPIA IN THE *AENEID* AND *SERENITY*

The golden age has been formulated in a number of ways in classical literature. Christine Perkell notes that Vergil imagines more than one version of the golden age across his poetry.[3] In the *Aeneid*, Vergil envisions two golden ages that offer peace, law, and order – but as the result of conquest. In Book 6, Aeneas' father Anchises speaks of the golden age of peace and prosperity coming to the future community of Augustan Rome. In Book 8, King Evander of Pallanteum recounts the first golden age, when Saturn was driven out of heaven by his son and settled, like Aeneas, as an exile in Latium. In both cases, past ways of life must be set aside in order to achieve a civilized society. Thus Vergil highlights the dilemmas inherent in questions such as who determines the right and wrong applications of power, who decides what constitutes civilized living, and whether loss of personal freedom is worth exchanging for promises of safety and security.

Aeneas learns about Saturn's golden age from Evander after he arrives on the shores of Italy. While they tour Evander's settlement, the site that is destined to become the city of Rome, Evander tells Aeneas the story of how Saturn founded the golden-age community in Latium after his exile from Olympus:

> The native fauns and Nymphs once occupied these groves,
> and a race of men formed from tree trunks and hard oak,
> for whom there was neither law nor culture, and they did not know how
> to yoke bulls or to amass wealth, or to be thrifty with what they acquired
> but branches and the hunt sustained them.
> Saturn first came down from ethereal Olympus,
> Fleeing the arms of Jove, an exile from his lost kingdom.
> He created order among a race untrained and scattered in
> the high mountains, and gave laws to them . . .
> Under this king's rule was the Golden Age men talk about,
> in calm peace he was ruling the peoples. (*Aeneid* 8.314–25)[4]

Vergil depicts Saturn as an exile who sought refuge from his son's violence: the *arma Iovis*, or the "arms of Jove." Thus, violence plays a role in the start of this story, and the inclusion of laws in Saturn's realm suggests that criminal behavior exists from the start as a possibility for Latium's inhabitants.[5]

Saturn is then described as collecting a *genus indocile*, or "untrained people," from the mountains for whom he established laws so as to maintain the peace. This peaceful state accords with Saturn's other main identity, which would have been known to the community of Augustan Rome, as an agricultural god: a vocation associated with peace. Saturn's ability to rule over the people with a gentle peace creates the Saturnian golden age (*Aen.* 8.319–27). But this peaceful state of existence proved to be unsustainable, and Evander's account describes an eventual decline into an inferior age, as the proto-Romans enter into a period where war and conflict become part of their existence. This narrative would have resonated with Vergil's audience, since the community had just experienced a succession of civil wars that ended the Republic.

The forecast of the return of a golden age in Book 6 offers stability and peace that will allow the Romans to dwell within a stable empire and conquer barbarians. Aeneas gets a glimpse of Rome's future when he visits the Underworld and his father Anchises shows him Rome's future descendants in this excerpt from the Parade of Heroes passage:

> This man, this is the one, Caesar Augustus,
> whom often you hear promised to you, the son of a god,
> who will found a golden age again in Latium,
> through lands once ruled over by Saturn,
> and will extend his empire over the Garamantes and the Indians,
> their land lies beyond the zodiac, beyond the sun's annual course,
> where sky-bearing Atlas rotates on his shoulder
> the heavens equipped with burning stars.
> Even now at his approach, the Caspian kingdoms and the Maeotian land
> shudder at the oracles of the gods, and the fearful mouths
> of the seven-fold Nile are stirred up.
> Nor truly did Hercules ever pass over so much land,
> although he pierced the bronze-footed deer,
> granted peace to the groves of Erymanthus,
> and made Lerna tremble with his bow:
> nor Bacchus, who, as the victor, guides his chariot,
> with his reins covered in vine-shoots,
> drives tigers from the tall peak of Nysa. (*Aeneid* 6.791–805)

The passage emphasizes that the Romans will civilize the world beyond Italy through conquest, which will then lead to a "golden age," or *aurea saecula*, under Augustus' reign (*Aen.* 6.791–5). Thus, Anchises explains how the emperor Augustus will return the people to a golden-age existence following their civil wars, just as Saturn had established his golden age by creating laws for Latium's inhabitants. But now Rome is an imperial city, and Augustus' reign includes extending command far to the East (6.788–95): to *Garamantas et Indos*, or "the Garamantes and the Indians" on the untamed frontier.

The references to widening imperial borders through Augustus' broadening of his command, however, set up the contrast between the expectations for a kind of golden-age stability where the society exists in a peaceful sort of stasis and the reality of maintaining peace only by continually expanding the borders through conquest. War must be waged abroad in order to maintain peace at home.[6] Throughout the *Aeneid*, there are references to the wars that lie in Rome's future. For example, Anchises, Aeneas' father, predicts the civil war between Caesar and Pompey (*Aen.* 6.828–31). The depiction of the Battle of Actium and Augustus' triumph occupies a central position on Aeneas' shield (8.675–723). At the end of the Parade of Heroes, however, Anchises reminds Aeneas that the Roman way is to impose habitual peace on conquered peoples (6.852). As Lee

Fratantuono notes, "The Roman is to rule the world, and to establish customs (law, tradition, all the richness of *mos*) in time of peace."[7]

Yet the future that Aeneas sees in Anchises' prophecy is not necessarily accurate, but rather "deceptively optimistic." James O'Hara points out that this prophecy, like many in the *Aeneid*, may not be as hopeful as it seems: "in this prophecy as in others, Vergil presents the hope that things will be better under Augustus and his deep fear and worry that this is only an illusion."[8] When Aeneas exits the Underworld, he will pass through the Gate of Ivory, or the "Gate of False Dreams." The idealized version of the past presented in *Aeneid* Book 6 has been replaced by a period of civil wars, and then the potential for a return to a golden age: Augustus promises better living conditions for the community through a secure and stable imperial government. The Romans and their deeds, as featured in this parade, appear to lead up to the glory of the Augustan Age. But that does not mean a permanent return to a golden age here, because an uncertain and vague future lies beyond the peace that marks the start of the Roman Empire.[9]

The "golden age" references in the *Aeneid* can be compared to a modern concept of utopian living, which seeks similar goals of better living through a society engineered to be safe, secure, and free from the problems that less civilized societies may have.[10] The opening sequence of *Serenity* shows how the Alliance too presents itself this way, thus justifying the civil war that the Alliance waged against the Browncoats who fought for independence.

Serenity begins with a scene of schoolchildren learning from their teacher (Tamara Taylor) about the benefits that the Alliance provides to all humankind. She assures the students that the Alliance is the best possible form of government for their society:

> Earth-that-was could no longer sustain our numbers, we were so many. We found a new solar system, dozens of planets and hundreds of moons, each one terraformed, a process taking decades, to support human life, to be new Earths. The Central Planets formed the Alliance. Ruled by an interplanetary parliament, the Alliance was a beacon of civilization. The savage outer planets were not so enlightened and refused Alliance control. The war was devastating, but the Alliance's victory over the Independents ensured a safer universe. And now everyone can enjoy the comfort and enlightenment of true civilization.

With all her talk of the "comfort and enlightenment" provided by the utopian civilization created by the Alliance, the teacher wins the approval of the majority of the students. Her characterization of the "savage outer planets," along with mention of the Alliance's success in putting the "Independents" under their domain, also evokes the *imperium sine fine* ("empire without end") that Jupiter promises to future Rome in the *Aeneid* (1.279). Like the extension of the Roman Empire's boundaries described at *Aen.* 6.791–5, a war expanded the Alliance's control of the planets in the solar system and thus offered civilization and peace to all.

But one child, River Tam (Hunter Ansley Wryn), challenges the idea that the Alliance has a right to impose its "beacon of civilization" on the "savage outer planets": "People don't like to be meddled with. We tell them what to do, what to think. Don't run. Don't walk. We're in their homes and in their heads and we haven't the right. We're meddlesome." River's sentiments on the Alliance's "meddling" encapsulate a key question also facing the Roman audience of the *Aeneid*: following a civil war, how much authority should the reigning government possess over individuals' lives? Central to the film's main plot is disagreement over the necessity of sacrificing freedom to the Alliance and the validity of its claim to provide "civilization" to the war's survivors.

In responding to River's objection, however, the teacher confirms River's criticism. After chastising River with "We're not telling people what to think. We're just trying to show them how," she jams a stylus into the child's forehead. A quick cut to an adult River (Summer Glau) in a government laboratory reveals that the schoolroom had been an induced hallucination; the Alliance has been experimenting on River's mind (see Figure 9.1). This abrupt reveal validates as reality River's warning about a society where citizens are being altered to suit the purposes of the government, and invalidates the teacher's representation of the Alliance as a benevolent ruling system. After River is rescued by Mal and the crew of *Serenity*, the Alliance will

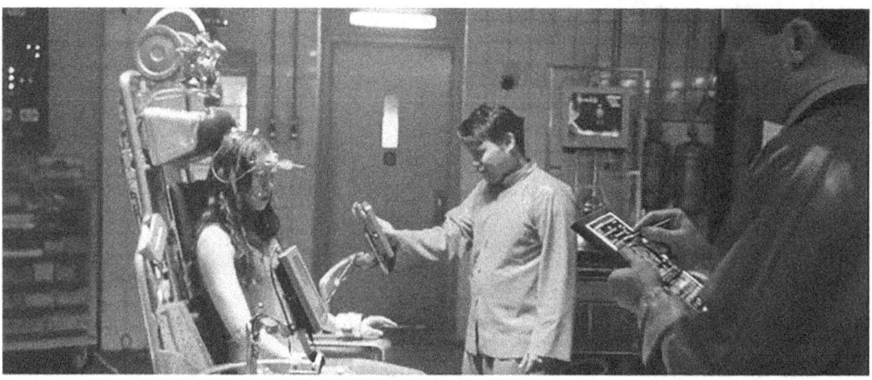

Figure 9.1 Alliance scientists attempt to impose their imperial-utopian worldview on River Tam (Summer Glau) in *Serenity* (2005). Universal Pictures.

engage in a relentless and brutal pursuit of their experimental subject, whose psychic abilities had allowed her to unwittingly gather sensitive information about another utopian Alliance project that will provide even more terrifying support to River's position that "we're in their homes and in their heads and we haven't the right."

Guided by what little information River can glean from the mind-control experiment that the Alliance performed on her, the crew ends up traveling to a planet, Miranda, where they find the exact opposite of the "comfort and enlightenment" that the teacher promised in the opening scene. When Mal and his crew arrive on the planet, they find a settlement fit for human habitation but curiously bereft of life – because it is full of corpses who died non-violent deaths. They discover a video recording made by a scientist, Dr. Caron (Sarah Paulson), who reveals what happened to the human population:

> It wasn't what we thought. There's been no war here and no terraforming event. The environment is stable. It's the Pax. The G-23 Paxilon Hydrochlorate that we added to the air processors. It was supposed to calm the population, weed out aggression. Well, it works. The people here stopped fighting. And then they stopped everything else. They stopped going to work, they stopped breeding, talking, eating. There's 30 million people here, and they all just let themselves die.

Thus, the crew learns that Miranda was part of a government experiment: to impose peace via chemicals. The experiment resulted in a failed attempt to create a peaceful society, in that too much Pax took away most inhabitants' will to live. The survivors had the opposite reaction, and became a violent, cannibalistic race known as the Reavers, who attack every settlement they encounter and wear the skins of those they rape and kill. The Alliance's attempt to bring peace through conquest has in fact created the most terrifying threat faced by all humanity, and the dystopian nature of the imperial Alliance has been fully revealed.

WHO WILL BRING ABOUT THIS BETTER WORLD – OR SAVE US FROM IT?

In the *Aeneid*, the weight of salvation falls on the shoulder of Aeneas. As the lone member of the Trojan royal family who escaped death or enslavement when the Greek army conquered his city, Aeneas must save the remnants of the Trojan people following the fall of Troy: as a duty to his fellow refugees, and to fulfill his fated establishment of the dynasty in Italy that will found and rule Rome. At first, he struggles to come to terms with his destiny to found a settlement in

Italy. He keeps trying to establish settlements at various stops along his journey, but each time he is driven away. By the time he reaches Italy, his crew has been sailing for seven years and his trust in the gods has been sorely tested. Once he sees the Parade of Heroes, however, and the glory of future Rome, his sense of *pietas*, or duty to the gods and community before individual needs, guides him to make the choices that will lead to the founding of the Roman Empire. As Gary Miles notes, "the *Aeneid* views Rome in terms of an idea or ideal, one that defines heroism in terms of service to the community, rather than single-minded pursuit of one's own reputation for martial prowess."[11] Aeneas recognizes that he needs to sacrifice his identity as a Trojan and his homeland in order to save his people and fulfill his destiny by defeating Turnus in Italy. As Paula James points out, Aeneas' new life is "foisted on him by higher powers."[12]

As *Serenity*'s captain, Mal too must determine how best to protect his crew – and whether the same sense of duty to the people of the universe that Aeneas feels toward the people of his wider community will impel Mal to make war on an oppressive ruling power, as Aeneas does in Italy. As an unreconstructed Independent, ever since the Unification War Mal has tried to stay on the periphery of the universe and under the radar of the Alliance, as much as his smuggling business will allow. He refuses to validate the legitimacy of the Alliance, but resists being thrust into the role of hero or savior of anyone but himself and (sometimes) his crew members. Mal's decision to rescue River has brought down the god-like fury of the Alliance upon him and his crew. Consequently, they sail around the universe looking for safe harbor but are driven away from any possible refuge as the Alliance's agent, a man known only as The Operative (Chiwetel Ejiofor), destroys any safe harbor they could hope to find. Mal only begins thinking about how he can make a better future for humanity at large once he learns about the Alliance's experiment with "Pax" on Miranda and realizes that he has a responsibility to expose the Alliance's attempts to control people's minds.

As the reluctant hero who finally embraces his duty to make war against a formidable tyrannical power in order to ensure a safe future for his fellow people, Mal embodies important qualities of Aeneas. However, his commitment to self-determination and rejection of higher authority – both human and divine – leaves out an important part of Aeneas' profile in the second half of the *Aeneid*. Such unquestioning embrace of a higher purpose is the primary characteristic of the film's antagonist, known only as The Operative, a ruthless assassin who admires the Alliance's plans to engineer humankind in order to make a better society and unquestioningly undertakes any and all missions to ensure its agenda. His sense of piety dictates that he must place the needs of the Alliance before all else. His own desire to rid the universe of "sin" makes him fond of commenting on his targets' flawed characters, just before killing them.

The Operative's obsession with creating "a world without sin" resonates with the return to a golden age in the *Aeneid*. Although the ancient Romans did not believe in the concept of sin in the Christian sense, there was a sense of *scelus*, or "an offense that incurs the wrath of the gods," such as unjustified war.[13] Thus, as depicted in the *Aeneid*, Augustus was the leader who could bring about a return to peace and the golden age, who would enable the community of Augustan Rome to begin to heal from their past trauma of *scelus* in the form of their civil wars, even as he conducts "justified" wars of conquest beyond Rome's borders to ensure stability and reaffirm the Roman Empire's supremacy.[14] Yet stability now depends on Augustus' ability to establish conquests and subsequently on the expansion and maintenance of the Empire's borders. So too, the Operative's resolve to kill anyone who stands in the way of the "comfort and enlightenment" that the Alliance offers evokes the dangers of believing blindly in a form of imperial control that requires constant policing of its borders and even invades people's minds. The Operative's character can function as a reminder that there is a darker side to Aeneas' mission: namely, the type of government that his descendant Augustus will institute, and the conflicts required to achieve the kind of peace that it promises.

After a particularly devastating attack on a settlement where Mal and his crew had hoped to find sanctuary from the furious pursuit of The Operative, the two engage in an illuminating ship-to-ship video conversation that establishes the values and stakes of these two combatants. The Operative explains his scorched-earth tactics and the ethics behind them: "I'm sorry. If your quarry goes to ground, leave no ground to go to. You should have taken my offer. Or did you think none of this was your fault?" Mal responds, "I don't murder children." The Operative's chilling response – "I do, if I have to" – proves that he has been so conditioned to believe in the Alliance's view of a better world that he follows orders without question, which Mal cannot understand:

Mal:	Why? Do you even know why they sent you?
The Operative:	It's not my place to ask. I believe in something greater than myself. A better world. A world without sin.

Mal:	So me and mine gotta lay down and die, so you can live in your better world?
The Operative:	I'm not going to live there. There's no place for me there, any more than there is for you. Malcolm, I'm a monster. What I do is evil. I have no illusions about it, but it must be done.

Just as Aeneas will not live to see the foundation of Rome and its prophesied "better world," not even The Operative sees himself living in the utopia promised by the Alliance. In particular, both heroes deal with the enemy in a way that reminds their audiences that the post-war future is not perfect, and that there should be anxiety and a desire to question the authorities in charge about what the future holds for those who served in the opposing faction of the war. There are some differences in the anxiety, however, that must be acknowledged: Aeneas' adventures which lead up to the founding of Rome make the community of Augustan Rome ask "Was the strife worth it?" whereas Mal's adventures, which may or may not lead to the take-down of the Alliance, make the audience ask, "Will the strife be worth it?"

The Operative's true belief in the promise of "a world without sin," where the Alliance commands total authority over the people, leads him to warn Mal: "You are fooling yourself, Captain. Nothing here is what it seems. You are not the plucky hero, the Alliance is not an evil empire, and this is not the grand arena." He then asks Mal, "Are you willing to die for your beliefs?" This challenge requires Mal to face and move past his fear of commitment to a higher cause than his own personal interest, much like Aeneas. Mal soon proves that he is willing to die for a cause greater than himself. The realization that dawns in Mal's character, which allows him to define himself as part of something greater, is in part due to the fact that he and his crew serve on the ship together not entirely by choice, and that *Serenity* functions not only as a sanctuary, but as a space where their characters evolve to the point where they come together to fight the unjust Alliance. As Lewis and Cho note, "interpersonal conflicts abound," yet the characters become "united under the project of collective political struggle."[15] Mal remarks to the crew that they are all "just folk" and that the war is long over; nevertheless, he and the crew become willing to entertain the idea of sacrificing themselves in battle.

Once Mal realizes what has happened on Miranda, he is determined to expose the conspiracy to cover up the government's wrong-doing by proving that the Alliance has destroyed an entire planet's population and lied to its citizens:

> This record here's about twelve years old. Parliament buried it and it stayed buried until River here dug it up. This is what they were afraid she knew. And they were right to fear. There's a universe of folk who're gonna know it, too. Someone has to speak for these people.

Here Mal makes the decision that he can no longer remain under the Alliance's radar. He convinces the crew to make public the knowledge of the Alliance's unethical experiments on Miranda and to put an end to the Alliance's dream of engineering a designer society: "Y'all got on this boat for different reasons, but y'all come to the same place. So now I'm asking more of you than I have before. Maybe all." Mal predicts that the Alliance will strike again if their crime against humanity is not exposed. "Sure as I know anything, I know this: they will try again. Maybe on another world, maybe on this very ground swept clean. A year from now, ten? They'll swing back to the belief that they can make people [pause] better." He then demonstrates his resolve to do something about the situation: "And I do not hold to that. So no more runnin'. I aim to misbehave."

Mal's questioning of the Alliance's motives and his rejection of the idea that the Alliance's centralized control of all the planets offers a better form of leadership than the previous system of governance resonate with a reading of the *Aeneid* that suggests uncertainty about Rome's future under Augustus' rule and thereafter. There is some dispute over whether, at the start of the Empire, Vergil and the community of Augustan Rome would have been reassured by the presence of the new regime, or if they would have been more hesitant to assign their trust to the change from Republic to Empire. Fratantuono argues for a lack of security: "For Virgil and the Romans of his day, there was, of course, no certainty that Augustus' reign would prove to be so calm and serene." Smith takes the opposite view:

> During the early to middle Augustan Age, when Vergil was writing the *Aeneid*, Rome was in the midst of a generally positive period. Civil wars had ended, and the empire's extensive building program was well underway. Romans were seeing the tangible symbols of a new order, and the sights they beheld underscored the constructive aspects of the *pax Augusta*.[16]

The opposing scholarly views demonstrate the complexity of the times. Whether or not the majority went along with the new Augustan regime, the imposed peace impacted the community of Augustan Rome in both positive and negative ways. *Serenity* presents the majority of the solar system as accepting the Alliance. Yet Mal and his crew fervently reject the idea that the Alliance can offer "comfort and enlightenment" to the survivors of the Unification War.

AT WHAT COST?

In the *Aeneid*, Vergil's prophetic characters consider the peace that allows Augustus to focus on the barbaric enemies menacing the edges of Rome's dominion and standing in the way of *imperium sine fine* to be worth the losses incurred through civil war. They imply that this peace is worth the costs of putting an end to that cycle of violence, even the loss of liberty associated with the Empire. But the epic's end previews the costs of this imperial project both for Romans and for Italians. *Serenity* too encourages its audience to calculate the price that a post-war society pays for the utopian promises of an imperialistic, centralized government that experiments on the population, then fails to take responsibility for its actions when disaster ensues. The price is being paid not only by the murdered colonists of Miranda, but also by the Reavers, who became monsters as a result of the Alliance's secret experiment, and by The Operative, whose indoctrination by the Alliance weaponized his sense of duty and faith in the Alliance's utopian promises.

Like the *Aeneid*, *Serenity* culminates in a final battle between two rivals who fight for control of the future. Both Mal and The Operative are driven by a sense of the righteousness of their cause; as in Vergil's epic with the fight between Turnus and Aeneas, only one set of values can be validated by victory in single combat. To reveal the truth about the population of Miranda and the creation of the Reavers, Mal and his crew must travel to a pirate broadcast station where they can stream Dr. Caron's video diary across the universe. As the rest of *Serenity*'s crew fights off the pursuing fleet of Reavers, The Operative makes one last attempt to protect his cause by confronting Mal in the station's control room.

In this conflict between two visions of the world – one that values liberty, another that values empire – both worldviews field a champion characterized by *pietas*, who puts his mission on behalf of a larger cause before his own interests, willing to sacrifice himself for a cause in which he believes. Aeneas will kill a rival, Turnus, in a final battle in order for the proto-Roman foundations to occur. Because Turnus fights to resist the new governance that the Trojans will impose on Latium, in some ways he can be considered similar to Mal, who resists the Alliance's rule. But Mal bears a stronger resemblance to Aeneas, because of his growing awareness that he can no longer just "look out for me and mine."

Also like Aeneas, Mal runs the risk of giving in to *furor* and killing an opponent who is already defeated. The Operative asks Mal

Figure 9.2 Mal (Nathan Fillion) kneels over his defeated foe The Operative (Chiwetel Ejiofor) after their climactic single combat in *Serenity* (2005). Universal Pictures.

in their final fight scene, "Do you know what your sin is, Mal?" to which Mal replies, "Ah Hell, I'm a fan of all seven. But right now, I'm gonna have to go with wrath." When Mal finally subdues The Operative at the end of the fight, he does not kill him, despite the fact The Operative has brought so much death and destruction to Mal's friends and allies (see Figure 9.2). Instead, he displays the mercy that Aeneas did not – at least, physically: "Expect you'd want to say your famous last words right now. Just one trouble. I ain't gonna kill you. Hell, I'm gonna grant your greatest wish. I'm gonna show you a world without sin." Then Mal shows The Operative Dr. Caron's video, killing his faith in the Alliance and its promises of a "better world." Just as the *Aeneid* demonstrates that there is no approaching golden age that does not require further war, likewise, Mal is determined to show The Operative that his world without sin does not exist.

As Paula James has noted, Whedon feels free to have his heroes redefine heroism, as does Vergil.[17] Aeneas finishes the fight with Turnus on his own terms, by ignoring Anchises' advice that the submissive should be spared (6.851–3).[18] Mal also finishes the fight on his own terms: The Operative is never submissive, but in the end he is spared. Although Mal chooses not to kill The Operative, there is a sense that they both will live in exile in the Alliance's new world. In the final scene of the film, Mal warns The Operative that he had better not see him ever again: "They take you down, I don't expect to grieve overmuch. Like to kill you myself, I see you again." The Operative reassures him: "You won't. There is nothing left to see."

CONCLUSION: THE FALSE PROMISE OF A "BETTER WORLD," POST-CIVIL WAR

Joss Whedon's oeuvre has become an established part of the academic dialogue for scholars who explore the interconnections between Classics and popular culture.[19] Both Whedon and Vergil present their audiences with a bigger and better vision of the future, as evidenced by Aeneas in his visit to the Underworld, when he sees the Parade of Heroes, and by the opening scene in *Serenity*, where the audience is shown how much the Alliance has done for humankind. Yet, also like the *Aeneid*, *Serenity* reveals that the golden age, or a utopian way of living, is not a lasting state of existence. The golden-age-gone-wrong scenario encourages its audience to think about the consequences of trying to create a perfect society by repressing or artificially eliminating aggression or labor. At the heart of both works is the question of the price a society will pay in chasing the promise of a golden age. *Serenity* encourages comparisons to the *Aeneid* through the characterizations of violence, the "evil empire" versus "free republic" dichotomy, and the golden-age-gone-wrong scenario.

Serenity can offer, if not closure for the epic's ending, an updated version of the story that focuses on post-war redemption as a means to a better world. Vergil and Whedon create a vision of the future that warns against societies founded through violence and bloodshed. But in both stories, the audience is led to the realization that things are not as they seem. Introducing modern perspectives on violence, vengeance, and post-war cultural resolution into consideration of Vergil's ancient epic allows the audience to connect a modern narrative, which calls into question how to establish political order from post-war turmoil, to what Vergil says about the future for the community of Augustan Rome.[20] In the *Aeneid*, the audience is left wondering what price the Romans will continue to pay for their new socio-political order and what additional sacrifices will be required in order to achieve peace. *Serenity* reveals the consequences for society of attempting a return to a golden age, and the violent means by which this "utopian" living is achieved.

Like the hero in Western films, Whedon's heroes face dilemmas that highlight the need to prioritize a sense of duty to the community at large, as opposed to the fulfilling of individual desires. Such choices do not appear remote from Aeneas' struggles to accept his fate and put the future of Rome before all else. In particular, Gross argues that the devastating losses Aeneas had experienced lead to "growing isolation, diminishing humanity and altered identity."[21]

Moreover, Putnam contends that the "humane concerns" of Aeneas have been completely displaced at the end of the work.[22] Aeneas will kill Turnus at the end of the *Aeneid*, and this does raise the question of how those who are not on board with the new regime will be dealt with and what this says about the regime. Whedon's heroes traverse the same emotional landscape as Aeneas whenever destiny shapes the course of their actions and whenever they must come to terms with the possibility of dying in battle, or with the fact that their choices will shape the future of their world. In films such as *Serenity* and television shows such as *Firefly* and *Buffy the Vampire Slayer*, Whedon has created heroic characters who, like Aeneas, possess the ability to inspire audience dialogue about how much of his or her own humanity a hero has to sacrifice in order to achieve a more secure and stable future.

NOTES

I would like to thank Meredith E. Safran for her insightful comments on my argument and the opportunity to publish in this volume. Avery D. Cahill and Velvet L. Yates also offered much constructive criticism on drafts.

1 Day (2016: 58–9).
2 Nappa (2005: 168). For more on Rome's violent foundation story see, for example, Rea (2008: 3–14, 130–1); Lowrie (2005: 950–2); Miles (1999: 175–97); L. Morgan (1998: 137–78); Feeney (1991: 150).
3 Perkell (2002: 28–34).
4 All Latin text is from Vergil (1990). All translations are my own.
5 Evans (2008: 165).
6 Evans (2008: 165). See also Green (2004: 236).
7 Fratantuono (2007: 194). See also Day (2016: 158), who argues that the "patriotic" display in the Parade of Heroes validates Augustus' rule.
8 O'Hara (1990; repr. 2014: 162).
9 Glei (1998: 125–6). See also Smith (2005: 87) for the association of Augustus and the golden age.
10 Evans (2008: 1). In using the terms "utopian" and "golden age," I am following Evans, who argues that both terms can suggest a society that exists in peace, without violence.
11 See Miles (1999: 234). See also Quint (1993: 56–9), for the need for the Trojans, and Aeneas in particular, to let go of the past.
12 James (2009: 242).
13 Wallace-Hadrill (1982: 24).
14 Wallace-Hadrill (1982: 24). See also Evans (2008: 67).
15 Lewis and Cho (2006: 89).
16 Fratantuono (2007: 4); Smith (2005: 176).

17 James (2009: 247, 252).
18 James (2009: 255).
19 Similarities between the heroine's quest in the TV show *Buffy the Vampire Slayer* (1997–2003) and Aeneas' struggle to face his adversaries have been documented: see, for example, Marshall (2003: 2) and James (2009: 239–55), who has argued that Aeneas serves as a "cultural companion" to Buffy.
20 Spence (2002: 50).
21 Gross (2003–4: 135–56) makes a case for a complete loss of Aeneas' identity and humanity at the end.
22 Putnam (1999: 226).

10 Turning Gold into Lead: Sexual Pathology and the De-mythologizing of Augustus in HBO's Rome *(2005–2007)*

Thomas J. West III

He transformed the Roman Republic into the Principate. He was hailed by his contemporaries as the harbinger of a new golden age of civil and political stability, reinforced by a return to appropriate gender and sexual mores. At the same time, in the popular imagination he remains something of an enigma, for the presence of the first Roman emperor within popular film and television has not been as pronounced as that of his successors Caligula, Claudius, and Nero. He was, of course, Augustus. Despite his prominence within ancient Roman history, he remains shrouded behind what Barbara Weiden Boyd has characterized as "The Augustan mask, in all its impenetrability and ominous power."[1] This mask has largely kept him from accruing the vexed aura that has attached itself to other imperial figures. When he does appear, as in the 1976 TV series *I, Claudius* (played by Brian Blessed) or in the 2003 TV film *Imperium: Augustus* (played by Peter O'Toole), he is typically depicted as an older statesman, long after the man and the myth had fused – but what of his formative years, before Octavian became Augustus?

HBO's *Rome* brings to the screen arguably the most fully fleshed depiction of the psychological development of this seminal figure. The series interprets Octavian in relation to his viciously sexual mother Atia and his variably timid and rebellious sister Octavia, and as the protégé of two of the Republic's leading men, Julius Caesar and Marc Antony. Although he begins the series in thrall to Atia and Antony, he gradually establishes control: first over himself, and then over everyone around him. Through his nuanced understanding of the workings of both politics and personal foibles, Octavian manages to seize control of the Republic and usher in a new regime. Whether it is the "golden" one proclaimed by poets and accepted by the classical tradition is up for debate.

Through two seasons, *Rome* mirrors this personal maturation in its chronicling of the decline and fall of the Roman Republic and the gradual emergence of the Principate under the undisputed leadership of the young Octavian, in his newly minted identity as Augustus. Via Octavian, *Rome* argues that the transition from a decaying and sexually unruly republic to a supposedly more stable and unified empire reflects the development and maturation from mother-dominated youth to master of his political and domestic domains. On the surface, the series ends with Octavian having established dominance over both of these aspects of his life, with his mother relegated to a subordinate status, his pseudo-father and arch-rival Marc Antony vanquished, and his wife Livia stationed demurely at his side. The destructive, disruptive sexuality of his family apparently has been brought back into its proper channels, paving the way for a new flowering of Roman power. However, the series goes to great pains to show that this is, in fact, a myth: that beneath the already-cultivated Augustan mask of male control and restraint seethes a darker strain of barely tamed sexual desires, symbolized by his privately sadomasochistic relationship with Livia.

Through this intertwining of the sexual and the political, which reflects the historiographic tradition of correlating the fortunes of Rome with the person of Augustus, *Rome* engages in a de-mythologizing of the "golden age" of Augustan Rome, showing how the moral underpinnings of that idealized period, the markers of its stability and its greatness, are hiding a counterfeit interior, like a gilded piece of inferior metal. In the process, the series utilizes a set of what Robert Rosenstone has termed "rules of engagement" with the world of Roman antiquity, to grapple with the larger question of how historical change takes place.[2] The fact that the restoration of Republican morals and civic stability proclaimed by the end of the series is merely a façade, papering over the roiling cauldron of sexual repression and personal strife, suggests that historical change is not so easily controlled. *Rome* peels away the layers of the carefully cultivated and seemingly impenetrable "Augustan mask" to expose his indulgence in precisely the types of gendered and sexual behaviors that he outwardly condemns. In doing so, the series claims that the powerful nature of epochal shift involves Octavian's seemingly dispassionate superego repressing the unruly id, represented by characters such as Atia and Antony. However, that powerful sexual unconscious always lurks beneath the surface of his placid exterior.

THE AUGUSTAN ENIGMA, GOLDEN-AGE RHETORIC, AND THE CINEMATIC EPIC TRADITION

The enigma of Rome's first emperor is rooted in the extant sources. With a few exceptions, ancient writers provide little concrete knowledge either about his youth or about the inner workings of his character. Mark Toher argues that authors such as Suetonius may offer glimpses into the motivations of the man, but they do not offer "any significant insight into the character of Augustus."[3] As Toher further observes, ancient biography often struggled to depict change in its subjects, which may explain in part why so little is known about Augustus' youth and why there is a signature lack of character development from the young Octavian to the figure of Augustus in the narratives that survive. Thus, even when modern scholars such as Meyer Reinhold attempt to tease out the complexities of Augustus' inner life, they still must rely on analyzing the actions that he took to speculate on his possible psychological motivations.[4]

Rome's articulation of its critique of the Augustan "golden-age" myth, and its concomitant argument about the nature of historical change, also draws on the Roman literary tradition that cultivated that myth. After his victory over the armies of Cleopatra and Antony at the Battle of Actium, followed by his assumption of unrivaled control over the Roman state, Augustus quickly ensured that his own age would be celebrated as not only a return to civil and political stability, but also the return of a golden age of moral and gender normality, in clear opposition to the instability and gendered chaos represented by his vanquished enemies.[5] The depths to which the Republic had sunk – or at least the way it was perceived to have done so – rendered the return of the golden age, combining the heights of glory and stability, all the more potent and psychologically needful.

Poets and historians alike, including Horace and Livy, praised Augustus for bringing about an end to the civil strife that had plagued the last years of the Republic for several decades. Andrew Wallace-Hadrill argues that "for Livy as for Horace, civil war and immorality are intertwined . . . War is regarded as the wages of sin; the termination of war is not a strictly military affair, but a religious crusade against sin that results in expiation."[6] It thus was crucial that the civil/political and the moral/sexual remain connected in the public imagination, and Augustus came to be understood as both the architect and the ultimate example of this newly minted golden age of Roman power, order, and peace.

Yet even in his own time, rumors of sexual dysfunction and hypocrisy seethed beneath the veneer of moral authority that he sought to impose on the rest of Roman society. Numerous ancient sources highlighted the emperor's perverse sexual proclivities, including acts of adultery, in which Livia too was supposed to have participated by procuring him lovers, and his particular desire for young virgins.[7] As meticulous as Augustus was in maintaining his public version of himself, some were determined to see him in a negative light. Even historians writing several generations after his death, such as Dio and Suetonius, emphasized the flaws in his sexual character.[8] The ruler who was supposed to usher in a golden age seemed to be a hypocrite whose propaganda merely served as a front for his own debauchery.

Rome thus falls within a tradition, established by Roman historiography and continued within film and television, of depicting the Roman world and its rulers in particular as full of sexual vice and perversion. During the golden age of the Hollywood historical epic in the 1950s and 1960s, such depictions ranged from the infantile delusions and rapacious sexuality of Nero and Poppaea in *Quo Vadis* (1951) to the sadistic and manipulative queerness of Crassus in *Spartacus* (1960). As scholars such as Monica S. Cyrino and Ina Rae Hark have suggested, for cinematic Romans sexuality marks their difference from the moral certitude of the Christians and slaves that serve as the films' ethical centers.[9]

Furthermore, the mid-century historical epic argues that the transgressive sexuality exhibited by the ancient Romans serves at least in part to explain the eventual fall of the empire. For films like *Quo Vadis*, the sexual corruption so conspicuously on display becomes the narrative explanation not just for the personal downfall of Nero and Poppaea, but also for why the empire itself, which appears to be at the apex of its political power, eventually collapsed. The morally upright Christians, these films suggest, represent the more hetero-productive, if somewhat plainer, future than that currently represented by the glittering, seductive, and erotically charged power of the Roman Empire. Again and again, the alleged golden age of Rome – marked by grand reconstructions of the city, the sartorial elegance of imperial figures such as Nero, and the brutal triumphalism of marching legions – is painted as rotten at its core, its political dominance slowly being eaten away by both its enslavement of other peoples and its indulgences, which become consistently wedded in the epic film imagination. *Spartacus*, for example, takes great pains to show how Crassus' ambitions to remake Rome in his own image exist in tandem with his desire to sexually dominate those around him, including the young slave Antoninus and Spartacus' wife Varinia.[10]

Rather than reading sexual perversion as merely an attempt to titillate contemporary audiences with the allure of the forbidden, Richard Armstrong is correct in arguing that sexuality and history remain intimately linked. He writes:

> It would be incorrect to assume that this "carnal knowledge" . . . invalidates historical understanding. For if consciousness is a feature of embodied subjects, *bodily egos* as Freud calls them, then sexuality is a genuine mode of understanding, even of historical understanding, due to its receptivity to the traces of human desire in the cultural archive.[11]

Though the perverse sexualities on display in a series like *Rome* may well be arousing, they also contain within them an acknowledgment that sex can and does influence the workings of history.

This understanding that sexuality remains intertwined with history was a claim that HBO, as a pay-cable network that combined the allure of explicit sex and violence with the badge of quality, was in a prime position to exploit. Situating *Rome* in its immediate cultural and industrial context allows for a more nuanced understanding of its rules of engagement with Roman antiquity. *Rome* was released in 2005, in the wake of other gritty, explicitly violent and sexual, yet prestigious drama series such as *Oz* (1997–2003), *The Sopranos* (1999–2007), and *The Wire* (2002–8). The first season of *Rome* coincided with another HBO series that took a revisionist approach to a well-established cinematic genre: *Deadwood* (2004–6), which combined the iconoclasm associated with revisionist Westerns of the post-New Hollywood with the genre conventions of the television Westerns of the 1950s and 1960s, producing a series that both worked within and broke with what viewers had come to expect of the genre.[12] Similarly, *Rome* challenged the conventions of the classic Hollywood epic – particularly the emphasis on the "great man" as an agent of historical change – while also drawing upon the soap-opera elements associated with a television drama such as *I, Claudius*.[13]

Rome's run also coincided with the resurgence of the epic within Hollywood cinema, inaugurated by the release of Ridley Scott's *Gladiator* (2000) and continuing with films such as *Troy* (2004), *Alexander* (2004), and *300* (2006). These newer films, like their predecessors in the mid-century cycle, continued to draw upon the idea that the ancient world was a playground for all manner of deviant sexualities, including the Orientalist fantasies on display in *Alexander* and *300*.[14] Furthermore, as Jerry Pierce has explained, the twenty-first-century resurgence of the genre also took as one of its primary thematic concerns the issue of masculinity, often juxtaposing powerful, hegemonic male heroes such as Maximus of *Gladiator* and Hector and Achilles of *Troy* with less straightforwardly masculine competitors, including Commodus and Paris.[15] Given the epic's interest in exploring the contours of masculinity, it comes as no surprise that *Rome*, as a self-conscious critique of that genre, should take an interest in Octavian's psychosexual development, particularly through his vexed relationships with the women in his life, with consequences for the series' vision of history.

FROM APRON STRINGS TO PUPPET STRINGS: OCTAVIAN AND WOMEN

Throughout *Rome*'s two seasons, Octavian's relationships with women remained marked by precisely the type of sexual deviance and strained power relations that have long been associated with the representation of ancient Rome in popular culture, further enabled by the HBO brand and its emphasis on boundary-pushing and the sexually risqué. Three women occupy central positions in Octavian's development from youth to man: his mother Atia, his sister Octavia, and, in the second season, his wife Livia. Throughout the first season, Octavian remains dominated by his mother, who simultaneously encourages him to become the man that she wants him to be and remains determined to keep him under her own control for use in furthering her political ambitions. It is thus worth noting that it is not until Octavian achieves victory on the battlefield in Season 2 that he is able to finally begin establishing his independence from Atia.

The first episode of the series sets up the fraught dynamic between mother and son during their introductory scene, in which Atia (Polly Walker) emerges languorously from her bath (see Figure 10.1). Illustrating Laura Mulvey's seminal observation that women within cinema are often rendered objects of visual spectacle and erotic contemplation, Atia halts the flow of narrative for several seconds as she exhibits her nudity for the camera's, and Octavian's, appreciation.[16] Given the way in which the camera weds its perspective to that of Octavian (Max Pirkis), the spectator becomes implicated in the deviance of this incestuous look, even as the scene also provides a means of condemning what has just occurred: for it gradually becomes apparent that this youth who has been looking at Atia and observing

Figure 10.1 The camera occupies the voyeuristic perspective of Octavian (Max Pirkis)as he gazes incestuously at his mother Atia (Polly Walker) in "The Stolen Eagle," Episode 1.1 of *Rome* (2005). HBO-BBC.

her nakedness is her son.[17] The relationship between mother and son is thus marked by a dangerous porousness, where the threat of incest seems to always lurk beneath the surface. Even at this early stage, the series makes clear that Octavian is at least partly driven by perverse desires: the result, it seems, of his mother's uncontrolled sexual impulses.[18]

According to Boyd, during *Rome*'s first season the lack of a suitable *paterfamilias* within the Julii family has led to both Octavian's vexed relationship with sexual activity and his lack of military and political control over his life, a situation that Atia does little to remedy.[19] Despite the fact that she frequently wants her son to behave in what she considers a more appropriately masculine manner – even going so far as to threaten to burn his books if he does not "penetrate" someone – Atia also utilizes him as a pawn in her political games. For example, in contradistinction to the sexual role appropriate for a Roman male citizen, she suggests that he should become his great-uncle Caesar's catamite if doing so will gain the family more political capital.[20] Her responsibility to either provide an appropriate male role model for her son (by, for example, marrying a respectable man) or inculcate the values appropriate to his class identity and his eventual role as *paterfamilias* remains subordinated to her own short-sighted political scheming. If her ambitions require Octavian to sacrifice his own fledgling normative masculinity, and thus his ability to act with political authority, that is a risk she proves more than willing to take.

The first season thus closely interweaves the political and the sexual. Atia's continued manipulation and mistreatment of both of her children leads, at least indirectly, to Octavia's incestuous seduction of her brother. Octavia (Kerry Condon) seeks out her brother due in part to her dysfunctional relationship with her mother; she also undertakes this ploy in an attempt to gain information for Atia's mortal enemy Servilia (Lindsay Duncan), who seeks to bring down Caesar, Atia, and the entire Julii clan. In undertaking this seduction, Octavia thus works directly against the interests of her own family, which could have consequences beyond the realm of the domestic. Octavia's weaponization of her sexuality remains an essential step in the closely interwoven set of plots and counterplots that eventually brings about Caesar's assassination and the concomitant dissolution of the Republic.

The siblings' responses to their dalliance reveals the extent to which Octavian has already mastered the ability to attain and maintain a dispassionate view on the world. While Octavia feels shame and revulsion, he responds with a cold, analytical attitude. The fits of wild emotion exhibited by others, his mother and Antony (James Purefoy) among them, do not inhibit him. This ability to detach himself from the world of the flesh – and the troubling emotions that follow – will allow Octavian to control the interpretation of such events more effectively, and eventually to establish dominance over Antony. He looks at the encounter with his sister as an experience, a means of understanding human nature; in his usual perceptive manner, he manages to discern why she has undertaken her seduction. Octavian thus reveals that he undertook this incestuous act of his own volition, not because he was manipulated by a woman.

Rome's first season, focused as it is on the Republic's decline and dissolution, follows the lead of the Roman historiographic tradition, especially the works of Tacitus, by suggesting that this process stems in part from the gendered deviance of its unruly women. The lack of a male figure to rein in Atia's excesses – Julius Caesar (Ciarán Hinds) seems unwilling to do so, and Antony is complicit in her sexual behavior – leads to a dangerous porousness in the boundaries that define the family. Though Atia responds with rage when she discovers that her children have engaged in incest, an act that endangers their political standing if news of it should emerge into the public sphere, her towering indignation reads as more than a little hypocritical, given that she has repeatedly engaged in illicit affairs with both slaves and nobles. She has thus failed in one of her primary duties: inculcating in her children socially appropriate understandings of sexual behavior.[21] This hypocrisy regarding sexuality will be echoed later in the series, when Octavian condemns gendered deviance as a type of vice, even while engaging in his own form of sexual perversion.

The beginning of the second season marks a significant shift in Octavian's relationship with the women in his life and in his relationship to his own gender identity, assisted by the change in casting after Octavian leaves for his education. Max Pirkis had imbued his characterization of the young Octavian with a faint note of spoiled and privileged petulance. Simon Woods, however, physiognomically marks the definitive transition from liminal, adolescent boyhood into full-fledged masculine adulthood. This older, sterner Octavian wastes no time in establishing control over the domestic sphere. While the first season consistently emphasized Atia's attempts to control her children, their home, and their political fortunes – often by resorting to both physical and emotional intimidation to achieve her ends – the second shows Octavian at last bringing his mother's disruptive and often destructive behavior under tighter regulation: a forecast of the control that he will exercise in his efforts to reinstate the "golden age" at Rome.

At the beginning of the second season, Atia seems to believe that she can still dominate her son, as she attempts to force Octavian to accept both her demands and those of her consort Antony. In Episode 2.5 ("Heroes of the Republic"), however, after Antony's ignominious defeat at Mutina and Octavian's rise to dominance, she recognizes that his political star is now in the ascendant and pleads with him to forgive her these transgressions. He coldly agrees to do so. However, the close-up on Atia's face, with its cunning, knowing smile, suggests that Octavian has not asserted nearly as much control as he would like to think. While Atia continues to emotionally manipulate her son, her posture of submission represents an intermediate stage of qualified success, cultivating at least the appearance of successful domination on Octavian's part and setting the stage for the further incidents of gendered ambiguity that will emerge in his relationship with his wife, Livia.[22]

Later, in Episode 2.8 ("A Necessary Fiction"), Octavian seeks to exert his gendered control over Roman society as a whole, but his attempts remain undercut by even his closest associates. On the one hand, he offers an "inspirational" history lesson to an audience of Roman women about the values that their predecessors have brought to the state, including their virtuous behavior, their civilizing influence upon men, and the fact that they provide stability at home so that Roman men can go out and conquer. On the other, the subsequent sarcastic comments of his friend Maecenas (Alex Wyndham), combined with the fact that Atia is at that moment copulating with Antony, and his sister is committing adultery with his general Agrippa (Allen Leech), ironize Octavian's statements. However, he soon exerts the same control over the domestic sphere that he commands on the public stage by demanding that his sister cease her illicit relationship with Agrippa. The collective bodies of women, both within his family and without, now provide him the means of attaining the control that he has been systematically denied throughout the preceding episodes. He has, at last, begun to take up his morally regulatory position of *paterfamilias*, both in his own family and in the Roman state that he will soon begin to shape according to his own vision.[23]

Episode 2.8 is also the one in which Octavian at last decides that he should find a wife, and ultimately settles on Livia (Alice Henley). Upon deciding that he will claim her, he demands that she divorce her current husband, a command that she eagerly obeys. At first, it seems that the young politician will at last be able to exert a measure of control over his sexual and gendered life, which he struggled to achieve over his mother and sister. However, the narrative juxtaposition of his assertion of control over his mother with his marriage suggests a "negative echo of the traditional Roman *manus* marriage," so that the control his mother once possessed over him has now passed into the hands of Livia.[24]

While Livia appears to be as meek and submissive as Atia is domineering and possessive, and she seems to offer Octavian the opportunity to control at once his political and his personal destiny, appearances are deceiving. Octavian might have established a modicum of control over his mother and sister, but the same does not ultimately hold true of his relationship with Livia. In one of the second season's more sexually provocative scenes, in Episode 2.9 ("Deus Impeditio Esuritori Nullus") Livia and Octavian engage in sadomasochistic sexual play that ultimately leaves him gasping and literally speechless (see Figure 10.2). This sexual play not only invests Livia with the position of power – she follows up her choking and slapping session with a list of political and domestic accomplishments they need to attain – but also stands in marked contrast to the public image that Octavian has sought to cultivate.

Indeed, this reversal of power even contradicts his own statement to Livia upon claiming her as his potential bride. He told her that he would sometimes strike her with his hand or a whip as a means of providing himself pleasure, to which she responded with a seemingly demure "yes, sir." The power positions here are ambiguous at

Figure 10.2 Octavian (Simon Woods) is rendered literally speechless during sex play with his secretly dominating wife Livia (Alice Henley) in "Deus Impeditio Esuritori Nullus," Episode 2.9 of *Rome* (2007). HBO-BBC.

best, for in previous encounters in the series, slapping has served as a means by which men reassert their authority over women, as when Caesar strikes Servilia in Episode 1.5 ("The Ram Has Touched The Wall").[25] The fact that Octavian remains largely the passive partner in this exchange with his wife suggests that he is not a practitioner of the traditional gender norms that he promotes to the broader Roman society. This encounter with Livia creates an ongoing tension between Octavian's clear need for the surrender and near-oblivion enabled by this particular form of sexuality, and his relentless desire to control every other aspect of his life, including his family and the state at large.

FROM THE PRIVATE SPHERE TO THE PUBLIC SPHERE: OCTAVIAN AND THE MASTERY OF ANTONY

Octavian's relationship with men, particularly Antony, is marked less by explicitly sexual dysfunction than by a gendered conflict that eventually radiates outward into the military and political realms. Episode 2.2, "Son of Hades," reveals the extent to which Antony seeks to occupy the de facto position of *paterfamilias* of the Julii, now that Caesar has been assassinated. When Octavian decides to give money to the plebs in order to buy their loyalty, both Atia and Antony respond with rage at this gesture, an indication of Octavian's growing independence; their emotionally overwrought reactions stand in clear juxtaposition to his coldly rational approach to politics. As with his response to his incestuous encounter with his sister, Octavian's intellectual abilities, made manifest through his cold, logical reasoning, allow him to distance himself from the emotions of a fraught situation and focus on the political consequences. It is precisely this analytical ability to examine the world around him, detached from bodily passions, that allows him to attain both military and political superiority over Antony and independence from his mother, which are key to his ability to claim control of the empire for himself.

One of the primary narrative arcs of the second season involves Octavian's recognition that he will need not only to establish command over his own family and to claim his place as its head by expelling Antony from Atia's bed, but also to beat him on the battlefield, which he does at the Battle of Mutina. The introduction of Simon Woods as the new, more adult Octavian occurs in the aftermath of this battle, and his portrayal in this episode (Episode 2.4, "Testudo et Lepus") highlights the extent to which he has at last emerged from his adolescence, in which he was dominated by his mother Atia, into full-fledged adulthood. As Boyd observes, "Octavian is reintroduced to the stage of Roman history no longer as a mama's boy or pleb's pupil, but as victor in the first of what would prove to be many conquests over a long career." Visually, his newly acquired superiority is heightened by the way in which he is positioned as looming over a kneeling Pullo in a low-angle shot.[26] The casting of an older actor, paired with his burgeoning military superiority on the battlefield, sets the stage for Octavian's gradual divorcement from his mother's influence and Antony's dominance. This personal and psychological development mirrors, and sets in motion, the far-reaching social and political changes through which the Empire emerges from the obsolescent Republic.

If Octavian's problematic relations with his own gendered identity remain largely confined to the shadows of the bedroom, those of Antony become increasingly public. Antony's dalliance with Cleopatra (Lyndsey Marshall) results in his increasingly "unmasculine" behavior, marked by adopting Egyptian dress, painting his eyes with make-up, and falling into a drug-induced stupor.[27] Octavian utilizes Antony's choices to his advantage in his bid to establish his own political hegemony by maligning Antony's manhood and thus his fitness for political authority. Throughout the second season, Octavian continues to assert his dominance over his erstwhile father-figure as the two men battle for control over the political and financial legacy left by Caesar, himself a father-figure for both Antony and Octavian. However, matters continue to favor Octavian, whose ruthlessness and emotionally dispassionate demeanor have enabled his political success. The second season suggests that only through the convoluted act of repression and transferal of desire, from mother to wife, from jealousy of the father-figure to control of the self, is Octavian able to attain his political success and usher in a new order. The stability of the state relies on the new ruler's ability to bring his own desires into line – even if, as has already been made clear, that appearance of control is built on a series of lies. Antony's great mistake is that he cannot recognize the fact that reliance upon brute strength and transparent emotion has no place in this newly forming political world.

READING SEX AS HISTORY: *ROME* AND THE HISTORICO-SEXUAL UNCONSCIOUS

Beyond mere titillation, the close intertwining of the sexual, the domestic, and the political is part of *Rome*'s understanding of how history works. As both Andrew B. R. Elliott and Christopher Lockett have observed, *Rome*'s emphasis on those historical actants typically elided from the epic, such as women, slaves, and plebs, poses a challenge to the "great man" theory of history.[28] These arguments shed light on the way in which *Rome*, in its critique of the traditional historiographic construct, also opens up alternative models of historical understanding. As the first season progresses, Octavia's successful seduction of her brother ultimately bears fruit, leading to Caesar's death and the subsequent political crisis. History does not simply flow of its own accord; sexual desire, when not properly contained and channeled, can initiate political and social chaos, leading to the fall of one system of political organization and the beginning of another. The first season of *Rome*, therefore, imagines the workings of history as following along the lines of sexual pathology. If the great families of Rome stand as the diseased and corrupt heart of the Republic, their actions – petty, selfish, and self-interested as they might be in origin and in execution – nevertheless have far-reaching consequences that radically destabilize the existing political and social order.

The second season, on the other hand, proposes that the characters must reform their behaviors in order to maintain the newfound stability of Augustan Rome. Since the political and the sexual/personal mirror the fall of the Republic and its rebirth into the alleged new "golden age" of the reign of Augustus, the younger generation must disavow, at least in their public lives, the sexual and gendered excesses that brought down their predecessors. The new historical actors that have emerged – including Octavian, Octavia, Agrippa, and Livia – exist uneasily in the shadow of the older rulers that preceded them. While their personal lives may be just as riddled with sexual hypocrisy and dysfunction as those of their progenitors, they have become more adept at concealing them. They still exist, of course, but they remain hidden away from public view.

Although Octavian emerges triumphant, the series cannot resist imbuing even his moment of greatest victory with layers of ambiguity and unease. Thus, the last scenes of the final episode highlight yet another way in which *Rome* challenges the myth of the golden age that has already begun to take shape under the Augustan regime. The scene in which the reconstituted Julii take their seats at the triumph celebrating Octavian's victory over Antony and Cleopatra is permeated by a profound sense of unease: Atia realizes that she has been displaced by Livia, and Octavian begins to reconfigure the past in his own image, painting himself as the restorer of Roman morals and Antony as his debauched enemy. These last moments signify the end of Atia's romantic hopes for Antony, even as they mark her vicarious political and personal victory, now that her son has at last achieved political dominance. As Octavia reminds her, she is now the mother to the *princeps*, or First Citizen.[29] This triumph, like Caesar's in the first season, is layered with ambivalence, for *Rome* has already revealed Octavian's carefully crafted public morality to be nothing more than a sham, a flimsy façade overlaying his own propensity for gendered sexual deviance.

What emerges from the two seasons of *Rome* is an engagement with the late Roman Republic, a pivotal point in the development of Western history, that highlights the moral ambiguity, psychosexual complexities, and gendered violence that, in the series' view, characterize moments of tremendous historical shifts in political and social organization. Just as the death of Caesar sparked the political instability of the second season, so Octavian's rise to power ushers in a new period, one characterized not by bloodshed on the battlefield, but rather by shrewder manipulation in the confines of the bedroom. Unlike Atia's desire, which radiated outward to cause political chaos, Octavian's remains focused inward, on repression rather than outward expression. The depiction of Octavian over two seasons as just as sexually deviant and flawed as the other characters indicates a complex knot of intertwined cultural ambivalences about sexuality and the "great man" theory of history: a portrait of the hypocrisy and political cunning that lurks beneath his mask as the protector of Roman moral virtues and founder of this "golden age" of the West.[30]

CONCLUSION

In revealing the base metal of moral hypocrisy beneath the alleged golden age of Augustus and its re-establishment of lapsed morality, *Rome* attempts to control what historian Theofilo F. Ruiz has termed "the terror of history": the sense that the past is a world of savagery and barbarity and that the process of history itself entails violence.[31] In drawing upon the psychosexual to paint this portrait of the shift from republican chaos to "golden" imperial stability, the series ultimately evokes the very dangers it seeks to repress. The darker forces of the psyche, embodied in Octavian/Augustus' fraught psychology, undercut the very stability that the series' narrative seems to have provided. Although the unruly and destructive id of the Republic – made so manifestly visible by Atia and Antony – has been tamed and repressed by Augustus' domineering superego, it always threatens to erupt and disturb the fragile stability of the golden age.

NOTES

1 Boyd (2015: 74).
2 Rosenstone (2006: 182).
3 Toher (2015: 225–37).
4 Reinhold (1980: 36–50).
5 Severy (2003: 38).
6 Wallace-Hadrill (1982: 26). For a further discussion of Horace, Livy, and Vergil, see Levick (2010: 251–87).
7 McCullough (2015: 134).
8 Levick (2010: 202–50), in which she discusses Augustus' self-fashioning.
9 Cyrino (2014: 619): "in *Spartacus* the scope of 'normal' sexuality is defined by the titular hero, the life-affirming and heteronormative father figure, the rebel slave, Spartacus, against the death-obsessed, family-less, and sexually 'deviant' elite Roman Crassus." See also Hark (1993).
10 Hark (1993: 166–7).
11 Armstrong (2006: 18).
12 Hark (2012: 5–15).
13 Lockett (2010: 104): "The series nevertheless offers, simultaneously, a counternarrative not just to the generic conventions of the 'toga movie,' but the historical epic more generally. The series works consistently

toward subtle dislocations of unitary and monolithic power and historical agency, traditionally located within *individuals* such as Caesar."

14 Lauwers, Dhont, and Huybrecht (2012: 84).

15 Pierce (2011: 27).

16 Mulvey (1975: 7).

17 Fitzgerald (2001) has suggested that films that take the ancient world as their subject typically offer spectators the opportunity to indulge in the illicit pleasures enjoyed by their Roman narrative surrogates, even as they also offer the opportunity to dissociate themselves from those pleasures by identifying with the more virtuous, if less exciting, Christian heroes.

18 Boyd (2008: 93–5).

19 Boyd (2008: 93–5).

20 Walters (1997: 30–2).

21 Strong (2008: 228).

22 McCullough (2015: 135).

23 Augoustakis (2015: 120). Augoustakis goes on to argue that "it is Atia who has to change, in order to conform to Octavian's new character; and her submission seems to reflect that of the women of Rome."

24 McCullough (2015: 135).

25 McCullough (2015: 135).

26 Boyd (2015: 75–6).

27 Kelly (2015: 179).

28 Elliott (2013: 584). Elliott suggests that "even the great nation-builders are reliant on chance and vicissitude . . . *Rome*'s history emerges as something that can only be ridden; it is an accident that explains how we got from then to now, rather than a carefully planned teleology designed and executed by great men forging a nation." Cf. Lockett (2010: 111).

29 Augoustakis (2015: 126) and Harrison (2015: 166).

30 Lockett (2010: 111). Lockett argues that *Rome* successfully moves historical agency and causality from the public to the personal. In regard to Brutus and his decision to join the plot to assassinate Caesar: "the assumption of his individual agency . . . becomes second to historically marginalized and indeed historically invisible actants – namely, women, plebs, and slaves, whose own actions and agency in *Rome* render the Great Men helpless to history's accidental progression." His comments relate equally well to Octavian/Augustus.

31 Ruiz (2011: 16). He suggests that "suspecting or knowing that there is probably no meaning or order in the universe, we combat this dark perspective by continuously making meaning, by imposing order on our chaotic and savage past, by constructing explanatory schemes that seek to justify and elucidate what is essentially inexplicable. These half-hearted attempts to explain the inexplicable and to make sense of human cruelty are what we call 'history.'"

11 The Dux Femina *Ends Westeros' Golden Age: Cersei Lannister as Agrippina the Younger in HBO's* Game of Thrones *(2011–)*

Meredith D. Prince

HBO's highly acclaimed and successful fantasy series *Game of Thrones* (2011–), based on George R. R. Martin's book series *A Song of Ice and Fire*, repeatedly reminds the viewer and characters that winter is coming. This event is correlated with the decline of morality, disintegrating order, and renewed conflict over the Iron Throne. In this shift from the golden age of summer to the iron age of winter, destruction and death await everyone. Fans and scholars alike have noted several historical models, especially from English history, for the various characters fighting, killing, and scheming to gain power through the Iron Throne. However, Martin's acknowledgment of his own "morbid fascination with ancient Rome, especially the late Republic and early Empire" suggests an ancient model.[1]

Rome's first emperor, Augustus, famously presided over a "golden age," but his dynasty ended two generations later with the reign of Nero, the last Julio-Claudian emperor. The moralizing discourse of Roman historiography, exemplified by the Roman historian Tacitus, associates the improper sexual behavior and power of the women of the imperial family with men's weakness, loss of autonomy, and the empire's corruption and decline. While medieval queens, including Margaret of Anjou and Isabella of France, may have influenced the characterization of Cersei Lannister (Lena Headey),[2] the wife of one king, mother of another, and only daughter of one of the most powerful and wealthy men in the Seven Kingdoms, Tacitus' literary construct of Agrippina the Younger, the sister of one emperor, wife of another, and mother to a third, offers a relevant and plausible framework for viewing Westeros' changing and declining fortunes. Compared to the medieval queens, parallels between Cersei and Agrippina are more numerous, specific, and striking, and resonate with Martin's passion for, and likely use of, imperial Rome to highlight the downfall of Rome's fictional descendants.[3]

Agrippina the Younger (12–59 CE), daughter of the successful and popular general Germanicus and of Augustus' granddaughter Agrippina the Elder, was closely connected to three successive Roman emperors of the Julio-Claudian dynasty: her brother Caligula (ruled 37–41 CE), her uncle/husband Claudius (ruled 41–54 CE), and her son Nero (ruled 54–68 CE).[4] The ancient sources, notably the second-century CE historian Tacitus and imperial biographer Suetonius, and the third-century CE Greek historian Dio Cassius, are universally hostile to Agrippina and Nero and obsessed with the horror and immorality of overly ambitious and sexual women. These authors portray her, in Judith Ginsburg's summary, "as the consummate schemer, lusting after power, manipulating men and women to her ends, and, when thwarted, retaliating with calculated ruthlessness."[5] Tacitus represents Agrippina as the quintessential *dux femina*, or "commander woman," "her every action . . . motivated by an unscrupulous desire to secure power for herself through her husband and her son, a woman prepared to use any and every means to obtain [power]."[6] This stereotype associates the Julio-Claudian women's "unnatural" power-grabbing with the dynasty's decline.[7] Agrippina personally instigated the worst-case scenario: promoting Nero as emperor, which led to the end of a dynasty and eventually to civil war.[8]

Cersei's actions in Season 1 parallel Agrippina's as the wife of the emperor Claudius in her attempts to influence her husband King Robert (Mark Addy) and through her schemes and efforts, including murder, to ensure that her son Joffrey (Jack Gleeson) succeeds to the throne. In Season 2, as mother of the new ruler, Cersei resembles Agrippina upon Nero's ascent to power, including attempts to display seemingly superior political and military knowledge and to control an increasingly sadistic teenage ruler. In Season 3, jealousy and rivalry with Margaery Tyrell (Natalie Dormer) for female influence in Joffrey's life initiate Cersei's downfall, much as Nero's paramours Acte and especially Poppaea contributed to Agrippina's. The breakdown of morality and increase in "feminine" lust for "masculine" power that Tacitus identifies as bringing ruin to ancient Rome do the same for Martin's fictional Westeros.

THE *DUX FEMINA*, HER HUSBAND, AND HER LOVERS

The *dux femina*'s "unnatural" masculine desire for power is framed by the cultural impossibility of a woman holding political power in her own right within Rome's patriarchal society. Agrippina could never become ruler; she could only exercise her will through men whom she could control. Agrippina reputedly dominated her husband Claudius and attempted to act as co-ruler. After their marriage, Tacitus notes how state affairs changed, as "all were subject to a woman," and that it was "a strict and almost masculine despotism." He continues, "Publicly, there was severity and more often arrogance; nothing immodest was done at home unless it achieved supremacy. Her huge desire for gold had the pretext that it was acquired as support for power" (*Ann.* 12.7).[9] The later imperial biographer Suetonius further highlights the power that Claudius' wives exerted over him, as he administered the empire more according to their wishes than his own judgment (*Claud.* 25).

Cersei's arrogance and masculine despotism over her husband, King Robert, as well as their tense relationship, are revealed within the first episodes of the series.[10] When her son Joffrey instigates a conflict with Ned Stark's daughter Arya (Maisie Williams) and gets bitten by her protective pet dire-wolf (Episode 1.2, "The Kingsroad"), Cersei orders that Arya be brought to Robert for punishment, instead of to her own father, who questions Cersei's orders. Although Robert yells at Cersei for speaking before he can respond, she repeats the cowardly bully Joffrey's lies about what happened and speaks more than Robert. When Robert decides that he and Ned (Sean Bean) will "discipline" their respective children, Cersei shifts tactics and subtly pressures him until Joffrey is absolved and blood exacted from the Starks via the execution of a family dire-wolf. Robert acquiesces, "As you will." Ned's disbelieving question to his close friend, "Is this your command?" emphasizes Cersei's unseemly control over her husband, the king.

Cersei again clashes with Ned in front of Robert, but with greater stakes, after Ned's wife Catelyn (Michelle Fairley) seizes Cersei's younger brother Tyrion (Peter Dinklage) on suspicion of murder, leading to Ned's swordfight with Cersei's twin brother Jaime (Nikolaj Coster-Waldau) in Episode 1.6 ("A Golden Crown"). Cersei again speaks first, issuing her demands to an injured Ned. Robert interrupts their argument by yelling, "Quiet, woman!" yet she questions whether he is properly handling her brothers' situation. When he again tells her "Hold your tongue," she retorts, "I should wear the armor and you the gown," making explicit the inversion of gender roles and how Cersei's behavior has emasculated him. Robert responds by slapping her. Although Robert, like Claudius, prefers to spend his time drinking, womanizing, and letting his Small Council administer the kingdom's business, he briefly reasserts himself as a man – but in an undignified manner for which he later expresses regret to Ned, not Cersei.[11]

Beyond direct self-assertion, sex was another means by which a *dux femina* might gain control, either outside of marriage or within the family, as the moral obligation of marital chastity did not prevent such a woman from using her sexuality to further her ambitions. Tacitus regards Agrippina's sexual proclivities as a way to obtain and retain power, including sexual relationships with Marcus Aurelius Lepidus, Claudius' freedman Pallas, and finally Claudius, at which point she was "experienced in every disgrace" (*Ann.* 14.2). In contrast to other imperial women who had been notorious for adultery or prostitution, such as Augustus' daughter Julia or Claudius' previous wife Messalina, Agrippina's incest is stressed over her adultery and signals "her destructive effect on the Roman state."[12] Agrippina was reputed to have committed incest with her brother Caligula, and her marriage to her uncle Claudius was also incestuous until the Senate passed a law allowing it.[13] Tacitus even considered the possibility that Agrippina attempted to commit incest with Nero, her son by her first husband (*Ann.* 14.2).

Like Agrippina, Cersei too commits adultery, which signals her failure as a wife and undermines her husband's ability to rule his family and, by extension, the realm itself.[14] The incestuous facet of her extramarital affairs is also central to her characterization. In Cersei's first scene of the series (Episode 1.1, "Winter is Coming") she converses intimately and anxiously with her twin brother Jaime about whether Jon Arynn, the recently deceased King's Hand, has "told someone." By the end of the episode, when Jaime pushes young Bran Stark (Isaac Hempstead Wright) out a tower window after he accidentally discovers them *in flagrante delicto*, Cersei's secret has been revealed: she is guilty of not only adultery, but also incest.[15] Although Cersei does not commit incest for power, she recognizes her greater susceptibility to blame because of it, preferring to repeatedly justify it to herself and others as adultery. This focus on incest aligns her particularly closely with Agrippina, whose incest with Caligula supposedly happened in their youth, when Cersei and Jaime's relationship also began.

Although a *dux femina* may desire to rule as a man would, her gender allows her only to extend her power past her husband's reign by promoting her son's loyalty and ensuring his succession. Although Nero was known not to be Claudius' son, Agrippina's marriage to her uncle positioned Nero as his heir, and she eagerly desired that Claudius choose Nero over his biological son Britannicus. Nero's adoption by Claudius and marriage to Claudius' daughter Octavia helped to secure his position. Yet Agrippina panicked and turned to murder when a drunken Claudius remarked that he was destined to marry unchaste but unpunished women (*Claudius* 43) and the freedman Narcissus promoted Britannicus as the heir (*Ann.* 12.64). Even without a secret paternity to hide, Agrippina worked fervently to thwart opposition to her son's succession.

By contrast, Cersei's three children, including the heir apparent, Joffrey, were supposedly fathered by her husband Robert – but all resulted from Cersei's incest with Jaime. Joffrey's paternity complicates issues of power and ruling, and his succession, due to his violent and rash nature, threatens the kingdom. John Arynn was killed for having discovered that Joffrey was the product of incest and not the rightful heir. Cersei schemes to further preserve her secret of Joffrey's illegitimacy by eliminating anyone who knows, or may know, of it. When Ned discovers the truth, he warns Cersei that, when Robert returns from hunting, he will reveal that all her children are Jaime's (Episode 1.7, "You Win or You Die"). But Cersei is already a step ahead, having employed adulterous incest to remove another threat to her ambitions for Joffrey: Robert himself, who returns from the hunt gored by a boar because of "too much wine," he claims. The squire who provided that wine is Cersei's cousin, Lancel Lannister (Eugene Simon), with whom she is revealed to be having an affair. Cersei's involvement in her husband's death is thus implied, through either having the wine doctored or having her lover ply Robert with an excess.

The series, which streamlines Cersei's numerous adulterous relationships in Martin's books into this other incestuous relationship, emphasizes this aspect of her sexuality and its destructive consequences.[16] The importance of the wine in Robert's fatal wounding also recalls Agrippina's poisoning of Claudius. When poisoned mushrooms failed, Claudius' doctor administered poison on a feather put down his throat (*Ann.* 12.65–7).[17] While both women rely on the knowledge or aid of another, each masterminds her husband's fatal poisoning and ensures it is carried out. When the courtier Varys (Conleth Hill) advises Ned to bend to Cersei's will, the king's upright friend exclaims "You want me to serve the woman who murdered my king?" (Episode 1.9, "Baelor"). Although Cersei may not literally have killed Robert, Ned reasonably believes that she was responsible.

Just as Agrippina maintained Nero's status as heir over Britannicus by eliminating threats to her son's claims, Cersei preserves the secret that would disbar Joffrey (and her) from ruling by not only eliminating her husband, but also imprisoning his loyal friend Ned Stark.[18] To ensure succession, the dying Robert had dictated his will to Ned, naming Ned as Lord Regent and Protector of the Realm until "my son Joffrey" – replaced by Ned with "my rightful heir" – should come of age (Episode 1.7). But Ned learns of Robert's death only after Joffrey already has ascended the throne. When Ned challenges Joffrey's claim, Cersei rips up Robert's document, much as Agrippina smoothed over the transition to Nero's rule by delaying the announcement of Claudius' death and ensuring that his will remained unread, in case he ultimately preferred his own son over Nero (*Ann.* 12.69). Cersei thus reflects Agrippina's political and sexual relationship with Claudius, her efforts to put Nero on the throne, and her rumored involvement with murdering her husband.

DUX FEMINA AS MOTHER TO THE MONSTROUS BOY-KING

While the ambitious Cersei holds sway, politically and domestically, over the cuckolded Robert in Season 1, as mother of the heir Cersei dotes on and overshadows her teenage son, whom the series has aged from the books to almost seventeen, the same age as Nero when he became emperor.[19] Agrippina, too, continued to exert her power as much as possible early in Nero's reign, transferring her energies from husband to son. Tacitus, however, comments that the Romans questioned how a mere seventeen-year-old, "who was ruled by a woman," could handle the external threat of Rome's inveterate enemies the Parthians (*Ann.* 13.6). Agrippina's role here is viewed suspiciously, and so is Cersei's.

While tending to the wound inflicted by Arya Stark's dire-wolf, Cersei advises Joffrey that, when he is king, "The truth will be what you make it . . . you are my darling boy, and the world will be exactly as you want it to be" (Episode 1.3, "Lord Snow"; see Figure 11.1). She also attempts to instruct him, usurping her husband's paternal role. Channeling her own father, the brilliant but ruthless general Tywin Lannister (Charles Dance), Cersei questions and corrects Joffrey on political and military matters. As Robert later notes, "You move

Figure 11.1 Cersei (Lena Headey) instructs Joffrey (Jack Gleeson) how to rule in "Lord Snow," Episode 1.3 of *Game of Thrones* (2011). HBO.

your lips and your father's voice comes out" (Episode 1.5, "The Wolf and the Lion"). Cersei's attempt to imitate her father in tutoring her son in masculine pursuits underscores the gendered deviance of the *dux femina*. Cersei displays superior knowledge to the inexperienced Joffrey and attempts to rule over him as she does her husband. But, as Robert questions and corrects her assumptions, the deficiencies in her knowledge and guidance become apparent, warning of flaws in Joffrey's eventual rule.

Cersei's influence grows when Joffrey becomes king. She speaks before and more than her son in public, and quickly discharges the veteran Lord Commander of the Guard to make way for Jaime. When Tywin informs his other son that Joffrey now rules, Tyrion remarks, "My sister rules, you mean" (Episode 1.8, "The Pointy End"). Cersei attempts to compel Ned Stark to renounce his regency and swear his loyalty to Joffrey publicly. So too Agrippina's removal of Marcus Junius Silanus marked the beginning of Nero's reign, since gossip reported that "the man, of mature age, guiltless, high-born, and from the descendants of the Caesars, should be preferred to Nero, who scarcely had left behind his childhood and obtained power through a crime" (*Ann.* 13.1). Both Agrippina and Cersei fiercely protect their own positions of power by immediately removing any threats to their sons ruling. But Joffrey's rash tendency to do what he wants regardless of consequences, most evident when he impetuously orders Ned Stark's execution, reveals Cersei's inability to control the monster that she has created. Cersei's failure to prevent or curb her son's behavior, or even to acknowledge it, impacts numerous individuals in King's Landing and plunges the kingdom into war.

Cersei continues to rule as regent in Season 2, meeting threats from outside and within. She participates in the Small Council's deliberations about the war refugees created by the rebellion of Ned's son Robb (Richard Madden) in Episode 2.1 ("The North Remembers") and refuses Robb's terms by ripping them up (Episode 2.2, "The Night Lands"). She strategizes with Tyrion as the fleet of her brother-in-law Stannis Baratheon (Stephen Dillane) approaches to lay his own claim to the Iron Throne. To her suggestion, "Rain fire from above," Tyrion responds, "You're quoting Father, aren't you?" (Episode 2.7, "A Man Without Honor"), but he implies that she is no substitute for their absent and more capable father, evident in her dismissal of others' suggestions and her anger and frustration when her plans do not work out. Meanwhile, she protects her interests and fights against those who threaten to expose the illegitimacy of Joffrey's rule and her own crimes. When inveterate schemer Petyr "Littlefinger" Baelish (Aiden Gillen) attempts to blackmail her by mentioning the affections of brothers and sisters, Cersei has him seized on the spot by her King's Guard and orders that he be killed – but then just as quickly changes her order, to demonstrate that "power is power," not "knowledge" (Episode 2.1).

Cersei desires power but she also needs to rule since Joffrey, like Nero, entrusts public and private business to his mother (*Nero* 9). Instead of taking interest in serious state matters, the inexperienced king delights in malicious behavior. When Joffrey hears of a local bard's bawdy song about his mother's emasculating treatment of his (supposed) father, he orders the bard's tongue cut out before an audience in the throne room and then leaves, stating, "I'm done for the day. I leave the rest of the matters to you, Mother" (Episode 1.10, "Fire and Blood"). On his name-day, Joffrey has men killed for entertainment and sport, while Cersei deals with the problems of running the kingdom – some of which have been exacerbated by having to manage the war that has resulted from Joffrey's actions and his ascension to the throne (Episode 2.1).

Joffrey's character clearly resonates with Roman historiography's depiction of Nero. Suetonius notes, "He practiced wantonness, lust, extravagance, greed, cruelty, at first gradually and secretly and as if from youthful misdirection, but then no one, moreover, doubted that those were the faults of his character, not of his age" (*Nero* 26). He further comments, "No distinction or limit was applied to killing whomever it was pleasing to, and for whatever reason ... He said that none of the emperors had known what they could do" (*Nero* 37). Joffrey's betrothed Sansa (Sophie Turner), Ned Stark's eldest daughter, is a particular victim of his torture; his behavior toward her parallels Nero's treatment of his wife and stepsister Octavia, especially toward the end of her life.[20] Joffrey tells Sansa that he has something to show her – her father's head, among those of other executed Stark loyalists – and reveals his plans to nevertheless impregnate her (Episode 1.10). After aiming his crossbow at Sansa and having her beaten as a message to her rebellious brother Robb, Joffrey is momentarily put in his place by his uncle Tyrion (Episode 2.4, "Garden of Bones"). Yet Joffrey reinforces his position by announcing, "The king can do as he likes."

Nero's advisers Burrus and Seneca worked together to curb his well-known cruelty: "so that more easily they might check the emperor's dangerous age, if he were to reject virtue, with permitted pleasures. Both had the same struggle against the fierceness of Agrippina" (*Ann.* 13.2). Cersei likewise has little but contempt for the philosophical Tyrion and his mercenary Bronn (Jerome Flynn), who attempt to channel Joffrey's idleness and cruelty by arranging a visit from several prostitutes as his name-day present (Episode 2.4). As Bronn says, "He's got nothing to do all day but pick wings off flies. Couldn't hurt to get some of the poison out." Joffrey, however, prefers to watch the women touch each other, then for one to slap the other; when he learns that his uncle has provided them, Joffrey makes one prostitute beat the other with escalating violence. When the rabble in King's Landing throw cow patties at Joffrey's carriage, he demands that everyone be killed (Episode 2.6, "The Old Gods and the New"). Tyrion slaps Joffrey, describing him as "a vicious idiot king," and manages temporarily to restrain him. But no one can save Joffrey, or the kingdom, from this cruelty.

Even the formidable Tywin Lannister's attempts to rein in Joffrey's sadism fail. When Joffrey and Tywin discuss matters of the kingdom in Season 3, Joffrey again shows that he is inept and unwilling to participate, yet easily offended when not consulted (Episode 3.7, "The Bear and the Maiden Fair"). During a Small Council meeting, Tyrion attempts to demean Joffrey's giddiness about the recent murders of Catelyn and Robb Stark by asking "Kill a few puppies today?" (Episode 3.10, "Mhysa"). Joffrey wants to serve her brother's head to Sansa; Cersei claims he is joking, but Joffrey insists "Everyone is mine to torment . . . I am the king." Tywin, whose military leadership and timely arrival saved King's Landing from Stannis Baratheon's attack, challenges him and notes to Tyrion, after Joffrey has threatened everyone and been led away by his mother, "You really think a crown gives you power?"

Despite these masculine interventions, Joffrey inclines to listen to his mother and even hide behind her, literally, when it suits his purposes. When Sansa talks back to Joffrey, he has the guard hit her because "my mother tells me a king should never strike his lady" and refuses to let Sansa return home since "Mother says I'm still to marry you" (Episode 1.10). Since Cersei "insists on keeping her alive," Sansa is merely beaten (Episode 2.4). He feigns reluctance in throwing over Sansa for Margaery Tyrell, but allows Cersei to pave the way for him to rescind his vow by emphasizing Sansa's traitorous family (Episode 2.10, "Valar Morghulis"). A swaggering Joffrey initially plans on fighting against Stannis' forces in the battle of Blackwater, and Tyrion agrees that Joffrey needs to be there, not "hiding behind his mother's skirts." But Cersei believes "his place is not on the battlefield" (Episode 2.8, "The Prince of Winterfell"), and Joffrey readily responds to her summons to safety when the battle seems to be going badly, even if it means destroying his soldiers' morale (Episode 2.9, "Blackwater"). Although his agreement with his mother is often a way of saving face or of justifying a course of action, Joffrey's frequent resort to "my mother said" demonstrates that she has exercised some influence over him.

Yet Joffrey can just as readily turn on her. He attempts to establish his authority by questioning Cersei about Robert's bastards and his "losing interest" in her (Episode 2.1).[21] After Cersei slaps him, he chillingly reminds her that such an action "is punishable by death. You will never do it again. Never." When Tyrion tells Cersei that Joffrey "needs to start acting like a king" (Episode 2.7), she claims she has tried, but "he doesn't listen to me." Tyrion notes, "It's hard to put a leash on a dog once you've put a crown on its head." Cersei briefly admits Joffrey's cruelty and speculates that his behavior is "the price for what we've done – for our sins."

Nero was at his best as emperor in the early years of his reign, when Agrippina was fairly successful in restraining him. The full extent of his cruelty emerged after her death, when he finally believed that he could do whatever he wanted with impunity and "he abandoned himself to all desires which, although poorly repressed, respect of whatever sort for his mother had hindered" (*Ann.* 14.13).[22] Joffrey, however, proves from the outset to be not much of a king and less of a warrior. His uncle Tyrion does not believe he belongs on the throne, and his grandfather Tywin criticizes his actions.[23] Joffrey is not only incompetent and naïve, but cowardly, cocky, entitled, and excessively cruel, and prefers to meet problems with whimpers and threats. Joffrey thus also resembles Agrippina's brother Caligula, who, even before becoming emperor, Suetonius claims was unable "to restrain his cruel and shameful nature; indeed, he most eagerly attended tortures and executions" (*Gaius* 11). Suetonius further notes Caligula's arrogance, cruelty (*Gaius* 34), and fearfulness (*Gaius* 51), while his comment to his own grandmother, "Remember that I may do everything to everyone" (*Gaius* 29), is echoed by Joffrey's assertions. Indeed, in the audio commentary to Episode 2.1, showrunners David Benioff and D. B. Weiss describe Joffrey's behavior and delight over the bloodshed at his name-day games as "Caligulan." Agrippina is depicted as reproducing her brother's worst impulses in her son, whom Tacitus and Suetonius describe as similarly vicious. Although Cersei has failed in her instruction, Joffrey's reliance on his mother to run things and her attempts to control him strongly mirror Nero's relationship with Agrippina.

THE *DUX FEMINA* FALTERS: FEMININE RIVALRY OVER THE BOY-KING

Agrippina's inability to compete for Nero's full attentions greatly contributed to her downfall and led to her supposed attempt to seduce her son. Agrippina lost her status with, and influence over, Nero when he fell in love: first with the freedwoman Acte, and then with Poppaea, the wife of his friend Otho. Nero took both women as mistresses due to the political impossibility of divorcing his stepsister Octavia while Agrippina still lived, in addition to their statuses: Acte was an ex-slave, Poppaea a married woman. After Cersei permits Joffrey to cast off Sansa and marry the ambitious Margaery Tyrell at the end of Season 2, feminine jealousy and rivalry similarly initiate Cersei's downfall in Season 3, as Margaery's flatteries work on Joffrey much as those of Acte and Poppaea affected Nero. Although Margaery can be viewed as a conflation of both Acte and Poppaea, she emerges as more of a Poppaea figure; both Poppaea and Margaery displace a ruler's mother to become empress or queen, then pay the ultimate price for their own "masculine" ambitions.

Margaery's determination to be Queen of the Seven Kingdoms emerges soon after her introduction in Season 2. The morning after the murder of her husband Renly Baratheon (Gethin Anthony), younger brother of Robert and one of the claimants of the Iron Throne, Littlefinger asks her, "Do you want to be a queen?" to which she responds, "No. I want to be the queen" (Episode 2.5, "The Ghosts of

Harrenhal"). Littlefinger notes this ambition, which he uses to ensure for the Lannisters the much-needed help of the Tyrells when fighting against Stannis. Tacitus, commenting on Poppaea's opportunistic promiscuity, explains that "from where benefit would be displayed, there she transferred her lust" (*Ann.* 13.45), implying that Poppaea's desire to become empress led to her affair and subsequent marriage with Nero. Margaery's ambition to become queen is realized when Joffrey tells her brother Loras to ask for whatever he wants as reward for aid from House Tyrell – which is marriage between their houses. When Joffrey asks Margaery if she wants this, she responds, "With all my heart, your grace. I have come to love you from afar. Tales of your courage and wisdom have never been far from my ears, and those tales have taken root deep inside of me" (Episode 2.10). Although Joffrey needs some persuading to break his vow to Sansa, Margaery immediately reveals her slyly manipulative ways and the steps she will take to accomplish her desires.

Tacitus explains of Poppaea's hold over Nero: "First she established herself through flatteries and artifice, feigning she was unequal to her passion and captivated by Nero's good looks; soon, with the emperor's love now fierce, she turned to haughtiness" (*Ann.* 13.46). As Poppaea realized that marriage to Nero was unlikely as long as Agrippina was alive, "she found fault with the emperor with frequent complaints and sometimes with humor called him a ward, who, dependent on another's commands, lacked not only the empire but also his freedom" (*Ann.* 14.1). Poppaea's encouragements contributed to Nero's eventual elimination of his mother and accusations of adultery against his wife Octavia, which led to her death. Although just as outspoken as Poppaea, Margaery refrains from nagging or encouraging Joffrey to do something as drastic as what Poppaea did with Nero. Yet Margaery similarly exerts the most persuasive force upon Joffrey.

Once betrothed to Joffrey, Margaery rivals Cersei as the female influence in Joffrey's life. Cersei justifiably fears that she is being usurped, that Joffrey is becoming immune to her. After Margaery's first effusive praise of Joffrey and declaration of love, he quickly takes to her. As she caresses his crossbow, she strokes his ego; showing an interest in his passion, she asks for a demonstration (Episode 3.2, "Dark Wings, Dark Words"; see Figure 11.2). Margaery, a cunning operator like Cersei, indulges Joffrey's whims and encourages his behavior, repeatedly emphasizing that he is the king, even after she has learned from Sansa that he is a "monster."[24] Unlike Cersei, who controls people through fear, Margaery knows how to manipulate

Figure 11.2 Margaery (Natalie Dormer) indulges Joffrey's (Jack Gleeson) passion in "Dark Wings, Dark Words," Episode 3.2 of *Game of Thrones* (2013). HBO.

the king, and people in general, into loving her, and she takes full advantage of his being smitten. Margaery does not directly attack a mother to her son, yet her fawning and encouragement subtly undermine Cersei and indirectly lead to Joffrey's violence toward others.[25]

During a fitting for Joffrey's wedding clothes, Cersei unsuccessfully attempts to use against Margaery the kind of subtle argument by which she had saved her son from Robert's punishment in Season 1 (Episode 3.2). Joffrey, who is thinking politically, sees the wealthy Margaery of House Tyrell as an "ideal match"; Cersei again asks what he thinks of her, noting Margaery's beauty, intelligence, and interest in the common people. Cersei's praise parallels Tacitus' of Poppaea, where he attributes to her similar qualities in his otherwise negative introductory portrait. He notes Poppaea's beauty, family, and wealth, and that "her conversation was charming, and she was clever. She displayed modesty but employed wantonness" (*Ann.* 13.45). Similarly, Cersei follows Margaery's assets with insults, claiming Margaery does everything "for a reason," including dressing "like a harlot." An impatient Joffrey responds that Margaery has done what she was told to, and "that's what intelligent women do – what they're told."

Cersei's inability to win him over further recalls Agrippina's ineffectual opposition to Nero's mistress Acte. As Tacitus notes, Agrippina "raged like a woman" because of Acte's lowly status and her role as competitor and potential in-law, and she "did not wait for her son's repentance or weariness. But the fouler the things she reproached him with, the more fiercely he was inflamed, until overcome with the power of love he cast off his obedience to his mother" (*Ann.* 13.13). Joffrey too asserts himself and attempts to escape his mother's control when pushed too far, too often; earlier, in Episode 3.1 ("Valar Dohaeris"), Joffrey defended Margaery's visit to an orphanage against Cersei's criticisms, a prelude to his developing resistance to his mother.

Events during a tour of the royal crypt offer the clearest proof of Joffrey's abandonment of his mother for his wife-to-be. Joffrey laughs about a Targaryen woman, from the previous royal family, being eaten by a dragon while her son watched; he is oblivious to the horrified reaction that his mother (or anyone else) may have. Margaery responds favorably to his "macabre" stories, as Cersei calls them, and again strokes his ego, exclaiming how the people adore him and how he led the defense of King's Landing (Episode 3.4, "And Now His Watch Is Ended"). Although Cersei is present, there is little interaction between mother and son, who ignores her plaintive "Wait" as Joffrey and Margaery proceed outside to meet a crowd shouting in acclamation.[26]

Cersei is reduced to approaching her father for help in her fragile position, explaining, "Margaery has her claws in Joffrey. She knows how to manipulate him" (Episode 3.4). Tywin sees this as positive and wishes that Cersei could do the same. He tells his daughter, "I don't distrust you because you're a woman. I distrust you because you're not as smart as you think you are. You've allowed that boy to ride roughshod over you and everyone else in this city." Tywin claims he will keep Joffrey from "doing what he likes," emphasizing the widening gap between Tywin's and Cersei's capabilities. As with Robert, Cersei's masculine pretensions are found to be deficient when measured against her father.

Margaery Tyrell is the heiress to a wealthy and prominent house whose support the Lannisters need on account of Robb Stark's war. But in the arrogant Cersei's eyes, the Tyrells are a lesser family that should tremble at the thought of crossing their betters. The increasingly desperate Cersei warns Margaery with a story about the former second-wealthiest family overextending itself and being killed when they rebelled against her father (Episode 3.8, "Second Sons"). While Poppaea urged Nero to eliminate his mother and remove Octavia, it is Cersei who threatens to kill Margaery rather than lose power over Joffrey and the kingdom. As Margaery's sway over Joffrey grows and she encourages him to take the reins as king – which can only detract from his mother's role – Cersei's power and political effectiveness progressively decline. As she loses control over son and kingdom, she descends into paranoia and drinking. Much as Poppaea's influence over Nero negatively affected Agrippina's position, so Margaery's rise contributes to Cersei's fall and underscores her failures as both a mother and a ruler. Although Margaery does not have to wait as long as Poppaea did to marry the ruler, the ambitions of both women ultimately lead to their deaths: Poppaea, kicked to death by Nero; and Margaery, killed in a fiery blast contrived by Cersei at the end of Season 6.

CONCLUSION

The Tacitean Agrippina was "designed to suggest the weakness of an emperor and a political system that could not control its women."[27] Casting Cersei in HBO's *Game of Thrones* as a *dux femina* on the model of Agrippina suggests, by analogy, that power was seized unjustly and that the wrong heir rules, resulting in the collapse of a house, the decline of the kingdom, and war. Unlike Agrippina, who was responsible for the best part of Nero's reign (relatively speaking), the arrogant Cersei sometimes proves politically naïve and ineffectual. Her desire for power and fierce loyalty to her family blind her to her own and Joffrey's faults, failings, incompetence, and their effects on the kingdom. She feels entitled to rule by her lineage, not her accomplishments – of which a woman can have none, at least at this point in the series, in this conventionally patriarchal society. Likewise, for Tacitus' Agrippina, "the ability to exercise control over her son is precisely what will make it possible for her to continue to exercise *potentia* in the public sphere."[28]

Yet Agrippina's influence proved unbearable; in 59 CE, after a failed attempt at killing her via a boating accident, Nero sent assassins to dispatch her (*Ann.* 14.3–8). She "was able to give the empire to her son, but was unable to endure him being the emperor" (*Ann.* 12.64). Agrippina proved too much for Nero, but Cersei not enough for Joffrey. Although Joffrey threatened Cersei when she slapped him (Episode 2.1), she avoided exerting the type of power and annoyance that would lead to her murder. Cersei's failures – as a mother, as a ruler – ultimately save her life but doom her son to a premature death. Early in Season 4, Joffrey met his end, poisoned at his and Margaery's wedding banquet by Margaery's grandmother, while Margaery remained queen and married Joffrey's younger brother Tommen. Cersei, although suffering her own punishments and reversals in Seasons 4–6, including the deaths of Tommen, her daughter, and her father, ultimately claimed the Iron Throne for herself at the end of Season 6.

Parallels with and variations on Agrippina and those connected closely to her similarly accentuate the faults of characters in *Game of Thrones* and their unfitness to rule. An oblivious and weak Robert allowed Cersei's rise to power, and eventually the succession of an illegitimate heir, with his drinking, whoring, and lack of control over her. Whereas Robert began his reign by successfully deposing the mad Targaryen king, Joffrey's reign is a disaster from the start. Joffrey is spoiled, cowardly, and cruel, a monster created and unleashed by his mother. Cersei's inability to effectively challenge Margaery or her father further relegates her to a supporting role and contributes to Joffrey's increasingly tyrannical behavior. The Lannisters may be the wealthiest and most powerful family in Westeros, but ultimately they are undone by their own corruption, immorality, and illegitimate rule. Both ancient Rome's Julio-Claudian dynasty and the fictional Lannister family are destroyed by women's "unnatural" lust for power and are implicated in a shift away from a golden age of order, peace, and morality to an iron age of disorder, war, and immorality.

NOTES

1 In the outdated "what I'm watching" section of his website, Martin (2005) thus explained why he watched the TV series *Empire* (and his enjoyment of HBO's *Rome*). Also see Anders (2013) on Martin's being "influenced" by Robert Graves' *I, Claudius* "to some extent" and his high opinion of the 1976 TV version.
2 See Frankel (2014: 96–7) on possible models.
3 On Cersei as an amalgamation, see Frankel (2014: 97–8).
4 On Agrippina the Younger, see Ginsburg (2006); on Nero, see Shotter (2008).
5 Ginsburg (2006: 4, revised by Erich Gruen).
6 Ginsburg (2006: 23).
7 L'Hoir (1994: 5–6). On earlier versions of the stereotype, see L'Hoir (1994: 24).
8 L'Hoir (1994: 19). Although Livy presents ambitious queens of Rome's original regal period, Tanaquil and Tullia, as king-makers, they are not, as L'Hoir (1994: 20) notes, "power-mad mothers" like Agrippina.
9 Translations of Tacitus and Suetonius are my own, from the text posted on <thelatinlibrary.com>, and aim for readability and the general sense of the Latin.

10 Their first scene together in Episode 1.1 implies an unhappy marriage. Upon arrival at the Starks' home, Cersei looks pained when greeting Ned. Robert wants to immediately visit the crypts, but Cersei ineffectually suggests he do so later. The next scene reveals that Robert was to marry Ned's sister, the reason for his visit to the crypts.
11 In Episode 1.3, Ned seems surprised that an absent Robert has entrusted "small matters" to the council. This resembles Claudius letting his freedmen run things; see Suetonius, *Claudius* 25, 29.
12 Ginsburg (2006: 117, 121). On Agrippina's sexual behavior and its significance within the Roman context, see Ginsburg (2006: 18–19, 116–30).
13 On Caligula, see Suetonius, *Gaius* 24; see Tacitus, *Annales* 12.5 on fears that their incest will be a "national calamity."
14 See Ginsburg (2006: 122–6) on Agrippina's adultery and its significance. Although not as predatory as imperial women on screen, Cersei recalls the scheming and sexually aggressive cinematic empresses of the 1950s, Poppaea in *Quo Vadis* (1951) and Messalina in *Demetrius and the Gladiators* (1954).
15 The showrunners David Benioff and D. B. Weiss note in the audio commentary for this episode that audiences of the original pilot were unaware of Cersei and Jaime's familial relationship, so they stressed that they were siblings/twins throughout the aired episode.
16 Cersei more frequently commits adultery for pleasure and political reasons in the books than in the series. She also is described more often as naked; strikingly, in the series, Cersei is not shown naked until she pays for her sexual transgressions in Season 5's "walk of shame."
17 On Agrippina's role in Claudius' murder, which varies in the sources from acting alone to using various agents, see Ginsburg (2006: 25–35).
18 Cersei is more murderous in the books, further resembling Agrippina, who, for example, eliminated Narcissus because of her hostility toward him (*Ann.* 13.1).
19 The series has aged all the children several years from the books; aging Joffrey from twelve to sixteen/seventeen aligns him with Nero.
20 See Suetonius, *Nero* 35; Shotter (2008: 127).
21 The order to execute Robert's bastards has been shifted from Cersei in the books to Joffrey here, further highlighting his nature and Cersei's ineffectual attempts to control him.
22 Shotter (2008: 129).
23 Tyrion thus can be equated with Claudius: both uncles of mad emperors and with their own physical deformities.
24 As Frankel (2014: 103) notes, one does not see this side of Margaery in the books.
25 In Episode 3.6 ("The Climb"), one of the name-day prostitutes, Ros (Esmé Bianco), ends up the object, and victim, of Joffrey's target practice with his crossbow, a pastime Margaery had heartily endorsed.

26 Their greeting the crowd visually recalls Nero doing the same in *Quo Vadis*; Joffrey's cruelty and the Lannisters' wealth, power, and depravity also evoke the stereotypically decadent, deviant, and tyrannical cinematic Romans.
27 Ginsburg (2006: 23).
28 Ginsburg (2006: 40).

12 *The Golden Aspects of Roman Imperialism in Film, 1914–2015*

Anise K. Strong

In Monty Python's *Life of Brian* (1979), the leader of the People's Front of Judea (PFJ) famously demands to know, "What have the Romans ever done for us?" Presumably he, like the audience reared on a "golden age" of Roman-themed films during the 1940s and especially the 1950s, expects to hear a list of examples of Roman oppression: the evils of slavery, crucifixion, religious persecution, possibly corruption and debauchery resulting from effeminate, secularized "over-civilization."[1] Hollywood's Rome was also associated with fascism and unorthodox sexual behaviors, both perceived as active dangers during the mid-twentieth century. Instead, the PFJ members point out the many advantages that ordinary Judeans benefit from under Roman rule: "the sanitation, the medicine, education, wine, public order, irrigation, roads" – in sum, the features of a highly organized, advanced society that claims the title of "civilization." This may be the sort of "civilization" that, as Tacitus would argue, is actually oppressive colonialism, but it does have its notable benefits for the ordinary citizen. In this reversal of audience assumptions from sword-and-sandal movies, the Pythons reflect upon the cinematic norms that shaped dominant representations of Roman imperialism in the twentieth century. The Roman Empire can serve as a simplistic metaphor for the evils of authoritarianism, but it has also been used by directors and screenwriters to celebrate the beneficial aspects of Roman civilization.

Such positive valuations of Roman imperialism as ennobling and civilizing – like the negative portrayals of the Romans as oppressive villains – are hardly offered naïvely. Rather, they are generally offered in order to defend or support contemporaneous social models: the producers' and consumers' own imperialist societies. During moments of social and political anxiety about the nature and effects of imperialism, modern media have sometimes turned to a particular vision of the Roman Empire as a potential model for, or at least a mirror of, contemporary society and its concerns. Filmmakers seeking to promote imperialism as beneficial or to defend its last remnants have focused on the unifying and meritocratic aspects of Roman society, rather than its oppressive aspects. Three positive aspects attributed to the Roman Empire in conventional Western historical narratives – law and order, multiculturalism, and warrior masculinity – are stated and echoed in Italian films of the 1910s to 1930s, American and British films from 1964 to 1980, and British and American films from 2000 to 2015. In order to explore the particular nuances of these optimistic representations of ancient Rome, this chapter will focus on *Cabiria* (1914), *Scipione l'Africano* (1937), *The Fall of the Roman Empire* (1964), *Life of Brian* (1979), and a trio of early twenty-first-century films set in Roman Britain: *Centurion* (2010), *The Eagle* (2011), and *The Last Legion* (2007).

THE RISE OF THE ITALIAN EMPIRE

Some of the earliest films to portray Roman imperialism in a somewhat favorable light were, unsurprisingly, produced in Italy, such as Guazzoni's series of Roman-era silent films in the 1910s. Especially under the later rule of Mussolini, these works explicitly glorified modern Italy's ancient Roman ancestors as the forerunners of militant authoritarian regimes that promoted the welfare of their own citizens while "civilizing" the barbarian "Other." In general, these films were set during the Roman Republic rather than the Principate or Imperial Period.[2] They praise the days of Rome's expansionist wars in Africa and emphasize Roman military glory and heroic generals, rather than the debauched emperors more commonly featured in Hollywood films of both the silent era and the epic heyday of the 1940s and 1950s. Two particularly famous films of the early Italian period are the silent film *Cabiria* (1914), directed by Giovanni Pastrone, and *Scipione l'Africano* (1937), directed by Carmine Gallone.[3] Both are set during the Second Punic War, a time when Rome was rapidly expanding its control over the Mediterranean and fighting against the North African merchant empire of the Carthaginians, who were not only ethnically distinct from Italian or Greek populations but also, according to Roman propaganda, allegedly baby-sacrificers.[4] The Second Punic War also loomed in Roman historical texts as a moment of extreme crisis and near-destruction for the Republic; only the strategy and heroism of individual Roman elite leaders were able to save Rome and defeat the great Carthaginian general Hannibal.

The 1914 film *Cabiria* suggests that Africans and Carthaginians are the paradigmatic savage barbarians who need to be conquered for their own good. Romans are represented as the forces of law and compassion: kindly masters and good parents who rescue women and children. In contrast, the African and Carthaginian characters are shown as not only sexually debauched and bestial, but also practitioners of human sacrifice and slave merchants. The stereotypically African king, dressed in animal skins and wearing large earrings, bows in submission before a Roman senator in his pristine white toga. Pastrone used Indian-style architectural elements to represent the Carthaginian temples, quite literally Orientalizing the villains as an exotic "Other" who deserved to be conquered by the civilized Romans.[5]

Roman imperialism thus justifies contemporary Italian imperialism, especially over foreign and implicitly inferior groups. For the film's message, that Roman domination is "inevitable" and resistance is futile, reflects the confidence of Italian nationalists at the time, who expected to conquer much of North Africa and regain their ancestral position as a great European power. Gabriele D'Annunzio, who took credit for the screenplay and wrote many of the intertitles, was a well-known Italian nationalist and militarist.[6] In the pamphlet that accompanied the film in Italy, D'Annunzio announced that "The blast of war transforms people into a kind of inflammable material which Rome strives to mold to his own likeness."[7] This Vergilian echo renders ancient Romans, and by extension modern Italians, as both conquerors and artists, effectively allowing contemporary Italians to claim the heritage both of classical Rome and of the Renaissance city-states.[8] At the same time, this is a motif of renewal through destruction, as the victims of Italian conquest must be consumed in flame before they can be refashioned as appropriate new citizens. Italy/Rome's new subjects implicitly themselves become the victims of the fiery immolation vividly depicted in *Cabiria*, but D'Annunzio reassures them that new life will somehow emerge, phoenix-like, from this "blast of war." This language also justifies the sort of "total war" that began in World War I and would become even more dominant as a military approach during World War II. The ends of "Roman civilization" justify whatever means are necessary.

Maria Wyke notes that this wildly successful film, which was released at the beginning of World War I in conjunction with Italian wartime victories in Africa, was used as a propagandistic and nationalistic tool.[9] It helped to remind Italians of their former greatness and assure them of the righteousness of their cause. The German subtitle of the film, "Struggle for World Dominion," made the connections to contemporaneous expansionist Italian movements and to the recent Italo-Turkish War all the more explicit.[10] It appears to have had its intended propagandistic effect; the Naples magazine *Film* reviewed it enthusiastically and declared that *Cabiria* was "a spark to ignite a fire of enthusiasm."[11] The primary outlet for such enthusiasm was presumably expansionist military conquest, in the grand tradition of the Roman Empire.

In the 1937 Mussolini-produced film *Scipione l'Africano*, Rome once again triumphs over a barbarian Africa. In this case, however, Rome is allegedly fighting not out of naked expansionist imperialism but from a desire for righteous vengeance. Rome's invasion of North Africa after twenty years of Hannibal's attacks in Italy serves as a metaphor for the 1930s Italian desire to avenge its ignominious late nineteenth-century defeat at the Battle of Adwa by Ethiopian tribesmen with inferior weapons. The prologue of *Scipione l'Africano* sets the scene:

> Toward the end of the third century, two great powers were struggling for mastery of the Mediterranean: Rome and Carthage. From the very beginning, the rivalry between the two nations became a dramatic life and death battle for both peoples concerned ... In fact, in the year 218 BC, Hannibal invaded the Italian peninsula from the Alps, with a vast army of men and elephants, leaving behind him a trail of death and destruction. In vain, Rome attempted to resist his unrelenting advance.[12]

War here is no longer portrayed as inherently virtuous, like the crusade against human sacrifice in *Cabiria*, but rather as a necessary evil against potential political oppressors. Scipio (Annibale Ninchi) proclaims, "To put an end to the war, there is no choice but to invade Africa." While World War I had demonstrated that war itself was inherently horrific and destructive, *Scipione* also represented war as a necessary step in order to ensure future peace and prosperity under a *Pax Romana* ("Roman peace"). The more negative perception of war may come from the horrors of World War I itself; Mussolini's expansionist desire must now be justified as a last resort.

The ancient Romans are cast here as patriots fighting to defend their homeland, illustrating Caprotti's observation that, during the 1930s, blatant propaganda was deemed unhelpful by the Italian fascist government. Rather, indirect delivery of subtler pro-fascist and pro-imperialist themes was strongly encouraged by Mussolini.[13] Thus *Scipione l'Africano* emphasizes a very particular view of the Roman state as a unified group of disparate Italians from every region of the peninsula, whose diversity and unity are explicitly praised; the wide variety of Mediterranean ethnic groups in the Roman Empire goes unmentioned. Victory will only be achieved by a united Italian front, another explicitly propagandistic and contemporary message. That united front is led by Scipio, who serves as a clear analogue for *Il Duce* himself. Scipio takes over from a weak group of quarreling political elites, much as Mussolini himself had seized power; he is hailed by the people with the "Roman salute," which soon became strongly associated with fascism.[14]

In contrast to the Romans' unification under the leadership of a single wise soldier and reliance on their training, sophisticated siege engines, and other technological elements, the Carthaginians, just as in *Cabiria*, are depicted as a savage barbarian mob that endangers humanity itself. Roman civilization includes not only the ubiquitous columns and togas, but also elected government and meritocratic military commands. The North Africans, in contrast, kidnap and abuse women, drink from animal troughs, and are described as "warriors" rather than as soldiers or legionaries in an organized army. The Carthaginian forces are strongly associated with the exotic and bestial elephant cavalry, yet Scipio himself virtuously stops a legionary from killing a mother elephant whose baby is beside her.[15] At the end of the film, Scipio announces that they will turn their swords into plowshares and begin to plant grain in North Africa, bringing prosperity to both lands. The Romans are quite explicitly the forces of progress and benevolent imperialism.

In the climax of the film, a wide shot of a field of African corpses after Roman victory at the Battle of Zama is immediately followed by the line, "The dead of Cannae are avenged. Hannibal is defeated." Similarly, two years before the release of *Scipione l'Africano*, Mussolini had explicitly used the shameful memory of the Battle of Adwa to spark his conquest of Ethiopia in 1935.[16] War is justified here as necessary to end barbarism and promote a universal authoritarian *Pax Romana*, now a *Pax Mussolinea*.

Despite its official support and patronage by Mussolini, *Scipione l'Africano* was a commercial flop. Mussolini's ban on dubbing Italian films into foreign languages also hurt its potential for wider distribution, but even in fascist Italy blatantly nationalistic approaches to mass media were not necessarily effective in achieving the goals of either audience support for authoritarian conquest or simple financial profit.[17] Wyke suggests that Italian audiences were not as easily manipulated as the fascist government may have hoped.[18] However, the popularity of a film may be due more to its quality than to its messaging. The wicked Romans of the various *Ben-Hurs* may simply have been more entertaining and appealing than the heroic ones of *Scipione*, or the Italian population may have been less receptive to militaristic and pro-imperialist films in the 1930s. Nevertheless, the key commonality between *Cabiria*, *Scipione*, and other Italian films of the period is the emphasis on ancient Rome as an inspirational source of heroic and martial power. The Romans are depicted not as aggressive, brutal expansionists, but rather as defenders of the Italian way of life and of civilization itself. Furthermore, the civilization that their conquests bring will be ultimately positive for rulers and subjects alike; everyone can benefit from Roman rule.

THE FALL OF THE BRITISH EMPIRE

Mussolini and his allies lost World War II, paving the way for decades of epic films in which the Romans represented thinly veiled versions of modern fascist regimes. Such films originated from not only American but also British and Italian film studios.[19] Films like *Ben-Hur* (1959), *Spartacus* (1960), and Christian-themed films like *Quo Vadis* (1951) and *The Robe* (1953) depicted Rome as a cruel empire that oppressed slaves and provincial subjects. While the Allies won World War II, their own overseas empires were significantly destabilized after the war, aided by local nationalist movements as well as a growing global distaste for imperialism. The contemporary British Empire rapidly dissolved or evolved, losing most of its remaining African and Asian possessions by the mid-1960s. During this period, a somewhat optimistic representation of ancient Rome briefly became a popular subgenre among British and American directors and writers.[20] These pro-Roman works can be interpreted as indirect defenses of the positive features of the decaying British Empire especially. They show awareness of common critiques of imperialism even as they attempt to mythologize and idealize that past.

The justification for a potentially beneficial empire was most clearly developed in *The Fall of the Roman Empire* (1964), directed by Anthony Mann. Although Mann was American, and the United States was in the process of establishing its own influence over the developing world, the cast and writers were largely British.[21] This film betrayed a somewhat muddled nature in both its accents and its values, wildly mixing the apparent ethnicities of its characters and trying to simultaneously promote both pacifism and imperialism. It was not a commercial success, perhaps due to the same issues of saturation that plagued the contemporaneous *Cleopatra*. The era of spectacle-laden epics set in the ancient Greco-Roman world seemed to be (temporarily) over. Contemporary reviews faulted *The Fall of the Roman Empire* for poor acting and a worse script, singling out John Ireland in his role as the Germanic barbarian leader as "an unkempt Beatle."[22] However, the film has gained scholarly recognition in recent years due to its strong influence on the more popular *Gladiator* (2000) and its unusual focus on the later era of Roman domination.

The potential of an imperial power to unify many peoples under one civic idea is advanced in an early dramatic speech by Marcus Aurelius (Alec Guinness), one of the canonical "Good Emperors." He rallies his troops by praising not just intra-Italian unity, but the empire as a mixing pot of many cultures, ethnicities, and religions, and wider cosmopolitan cooperation (see Figure 12.1):

> Commoners, consuls, princes, you have come from the deserts of Egypt, from the mountains of Armenia, from the forests of Gaul and the prairies of Spain. You do not resemble each other, nor do you wear the same clothes, nor sing the same songs nor worship the same gods. Yet, like a mighty tree with green leaves and black roots, you are the unity which is Rome. Look about you

Figure 12.1 The diverse Roman legions in *The Fall of the Roman Empire* (1964). Paramount.

> and look at yourselves and see the greatness of Rome . . . Wherever you live, whatever the color of your skin, when peace is achieved, it will bring to all, all, the supreme right of Roman citizenship. No longer provinces or colonies . . . but a family of equal nations.

In order for Rome to triumph, it must, in other words, become a commonwealth much like the modern form of the British Empire: a "family of equal nations" in which civic status pre-empts ethnic identity. Within the context of the American Civil Rights movement, such a speech also emphasizes the ideal of equal treatment under the law. Roman citizenship is anachronistically presented as a right available to all within the Empire. Roman law and justice, like their British parallels, are viewed as inherently superior to the cultures and governmental systems of subject societies. While each nation is allowed to preserve its own cultural traditions and religion, British or American leadership will nevertheless dominate. The structure of Aurelius' metaphorical tree enforces a political unity for each of its disparate leaves.

This emphasis on success through subordinated diversity is somewhat ironic given the themes and plots of the film itself, which focuses on the collapse of the Roman Empire due to mismanagement by Aurelius' successor Commodus (Christopher Plummer) and his intolerance toward provincial citizens. To the extent that it is a political allegory, *The Fall of the Roman Empire* serves less as a triumphalist celebration of anti-imperialism and civil rights movements around the world than as an apocalyptic warning of the consequences of racial persecution and imperialist oppression. The potential evils of the Roman Empire, especially the risks of one-man authoritarian government, are certainly addressed; Mann would disagree strongly with the fascist ideals of the earlier Italian films.[23] However, Aurelius' speech also idealizes Rome as potentially the best possible form of government and as a pinnacle of human civilization. While the rest of the film demonstrates the flaws in relying on hereditary succession, Western imperialism itself can still triumph over the barbarian hordes.

Within the film, Roman imperialism also has the potential to bring wealth and meritocratic advancement to the unified and diverse masses, exchanging fascism for liberal progressivism. The heroes of the film are explicitly men of low birth, including the ex-slave Timonides (James Mason), one of Aurelius' chief deputies, and the general Gaius Metellus Livius (Stephen Boyd), an anachronistically named soldier of non-senatorial origin. At the same time, the movie suggests that social promotion comes primarily through the military, continuing to link the empire with traditional masculine virtues in the same way that Scipio was represented as a "man's man" in *Scipio l'Africano*. Timonides' principal virtuous act in the film is to persuade the Senate to allow captured Germanic prisoners to become farmers in Italy, rather than executing them; he promotes the notion of a "human frontier" rather than a military one. This again recasts imperialism in the idealized British model rather than the Italian fascist one; the heap of African corpses is replaced by the image of successfully tamed barbarians. Furthermore, Timonides is able to calm down the Germans by undergoing one of their traditional rituals of bravery, thus honoring and acknowledging their cultural values. *The Fall of the Roman Empire* tries its best to walk a difficult line between its celebration of multiculturalism and a firm belief in the potential value of well-ruled and well-organized empires.

While acknowledging the lack of freedom and the problems of imperialist oppression, in *Life of Brian* the British Pythons famously raise the question of whether the benefits of the Roman Empire significantly outweigh its disadvantages. Thus, they invoke the model of their own faded British Empire by stressing the social services that the Romans brought to their conquered subjects. The Roman forces also are better organized, better educated, and more reasonable than the bitterly divided, illogical, argumentative Judeans. The Romans in the film represent not only better roads but also the rule of law, the guarantee of security, and the victory of proper grammar. Without imperialist rule, societies will simply collapse into civil war, the Pythons suggest. Even incompetent Roman governors are still wiser and more reasonable than Reg (John Cleese), the leader of the People's Front of Judea. "Always Look on the Bright Side of Life" was apparently a favorite song among British troops serving in the Falklands War in 1982, one of the last gasps of British imperialism.[24] (While within the film this song is sung as a finale number by the varied victims of crucifixion, it became a popular hit in Britain as a general celebration of optimism under desperate circumstances.) The overall impression left by *Life of Brian* is that while Roman (and British) rule may not be wholly benevolent or beneficial, it is significantly superior to the alternatives.

THE DEFENSE OF NEW IMPERIALISM

After a hiatus in the late twentieth century, a new golden age of classical reception on screen sparked by Ridley Scott's 2000 film *Gladiator* has included films that unite the themes of the wartime Italian films and the 1960s–70s "melting pot" eras, glorifying Rome both as the defender of order against savage barbarians and also potentially as a center of ethnic and religious diversity.[25] The definition of a heroic Roman expands significantly to include non-white characters and women, but it is still framed in relationship to the savage "Others" who lurk just beyond the geographical and temporal borders of the Empire. Such a dichotomy may reflect contemporaneous fears of nebulous foreign terrorists, as the US and Great Britain united against modern alleged "barbarians." Modern anti-terrorist media campaigns often stressed both the diverse nature of these two nations' populations and their political unity under traditional Anglo-American values and laws. Apart from *Gladiator*, these films all were produced and released in a post-9/11 framework, with potential threats lurking around every border. At the same time, distrust in government and a lack of faith in government's leaders have also pervaded the cultural discourse in both the United States and the United Kingdom. A desire to return to the "golden age" of the 1950s may also have sparked interest in films that emphasized the glory days of martial success and individual heroism in the ancient Roman world, like *Ben-Hur* or *Spartacus*.[26]

The opening battle scene of *Gladiator* and the protagonist Maximus' opening speech depict Rome as the light against the encroaching Germanic darkness, which is explicitly both "brutal and cruel." At the same time, little concrete reason is provided for idealizing Roman rule in the way that Aurelius' specific praise of multiculturalism offers in *The Fall of the Roman Empire*. In contrast to Mann's film, the Germans in *Gladiator* are essentially anonymous monsters rather than individualized characters with their own customs and agendas.

This one last battle, according to the opening narration of *Gladiator*, will establish perpetual peace for all. Echoing Scipio's climactic proclamation that the Romans and their new North African subjects will plant grain together after the war is over, *Gladiator*'s protagonist Maximus (Russell Crowe) exhorts his troops before the battle by telling them that in three weeks he will be planting his fields. His desire is to abandon the fields of blood and focus on the black dirt of his farm, explicitly preferring peace to war. Roman superiority is marked within this battle by technological advantages and tight organization, unlike the mob of crazed German barbarians who attack from the woods. Once again, order itself is represented as a virtue worthy of admiration and imitation; this is a sharp reversal of the demonization of fascist militaristic precision depicted in such earlier films as Kubrick's 1960 *Spartacus*. While the rest of the film echoes *The Fall of the Roman Empire* in its depiction of internal corruption and betrayal within Roman society, the Roman world is still presented as superior to what lies beyond its borders.

Support for the potential benefits of Roman order is further developed in three recent films centering on life in Roman Britain. In each of these films, the Romans are presented as civilized and comparatively heroic frontier soldiers, defending themselves from the savage barbarian Picts.[27] Unlike the earlier Italian films like *Cabiria* or *Scipione*, *The Eagle* (2011), *Centurion* (2010), and *The Last Legion* (2007) take place on the frontiers of the Roman Empire and feature a diminished and weakened imperial power, kept afloat largely by its brave legions. Having been filmed in the last decade, during a time of uncertainty for both America and Britain about their global roles, these films glorify a time when men fought for civilization and order against clearly uncivilized, exoticized "bad guys." At the same time, these films allow for somewhat more complex ruminations on the nature of loyalty and the moral authority of governments, given various morally questionable and politically disputed wars fought by the filmmakers' governments since the 1970s.

Neither *The Eagle* nor *Centurion* exalts imperialism as innately beneficial, unlike their Italian predecessors. However, both films still depict some values associated with Rome in a positive manner, especially the quality of soldiers and unit loyalty that the Romans produced. "I am a soldier of Rome: I will not yield," proclaims the hero of *Centurion* (Michael Fassbender). Marcus Aquila (Channing Tatum), the hero of *The Eagle*, is defined by his honor and his emphasis on the legions as an "elite" Marine-like force.[28] Echoing the earlier *Gladiator*, the directors and screenwriters focus on a narrow, militarized vision of masculinity that adheres to the Roman ideal of *virtus* (manly excellence).[29] To be a good Roman is to be male, physically tough, and loyal to your comrades. In contrast to other popular historical eras in film and television over the past decade, such as Regency England or 1960s America, these new Roman films offer a positive and simplistic perspective on male roles in society and male virtue. While not necessarily fascist, these ideals emphasize the same conservative vision of masculinity, relying on charisma and strength rather than on intelligence or cunning. At the same time, the far greater ethnic diversity present in these teams of legionaries suggests that "Romanness" is no longer limited to people of ethnically Italian descent, as implied by the earlier Italian films.

Within the framework of this characterization of masculinity, focus shifts from the advantages or disadvantages of specific social or governmental systems to the individual heroism and group loyalties of their characters, largely eliminating or ignoring the role of birth families in favor of exalting families created by choice, especially bonds of brotherhood. The heroes in *Centurion* are a motley group of Italian, British, and other Roman citizens whose inter-ethnic differences are irrelevant as they band together to fight against Pictish savages. In *The Eagle*, although Aquila's male British slave Esca (Jamie Bell) speaks out about the evils of Roman conquest and slavery, he also works with Aquila to fight against the greater threat of the Picts who practice human sacrifice and cannibalism; they even literally eat babies. Over the course of *The Eagle*, Aquila and Esca become each other's loyal companion.

Yet this abstract sense of Roman military culture as beneficial in shaping good men decidedly does not extend to representation of the policies that Roman officials pursue through that military. When the Roman soldier Aquila in *The Eagle* exalts Roman honor, his British companion Esca responds by noting that the Romans killed his entire family during a rebellion. The Roman leaders at the end of *Centurion* attempt to murder the hero in order to cover up their military defeat. He escapes and finds a new life as a "fugitive of Rome" with a blonde Pictish woman (Imogen Poots), who has been cast out as a witch by her people; while "Othered," she nonetheless rejects the savagery of the "barbarians." At the same time, Roman culture is still depicted as a more positive than negative force. While the leadership may be corrupt, individual soldiers and units still uphold traditional virtues and behave responsibly toward their fellow Romans. Even more than in earlier films, Rome represents the forces of civilization against savagery, even if it is perhaps the lesser of two evils. In *The Eagle*, a compromise can even be achieved: between Aquila and Esca, between Roman military loyalty and the British personal bonds of loyalty and friendship. Both characters can remain true to their cultures while also embracing their relationship with each other.

While *The Eagle* and *Centurion* are set in a strong but flawed Roman Empire, *The Last Legion* takes place in a rapidly collapsing Roman Empire that seeks to preserve some small fragments of its former greatness. The plot is very loosely based on the life of Romulus Augustulus, one of the last emperors of Rome, which has been somewhat unharmoniously grafted onto the Arthurian mythos of Britain. Britain thus has the opportunity to inherit the best aspects of Roman imperialism while abandoning its alleged decadence and corruption.

Figure 12.2 Diverse Roman officers in *The Last Legion* (2007). Dino de Laurentiis Company.

The film begins with a cinematically very traditional Roman parade, echoing similar scenes in films like *Ben-Hur* or *Quo Vadis*. In this case, the parade marks the coronation of the young boy-emperor Romulus Augustulus (Thomas Sangster), who is acclaimed by an ethnically mixed group of civilians and soldiers while the wealth and pomp of the Empire are on full display, recalling the old glory days of triumphal imperialism. When the city of Rome soon thereafter collapses under barbarian onslaught, a small squadron of brave Roman bodyguards and legionaries rescues Romulus and escapes with him to Britannia (see Figure 12.2). This force is so ahistorically diverse that it includes noted Bollywood actress Aishwarya Rai as a female warrior from the Indian province of Kerala, who has, for no clear reason, joined the guards of the Eastern Roman Empire. The film also features an African character named Batiatus and a Byzantine ambassador played by Alexander Siddig, an ethnically Sudanese actor. Such casting takes the idea of the Roman cosmopolitan meritocracy to an extreme, creating an idealized Rome for today rather than reflecting the more realistically prejudiced society of Roman antiquity.

The brave and motley group of bodyguards successfully defends the young blond Romulus from both Germanic barbarians and native Britons, just as earlier cinematic armies defeated earlier groups of Germans. However, in this case they are unable to save or restore the government itself, managing to barely escape with their lives from what is represented as an unstoppable barbarian force. Our heroes eventually establish a new successor kingdom in Britannia, which is revealed in the epilogue to be the kingdom of King Arthur. Hadrian's Wall is described explicitly as "a monument to law and order," further underscoring the anti-barbarian messaging. Colin Firth, playing the leader of Romulus' protectors, echoes *Gladiator* in a climactic speech where he proclaims, "Remember that there was such a thing as a Roman soldier, with a Roman sword, and a Roman heart! Hail Caesar!" Even as the empire collapses, its memory is seen as worthy of commemoration. At the same time, it is specifically Roman military prowess that is venerated in all three of these films, rather than Rome's prosperity, culture, or legal system. The Roman Empire becomes a useful tool in these films for invoking an ethic of the heroic warrior code defined by the loyalty of the squad or pair of soldiers, rather than by the individual prowess of valiant heroes such as those seen in medieval or early modern-era films.

WHAT PORTRAYALS OF IMPERIALISM AS "GOLDEN" AVOID

However, there are some glaring thematic omissions from such positive portrayals of Roman imperialism. For example, the Republican setting of *Cabiria* and *Scipione* conveniently allows these films to dodge the problem of Christianity and Roman persecution. Most pre-2000 films set in Roman antiquity treat Christianity and Christian characters as unambiguously righteous and virtuous, ranging from the conversion narratives of *Ben-Hur* and *Quo Vadis* to even more explicitly Christian films like *The Sign of the Cross* (1932). In a conflict between polytheist Romans and Christians in twentieth-century films, the Romans are almost inevitably the villains. As a result, pro-Roman films rarely feature such themes, which would necessitate justifying religious persecution of Christians. Even in films set after the dawn of Christianity, religion is largely absent from the picture in most pro-Roman films. In *The Fall of the Roman Empire*, Timonides is a crypto-Christian, but his faith only lightly informs his moral choices and does not form a major arc within the film. While Christianity forms the major theme of Monty Python's *Life of Brian*, much of the Pythons' humor is targeted at religion.

The pro-Roman films of recent decades tend to offer a nebulous and hazy celebration of polytheism, while making no mention of Christianity. This absence is particularly striking in *Gladiator*. A scene in which Maximus saw condemned Christians fed to the lions in the arena was deleted from the final film.[30] Indeed, one of Commodus' historical assassins, the concubine Marcia, was a known supporter of Christians and in fact Commodus himself presided over an era of Christian toleration.[31] However, such a message would interfere with the theme of Commodus' villainy and the film's emphasis on a more universalist and inchoate approach to religion. If Rome is corrupt in *Gladiator*, it is largely the result of Commodus' autocratic rule, rather than as a symptom of any systemic oppression. Under a good ruler or an idealized return to the Republic, Roman rule might be entirely beneficial, *Gladiator* suggests.

Another major issue that *Life of Brian* almost entirely ignores is slavery, one of the traditional evils of cinematic Rome. So too *Gladiator*, like earlier pro-imperialist films, significantly erases or diminishes this common critique of Roman society connected to imperialism and the Empire. While the gladiators are treated harshly as slaves, there is almost no other critique or presence of the slavery endemic within the Roman world. Maximus has a "servant," the ironically named Cicero (Tommy Flanagan), who remains loyal to Maximus and dies trying to rescue him; the imperial household similarly, according to the screenplay, has "servants" and "tall African servants," rather than the slaves who would have surrounded nobles like Lucilla (Connie Nielsen) and Lucius (Spencer Treat Clark) in reality.[32] Forcing men to fight and die for entertainment is cruel and evil, within the context of *Gladiator*, but the film glosses over the basic economic inequities and injustices of the Roman world. Who works Maximus' farm for him while he is away at war? The presumptive slave steward and field hands do not appear in his gauzy visions of the past.

In both *The Eagle* and *Centurion*, the Roman Empire is also apparently inhabited almost entirely by men, which contributes to these films' focus on the nature and worth of masculinity. The main protagonists in all these movies are all straight white men; leadership roles are still reserved for a conventional elite, despite the more diverse leadership of the actual Roman Empire itself. For instance, there is not a single named female character in *The Eagle*, despite the presence of prominent female characters in its source material, Rosemary Sutcliff's novel *The Eagle of the Ninth* (1954). Etain (Olga Kurylenko), the most significant woman in *Centurion*, is a mute barbarian scout whose tongue was ripped out by Roman soldiers. She is also eventually revealed to be a rape victim whose suffering motivates both her and her fellow Picts to fight against the Romans; her own perspective on the vices of Roman rule is never directly given to the audience. While Etain serves as a symbolic rebuke to the dangers of imperialist conquest, her revenge seems inappropriately brutal and outside the bounds of civilized behavior, as well as driven by emotion rather than rationality. Rape is not presented as a uniquely Roman or uniquely imperialist practice, but rather as one of the general awful consequences of war and conquest. *Centurion*'s other female character, the alleged witch Arianne, is also largely presented as a subordinate foil for the male characters.

In *The Last Legion*, Rai serves both as a token female warrior, somewhat like *Centurion*'s Etain, and as an implicit reference to the success and cosmopolitan nature of the modern British Empire and its conquest of India, a nod to diversity also invoked in *Centurion*. In this mythical retelling of the founding of Arthurian Britain, the best of these two imperial regimes can meet in the romantic union of the impeccably English Firth and the exotic Rai.

CONCLUSION

At the end of *The Last Legion*, Ben Kingsley as Merlin inverts the assessment by Tacitus (*Agricola* 30) in his epilogic narration, proclaiming, "The last of the Romans found a home here in Britannia and after years of turmoil, they brought peace to the land." (Kingsley here sharply inverts the message he had famously delivered as the titular anti-imperialist character of *Gandhi* [1982].) Rather than making Britannia an empty wasteland, the Romans are described as the new force of civilization, imposing right over might in the reign of King Arthur. This transformative message has more than a little in common with the beneficent imperialism of Italian fascist films in the early twentieth century. However, it presents Roman civilization as the endangered force under siege, forced to transplant itself to a more hospitable land, rather than as a successful expansionist conqueror. Roman imperialism's claim to be a force for good is still undoubtedly questioned, especially in the twenty-first century, and especially when works of classical reception directly address issues of slavery and patriarchal oppression. However, the "evil empire" is not and has never been the only representation of the Roman Empire.

As the United States and Great Britain again adopt a more aggressive military stance and often see themselves as the guardians of a nebulously defined "Western civilization," it is unsurprising that once again Anglo-American media might choose to emphasize all the things that the Romans have done "for us." In a political moment where authoritarian and nationalist movements seem to be gaining strength around the world, the valorization of these aspects of Roman society harken back to the propagandistic films of Mussolini. In particular, although these films all celebrate the multicultural, multi-ethnic nature of the Roman Empire, they emphasize that Roman-style peace can be best achieved through the brilliance and strength of a male European autocratic ruler who imposes order and Western technology on his subjects, while allowing them to maintain unthreatening quaint cultural practices. There are many lessons that modern audiences might receive through popular representations of ancient Rome; this particular one is perhaps even more dangerous than the notion that all Romans were debauched hedonists who burned Christians for their idle amusement.

NOTES

1 E.g. Winkler (1995), Cyrino (2005), Wyke (1997, repr. 2013; 1999).
2 Roman imperialist expansion begins by the third century BCE; the period of one-man rule beginning with Augustus in 31 BCE is more accurately termed the Principate, but often popularly described as the Empire.
3 Wyke (1997, repr. 2013: 20–4).
4 Miles (2011: 260–79).
5 Dorgerloh (2013: 234).
6 Dorgerloh (2013: 230). For further bibliography on *Cabiria*, see Morcillo (2015: 160 n59).
7 Pastrone as transcribed in Wyke (1997, repr. 2013: 188).
8 Vergil, *Aeneid* 6.848–53: "Other peoples, I know certainly, create living features out of marble ... But you, Roman, remember, rule over the nations with your might" (my translation).
9 Wyke (1997, repr. 2013: 21).
10 Dorgerloh (2013: 232).
11 Cited in Wyke (1999: 202).
12 As transcribed in Wyke (1997, repr. 2013).
13 Caprotti (2009: 387).
14 Caprotti (2009: 392).
15 Caprotti (2009: 394).
16 Caprotti (2009: 393).
17 Liehm (1984: 7).
18 Wyke (1997, repr. 2013: 20–2).
19 Wyke (1997, repr. 2013: 51–2).
20 Besides the works discussed here, other examples include *A Funny Thing Happened on the Way to the Forum* (1966), *I, Claudius* (1976), and, to some extent, *Cleopatra* (1963).
21 See Winkler (1995; 2009b) for the fullest treatment of this film.
22 Crowther (1964).
23 Ward (2009: 52).
24 Bhaskar (2009).
25 Cyrino (2004: 125).
26 Boyle (2011: 149–52).

27 The Picts in these films, which echo many elements of traditional Westerns, can be interpreted as replacements for Native Americans, who are a less acceptable target for vilification in the modern world. Ancient barbarians can conveniently replace nineteenth-century caricatures of Native Americans, presumably under the theory that the only people possibly offended will be the Scots. See Keen (2014: 5–6) for more details.
28 Faraci (2011).
29 Barker (2008: 171–2).
30 Solomon (2004: 12).
31 Strong (2014: 2–3).
32 Franzoni (2000: scene 187).

13 Broken Eagles: The Iron Age of Imperial Roman Warfare in Post-9/11 Film

Alex McAuley

A comparison of two very different battles serves to illustrate how the depiction of ancient warfare on film has changed during the decades separating the golden age of Classics on screen in the 1950s and 1960s from its post-2000 revival thanks to Ridley Scott's *Gladiator*. The first example is the climactic end to Stanley Kubrick's *Spartacus* (1960), in which two massed armies align themselves for the rhythmic dance of ancient warfare on the plains of Campania, where the historical Spartacus met his end in 71 BCE. Jon Solomon captures the scene's ambience perfectly: "in all of filmdom there is no better exhibition of Roman military genius ... the Roman cohorts and maniples, machinelike and crimson-cloaked, maneuver into perfectly straight phalanxes of icy death."[1] Juxtaposed with such calculating, faceless military might is the ragged but ardent slave army. In the end, their fervor for freedom cannot best the unflinching precision of Crassus' legions.

In the second example, the ominous forests of the Scottish Highlands circa 117 CE set the moody stage for the second major battle scene of Neil Marshall's *Centurion* (2010). Amid the fog and rain, the camera catches furtive glimpses of native Picts spreading through their ancestral lands. Weapons in hand, they wait as the unsuspecting Roman column marches deeper into the shadows of the forest, tipped off by Etain (Olga Kurylenko), their mute spy planted among the Ninth Legion. A tree falls to block the legion's way; as the soldiers are forming themselves up, suddenly flaming bales roll at them from both sides, breaking apart the unprepared ranks. Brutal slaughter follows as the Picts attack, beheading the hated Romans as they advance steadily toward the general of the Ninth Legion, Titus Flavius Virilus (Dominic West). The scene ends with the protagonist, Quintus Dias (Michael Fassbender), hiding among the dead to save his own life as Virilus is carried off by the Pictish guerrillas. So much for the grandeur that was Rome.

The fundamental shift in contemporary perceptions and depictions of ancient warfare over these fifty years is a direct reflection of the changes in modern warfare that began with the Vietnam War and continued during the post-9/11 "War on Terror."[2] This evolution of contemporary conflict has been well noted in military circles, where numerous works have explored the emergence since the Vietnam era of "non-traditional" or "unconventional" warfare, which has become significantly more complicated with the occupations of Iraq and Afghanistan.[3] A fundamental shift in the psychology of warfare and killing since Vietnam has increasingly dehumanized the enemy and shifted guilt for combat from the individual to the collective unit.[4] The unclear line between friend and foe, the prevalence of ambushes, kidnappings, and civilian attacks, along with the uncertain convictions of soldiers themselves, have created a vastly different and more ambiguous kind of conflict than the neat Cold-War binary of *Spartacus*. The golden age of righteously justified warfare against a clear, villainous enemy has faded, giving way to a gritty iron age in which the only constants in armed conflict are violence and privation in a struggle against an unclear enemy.

Capturing this new climate of warfare in an ancient context was precisely *Centurion* director Neil Marshall's intent:

> My dad was in the army, my granddad was in the army, so I definitely have an affinity for soldiers and the like. And so my film is about the individual. It's about the fact that, regardless of what you may think about these campaigns, be it Rome, be it what's going on in Afghanistan, whatever . . . that's primarily what the story's about – this bunch of guys who are betrayed and become disillusioned by the job they're doing and just want to get home.[5]

This depiction of Roman soldiers as betrayed, disillusioned, and desperate for a return to peace and tranquility stands at a vast remove from the robotic, emotionless soldiers of *Spartacus* and dozens of other films like it. The messy experience of Vietnam, echoed in the conflicts in Iraq, Afghanistan, and now Syria, has rendered the ability to distinguish enemy from ally between uncertain and impossible. Such contemporary changes in warfare manifest themselves clearly in films set in Roman antiquity that have been produced since 9/11.

This chapter examines the impact of this paradigm shift on contemporary depictions of the Roman army and its soldiers: first, by considering the "golden age" of Roman warfare as shown by films from the 1950s and 1960s in contrast with the dystopic view of *Centurion* and *The Eagle* (2011). Then follows the depiction of the individual Roman soldier in each era: the transition from the faceless, nameless automaton of the golden age of peplum to the jaded veterans of contemporary films who suffer from a haranguing conscience about their mission and from post-traumatic stress disorder (PTSD). Lastly, the broader contemporary context for these post-9/11 depictions of antiquity comes into focus: the growing body of films about the War on Terror, with which films like *Centurion* and *The Eagle* have far more in common than with their golden-age predecessors.

THE GOLDEN OLD DAYS

The period stretching roughly from the close of World War II until the glorious failure that was 1963's *Cleopatra* is widely held to be the golden age of the ancient world in popular cinema, in both the North American and European markets. In these years, Hollywood produced most of its canon of wildly successful big-budget blockbusters set in antiquity, including *The Robe* (1953), *Ben-Hur* (1959), and *Spartacus*. Across the Atlantic, Italian film studios were producing classically themed films by the dozens, from one-off epics like *Annibale* (1959) and *Romolo e Remo* (1961) to the serialized offerings recounting the adventures of Hercules and knock-off heroes like Maciste. This era merits the "golden" moniker by virtue of the genre's pervasiveness: the commercial success of one studio's epic led to emulation by another in a repeating cycle of swelling budgets and revenues. Underpinning this profitability is the morality of the conflict itself: filmmakers and studios clearly placed themselves on the side of the "good guys" in the conflict, tying their works into an oppositional political narrative.

This "golden age" took place in the context of the clean binary of the Cold War, generating thematic similarity. Images of warfare were fresh in the minds of audiences and filmmakers alike, given the intimate documentation of World War II's atrocities in film and photography; perhaps there is some attempt to depict a cleaner, more comprehensible, more civilized form of ancient warfare after the sobering experience of modern conflicts. Whether such depictions are the product of nostalgia or contemporary idealization of warfare, the dialogue between ancient and modern concerns persists.

Warfare as depicted by these golden-age films was a rather straightforward affair – in a word, "conventional." In the victory of Caesar against Pompey in *Cleopatra*, clashes with the Dacians in *The Fall of the Roman Empire* (1964), the Battle of Cannae in *Annibale*, or the naval equivalent in *Ben-Hur*, armies lined up against other armies *en masse* in a location that limited collateral damage; the two sides of the conflict were handily delineated for the viewer by distinct cloaks, shields, or armor; and at the sound of a trumpet, battle was engaged. The clash of men and arms was typically depicted by wide-angle shots of troop formations combined with quick cuts to close combat between small groups of soldiers until a clear victor was decided. The scene that followed returned the principal characters to the foreground as they discussed the consequences of their success or failure, and the narrative proceeded. The same is true of Greek-themed films such as *The 300 Spartans* (1962) and *Alexander the Great* (1956).

Such clean and coherent depictions of pitched warfare between two opposing sides logically reflect the Cold-War context. A great deal has been written on how the Cold War left its mark on contemporary depictions of antiquity in the 1950s and 1960s, ranging from *The 300 Spartans*' appeal for NATO unity against the Soviet Union's encroachment in Europe to *Spartacus*' thinly veiled commentary on liberty versus absolutism.[6] Warfare in such films became a facet of the broader morality drama that pitted capitalist, Christian America against atheistic, totalitarian Russia in various ancient Greek and Roman contexts. As contemporary political conflicts were grafted onto antiquity, contemporary attitudes toward warfare were carried over as well. The clarity offered by such contemporary resonance easily led audiences to identify with one side over another, be it the Christians of *Demetrius and the Gladiators* (1954) or the rebel slave army of *Spartacus*.

Thus ancient warfare becomes, as von Clausewitz famously observed, "the continuation of politics by other means." Political clashes with at least understandable, if not necessarily sympathetic, causes led to military clashes; a victor was decided in combat; and then the narrative of the film resumed. This approach to screening ancient warfare was not unique to the 1950s and 1960s, of course, as the clear ideological lines that were drawn on either side of World Wars I and II presented themselves as clearly in *Cabiria* (1914) and in *Scipione l'Africano* (1937). In this sense, perhaps there is more similarity between the propagandistic function of films like the Italian *Cabiria* and the American *Spartacus* than may be comfortable to admit. The contemporary resonance of ancient warfare as depicted is the same in mechanism, if not precise content, and the device resonated with nationalistic Italian audiences as it did with the American filmgoers of the 1950s and 1960s.[7]

THE NEW IRON DAYS

Conventional, neat, contained, intelligible: none of these terms describe either post-9/11 warfare or its ancient echoes on screen. In a sense, there has been a transition from a golden age of cinematic warfare to an iron one. After the Cold War and the collapse of the Soviet Union, the type of warfare fought between two major opposing powers was widely considered obsolete.[8] Wars were no longer fought against an entire opposing state, but rather a regime, a group within a nation, or even an individual figure of authority – a distinction made by President Bill Clinton when describing American intervention in Serbia as not being a conflict against the Serbians themselves, only one against their leadership.[9] The identification of the enemy thus became more complicated and nuanced, a problem compounded by the resurgence in collateral damage that came with post-9/11 conflicts.

Attitudes about the enemy also changed. In World Wars I and II, the clear distinction between friend and foe engendered a respect bordering on admiration for the enemy among combatants. As T. E. Lawrence writes of the German soldiers who resisted his Arab troops, "I grew proud of the enemy who had killed my brothers . . . There was no haste, no crying, no hesitation. They were glorious."[10] To some extent, this distinction had frayed in the Korean War; by the time of the Vietnam War, it had collapsed entirely. As Edward Doyle describes in his memoirs, published in *Soldier of Fortune* magazine in 1983:

> The often subtle nuances and indicates used by interrogators to identify VC [Viet Cong Regulars] from civilian, combatant from non-combatant, were a luxury they felt they could not afford. The decision, VC or not VC, often had to be reached in a split second . . . The soldiers never found out whether the Vietnamese was VC or not. Such was the perplexity of a war in which the enemy was not a foreign force but lived and fought among the people.[11]

Such ambiguity was the product of new styles of combat. Instead of the pitched battles of massed armies for which the Cold-War-era militaries had trained, now guerrilla tactics of ambushes, surprise attacks, intimidation, and hostage-taking were employed by an enemy increasingly difficult to distinguish from the civilian populace. Technologically superior armies found that even irregular, haphazardly trained fighters put up a difficult fight. The clear tones of black and white that had colored warfare gave way to the post-Vietnam world's disturbing shades of grey.

Such messy warfare is depicted by the duo of Rosemary Sutcliff-inspired films based on the legend of the Ninth Legion: 2010's *Centurion* and 2011's *The Eagle*.[12] Gone are the neat depictions of Romans fighting against their barbaric enemies in every corner of the Empire, as the grit, confusion, and brutality of contemporary warfare are retrojected onto Roman Britain. In this new paradigm of ancient warfare, a lone but highly talented Roman solider must venture into the wilds of the Highlands in order to retrieve his ambushed legion's eagle standard, thus avenging Roman honor. In the process, each protagonist – Quintus Dias in *Centurion* and the aptly named Aquila (Channing Tatum) in *The Eagle* – must confront the results of the brutal Roman occupation first-hand "beyond the wall": the survivors of Roman atrocities, Roman veterans who deserted, and the suspect loyalties of native guides. In the process of recovering the eagle, Aquila recovers himself.

By contrast, post-2000 films set in the Greek world, among them *300* (2006) and *Alexander* (2004), tend to depict the victory of a charismatic group of talented, individualistic fighters against the uniform forces of outside (generally Eastern) imperialism. Such films are narratives of resistance and questing, not occupation, and are comparable to the slew of mythologically themed films such as *Immortals* (2011) and *Hercules* (2014) that have also grown in popularity. Films set in Roman antiquity, such as *Centurion*, *The Eagle*, and even perhaps *King Arthur* (2004) and *The Last Legion* (2007), view ancient conflicts from the other side: the struggle to retain Roman imperial control of the ends of the empire against the "un-Roman" (read: "un-civilized") native subjects. In locating such films on the margins of empire and narrating the side of the imperialists, these directors suggest an eerily familiar setting to the post-9/11 American or British viewer.

The contemporary resonance of such narratives is not subtle – as the directors intended. Marshall states that *Centurion* is about "a superpower invading a country and encountering guerrilla warfare," leading *The Guardian*'s Charlotte Higgins to note that "Rome gives us an ideal template for thinking about that other Empire, the United States."[13] Kevin MacDonald, director of *The Eagle*, states that he was "interested in making it like a documentary . . . The Romans are like a tank rolling through a Vietnamese village, you've got disjunction of level of fighting know-how."[14] The Romans, for all of their superior weapons, training, and discipline, are recurrently unable to overcome the tenacious Picts because of such unconventional warfare. Quintus Dias notes this glumly at the very beginning of *Centurion*: "this is a new kind of war. A war without honor. A war without end."

Much like the Americans in Vietnam or the Coalition forces in Iraq or Afghanistan, the conventionally trained Roman legions in Britain were never intended to fight this type of warfare. The native "insurgents" of *Centurion* and *The Eagle*, much like their Iraqi or Afghan counterparts, avoid pitched battles like those in *Spartacus*, preferring evasive, small-scale, guerrilla ambushes. Quintus Dias observes that "they will not be drawn into open combat. They pick at the scab until we bleed, hiding in the shadows like animals, striking hard and then falling back into the night." The opening scenes of each film enact the dangers posed by this unaccustomed kind of warfare, as the Roman garrison is ambushed under cover of darkness in order for the unsuspecting Roman soldiers to be slaughtered as they sleep. The Romans, in each case, only put forward a hasty and disorganized response to such unconventional tactics. The incompatibility of the Roman legions with such warfare is patent in *Centurion*'s ambush scene, described at the outset of this chapter (see Figure 13.1): the well-armored, orderly Roman column falls victim to the ambush of Pictish warriors sneaking through the forest and lying in wait along their marching route. Flaming bales striking the Roman flanks evoke images of improvised explosive devices (IEDs) detonating along Coalition patrol routes in Afghanistan or Iraq, as recounted in the news media.

Figure 13.1 This ambush of the Ninth Legion evokes roadside ambushes as occurred during the invasions of Iraq and Afghanistan, in *Centurion* (2010). Celador Films / Canal+ / Warner.

These films' depiction of unconventional ancient warfare is accompanied by what audiences may well recognize as wartime atrocities. After such ambushes, "insurgent" forces take Roman hostages and, in *The Eagle*, parade them around in front of the Roman fort before brutally beheading their captives: an all-too-contemporary image. After General Virilus' capture in *Centurion*, the weakened soldier is publicly executed by being forced to fight the fearsome Etain to the death in the Pictish camp as her comrades cheer her on. Quintus Dias is likewise tortured and interrogated in captivity before escaping; Aquila has a similar experience at the hands of the Seal People.

Non-Roman characters allude to similar atrocities committed by the Romans during occupation, but not depicted on screen. The druid of *The Eagle* shouts at the Romans in the besieged camp "you have stolen our lands and killed our sons, you have defiled our daughters, I curse you." Esca (Jamie Bell), Aquila's guide-*cum*-sidekick in the same film, recounts his own experience of Roman brutality:

> Seven years ago, you took our lands when we rose against you. My father and two brothers died. My mother also. My father killed her before the legionaries broke through, he knew what they would do to her. She knelt in front him while he slit her throat. Rome also did that.

In *Centurion*, the muteness of Etain, the Pictish tracker, is also explained by a Roman atrocity. As a child, her village was destroyed as an example of what happens when Roman rule is resisted. The Romans put out her father's eyes, raped and killed her mother, and raped little Etain as well before cutting out her tongue so that she might not speak ill of Rome in the future. Gorlacon (Ulrich Thomsen), the Pictish chieftain and leader of the resistance, had been introduced as a farmer – until the murder of his wife led him to put down the plow and take up the sword.

This dark and messy conflict is a far cry from the neat battle lines of *Spartacus* and *The Fall of the Roman Empire*, reflecting the ambiguity and confusion of contemporary wars of occupation instead of the more comprehensible conflicts among nations that characterized both the Cold War and the ancient-world films through which its ideology was filtered. In these post-9/11 depictions of antiquity, armies that were designed for large-scale battles are recurrently stuck in smaller-scale engagements. Most battle scenes have at most fifty combatants on each side, generating an intimacy that aligns with the prevalence of squad- or platoon-based engagements in contemporary theaters of operation. There are no more monolithically decisive battles with thousands on either side. Instead, these conflicts are resolved by numerous intermittent clashes between smaller groups that often spill off the battlefield and blur the line between civilian and combatant.

ROMAN MARINES: SCREENING ANCIENT PTSD

Vastly different types of soldier are suited to these vastly different types of war. The image of the Roman legionary that dominates films from the 1950s and 1960s is that of the faceless, emotionless professional, the consummate soldier fighting for the consummate empire. The average legionary in such films is equally capable and robotic, highly disciplined and well trained in the arts of war. Consider the statuesque Roman soldiers who line the route of Judah Ben-Hur's triumphal procession; so too the legionaries of Caesar, Antony, and Octavian in *Cleopatra* are clearly intended to contrast with the garishly exotic soldiers of the Egyptian queen. The same trope is found among the soldiers who cast the Christians into the arena in *The Sign of the Cross* (1932) and those who lead the tribune Marcellus to his death on the archery range at the behest of Caligula in *The Robe*. The depiction of Roman soldiers throughout these films, and extending to the Praetorians of *Gladiator*, is remarkably consistent: faceless, unflinching, executing their orders without hesitation or reflection. They generally have little or no dialogue, are brutally effective, and, more often than not, are undefeated on the battlefield.

Soldiers such as Aquila of *The Eagle* and Quintus Dias of *Centurion*, however, have more in common with the American GIs of *Jarhead* (2005) or *The Hurt Locker* (2008) than they do with their generic golden-age Roman predecessors – again, by design. Kevin MacDonald placed a similar emphasis on the individual soldier in *The Eagle* as did Neil Marshall in *Centurion*, though MacDonald had a more specific image in mind: "in order to make it feel like it has some kind of resonance today – to see Channing [Tatum] as an American soldier, as a Marine – it makes you see Rome in a new, fresh way."[15] Indeed, the lens of contemporary combatants in Iraq or Afghanistan, or of older veterans from the Vietnam era, does offer viewers a new, fresh way to think of the ancient Roman legionary. In the process, they are exposed to a grittier side of ancient warfare previously obscured by the preference for large-scale set-piece battles between opposing states.

The controversy and the moral ambiguity surrounding these contemporary conflicts has focused attention on the psychological experience of the individual soldier both during and after war. While the horrors and trauma of the battlefield are hardly new, Dave Grossman explains:

> Since World War II a new era has quietly dawned in modern warfare: an era of psychological warfare, conducted not upon the enemy but upon one's own troops . . . [N]ever in American history has the combination of psychological blows inflicted on a group of returning warriors been so intense as since the Vietnam era.[16]

This psychological warfare is fought on two fronts: first, the conditioning of contemporary soldiers by their own military, with the goal of desensitizing them to the trauma of conflict and bloodshed; then, the internalization of these experiences on the home front amid widespread domestic criticism of the conflicts and their combatants. This combination of wartime trauma and peacetime controversy has created an all-too-populous class of walking wounded suffering from PTSD, surviving combatants who can nevertheless be counted among the casualties of this new kind of warfare.[17]

MacDonald and Marshall are clearly engaging with this discourse surrounding the experience of contemporary combat in the War on Terror and its lasting effects on combatants. The former's interest in the American Marine is underlined by the prevalence of American accents in *The Eagle*, leading the viewer to identify Roman combatants with twenty-first-century GIs. Each film's protagonist is shown struggling with his experience of combat in this horrific new "iron age" of warfare. *Centurion*'s Quintus Dias is taken prisoner at the beginning of the film, then tortured with an ancient equivalent of waterboarding, and barely manages to escape back to Roman lines. His new commanding officer Virilus is aware of the lasting damage that such experiences can bring about on a soldier's psyche. Sitting down next to him, Virilus asks how Dias is doing and cautions him that "sometimes there are scars that can't be seen."

The Eagle addresses the subject of PTSD rather more directly. After being badly wounded in the defense of a northern outpost, Aquila recovers in the genteel civility of his uncle's villa in Roman Britain. Although he is discharged from the army with the Roman equivalent of a Purple Heart, he has trouble escaping the memories of his service. He suffers from recurring nightmares during his convalescence: images of the men who died under his command and the savagery of those who killed his father, combined with the eagle falling. Other Roman soldiers suffer as well. Much later in the film, Aquila and Esca come across the veteran legionary L. Caius Metellus (Mark Strong), who describes the horrors that befell the legion during his service. Scarred and battered by the experience of seeing the feet of his dead comrades being severed and his officers executed as human sacrifices, he fled and never returned to the Roman fold. When Aquila calls him a coward, Metellus retorts "you weren't here, you don't know what it was like."

This darker kind of warfare at the edge of the Roman world can bring out the worst in Roman soldiers, and it is fascinating to see how some of the agents of Rome's military might devolve into cowards, thieves, and murderers. Quintus Dias' ragged band of Roman survivors in *Centurion* include decidedly unsavory characters; the worst two betray each other after they attempt to escape and save themselves. Another of the soldiers muses that "this was supposed to be my last tour" before daydreaming of his retirement in Tuscany, evoking the sympathy of the modern viewer despite the historical inaccuracy of this plan for a legionary in the Imperial Period. Somewhat more optimistically, Aquila's recovery of his father's eagle is thanks to the assistance of old Roman soldiers who had broken ranks and fled when the legion was first ambushed. Their redemption translates into the success of his mission.

After witnessing the darker side of Roman imperialism from the side of the conquered and upon hearing, from both allies and captors, tales of Roman brutality toward those who resist their rule, Aquila quickly becomes disillusioned, both with his mission in Roman Britain in particular and with his allegiance to Rome. Early in *The Eagle*, as Aquila recovers in his uncle's villa, his uncle hosts a dinner party at which the conversation turns to the glory that comes from a soldier serving Rome, courageously and faithfully. Aquila's uncle (Donald Sutherland) turns to him and assures him, "you did, son." Aquila responds furiously, shouting "for what? For what!" Deep behind enemy lines, Aquila literally steps into the shoes of the occupied when he poses as Esca's slave in order to gain entry into the village of the Seal People, where his treatment reveals the depth of resentment for Roman rule.

Aquila's disillusionment becomes patent after he and his band of veterans manage to recover the eagle of the Ninth in the film's climactic battle. Following his victory, he pays tribute to the men who fought and died in the name of honor – Britons and Romans alike – and prays "may peace and honor follow you, may you know no more strife." Aquila has realized that mutual loss is the product of this new kind of warfare, and in the end, he turns his back on Rome. Returning the eagle to the Roman governor redeems his family's honor, but Aquila retains little respect for Rome. At the governor's headquarters, he boldly asserts that the slave Esca knows more about honor and freedom than the son of the governor ever will, then walks out with his companion.

Centurion depicts Quintus Dias' shifting loyalties more directly, as the narrative essentially traces his abandonment of the Roman cause; much like Aquila, witnessing both sides of the Roman occupation of Britain scars him. Early in the film, even General Virilus admits that "the conquest of Britain is a lost cause." Instead of belief in the mission, he expresses his loyalty to the men under his command. Fraternity among soldiers as a unifying substitute for their belief in the war itself pervades Vietnam-era films, notably *Platoon* (1986) and *Full Metal Jacket* (1987). Dias' pursuit of the eagle is driven by the promise he made to Virilus; after returning the eagle to Roman headquarters, he feels no further allegiance to the corrupt, deceptive Roman administration. Indeed, rather than admitting the defeat of an entire legion and thereby risking further revolt by the emboldened Picts, the governor Agricola (Paul Freeman) prefers that the fate of the Ninth remain a mystery and plots to cover up the entire affair by killing Dias, who manages to foil the attempt and escape. Embittered after his betrayal by Rome, Dias then flees to "where I belong," as he tells Agricola's daughter: with the Pictish accused witch Arianne (Imogen Poots), herself an exile from her community. While initially he described himself as "a soldier of Rome," by the film's end Dias' loyalties have changed: "My name is Quintus Dias, and I am a fugitive of Rome." Like Aquila, Dias' experience of brutality in service of questionable objectives evacuates his faith in Rome.

CONCLUSION: BROKEN EAGLES, THEN AND NOW

Both the new kind of warfare and the experiences of individual soldiers depicted in *Centurion* and *The Eagle* fit into broader trends of post-9/11 war films. Aquila and Dias find an unlikely fellow in, for instance, Chief Warrant Officer Roy Miller (Matt Damon), who undergoes a similar story of disillusionment in Paul Greengrass' *Green Zone* (2010). Miller gradually realizes that the alleged weapons of mass destruction that justified the second invasion of Iraq never existed. The psychological scars of the two Roman protagonists resemble those of Chris Kyle (Bradley Cooper), the protagonist of Clint Eastwood's blockbuster *American Sniper* (2014), which depicts the Navy SEAL's inability to readjust to civilian life with his family after participating in the war in Iraq. The moral ambiguity of such wars and their impact on the individual soldier echo the ambivalence of Anthony Swofford (Jake Gyllenhaal) in *Jarhead*; the desperate measures taken to survive behind enemy lines find their modern equivalent in *Lone Survivor* (2013); and the shift away from large-scale combat and toward small special-forces operations to avenge past injustices also drives *Seal Team Six* (2012) and *Zero Dark Thirty* (2012).[18]

Beyond warfare itself, *Centurion* and *The Eagle* align with the more general characteristics of post-9/11 films.[19] Both are set on the fringes of the civilized world, at the intersection of two very different ways of life, and thus engage with the "clash of civilizations" theme that has dominated Hollywood releases – whether historical or otherworldly – ranging from *War of the Worlds* (2005) to *Kingdom of Heaven* (2005). Both are set "after the fall," when the golden age of Rome has passed and the Romans are instead fighting to preserve, rather than to win, their empire.[20] Fighting for survival in desperate and uncivilized conditions aligns them with the swelling ranks of post-apocalyptic films that have dominated the box office since the turn of the century, including *28 Days Later* (2002), *I Am Legend* (2007), and *The Book of Eli* (2010). The fear and anxiety that become paranoia, roused by the uncertain loyalties of Dias and Aquila's native companions and their betrayal by Roman officials, also describe the conspiratorial tones of *V for Vendetta* (2005), *Good Night and Good Luck* (2005), and *Batman Begins* (2005).[21]

This alignment of *The Eagle* and *Centurion* with the tropes that dominate post-9/11 cinema reflects Kevin MacDonald's and Neil Marshall's intent to use Roman Britain as a space for exploring these contemporary preoccupations with the clash of civilizations, occupation of territories by foreign armies, and the justifications thereof. While making a film set in his own historical backyard, Marshall nevertheless chose to frame it as a parable of the American experience in Iraq, as did Kevin MacDonald. In so doing, they discard the glory and the grandeur of the golden age of sword-and-sandal films in Hollywood in exchange for the gritty uncertainty of contemporary conflicts in an ancient setting. Gone is the idealistic certainty of conventional warfare. In its place arises a confusing, multipolar, and brutally violent iron age akin to that described by Hesiod in his archaic Greek poem *Works and Days*: a war, and a world, without honor – only moral uncertainty.

Yet in the process these directors have, perhaps unwittingly, raised popular awareness of an aspect of ancient Roman history that is often confined to academic circles. The ancient Greeks and Romans did indeed fight such brutal wars as those depicted in contemporary films, including "guerrilla-style" campaigns waged everywhere from Bactria, by Alexander the Great, to Britain in the Roman Imperial Period.[22] In a sense, the changing character of contemporary warfare has stimulated a rediscovery of certain facets of ancient conflict that have been either glossed over or ignored in popular media.

Beyond modes of depiction, the subject matter of contemporary films set in antiquity, including the works of Marshall and MacDonald, has profoundly changed since the mid-twentieth-century golden age of ancient-world epics. Creating a parallel between modern soldiers in Afghanistan or Iraq and their ancient counterparts in Roman Britain helps audiences to imagine experiences that are obscured by the limitations of extant sources. The lesson, then, is not that the golden age of ancient warfare faded as contemporary conflicts took on a vastly different character than their Cold-War antecedents; but rather that even in the farthest extremes of Roman Britain, the present always lurks in such ancient shadows, and leads us to perceive antiquity with different eyes.

NOTES

My thanks go to Meredith E. Safran for her kind invitation to contribute to this volume, as well as her past and present editorial insight. The structure of this discussion and its emphasis on the psychological shifts in contemporary warfare are thanks to the guidance of my colleague C. W. Marshall at the University of British Columbia, to whom I am immensely grateful. All errors, omissions, oversights, and infelicities remain, of course, mine alone.

1 Solomon (2001: 53–5).

2 Throughout this chapter "War on Terror" serves as familiar shorthand for the conflicts that have arisen since the attacks on the Pentagon, Twin Towers, and United Airlines Flight 93 on September 11, 2001. The "War on Terror," although a somewhat nebulous appellation for the invasions of Iraq, Afghanistan, the war against ISIS, and various conflicts associated with the Arab Spring, has been ubiquitous in the media.

3 Many studies of non-traditional warfare have proliferated since the 2000s: see, for example, Schilling (2002) and Duyvesten and Angstrom (2005), who trace the notion back to an allusion by John F. Kennedy. The concept is elaborated in the US Army's 2010 *Special Forces Unconventional Warfare Training Manual* compiled by the United States Department of the Army.

4 See Grossman (2009: 251–64) on the psychological shifts in the Vietnam War and (2009: 149–56) on the notion of "Group Absolution."

5 Quoted in Henney (2010).
6 For a survey of this morality drama, see Llewellyn-Jones (2009: 566–72), Winkler (2001b), and Wyke (1997: 1–34, 147–82). Solomon (1978; rev. 2001) describes this Cold-War context in depth in the context of each individual film. Cyrino (2005: 1–81) provides an overview of the epoch as a whole.
7 See Solomon (2001: 4–8, 47–9) on *Cabiria* and its reception among contemporary Italian audiences.
8 McInnes (2005) provides an overview of the changing military climate since 9/11, as do Angstrom (2005) and Duyvestyn (2005), all in Duyvesten and Angstrom (2005). The edited volume of Kassimeris and Buckley (2010) places these changes in a longer chronological context.
9 McInnes (2005: 114).
10 Quoted in Grossman (2009: 198); see also his discussion on the preceding pages.
11 Quoted in Grossman (2009: 198–9).
12 The *Legio IX Hispania* was a Roman legion attested since Caesar's invasion of Gaul in 58 BCE. The legion then proceeded to serve under Augustus at Actium and later in Spain and perhaps on the Rhine, before serving in campaigns along the Danube until the death of Augustus in 14 CE. In 43 CE the legion was stationed in Britain, where it remained until its last conventional attestation at York in 108/109 CE. The legend of the Ninth Legion emerged from Mommsen's hypothesis that it was destroyed by the Britons after its last attestation and was later popularized in Rosemary Sutcliff's 1954 novel *The Eagle of the Ninth*, which provides the narrative basis for these two films. For recent interpretations of the Legion's historical fate, see Keppie (1989), Sijpestijn (1996), and Campbell (2010).
13 Higgins (2010). The entire article is well worth reading, and notes that these two films turn "the traditional Roman epic on its head." Also noteworthy is Mary Beard's remarkable comparison of Boudicca to the Taliban, quoted in the same article.
14 Quoted in Faraci (2011).
15 MacDonald, quoted in Faraci (2011).
16 Grossman (2009: 253, 282). See also *Shake Hands with the Devil*, the memoirs of the Canadian Lieutenant-General Roméo Dallaire, commander of the United Nations peacekeeping forces during the Rwandan genocide, on the ravages of this new kind of warfare and their lasting impacts on its combatants (published in 2003 and adapted into both a documentary in 2007 and a feature film, *Hotel Rwanda*, in 2005).
17 For a fascinating discussion of ancient cases of PTSD, see Melchior (2011).
18 For an overview of the evolution of war films after 9/11 in general, see Toffoletti and Grace (2010).

19 Rich (2004) provides a succinct and early overview of shifts in popular culture since 9/11; for more recent treatments, see the edited volumes of Schopp and Hill (2009) and Birkenstein, Froula, and Randell (2010). This reappraisal of the post-9/11 culture of film and television contrasts heavily with the golden-age ideal of antiquity in cinema as described by Solomon (1978; rev. 2001) and Llewellyn-Jones (2009).

20 Prince (2009) describes many of these trends in greater detail, as does Nilges (2010).

21 For this notion of fear and conspiracy dominating post-9/11 cinema, see especially Altheide (2010).

22 Holt (2005) provides the best example of a contemporary approach to Alexander's campaigns in Bactria as guerrilla warfare – though he does so with a heavy dose of presentism and retrojection. In the context of Roman Britain, the campaigns of Caratacus and Boudicca could fit the mold as well.

14 *Dreaming of Rome with Ridley Scott's* Gladiator *(2000)*

Matthew Taylor

"There was once a dream that was Rome. You could only whisper it; anything more than a whisper and it would vanish, it was so fragile. And I fear it will not survive the winter." With these words from the opening act of *Gladiator* (2000), the aging emperor Marcus Aurelius (Richard Harris) confides in his general Maximus (Russell Crowe) that he wishes to make imperial Rome a republic once more, and for Maximus to be the agent of this transition. *Gladiator*'s central revenge-plot finds both its beginning and its resolution in this dream of the Republic: it is to prevent this transition and secure his imperial inheritance that Commodus (Joaquin Phoenix) murders Aurelius and orders the deaths of Maximus and his family. As Maximus struggles to return to Rome, exact his revenge, and depose Commodus, the political question of republic versus empire is linked inextricably to the progression of both the film's hero and its narrative: Maximus' last words at its climax, delivered over the corpse of his rival, promise the fulfillment of Aurelius' nostalgic desire.[1]

What does it mean to champion Rome's republic in the context of a Hollywood epic at the turn of the twenty-first century? Film critics, Classicists, and postcolonial theorists have regarded the film's ordering of its world through a discourse of republic as part of "a broader tradition in which [America] returns to Rome in order to speak its own history."[2] Whether *Gladiator*'s Rome allegorizes an America "corrupt at its heart, based on enslavement, dedicated to sustaining pointless wars," portrays a "conflict between two competing visions of what kind of superpower Rome, or by analogy America, should be," or is "a film that is both *about* empire and *of* it – depicting Roman imperial rule while enacting US global cultural capitalism,"[3] critics agree that the Republic serves as a point of reflection or refraction for contemporary perspectives on America, based upon a strong identification between America's democratic republic and the historical example of Rome.

This chapter further examines *Gladiator*'s figuration of the Roman Republic, to show how it articulates a surprisingly ambivalent perspective on the enterprise of speaking America through Rome. Richard Rushton has already demonstrated that *Gladiator* is capable of speaking in a double voice, arguing that it presents a critique of spectacle even as it indulges in "spectacular engulfment." Rushton provides two useful frames for interpreting *Gladiator*: that "[t]he film offers its own extra-diegetic comments – we might say that the film has a 'voice' – on the moral and political value of 'spectacle' as it takes place within the diegesis" and that "it provides a position from which audiences can criticize this use of spectacle . . . [placing] in question its own representational strategies."[4] Rushton's argument turns on the self-reflexive nature of a film that entertains its audience with visceral spectacle, even as its dialogue presents a critique of spectacular entertainments. This chapter suggests that *Gladiator* similarly enacts and critiques a nostalgia for Rome more broadly.

Gladiator's release in 2000, after several decades without any similar epics set in the ancient Greco-Roman world, all but necessitated its reception as the return of a Hollywood tradition, and thus infuses it with a nostalgic character even as the film itself enacts its nostalgia for Rome's past. Indeed, critics and scholars have characterized *Gladiator* as the start of a new "golden age," one that evokes another classical model even as it emplots the cinema of the 1950s and 1960s as an object of desire. This new golden age has perhaps seen its natural culmination in the release of Joel and Ethan Coen's *Hail, Caesar!* (2016), a more obviously cynical examination of Hollywood's past that grounds its own nostalgia in dramatizing a production of a *Ben-Hur*-esque Roman epic. *Hail, Caesar!* undermines the artifice of these 1950s Roman–Christian conversion narratives by granting the audience insight into the insincerity of their manufacture. In particular, the transcendent performance of Baird Whitlock (George Clooney) is offset by his imbecilic and mercurial behavior off set, exposing the generic and cynical nature of such Hollywood productions.

Gladiator's cascading *mise en abyme* – its celebration as a return of the past, even as its own plot plays out the ambivalence of idealizing the past – may in fact be best understood within the classical trope of the golden age, a complex of belated perspective and unrequitable yearning for the conditions of an earlier time that has been retrospectively valued as optimal. *Gladiator* itself contains elements of a classical golden-age discourse, simultaneously idealizing the past and implicitly foreclosing on the possibility of its return. This discourse operates on two levels within the film, both as a narrative thematic that posits Rome's republic as an irretrievable golden age, and in a set of meta-cinematics that expose the film's unreality even as they harken back to its Hollywood precursors. *Gladiator*'s formal and textual nostalgia, and its inherent cynicism regarding both, provide a critical perspective on America's tendency to view itself through Rome's past, demonstrating how phantasmic the dream of such a Roman past really is.

A TALE OF TWO ROMES

Gladiator begins by promising the achievement of one kind of golden age – one in which warfare ends in victory and only peace remains – only to undercut that promise with a sense of foreboding. This "defeat in victory," focalized through both Maximus and Aurelius, sets up their competing and equally illusory versions of "the dream that was Rome." Before the picture fades in, the audience is confronted with title cards establishing an interpretive context for Marcus Aurelius' Germanian wars in 180 CE: "Just one final stronghold stands in the way of Roman victory and the promise of peace throughout the Empire." The camera then surveys Maximus' army: a formidable spectacle of Rome's military machine, clad in steel, orderly in their ranks, a relentless, civilizing force. By contrast, the Germans emerge from the forest a ragged horde of hairy, yelling humanity: savage barbarians who must be tamed. The Germans are defeated soundly by a combination of Roman discipline and strategy, pinned in the center by a well-ordered infantry advance and outmaneuvered by Maximus' cavalry in the flanks and rear.

As the camera follows Maximus on his charge through the woods and through the arc of the battle, it is easy to identify with his personal struggle and the Roman cause. Yet in the gritty cinematography, in the gradual ramping down of the film-speed in later shots where men deliver brutal finishing blows, and in Maximus' haunted face at the close of hostilities, *Gladiator* does not present this remarkable set-piece as the glorious conclusion to the conquests heralded at its opening. By slowing down time, the film permits the audience to confront both the vicious reality of how an empire achieves its

Figure 14.1 Marcus Aurelius (Richard Harris) meditates on the peace wrought in his name in *Gladiator* (2000). Universal Studios/DreamWorks.

promised peace and their own engagement with the film's spectacular violence.[5] Any enjoyment of the carnage is threatened by the shot of Aurelius as he surveys the battlefield: whether Harris' face communicates relief, resignation, or mourning, this image potentially upsets audience satisfaction while laying the groundwork for Aurelius' disillusionment with contemporary Rome (see Figure 14.1).

Aurelius' meeting with Maximus in the Roman camp later that night addresses this disillusionment. The first dream of Rome to be exposed as chimerical is Maximus': that of the righteous empire whose conquests bring peace. Aurelius puts the righteousness of Rome's imperialism into doubt, lamenting that "For 25 years, I have conquered, spilt blood, expanded the empire. Since I became Caesar, I've known four years without war . . . And for what? I brought the sword, nothing more." Maximus, desperate to find a purpose for the deaths of men under his command, advocates for Rome as a civilizing power: "I've seen much of the rest of the world. It is brutal, and cruel, and dark. Rome is the light." "Yet you have never been there," replies Aurelius, "You have not seen what it has become!" He suggests that the Rome – inseparable as place and idea – for which Maximus has been fighting has degenerated, and that Maximus, who has never seen the place itself, doesn't realize that he has been fighting for an illusion: an idea that no longer exists.

In its place, Aurelius attempts to substitute his own nostalgic dream of Rome as a republic, redeemed by being returned to its "people." Aurelius is disillusioned with the present, fearful for the future, nostalgic for the past; his speech is thin on detail but full of affective rhetoric. He mourns for "the dream that was Rome" and yearns to be remembered as the "emperor who gave Rome back her true self." His speech culminates in charging Maximus to follow him as "protector of Rome" and to "give power back to the people of Rome and end the corruption that has crippled it." For Aurelius, this is not a question of Rome giving up the empire that his sword has pacified – merely a change in who wields that sword. Although critics have questioned the implication that a righteous, democratic government might somehow justify Rome's bloody conquests, Aurelius nevertheless establishes the stakes of the film in simple terms. In the words of Roger Ebert, "[t]he moral backbone of the story is easily mastered."[6]

The introduction of Aurelius' imperial heir adds significant weight to the emperor's claims about Rome's corruption. Immediately after the battle, Commodus and his sister Lucilla (Connie Nielsen) are conveyed to the front in an armored coach, sprawled amid fine colored silks. In his pristine purple splendor, Commodus contrasts sharply with the ranks of bloodied and muddied soldiers. He embraces his father and declares, "I shall sacrifice a hundred bulls to honor your triumph." Aurelius makes his preference for Maximus' deeds over Commodus' bluster clear: "Save the bulls. Honor Maximus. He won the battle." Beyond prefiguring the rivalry between these "sons" of Aurelius, the scene contrasts Maximus' self-sacrifice, standing for the moral integrity of Aurelius' dream of Republican Rome, with Commodus' profligacy, as the embodiment of its corrupted empire. As Joy Connolly has noted about Rome's place in Western political thought, "Rome has always symbolized both heroic self-sacrifice and thrift (the heroic Cincinnatus / George Washington) as well as self-indulgence (Nero / King George)."[7]

Connolly's Cincinnatus/Nero dichotomy structures an audience's encounter with *Gladiator* in general, since these figures also function as metonyms for republic and empire. Nero is most often remembered as an immature and disinterested tyrant who ascended to the imperial throne by means of intrigue, incestuous marriage, and poison, and who devoted more time to the theater and chariot-races than to the business of managing the empire. That memory has been powerfully shaped by the character's appearances in films and television programs, including *The Sign of the Cross* (1932), *Quo Vadis* (1951), and *I, Claudius* (1976). Commodus' Neronian tendencies have already been indicated by his leers toward his sister and his preference for luxury and spectacle. As the film progresses, he will become more closely aligned with Nero and his empire further figured as corrupt.

By contrast, the Republican hero Cincinnatus has long been invoked as a positive exemplar and "rich lode of precious belief" in America's moralizing political discourse.[8] Cincinnatus was famed for leaving a quiet life on his farm in order to lead Rome's armies to victory as *dictator*, then returning his extraordinary powers to the state and himself to his farm after the need for emergency action had passed. George Washington was compared favorably to Cincinnatus for not parlaying his own military command into supreme leadership of the fledgling United States.[9] Maximus, too, is a capable general who serves Rome but dreams of nothing more than tending the fields of his own farm in Spain. When offered Aurelius' place at the head of the empire, Maximus refuses: "With all my heart, no." "Maximus," replies the emperor, "that is why it must be you."

But a republic, too, is susceptible to corruption, and not all Romans are Cincinnatus. Following the battle, the obsequious Commodus introduces Maximus to two senators in camp: Gaius (John Shrapnel) and Falco (David Schofield). Commodus sardonically warns Maximus to take care, lest Gaius beguile him with ideas of "Republic! Republic! Republic!" Gaius pointedly reminds them that "Rome *was* founded as a republic" – a self-serving appropriation of history, since ancient Romans (and many modern audience members) knew quite well that Rome began as a monarchy. But the line serves to conjure the Republic as the originary condition of Rome and a viable alternative to the current rule of the emperor. The senators then put the question to Maximus as a simple dichotomy – "Where do you stand? Emperor or Senate?" – thus aligning republic with senatorial rule, and potentially undercutting Aurelius' later claims that it affords power to the people.

Where an audience member stands on this question may turn on their estimation of Gaius and Falco, in relation to Commodus and Maximus. The latter, still in his armor and bloody from the work of the day, contrasts with the two senators, sipping wine in their ornate togas. Like Commodus, these men do not participate in the bloody work of empire, but they do enjoy the privilege and excess born of it, and their self-interest in advocating the return of the Republic is plain. Maximus' lack of interest in the debate does their case no favors, yet Commodus' apparent scorn for their opinion may have a counterbalancing effect. This short confrontation lays the groundwork both for Aurelius' conversation with Maximus and for his subsequent scene with Commodus, in which Aurelius acknowledges that a return to republic means government by the Senate. Although this acknowledgment may deflate the populist rhetoric of Aurelius' previous scene with Maximus, Commodus' patricidal response is sufficient to cast his own reign – and thus the continuation of empire – in a negative light.

After Aurelius dies, the film's remaining republicanism is focused through the upright senator Gracchus (Derek Jacobi), who similarly embodies the double figure of Rome. As Jon Solomon first observed, the name "Gracchus" carries immediate associations with stout republicanism, as with a similar Gracchus played by Charles Laughton in Stanley Kubrick's *Spartacus* (1960).[10] Both characters pay tribute to the Roman brothers of the late second century BCE, Tiberius and Gaius Gracchus. Although they were from a senatorial family, the Gracchi advocated for a radical redistribution of wealth in the form of public land, which had been concentrated in the hands of the rich ruling class. Bypassing the traditional structure of government, they brought legislation directly to the people and were branded as dangerous demagogues by the rest of the Senate.[11]

In *Gladiator*, as Commodus shows increasing disinterest in civic governance and fritters away public funds on his extravagant games, Gracchus becomes the primary voice of the disgruntled Senate and an advocate for their return to power. Unlike Gaius and Falco, whose commitment to a revived republic is portrayed as self-serving, Gracchus seems to care genuinely for the greater good of the city, joining Maximus and Lucilla's conspiracy to oust Commodus and accepting the task of realizing Aurelius' dream upon Maximus' death. Yet Jacobi also carries with him the memory of another Roman: the Emperor Claudius, whom he portrayed in *I, Claudius*. While arguably the most sympathetic of that miniseries' emperors, Claudius was still a figure of privilege and preferment, and a symbol of the susceptibility of imperial rule to manipulation and machination.

Thus, while *Gladiator* does offer a simple political dichotomy in which to situate the personal struggles of its hero, several internal elements also unsettle and problematize that simplicity. Jacobi's star text is an apt metaphor for the complexity of Western engagement with Rome, and Aurelius ponders whether he himself will be remembered as "the warrior, the philosopher, [or] the tyrant." That Aurelius could be remembered as all these things points to the multivalent nature of Rome in the Western imagination: at once a place of philosophical enlightenment, political idealism, violent atrocity, and sensual indulgence.

AMERICA'S ROMAN REPUBLIC

Like all films about the Greco-Roman world, *Gladiator* is inherently nostalgic; by fabricating Aurelius' yearning for Republican Rome, it makes that nostalgia explicit and dramatic. *Gladiator* thus leverages contemporary American political tastes to figure Rome's earlier past as an object of desire against the corruption and deviance associated with the image of its far more long-lived and influential empire. Aurelius and Maximus may speak in terms that would be familiar to educated Romans,[12] but more importantly they permit a modern audience to perceive the fragility of imperial ideology even as they valorize Rome's republican history. And yet, as Connolly further observes, "at any given time the republic is always a double signifier . . . [I]ts ideal condition has been understood on the one hand as unity, consensus, and homogeneity, and on the other, as intense and relentless internal conflict."[13]

While Aurelius' and Gracchus' characterizations of the Republic may appeal immediately to the general public, several Classicists have already critiqued their nostalgia. Allen Ward has called *Gladiator*'s republican ideology "an instance of pandering to an American audience," while Martin Winkler has labeled its articulation as the opposite to empire a "facile dichotomy." Peter Rose, meanwhile, has attacked the vague oversimplifications of Aurelius' vision, calling it "utopian pseudo-populism" and "enlightened paternalism."[14] Much of this criticism rests on the sense that Aurelius' republic is overidentified with a virtuous idea of America united in democracy, rather than a more accurate understanding of republican political arrangements (both Roman and American), wherein the sovereign power of the people is directed by an elected body of representatives, often in tension with the electorate's desires.

But *Gladiator* actually does offer its audience a position from which to question the plausibility of Aurelius' vision, including the possibility that government by a senatorial elite will not actually "give power back to the people of Rome and end the corruption that has crippled it." If Aurelius' plan does not evoke a viewer's immediate skepticism (either from historical knowledge of Rome or from contemporary opinion of American politics), Gaius and Falco hardly seem likely to be champions of the people. Commodus later explicitly critiques the Senate's elite status and questionable populism when Gracchus self-righteously claims that the Senate are the people: "chosen from among the people, to speak for the people." Commodus spits back, "I doubt if any of the people eat so well as you, Gracchus. Or have such splendid mistresses, Gaius," a nod to the plutocracy that was the historical reality of the Republic and the potential future of *Gladiator*'s Rome.

Indeed, on closer scrutiny Gracchus may be quite deserving of Commodus' scorn. As Rose observes, even this supposed "best man in the Senate" offers condescending remarks about the Roman "mob" and its blind passion for the arena, undercutting hope that he might foster a better, fairer Rome for its people.[15] When he deigns to join the mob at their entertainments, Gracchus tells a colleague "I may not be a man of the people, but I do try to be for the people." This line, "voicing both the political and rhetorical form of representative democracy,"[16] pays tribute to the stirring rhetoric of Lincoln's Gettysburg Address, yet also emphasizes Gracchus' socio-political distance from the people he represents and renders the solemn duty of Aurelius' dream as something he merely "tries" to do. Of course, Gracchus' cynical comments about the people are also borne out by the film, which shows them happily thirsting for blood in the Colosseum and interested in Maximus as a gladiator, not a political savior. Even as the film celebrates "the people" as the wellspring of republican democracy, it also condemns them for accepting bread and circuses instead.

Maximus himself is decidedly ambivalent about the Republic, and politics in general.[17] His dying command at the close of the film – indeed, any passion he shows for the restitution of the Republic – is driven not by any fervent belief but by his dutiful commitment to honoring "the wishes of Marcus Aurelius." The world for which Maximus personally yearns is his farm, where he works the land and harvests crops as the reward for his labor. He repeatedly articulates his quest to confront and kill Commodus as a personal vendetta, not public service. In probably his second-most-quoted speech, Maximus stands before Commodus on the sands of the arena, names himself the "loyal servant to the true emperor, Marcus Aurelius," and promises "I will have my vengeance, in this life or the next." No mention is made of the Republic. Later, when Gracchus asks why he would cede Rome to the Senate upon ousting the emperor, Maximus only reiterates his commitment to vengeance and his disinterest in Roman government: "Because that was the last wish of a dying man. I will kill Commodus. The fate of Rome I leave to you."

THE REPUBLIC AS GOLDEN AGE

Gladiator is peppered with hints that Aurelius' dream is nothing more than that: the vision of a dying man scared of what history will make of him; a vision shared neither by his natural son nor by his appointed heir; and a vision that the Senate is ill-equipped to realize. Indeed, the air of triumph suffusing the film's end is fundamentally upset by knowledge of Roman history: Commodus was murdered in his bath, not the arena, and his end precipitated not a rebirth of the Republic, but a civil war that ended in a new imperial dynasty. Aurelius' dream is problematized by the film, denied by history, and so revealed as the nostalgic illusion it really is. It thus partakes in a truly classical type of golden-age discourse, figuring the Republic as a previous, mythical time when things were magically better than they are in the present.

The classical world's most famous picture of the golden age comes from the archaic poet Hesiod's *Works and Days*, in which five races of men – golden, silver, bronze, heroic, and iron – succeed each other, their lives devolving in quality and happiness relative to that first age. Hesiod's vision of the golden past is fantastical: a life of ease, peace, and community, in which people are better able to co-exist with one another (111–20). Hesiod offered his golden age as a contrast to his own reality, that of "iron age" Greece (174–8), where life is brutish and short, and where, as Jean-Pierre Vernant famously interprets it, *dikē* (justice) risks succumbing to *hubris*: outrageous behavior that violates the natural or social order (perhaps in *Gladiator* embodied by Commodus).[18] When Aurelius speaks longingly of the dream that was Rome, and cynically of "the sword" that his reign has brought to the world, he, too, imagines a past lacking in evils, where a different arrangement of things allowed men to be better than they are in his own time. Like Hesiod's golden age, Aurelius' vision of republic is both nostalgic and fictional.

During their private scene in the camp, Maximus articulates a different and more distinctly Roman golden-age vision. His desire to return to his farm in Spain and his vivid description of rustic life recall the end of the second of Vergil's *Georgics*, a poem that paints a beguiling picture of Rome's pastoral history. While Vergil characterizes the land of this time as an easy companion to man's well-being, when "willing fields bore fruit of their own accord" (500–1), the

Roman farmer worked – plowing, harvesting, and husbanding – and cared not for politics, the courts, or the battlefield. Working the land is positioned as a desirable alternative to the blare of war horns and the clang of swords (532–40), the very life of iron that Maximus wishes to escape.[19] Its hardworking solipsism has nothing to do, however, with Aurelius' dream of grand political rebirth.

Maximus' dream is brutally denied him when Commodus' soldiers arrive at his farm ahead of him, slaughtering his family and burning his property. The place to which he wished to return no longer exists, rendering his dream truly utopian in the fullest dimensions of the term: both eu-topian and ou-topian, a vision of a better place and of a place that does not actually exist.[20] Both terms are based on the ancient Greek *topos* (place), modified by a prefix: eutopia by *eu-* ("good" or "well") and utopia by *ou-*, which negates what follows. This doubled effect could extend to Aurelius' dream of Rome, a place he claims Maximus can't ever visit, since it has been fundamentally changed by corruption. Indeed, the Rome that Maximus will experience later in the film is precisely the Rome that Aurelius wishes to change.

THE FRAGILITY OF ROME

Even as its characters yearn for places that no longer exist, and as its dialogue disturbs Aurelius' dreams of both past and future, *Gladiator* itself famously interferes with the suspension of disbelief customarily asked of an audience engaging with a fictive world on screen. By demanding, both in the marketing of the film and through characters within the film itself, that the digitally fabricated setting and action be marveled at – that its fictiveness be consciously acknowledged – *Gladiator* upsets easy identification with Aurelius' Rome as reality, and thus his dream as realistic. As a representation of reality, *Gladiator* exposes – even celebrates – both the excess and the insufficiency of mimetic practices, drawing attention to the nature of such representations as "the mind's image of the external thing," rather than an objective reflection of reality.[21] It might even point up the "hyperreality" of Rome, both as portrayed in the film and as constructed in Western imaginations. Jean Baudrillard coined the term "hyperreality" to denote "models of a real without origin or reality . . . [which come to be substituted] for the real itself."[22] The Colosseum of *Gladiator* might be called "hyperreal" to the extent that it is an imaginative reconstruction that now programs popular understanding of what Rome actually looked like.

The intense focus placed on *Gladiator*'s Colosseum similarly draws attention to the film's status as a product of high technology. In showcasing the genius of Roman engineering, from terrifying siege artillery to the Colosseum with its lifts and trapdoors, *Gladiator* makes a spectacle of Hollywood's ability to represent such imagery on the big screen. As Alastair Blanshard and Kim Shahabudin note, "pre-publicity for the film actively recruited the prospective cinema audience as fans rather than just viewers, knowing conspirators in the film's re-presentation of a Rome that never did, and never could exist."[23] Indeed, the teaser trailer includes at least four shots that make the computer-generated Colosseum their focus. Leslie Felperin describes *Gladiator*'s architecture as "illusions standing in for ephemeral structures, projections of the melancholic Piranesian ruins they would become," referring to the eighteenth-century etchings by Giovanni Battista Piranesi, whose romantic visions of the Rome of his time mediate subsequent imaginings of the city in its heyday.[24] The Colosseum thus functions as a perfect allegory for *Gladiator*'s larger, hyperreal Rome (both the place and the idea): its digital reconstruction functions as a referent to something that no longer exists – something that certainly did exist in some form, but which is now approachable only as a reconstruction. *Gladiator*'s hyperconsciousness of its hyperreality emerges clearly in Juba's (Djimon Hounsou) breathless remark upon first seeing the Colosseum: "I did not know men could build such things" (see Figure 14.2).

Gladiator occupies a pivotal place in the history of the development of computer-generated imagery (CGI) in film, as discussed in Michael Allen's influential 2002 essay, "The Impact of Digital Technologies on Film Aesthetics." Building on André Bazin's arguments that cinema's power as a photographic art lies in its ability to convince the audience that what they see correlates with reality, Allen examines the development of filmic techniques (such as shot duration, montage, and camera movement) used in the 1990s to integrate digital material convincingly into the representational world of film.[25] According to Allen, "[t]he success or failure of any digital image lies in the degree to which it persuades its spectator that it is not digital, but *is* photographic," yet Allen also marks as significant how *Gladiator*'s digital images are used both to beguile the audience and to impress them with its technological artifice: "they both confirm the spacial [sic] reality of the scenes in which they appear and simultaneously announce their amazing presence as illusion."[26] Allen cites the famous shot of Maximus and his gladiatorial brothers stepping onto the sands of the Colosseum for the first time, which

Figure 14.2 Through the reactions of Juba (Djimon Hounsou) and Maximus (Russell Crowe), the camera invites viewers to marvel at the Colosseum in *Gladiator* (2000). Universal Studios/DreamWorks.

employs a 180-degree camera move that serves both to "reinforce our belief in the reality of the scene" and also to highlight the genius of its digital composition.[27]

This peculiar ability of film to refer to its own artifice, first capturing the audience with a representation and then evacuating it of authenticity, renders it a particularly powerful medium for drawing attention to the (o)utopian nature of the golden age. *Gladiator* could be said to leverage the fragility of the digital image to demonstrate the fragility of Aurelius' dream. Ironically, the valorization of technology is where America's utopian dreams split definitively from classical forebears, since in classical literature technology is a hallmark of the rupture that ends a golden age. For example, the Roman poet Tibullus mourns for a time when "the pine had not yet defied the dark-blue waves" (1.3.35–8), permitting man to travel long distances and to engage in exchange with other societies: globalization in microcosm. Ovid's *Metamorphoses* expands on this conceit to lament the advent of "harmful iron, and gold more harmful than iron" (1.141), figuring capital as a greater threat to human happiness than war. The role of trade and communication as harbingers of the golden age's end provides a metaphor for *Gladiator*'s technological and financial achievements, since its international success, as Vilashini Cooppan notes, allowed it to enact "US global cultural capitalism" even as it examined the darker side of Roman imperialism.[28] To watch *Gladiator* is to participate in contemporary mechanisms of cultural, technological, and financial progress and domination – and thus to deny the possibility of returning to the simpler, better time of which Aurelius dreams.

GLADIATOR AS HARBINGER OF A NEW GOLDEN AGE?

Gladiator also occupies a special position in the history of films about the ancient Greco-Roman world, as it is often credited with the rebirth of Hollywood's interest in making such films.[29] Such characterizations are generally tinged with their own nostalgia for the period of high cinematic production of the mid-twentieth century, and thus are themselves manifestations of a type of golden-age discourse that imagines a previous time as a spectacular heyday and longs for its return. This reception of *Gladiator* is demonstrated most readily in the evolution of Jon Solomon's landmark text, *The Ancient World in the Cinema*. In the epilogue to the 2001 revised edition, he argues that his prediction of a renaissance in classical cinema, made in the 1978 edition, has at last come true, citing the box-office success of *Gladiator* as particular proof.[30] If production trends necessitated that his 1978 text be mainly retrospective in character, the success of *Gladiator* allowed Solomon to look forward in 2001; so, too, film scholar Richard Rushton argues that *Gladiator*'s narrative structure embodies a return to a mode of "classical Hollywood storytelling" that promises to cure the apparent devolution of modern cinema.[31]

This overdetermination of the word "classical" – referring both to the ancient Greco-Roman world and to a certain period of Hollywood cultural production – unites critical perspectives by belying their golden-age tendencies. The very idea of classicism, of canonizing certain works or periods of production as supreme achievements of human civilization, implicitly invokes golden-age discourse, fixing certain times and products as valuable and worthy of remembrance, imitation, and study. Thus the release of *Gladiator* might offer scholars the opportunity for a radical encounter with their own nostalgia, whether for film or philology, and one that has the potential to expose "the sedimented reading habits and categories developed by [certain] inherited interpretative traditions."[32] Classicists should heed Miriam Leonard in recognizing that "reception studies provide the opportunity for a rigorous analysis of the 'historical unconscious' of classical studies."[33] Leonard's approach would direct our critical attention to the contexts that mediate our response to *Gladiator*; beyond canonical texts and films, these might include anxieties about the future of Classics and desires for the return of its former importance. But what form might such a return actually take? We might ponder, for example, whether it is possible for our discipline to regain its old prominence without bending to the prescriptions of *Who Killed Homer?*, reviving dreams of the past that might be better left dismantled.[34]

Even while celebrating the success of *Gladiator* and the opportunities it brings for our discipline, as teachers and scholars we should also interrogate our own golden-age thinking. We are taught to approach the golden-age discourses of Hesiod, Vergil, Tibullus, and Ovid as critical commentary on the authors' own times rather than an authentic vision of their pasts. Shouldn't we examine our own impulse to situate *Gladiator* as the return of something better, especially if it contains so many nods within itself to the inauthenticity of golden-age nostalgia? Leonard argues that a hybrid historical approach to reception could make Classics "a dynamic political force," a comment that itself bears the hint of loss and the hope of renewal, just as Aurelius hopes to condition his own remembrance as "the emperor who gave Rome back her true self."[35] Moreover, the "golden-age" trope is itself a type of hyperreality: the interpretation of a text (*Works and Days*) by one scholar (Vernant) that has come to precondition later interpretations of similar texts.[36] To approach *Gladiator* as a golden-age discourse is, to some extent, to reify such discourse as a cultural trope. Our interpretive traditions heap sediment upon sediment; the temptation to submit to them might cause us to rethink how naïvely Hesiod's and Vergil's audiences might have submitted to their own nostalgic visions of the past.

CONCLUSION

History bore out Solomon's prediction, insofar as *Gladiator* was followed by films such as *Troy* (2004), *Alexander* (2004), and *300* (2006). But is what *Gladiator* has brought us truly a golden age? Hesiod's model might characterize the current spate of films and television series – including, most notably, the *300* movies and STARZ's *Spartacus* (2010–13) – as expressions of a new age of bronze, products by and about the race of men who "are busied with the lamentable deeds of Ares and acts of *hubris*" (145–6). To paraphrase Vernant, have we "moved from the juridical and religious plane to that of manifestations of brute force, physical energy, and the terror that the warrior inspires"?[37] The dominance of the revenge-narrative in *Gladiator* spatters with moral ambiguity Aurelius' dream of the people's due: peace, without corruption. Thus, the film admits a critical eye and voice into its own operations from its very narrative foundations.

Gladiator is a film marked by contradictions, one that enacts a studied ambivalence about nostalgia for Rome even while exploiting it. As a text produced, marketed, and consumed at a certain time and within a specific context, it is enmeshed in a web of publicity, reception, and scholarship that has only complicated its perspective on the ancient Greco-Roman world further. *Gladiator* yearns for the past, produces the past for us, betrays the fragile fantasy of that past, and exposes our investment in it. The film lays bare the conceits of golden-age thinking in all its affective beguilements and intellectual pitfalls, undermining Aurelius' nostalgic hope with its narrative even as its formal qualities and critical reception reveal our own nostalgic perspective on cinema. It shows us how unexamined golden-age perspectives congeal into hyperreality, rendering as unproblematically true a vision of the past that is the result of sedimented habits of reading and desiring. Aurelius himself warns Maximus that his dream of Rome cannot survive more than a whisper. Yet if his problematic vision of the past sustains our own identities – as Westerners, as members of a republic, or as scholars – perhaps it is *Gladiator* itself that whispers most loudly.

NOTES

I would like to offer special thanks to Meredith E. Safran for her tireless and creative work as editor. Any strengths of this chapter owe much to her interventions and suggestions; any infelicities remain my own. My thanks also (and as ever) to Lisl Walsh.

1 Rushton (2001: 41) classifies both the revenge and republic plot-lines as "positive" plots that the audience wishes to see satisfied. The original teaser for *Gladiator* suggested a plot entirely about the rivalry of these two men as heirs to Aurelius.
2 Cooppan (2005: 90–1); she also offers a survey of said tradition (2005: 82–3).
3 Felperin (2000), Cyrino (2005: 239–40), and Cooppan (2005: 84), emphasis in original, respectively.

4 Rushton (2001: 35, 43).
5 Manohla Dargis (2000) called *Gladiator* "a film in which the inherent frisson of movie violence is continually negated by its horror, by crushed heads and pulverized bodies delivered in unblinking close-up."
6 Ebert (2000b).
7 Connolly (2015: 61).
8 Brown (1957: 29).
9 For Cincinnatus, see Livy 2.36–7; comparisons to Washington (and others) in Shalev (2009: 217–40). Even Arnold Schwarzenegger, in a 2012 interview that he gave in the "By the Book" column in the *New York Times*' Sunday Book Review after serving as California governor, expressed his admiration for Cincinnatus – and his desire to play the ancient Roman in a film.
10 Solomon (2001: 94–5).
11 The Roman historian Sallust commended them for trying "to set free the working class and expose the crimes of the few" (*Jug.* 42.1). According to Connolly (2015: 92–102), Sallust employed figures like the Gracchi as stock reformers, yet was genuinely concerned about the damage caused by corruption and economic inequality.
12 Maximus' sentiments resemble imperial ideology from authors such as Vergil (*Aen.* 1.279, 6.851–3) and Julius Caesar (discussed at length by Riggsby 2006). Aurelius' laments echo Tacitus' famous condemnation from *Agricola* 30: "they make a desert and call it peace."
13 Connolly (2015: 61).
14 Ward (2004: 35); Winkler (2004b: 109); Rose (2004: 159).
15 Rose (2004: 161).
16 Cooppan (2005: 90).
17 *Contra* Rushton (2001: 41), who pigeonholes Maximus as a straightforward advocate for democracy.
18 Vernant (2006: 25).
19 Vergil's utopia may be no less naïve (or ironic) than Aurelius': he imagines Rome fortifying her seven hills without the intervention of violence and warfare (534–5) and mentions "Remus and his brother" (533), Rome's first case of fratricide over political disagreement. Tibullus 1.1 echoes Vergil's mixture of toil and natural plenty; Ovid *Met.* 1.89–112 presents a vision closer to Hesiod, where "food was produced with no one compelling it" (1.103).
20 The homophony of these two words often causes the distinction to be elided, especially with respect to Sir Thomas More's 1516 *Utopia* (2003), which was both eutopian and outopian in its conceits.
21 Putnam (1981: 57).
22 Baudrillard (1988: 166–7).
23 Blanshard and Shahabudin (2011: 225–6).
24 Felperin (2000).
25 Allen (2002), citing Bazin (1960).

26 Allen (2002: 110–14, emphasis in original).
27 Allen (2002: 114). See also Rushton (2001: 40). Roger Ebert (2000b; 2000c) criticized the CGI as "shabby" and lamented the film's washed-out color palette. Belton (2008) argues that conspicuous color-grading can also interrupt an audience's faith in film's representative capacity.
28 Cooppan (2005: 84).
29 See for example Cyrino (2005: 238) and Blanshard and Shahabudin (2011: 216).
30 Solomon (2001: 325–6). *Gladiator*'s influence on the second edition is also evident in Solomon's revised discussion of previous films. *Spartacus*' Gracchus is no longer one of "two patricians" (Solomon 1978: 34) but "the self aware, populist patrician" (Solomon 2001: 51), arguably the result of comparison with Jacobi in *Gladiator*.
31 Rushton (2001: 38–9), arguing that *Gladiator* fits the schema outlined by Thompson (1999).
32 Jameson (1981: 9), quoted by Leonard (2006: 117).
33 Leonard (2006: 116).
34 Hanson and Heath (1998); see the review by Connolly (1998). These questions and incumbent challenges are now being addressed with much talent and drive in the online journal *Eidolon*.
35 Leonard (2006: 126).
36 On Vernant's vexed historicism, see Loraux (1993).
37 Vernant (2006: 35–6).

Filmography

28 Days Later (2002). Directed by Danny Boyle. Fox Searchlight.

The 100 (2014–). Created by Jason Rothenberg. Bonanza Productions/Alloy Entertainment/Warner Bros. Television.

300 (2006). Directed by Zack Snyder. Warner Bros./Legendary Pictures.

300: Rise of an Empire (2014). Directed by Noam Murro. Warner Bros./ Legendary Pictures.

The 300 Spartans (1962). Directed by Rudolph Maté. Twentieth Century Fox.

Alexander (2004). Directed by Oliver Stone. Warner Bros.

Alexander the Great (1956). Directed by Robert Rossen. Rossen Films/ C. B. Films.

An American in Paris (1951). Directed by Vincente Minnelli. Metro-Goldwyn-Mayer.

American Sniper (2014). Directed by Clint Eastwood. Warner Bros.

Anchors Aweigh (1945). Directed by George Sidney. Metro-Goldwyn-Mayer.

Annibale (1959). Directed by Edgar G. Ulmer and Carlo Ludovico Bragaglia. Liber Films.

The Avengers (2012). Directed by Joss Whedon. Walt Disney Studios Motion Pictures.

The Avengers: Age of Ultron (2015). Directed by Joss Whedon. Walt Disney Studios Motion Pictures.

Avengers: Infinity War (2018). Directed by Anthony Russo and Joe Russo. Walt Disney Studios Motion Pictures.

The Band Wagon (1953). Directed by Vincente Minnelli. Metro-Goldwyn-Mayer.

Barton Fink (1991). Directed by Joel Coen. Circle Films/Working Title Films.

Batman Begins (2005). Directed by Christopher Nolan. Legendary Pictures/ Warner Bros.

Batman v. Superman: Dawn of Justice (2016). Directed by Zack Snyder. Warner Bros.

La Battaglia di Maratona (1959), a.k.a. *The Giant of Marathon* (1960). Directed by Jacques Tourneur and Mario Bava. Titanus/Galatea.

Beauty and the Beast (2017). Directed by Bill Condon. Mandeville Films/Walt Disney Pictures.

Ben-Hur (1959). Directed by William Wyler. Metro-Goldwyn-Mayer.

Bill and Ted's Excellent Adventure (1989). Directed by Stephen Herek. Metro-Goldwyn-Mayer.

The Book of Eli (2010). Directed by the Hughes Brothers. Warner Bros.

Brigadoon (1954). Directed by Vincente Minnelli. Metro-Goldwyn-Mayer.

Broken Arrow (1950). Directed by Delmer Daves. Twentieth Century Fox.

Buffy the Vampire Slayer (1997–2003). Created by Joss Whedon. Mutant Enemy, Twentieth Century Fox Television.

Cabiria (1914). Directed by Giovanni Pastrone. Itala Film.

Captain America: Civil War (2016). Directed by Anthony Russo and Joe Russo. Walt Disney Studios Motion Pictures.

Centurion (2010). Directed by Neil Marshall. Celador Films/Canal+/Warner.

Cheyenne Autumn (1964). Directed by John Ford. Warner Bros./Fort-Smith Productions.

Cleopatra (1963). Directed by Joseph Mankiewiecz. Twentieth Century Fox.

Cover Girl (1944). Directed by Charles Vidor. Columbia Pictures.

Crest of the Wave (1954). Directed by John Boulting and Roy Boulting. Boulting Brothers/Metro-Goldwyn-Mayer.

The Cross of Lorraine (1943). Directed by Tay Garnett. Metro-Goldwyn-Mayer.

"Dancing: A Man's Game" (1958). Directed by William A. Graham and Gene Kelly. *Omnibus*, December 21. Created by Robert Saudek and the Ford Foundation.

The Dark Knight (2008). Directed by Christopher Nolan. Warner Bros.

The Dark Knight Rises (2012). Directed by Christopher Nolan. Warner Bros.

Deadwood (2004–6). Created by David Milch. HBO.

Demetrius and the Gladiators (1954). Directed by Delmer Daves. Twentieth Century Fox.

The Devil Makes Three (1952). Directed by Andrew Marton. Metro-Goldwyn-Mayer.

Down to Earth (1947). Directed by Alexander Hall. Columbia Pictures.

A Dream of Passion (1978). Directed by Jules Dassin. Bren/Melinafilm.

The Eagle (2011). Directed by Kevin MacDonald. Focus Features/Universal Pictures.

The Fall of the Roman Empire (1964). Directed by Anthony Mann. Paramount Pictures.

Firefly: The Series (2002). Created by Joss Whedon. Mutant Enemy, Twentieth Century Fox Television.

The Flintstones (1994). Directed by Brian Levant. Universal Pictures.

For Me and My Gal (1942). Directed by Busby Berkeley. Metro-Goldwyn-Mayer.

Fort Apache (1948). Directed by John Ford. Argosy Pictures.

Full Metal Jacket (1987). Directed by Stanley Kubrick. Warner Bros.

A Funny Thing Happened on the Way to the Forum (1966). Directed by Richard Lester. United Artists.

Game of Thrones (2011–). Created by David Benioff and D. B. Weiss. HBO.

Gandhi (1982). Directed by Richard Attenborough. International Film Investors/National Film Development Corporation of India (NFDC)/ Goldcrest Films International/Indo-British Films.

The Giants of Thessaly (1960). Directed by Riccardo Freda. Alexandra Produzioni Cinematografiche/Societé Cinématographique Lyre.

Gilda (1945). Directed by Charles Vidor. Columbia Pictures.

Gladiator (2000). Directed by Ridley Scott. Universal Studios/DreamWorks.

"Going Back to Xanadu" (2008). Documentary extra, DVD. Universal Studios Home Video.

Good Night and Good Luck (2005). Directed by George Clooney. Summit/ Lionsgate.

Grease (1978). Directed by Randal Kleiser. Paramount Pictures/Robert Stigwood Organization/Allan Carr Production.

Green Zone (2010). Directed by Paul Greengrass. Universal Pictures.

Hail, Caesar! (2016). Directed by Ethan Coen and Joel Coen. Universal Pictures/Working Title Films.

Happy Days (1974–84). Created by Garry Marshall. Henderson Productions/ Miller-Milkis Productions/Miller-Milkis-Boyett Productions/Paramount Television.

Hercules (1959). Directed by Pietro Francisci. Embassy Pictures/Galatea Film.

Hercules (2014). Directed by Brett Ratner. Paramount/Metro-Goldwyn-Mayer.

Hercules Action Pack: Hercules and the Lost Kingdom, Hercules and the Circle of Fire, Hercules in the Underworld, Hercules in the Maze of the Minotaur (1994). Renaissance Pictures and Universal Television.

Hercules Against the Barbarians (1964). Directed by Domenico Paolella. Jonia Films.

Hercules Against the Moon Men (1964). Directed by Giacomo Gentilomo. Nike Cinematografica/Comptoir Français de Productions Cinématographiques.

Hercules and the Amazon Women (1994). Directed by Bill L. Norton. Renaissance Pictures and Universal Television.

Hercules: The Legendary Journeys (1995–9). Created by Christian Williams. Renaissance Pictures/MCA Television.

Hercules Unchained (1960). Directed by Pietro Francisci. Galatea Film/Lux Film.

High Noon (1952). Directed by Fred Zinnemann. United Artists.

Hotel Rwanda (2005). Directed by Terry George. Lionsgate.

The Hudsucker Proxy (1994). Directed by Joel Coen. Silver Pictures/ Working Title Films.

The Hurt Locker (2008). Directed by Kathryn Bigelow. Summit Entertainment.
I Am Legend (2007). Directed by Francis Lawrence. Warner Bros.
I, Claudius (1976). Directed by Herbert Wise. BBC.
Immortals (2011). Directed by Tarsem Singh. Relativity.
Imperium: Augustus (2003). Directed by Roger Young. EOS Entertainment.
Inside Llewyn Davis (2013). Directed by Ethan Coen and Joel Coen. CBS Films/Studio Canal.
The Iron Horse (1924). Directed by John Ford. Fox Film Corporation.
Iron Man (2008). Direct by Jon Favreau. Paramount Pictures.
Iron Man 3 (2013). Directed by Shane Black. Walt Disney Studios Motion Pictures.
It's Always Fair Weather (1955). Directed by Stanley Donen and Gene Kelly. Metro-Goldwyn-Mayer.
Jarhead (2005). Directed by Sam Mendes. Universal Pictures.
Jason and the Argonauts (1963). Directed by Don Chaffey. Columbia Pictures.
Jason and the Argonauts (2000). Directed by Nick Willing. Hallmark Entertainment.
King Arthur (2004). Directed by Antoine Fuqua. Touchstone Pictures/Jerry Bruckheimer Films.
Kingdom of Heaven (2005). Directed by Ridley Scott. Twentieth Century Fox.
The Lady from Shanghai (1947). Directed by Orson Welles. Columbia Pictures.
The Last Legion (2007). Directed by Doug Lefler. Dino de Laurentiis Company.
Life of Brian (1979). Directed by Terry Jones. HandMade Films.
Living in a Big Way (1947). Directed by Gregory LaCava. Metro-Goldwyn-Mayer.
Lone Survivor (2013). Directed by Peter Berg. Universal Pictures.
The Man Who Shot Liberty Valance (1962). Directed by John Ford. Paramount Pictures.
Medea (1969). Directed by Pier Paolo Pasolini. San Marco.
Medea (1988). Directed by Lars Von Trier. Danmarks Radio.
Midnight in Paris (2011). Directed by Woody Allen. Mediapro/Versátil Cinema/Gravier Productions/Pontchartrain Productions/Televisió de Catalunya (TV3).
Miller's Crossing (1990). Directed by Joel Coen. Circle Films/Twentieth Century Fox.
Never on Sunday (1960). Directed by Jules Dassin. Lopert Pictures Corporation/Metro-Goldwyn-Mayer.
O Brother, Where Art Thou? (2000). Directed by Joel Coen. Touchstone Pictures/Universal Pictures.
"Olivia Newton-John: Hollywood Nights" (1980). Directed by Jeff Margolis. Jackson Productions/L.K. Productions.
Olympia Part 1: Festival of the Nations (1938). Directed by Leni Riefenstahl. Olympia Film GmbH.

On the Town (1949). Directed by Stanley Donen and Gene Kelly. Metro-Goldwyn-Mayer.
Oz (1997–2003). Created by Tom Fontana. HBO.
Phaedra (1962). Directed by Jules Dassin. Joele/Jorilie/Melinafilm/Lopert Pictures Corporation.
The Pirate (1948). Directed by Vincente Minnelli. Metro-Goldwyn-Mayer.
Platoon (1986). Directed by Oliver Stone. Orion Pictures.
Quo Vadis (1951). Directed by Mervyn LeRoy. Metro-Goldwyn-Mayer.
Raiders of the Lost Ark (1981). Directed by Steven Spielberg. Paramount Pictures.
Red River (1948). Directed by Howard Hawks and Arthur Rosson. United Artists.
The Robe (1953). Directed by Henry Koster. Twentieth Century Fox.
Roller Boogie (1979). Directed by Mark L. Lester. Compass International Pictures.
Rome (2005–7). Created by Bruno Heller, William J. MacDonald, and John Milius. HBO-BBC.
Romolo e Remo (1961). Directed by Sergio Corbucci. Titan Films.
Saturday Night Fever (1977). Directed by John Badham. Robert Stigwood Organization.
Scipione l'Africano (1937). Directed by Carmine Gallone. Consorzione "Scipio l'Africano"/Ente Nazionale Industrie Cinematografiche.
Seal Team Six (2012). Directed by John Stockwell. Voltage Pictures/The Weinstein Company.
The Searchers (1956). Directed by John Ford. Warner Bros.
Serenity (2005). Directed by Joss Whedon. Universal Pictures.
Seven Brides for Seven Brothers (1954). Directed by Stanley Donen. Metro-Goldwyn-Mayer.
The Seventh Seal (1957). Directed by Ingmar Bergman. AB Svensk Filmindustri.
Shake Hands with the Devil (2007). Directed by Roger Spottiswoode. Seville Pictures/Regent.
Shane (1953). Directed by George Stevens. Paramount Pictures.
The Sign of the Cross (1932). Directed by Cecil B. DeMille. Paramount Pictures.
Singin' in the Rain (1952). Directed by Stanley Donen and Gene Kelly. Metro-Goldwyn-Mayer.
Skatetown, U.S.A. (1979). Directed by William A. Levey. KBC/Rastar Pictures/Skatetown.
Socrate (1971). Directed by Roberto Rossellini. Radiotelevisione Italiana.
The Sopranos (1999–2007). Created by David Chase. HBO.
Spartacus (1960). Directed by Stanley Kubrick. Bryna Productions/Universal Studios.
Spartacus: Blood and Sand (2010–13). Created by Stephen S. DeKnight. Tapert Donen Raimi/STARZ.

"A Special Olivia Newton-John" (1976). Directed by Norman Campbell. ABC.

Spider-Man (2002). Directed by Sam Raimi. Columbia Pictures.

Spider-Man 2 (2004). Directed by Sam Raimi. Columbia Pictures.

Spider-Man 3 (2007). Directed by Sam Raimi. Columbia Pictures.

Sullivan's Travels (1941). Directed by Preston Sturges. Paramount Pictures.

Summer Stock (1950). Directed by Charles Walters. Metro-Goldwyn-Mayer.

Superman Returns (2006). Directed by Bryan Singer. Warner Bros./ Legendary Entertainment.

Talking Dead (2011– . Hosted by Chris Hardwick. AMC.

That's Entertainment! (1974). Directed by Jack Haley Jr. Metro-Goldwyn-Mayer.

That's Entertainment, Part II (1976). Directed by Gene Kelly. Metro-Goldwyn-Mayer.

Thousands Cheer (1943). Directed by George Sidney. Metro-Goldwyn-Mayer.

Triumph of the Will (1935). Directed by Leni Riefenstahl. Leni Riefenstahl-Produktion.

Troy (2004). Directed by Wolfgang Petersen. Warner Bros.

V for Vendetta (2005). Directed by the Wachowski Brothers. Warner Bros.

The Virginian (1929). Directed by Victor Fleming. Paramount Pictures.

Wagon Master (1950). Directed by John Ford. Argosy Pictures.

The Walking Dead (2010–). Created by Frank Darabont. AMC.

War of the Worlds (2005). Directed by Steven Spielberg. Paramount/ DreamWorks.

The Wire (2002–8). Created by David Simon. HBO.

Wonder Woman (2017). Directed by Patty Jenkins. Warner Bros.

X2 (2003). Directed by Bryan Singer. Twentieth Century Fox.

Xanadu (1980). Directed by Robert Greenwald. Universal Pictures.

Xena: Warrior Princess (1995–2001). Created by John Schulian and Rob Tapert. Renaissance Pictures/MCA Television.

X-Men (2000). Directed by Bryan Singer. Twentieth Century Fox.

X-Men: Apocalypse (2016). Directed by Bryan Singer. Twentieth Century Fox.

X-Men: Dark Phoenix (2018). Directed by Simon Kinberg. Twentieth Century Fox.

X-Men: Days of Future Past (2014). Directed by Bryan Singer. Twentieth Century Fox.

X-Men: First Class (2011). Directed by Matthew Vaughn. Twentieth Century Fox.

X-Men: The Last Stand (2006). Directed by Brett Ratner. Twentieth Century Fox.

Zero Dark Thirty (2012). Directed by Kathryn Bigelow. Columbia Pictures.

Ziegfield Follies (1946). Directed by Lemuel Ayers, Roy Del Ruth, Robert Lewis, Vincente Minnelli, George Sidney, Merrill Pye, and Charles Walters. Metro-Goldwyn-Mayer.

Bibliography

Aeschylus (2009). *Persians. Seven against Thebes. Suppliants. Prometheus Bound*, ed. and trans. Alan H. Sommerstein. Loeb Classical Library. Cambridge, MA: Harvard University Press.

Alexander, Beatrice (1947). *Famous Myths of the Golden Age*. New York: Random House.

Allen, Michael (2002). "The Impact of Digital Technologies on Film Aesthetics," in Dan Harries (ed.), *The New Media Book*. London: British Film Institute, 109–18.

Allen, Thomas W. and David B. Munro (eds) (1920). *Homeri Opera*. Oxford: Oxford University Press.

Alpers, Paul (1997). *What is Pastoral?* Chicago: University of Chicago Press.

Altheide, David L. (2010). "Fear, Terrorism, and Popular Culture," in Jeff Birkenstein, Anna Froula, and Karen Randell (eds), *Reframing 9/11: Popular Culture and the "War on Terror."* New York: Continuum, 11–22.

Altman, Rick (1987). *The American Film Musical*. Bloomington: Indiana University Press.

Ames, Christopher (1992). "Modernism and Tradition: The Legacies of Belatedness." *Studies in the Literary Imagination* 25.2: 39–62.

Anders, Charlie Jane (2013). "George R. R. Martin: The Complete Unedited Interview." July 23, <http://observationdeck.kinja.com/george-r-r-martin-the-complete-unedited-interview-886117845> (last accessed January 4, 2018).

Anderson, William S. (1958). "Calypso and Elysium." *Classical Journal* 54.1: 2–11.

Angstrom, Jan (2005). "Introduction: Debating the Nature of Modern War", in Isabelle Duyvesten and Jan Angstrom (eds), *Rethinking the Nature of War*. London: Frank Cass, 1–28.

Aperlo, Peter (2013). *300: Rise of an Empire. The Art of the Film*. London: Titan Books.

Armstrong, Richard H. (2006). *A Compulsion for Antiquity: Freud and the Ancient World*. Ithaca: Cornell University Press.

Arthur, Marilyn (1982). "Cultural Strategies in Hesiod's *Theogony*: Law, Family, Society." *Arethusa* 15.1/2: 63–82.

Arthur, Marilyn (1983). "Dream of a World Without Women." *Arethusa* 16.1–2: 97–116.

Arthur, Marilyn (1984). "Early Greece: The Origins of the Western Attitude Toward Women," in John Peradotto and J. P. Sullivan (eds), *Women in the Ancient World: The Arethusa Papers*. Albany: State University of New York Press, 7–58.

Augoustakis, Antony (2015). "Effigies of Atia and Servilia: Effacing the Female Body in *Rome*," in Monica S. Cyrino (ed.), *Rome, Season Two: Trial and Triumph*. Edinburgh: Edinburgh University Press, 117–27.

Babbitt, Frank Cole (trans.) (1931). "The Sayings of Spartan Women," in *Plutarch: Moralia, Volume III*. Loeb Classical Library. Cambridge, MA: Harvard University Press, 454–69.

Baertschi, Annette M. (2014). "Rebel and Martyr: The *Medea* of Lars Von Trier," in Konstantinos P. Nikoloutsos (ed.), *Ancient Greek Women in Film*. New York: Oxford University Press, 117–38.

Bakewell, Geoffrey W. (2002). "Oedipus Tex: *Lone Star*, Tragedy, and Postmodernism." *Classical and Modern Literature* 22.1: 35–48.

Baldry, H. C. (1953). "The Idler's Paradise in Attic Comedy." *Greece & Rome* 22.65: 49–60.

Baldwin, James (1887). *A Story of the Golden Age of Greek Heroes*. New York: Charles Scribner's Sons.

Barker, Duncan (1996). "'The Golden Age is Proclaimed'? The *Carmen Saeculare* and the Renascence of the Golden Age." *Classical Quarterly* 46.2: 434–46.

Barker, Elton and Joel Christensen (2013). *Homer: A Beginner's Guide*. London: Oneworld.

Barker, Jennifer (2008). "'A Hero Will Rise': The Myth of the Fascist Man in *Fight Club* and *Gladiator*." *Literature/Film Quarterly* 36.3: 171–87.

Barter, Judith A. (2016). "Prairie Pastoral," in Judith A. Barter (ed.), *America After the Fall: Painting in the 1930s*. Chicago: Art Institute of Chicago, 28–53.

Baudrillard, Jean (1988). *Selected Writings*. Stanford: Stanford University Press.

Bazin, André (1960). "The Ontology of the Photographic Image." *Film Quarterly* 13.4: 4–9.

Beach, Richard and James D. Marshall (1991). *Teaching Literature in the Secondary School*. San Diego, CA: Harcourt Brace Jovanovich.

Bean, Robin (1963). "*Phaedra*." *Films and Filming* 9.4: 46–7.

Beatrice, Alexander (1947). *Famous Myths of the Golden Age*. New York: Random House.

Beekes, Robert S. P. (2010). *Etymological Dictionary of Greek*. Leiden: Brill.

Belton, John (2008). "Painting by the Numbers: The Digital Intermediate." *Film Quarterly* 61.3: 58–65.

Benario, Herbert W. (1964). "Tacitus and the Principate." *Classical Journal* 60.3: 97–106.

Berger, Stefan (2008). "National Movements," in Stefan Berger (ed.), *A Companion to Nineteenth-Century Europe, 1789–1914*. Hoboken, NJ: Wiley, 178–92.

Bhaskar, Sanjeev (2009). "What Did the *Life of Brian* Ever Do for Us?" November 29, <http://www.telegraph.co.uk/culture/film/6679546/What-did-Life-of-Brian-ever-do-for-us.html> (last accessed December 26, 2017).

Birkenstein, Jeff, Anna Froula, and Karen Randell (eds) (2010). *Reframing 9/11: Popular Culture and the "War on Terror."* New York: Continuum.

Bishop, Kyle William (2010). *American Zombie Gothic: The Rise and Fall (and Rise) of the Walking Dead in Popular Culture*. Jefferson, NC: McFarland.

Blanshard, Alastair (2005). *Hercules: A Heroic Life*. London: Granta.

Blanshard, Alastair J. L. and Kim Shahabudin (2011). *Classics on Screen: Ancient Greece and Rome on Film*. Exeter: Bristol Classical Press.

Blondell, Ruby (2005). "How to Kill an Amazon," in Ruby Blondell and Mary-Kay Gamel (eds), *Ancient Mediterranean Women in Modern Mass Media. Helios* 32.2: 73–103.

Blondell, Ruby (2007). "Hercules Psychotherapist," in Wendy Haslan, Angela Ndalianis, and Chris Mackie (eds), *Super/Heroes*. Washington, DC: New Academia Publishing, 239–49.

Blundell, Mary Whitlock and Kirk Ormand (1997). "Western Values, or the Peoples [*sic*] Homer: *Unforgiven* as a Reading of the *Iliad*." *Poetics Today* 18.4: 533–69.

Boccaccio, Giovanni (2013). *Decameron*, trans. Wayne A. Rebhorn. New York: W. W. Norton.

Boedeker, Deborah (2002). "Epic Heritage and Mythical Patterns in Herodotus," in Egbert J. Bakker, Irene J. F. de Jong, and Hans van Wees (eds), *Brill's Companion to Herodotus*. Leiden: Brill, 97–116.

Boedeker, Deborah D. and Kurt A. Raaflaub (eds) (1998). *Democracy, Empire, and the Arts in Fifth-Century Athens*. Cambridge, MA: Harvard University Press.

Bondanella, Peter (2009). *A History of Italian Cinema*. New York: Bloomsbury.

Borgeaud, Philippe (1989). *The Cult of Pan in Ancient Greece*, trans. Kathleen Atlass and James Redfield. Chicago: University of Chicago Press.

Box Office Mojo (2007). *300*. March 11, <http://www.boxofficemojo.com/movies/?id=300.htm> (last accessed December 26, 2017).

Box Office Mojo (n.d). "Musical: 1974–Present, Live Action Only." <http://www.boxofficemojo.com/genres/chart/?id=musical.htm> (last accessed December 26, 2017)

Boyd, Barbara Weiden (2008). "Becoming Augustus: The Education of Octavian," in Monica S. Cyrino (ed.), *Rome, Season One: History Makes Television*. Oxford: Wiley, 87–99.

Boyd, Barbara Weiden (2015). "The Triumvirate of the Ring in *Rome*," in Monica S. Cyrino (ed.), *Rome, Season Two: Trial and Triumph*. Edinburgh: Edinburgh University Press, 74–87.

Boyle, A. J. (1987). *Seneca's Phaedra: Introduction, Text, Translation and Notes*. Liverpool: Francis Cairns.

Boyle, A. J. (2014). *Seneca: Medea*. Oxford: Oxford University Press.

Boyle, Brenda M. (2011). "Rescuing Masculinity: Captivity, Rescue and Gender in American War Narratives." *The Journal of American Culture* 34.2: 149–60.

Boym, Svetlana (2001). *The Future of Nostalgia*. New York: Basic Books.

Bradford, Ernie (1980). *The Battle for the West: Thermopylae*. Boston, MA: Da Capo Press.

Brazouski, Antoinette and Mary J. Klatt (1994). *Children's Books on Ancient Greek and Roman Mythology: An Annotated Bibliography*. Santa Barbara: Greenwood.

Brideson, Cynthia and Sara Brideson (2017). *He's Got Rhythm: The Life and Career of Gene Kelly*. Lexington: University of Kentucky Press.

Briggs, Ward (2008). "Layered Allusion in *Gladiator*." *Arion* 15.3: 9–38.

Briley, Ron (2008). "*The Dark Knight*: An Allegory of America in the Age of Bush?" *History News Network*. August 25, <http://historynewsnetwork.org/article/53504> (last accessed January 4, 2018).

Brown, A. S. (1998). "From the Golden Age to the Isles of the Blest." *Mnemosyne* ser. 4, 51.4: 385–410.

Brown, W. Burlie (1957). "The Cincinnatus Image in Presidential Politics." *Agricultural History* 13: 23–9.

Buell, Lawrence (1989). "American Pastoral Ideology Reappraised." *American Literary History* 1.1: 1–29.

Campbell, Duncan B. (2010). "The Fate of the Ninth: The Curious Disappearance of the Legio VIIII Hispana." *Ancient Warfare Magazine* 4.5: 48–53.

Camus, Albert (1947, trans. 1948). *The Plague*, trans. Stuart Gilbert. New York: Vintage.

Caprotti, Federico (2009). "Scipio Africanus: Film, Internal Colonization and Empire." *cultural geographies* 16.3: 381–401.

Cartledge, Paul (2003). *The Spartans*. New York: Overlook Press.

Cartledge, Paul (2004). "What Have the Spartans Done for Us? Sparta's Contribution to Western Civilization." *Greece & Rome* 51.2: 164–79.

Cartledge, Paul (2006). "Spartan Traditions and Receptions." *Hermathena* 181: 41–9.

Cartledge, Paul (2007). *Thermopylae: The Battle That Changed the World*. New York: Vintage.

Cary, Earnest (trans.) (1947). *Dionysius of Halicarnassus: Roman Antiquities, Volume VI: Books 9.25–10*. Loeb Classical Library. Cambridge, MA: Harvard University Press.

Cato and Varro (1934). *On Agriculture*, trans. W. D. Hooper and Harrison Boyd Ash. Loeb Classical Library. Cambridge, MA: Harvard University Press.

Catullus (1962). *Catullus, Tibullus, and Pervigilium Veneris*, trans. F. W. Cornish. Loeb Classical Library. Cambridge, MA: Harvard University Press.

Cawelti, John G. (1971). *The Six-Gun Mystique*. Bowling Green, OH: Bowling Green University Popular Press.

Chadwell, Sean (2004). "Inventing that 'Old Time' Style." *Journal of Popular Film and Television* 32: 3–9.

Chapoutot, Johann (2016). *Greeks, Romans, Germans: How the Nazis Usurped Europe's Classical Past*, trans. Richard R. Nybakken. Los Angeles and Berkeley: University of California Press.

Chaw, Walter (2007). Review of *300*. *Film Freak Central*. April 2, <http://www.filmfreakcentral.net/ffc/2013/09/300.html> (last accessed June 9, 2018).

Christesen, Paul (2004). "Utopia on the Eurotas: Economic Aspects of the Spartan Mirage," in Thomas J. Figueira (ed.), *Spartan Society*. Swansea: Classical Press of Wales, 309–37.

ClassicTVHits.com (n.d.) <http://www.classictvhits.com/tvratings/index.htm> (last accessed December 26, 2017).

Clauss, James J. (1993). *The Best of the Argonauts*. Berkeley: University of California Press.

Clauss, James J. (1999). "Descent into Hell: Mythic Paradigms in *The Searchers*." *Journal of Popular Film and Television* 27.3: 2–17.

Clauss, James J. (2008). "*Hercules Unchained*: *Contaminatio*, *Nostos*, *Katabasis*, and the Surreal." *Arethusa* 41.1: 51–66.

Clough, Emma (2004). "Loyalty and Liberty: Thermopylae in the Western Imagination," in Thomas J. Figueira (ed.), *Spartan Society*. Swansea: Classical Press of Wales, 363–84.

Cohan, Steven (2005). *Incongruous Entertainment: Camp, Cultural Value, and the MGM Musical*. Durham, NC: Duke University Press.

Cohen, Ronald D. (2003). *Rainbow Quest: The Folk Music Revival and American Society, 1940–1970*. Amherst: University of Massachusetts Press.

Collias, Nick (2014). "Fit for Battle: The New Bodies of *300: Rise of an Empire*." Bodybuilding.com. March 9, <https://www.bodybuilding.com/fun/fit-for-battle-the-new-bodies-of-300-rise-of-an-empire.html> (last accessed December 26, 2017).

Collis, Clark (2007). "Why People Love *Xanadu*." *Entertainment Weekly*. July 6, <ew.com/article/2007/07/06/why-people-love-xanadu/> (last accessed January 16, 2018).

Connolly, Joy (1998). Review of Hanson and Heath (1998). *Bryn Mawr Classical Review*. May 13, <http://bmcr.brynmawr.edu/1998/98.5.13.html> (last accessed December 26, 2017).

Connolly, Joy (2015). *The Life of Roman Republicanism*. Princeton: Princeton University Press.

Coontz, Stephanie (2011). *A Strange Stirring: The Feminine Mystique and American Women at the Dawn of the 1960s*. New York: Basic Books.

Cooppan, Vilashini (2005). "The Ruins of Empire: The National and Global Politics of America's Return to Rome," in Ania Loomba, Suvir Kaul, Matti Bunzl, Antoinette Burton, and Jed Etsy (eds), *Postcolonial Studies and Beyond*. Durham, NC: Duke University Press, 80–100.

Cornelius, Michael G. (2011). "Introduction," in Michael G. Cornelius (ed.), *Of Muscles and Men*. Jefferson, NC: McFarland, 1–14.

Cornish, F. W. (trans.) (1962). *Catullus, Tibullus, and Pervigilium Veneris*. Loeb Classical Library. Cambridge, MA: Harvard University Press.

Cortese, James (1976). "Bourgeois Myth and Anti-Myth: The Western Hero of the Fifties." *SubStance* 5.15: 122–32.

Cribriore, Raffaella (2001). *Gymnastics of the Mind: Greek Education in Hellenistic and Roman Egypt*. Princeton: Princeton University Press.

Crowther, Bosley (1964). "Romans Versus Barbarians: Spectacles and Melees in 'Fall of Empire.'" *New York Times*. March 27, <http://www.nytimes.com/movie/review?res=9F02E6DA1138E13ABC4F51DFB566838F679EDE> (last accessed December 26, 2017).

Cyrino, Monica S. (2004). "*Gladiator* and Contemporary American Society," in Martin M. Winkler (ed.), *Gladiator: Film and History*. Malden, MA: Wiley-Blackwell, 124–49.

Cyrino, Monica S. (2005). *Big Screen Rome*. Oxford: Blackwell.

Cyrino, Monica S. (2011). "'This is Sparta!': The Reinvention of Epic in Zack Snyder's *300*," in Robert Burgoyne (ed.), *The Epic Film in World Culture*. London and New York: Routledge, 19–38.

Cyrino, Monica S. (2014). "Ancient Sexuality on Screen," in Thomas K. Hubbard (ed.), *A Companion to Greek and Roman Sexualities*. Malden, MA: Wiley-Blackwell, 613–28.

Dallaire, Roméo (2003). *Shake Hands with the Devil: The Failure of Humanity in Rwanda*. Toronto: Arrow.

Dargis, Manohla (2000). "Saving General Maximus." *LA Weekly*. May 3, <http://www.laweekly.com/film/saving-general-maximus-2131976> (last accessed December 26, 2017).

Dassin, Jules (2007). Interview at the Los Angeles County Museum of Art (LACMA), filmed 2004. DVD extra on *The Naked City*. Criterion Collection.

Dawson, Doyne (1992). *Cities of the Gods: Communist Utopias in Greek Thought*. New York: Oxford University Press.

Day, Kirsten (2008). "'What Makes a Man to Wander?': *The Searchers* as a Western *Odyssey*." *Celluloid Classics: New Perspectives on Classical Antiquity in Modern Cinema* (= *Arethusa* 41.1): 11–49.

Day, Kirsten (2016). *Cowboy Classics: The Roots of the American Western in the Epic Tradition*. Edinburgh: Edinburgh University Press.

Defoe, Daniel (2013 [1722]). *Journal of the Plague Year*, with introduction and notes by Cynthia Wall. London: Penguin.

Demont, Paul (2013). "The Causes of the Athenian Plague and Thucydides," in Antonis Tsakmakis and Melina Tamiolaki (eds), *Thucydides between History and Literature*. Berlin and Boston, MA: De Gruyter, 73–87.

Dewing, H. B. (trans.) (1914). *Procopius: History of the Wars, Volume I: Books 1–2 (Persian Wars)*. Loeb Classical Library. Cambridge, MA: Harvard University Press.

Diggle, James (ed.) (1984). *Euripidis fabulae*. Oxford: Clarendon Press.

Dika, Vera (2003). *Recycled Culture in Contemporary Art and Film: The Uses of Nostalgia*. New York: Cambridge University Press.

Dionysius of Halicarnassus (1947). *Roman Antiquities, Volume VI: Books 9.25–10*, trans. Earnest Cary. Loeb Classical Library. Cambridge, MA: Harvard University Press.

Doman, Katie (2005). "Something Old, Something New: The Carter Family's Bristol Sessions," in Charles K. Wolfe and Ted Olson (eds), *The Bristol Sessions: Writings about the Big Bang of Country Music*. Jefferson, NC: McFarland, 66–86.

Dominik, William J. (1996). "Reading Vergil's *Aeneid*: The Gates of Sleep (6.893–8)." *Maia* 48.2: 129–38.

Donatus, Aelius (1996, rev. 2014). *Life of Virgil*, trans. David Wilson-Okamura. <virgil.org/vitae> (last accessed December 10, 2017).

Dorgerloh, Annette (2013). "Competing Ancient Worlds in Early Historical Film: The Example of *Cabiria* (1914)," in Pantelis Michelakis and Maria Wyke (eds), *The Ancient World in Silent Cinema*. Cambridge: Cambridge University Press, 229–46.

Dougherty, Carol (2001). *The Raft of Odysseus: The Ethnographic Imagination of Homer's Odyssey*. Oxford: Oxford University Press.

Dougherty, Carol (2006). *Prometheus*. London: Routledge.

Durman, Chris (2008). "African American Old-Time String Band Music: A Selective Discography."*Notes: Quarterly Journal of the Music Library Association* 64.4: 797–808.

Duyvesten, Isabelle (2005). "Rethinking the Nature Of War: Some Conclusions," in Isabelle Duyvesten and Jan Angstrom (eds), *Rethinking the Nature of War*. London: Frank Cass, 225–41.

Duyvesteyn, Isabelle and Jan Angstrom (eds) (2005). *Rethinking the Nature of War*. London: Frank Cass.

Dwyer, Michael D. (2015). *Back to the Fifties: Nostalgia, Hollywood Film, and Popular Music of the Seventies and Eighties*. New York: Oxford University Press.

Dyer, Richard (1979). "In Defence of Disco." *Gay Left* 8: 20–3. <http://www.gayleft1970s.org/issues/issue08.asp> (last accessed December 26, 2017).

Dyer, Richard (1981). "Entertainment and Utopia," in Rick Altman (ed.), *Genre: The Musical*. London, Boston, and Henley: Routledge & Kegan Paul, 175–89.

Dyer, Richard (2011). "'I Seem to Find the Happiness I Seek': Heterosexuality and Dance in the Musical," in Richard Dyer, *In the Space of a Song: The Use of Song in Film*. New York: Routledge, 89–100.

Ebert, Roger (2000a). "*O Brother, Where Art Thou*." December 29, <http://www.rogerebert.com/reviews/o-brother-where-art-thou-2000> (last accessed December 26, 2017).

Ebert, Roger (2000b). "*Gladiator*." May 5, <http://www.rogerebert.com/reviews/gladiator-2000> (last accessed December 26, 2017).

Ebert Roger (2000c). "Ebert Has No Remorse for Review of *Gladiator*." *The Victoria Advocate*. May 21, <https://news.google.com/newspapers?nid=861&dat=20000521&id=RQxIAAAAIBAJ&sjid=xYAMAAAAIBAJ&pg=5195,4874768&hl=en> (last accessed January 4, 2018).

Echols, Alice (2010). *Hot Stuff: Disco and the Remaking of American Culture*. New York: W. W. Norton.

Ehrbar, Ned (2014). "Interview: New *300* Star Eva Green Doesn't Always Want to Show Her Boobs." *Metro*. March 3, <http://www.metro.us/entertainment/new-300-star-eva-green-doesn-t-always-want-to-show-her-boobs-metro/tmWncc---d6zzznRfoOvVs/> (last accessed December 26, 2017).

Eleftheriotis, Dimitris (2012). "The Foreignness of Jules Dassin: Notes on Cosmopolitan Authorship." *Screen* 53.4: 339–58.

Elliott, Andrew B. R. (2013). "Rewriting European History: National and Transnational Identities in HBO's *Rome*." *Historical Journal of Film, Radio, and Television* 33: 576–93.

Ellis, Stephen (2013). "Bruce Molsky with Stephen Ellis and David Ross." *The Brooklyn Rail*. November 5, <http://www.brooklynrail.org/2013/11/music/bruce-molsky-with-stephen-ellis-and-david-ross> (last accessed December 26, 2017).

Elston, M. Melissa (2009). "Xerxes in Drag: Post-9/11 Marginalization and (Mis)Identification in *300*." *disClosure: A Journal of Social Theory* 18: 58–74.

Euripides (1984). *Euripidis fabulae*, ed. James Diggle. Oxford: Clarendon Press.

Evans, Rhiannon (2008). *Utopia Antiqua: Readings of the Golden Age and Decline at Rome*. London: Routledge.

Evelyn-White, Hugh G. (trans.) (1914; repr. 1982). *Hesiod: The Homeric Hymns and Homerica*. Loeb Classical Library. Cambridge, MA: Harvard University Press.

Evslin, Bernard (2012). *Gods, Heroes, and Monsters of the Greek Myths*. New York: Open Road Integrated Media.

Failes, Ian (2014). "Inside the Battles of *300: Rise of an Empire*." *Fxguide*. March 23, <https://www.fxguide.com/featured/inside-the-battles-of-300-rise-of-an-empire/> (last accessed December 26, 2017).

Fantham, Elaine, Helene Peet Foley, Natalie Boymel Kampen, Sarah B. Pomeroy, and H. Alan Shapiro (1994). *Women in the Classical World: Image and Text*. New York: Oxford University Press.

Fantuzzi, Marco and Theodore D. Papanghelis (eds) (2006). *Brill's Companion to Greek and Latin Pastoral*. Leiden: Brill.

Faraci, Devin (2011). "The Badass Interview: Kevin Macdonald, Director of *The Eagle*, Talks Rome, Vietnam, and Afghanistan." *Birth.Movies.Death*. February 9, <http://birthmoviesdeath.com/2011/02/09/the-badass-interview-kevin-macdonald-director-of-the-eagle-talks-rome-vietn> (last accessed December 26, 2017).

Feeney, Denis (1991). *The Gods in Epic: Poets and Critics of the Classical Tradition*. Oxford: Oxford University Press.

Felperin, Lesley (2000). "Decline and Brawl." *Sight and Sound* 10:6. <http://old.bfi.org.uk/sightandsound/review/374> (last accessed December 26, 2017).

Felski, Rita (ed.) (2008). *Rethinking Tragedy*. Baltimore: Johns Hopkins University Press.

Fenin, George N. and William K. Everson (1973). *The Western: From Silents to the Seventies*. New York: Grossman.

Ferguson, John (1975). *Utopias of the Classical World*. Ithaca: Cornell University Press.

Ferris, David (2000). *Silent Urns: Romanticism, Hellenism, Modernity*. Stanford: Stanford University Press.

Feuer, Jane (1977). "The Self-Reflexive Musical and the Myth of Entertainment," in Barry Keith Grant (ed.), *Film Genre Reader*. Austin: University of Texas Press, 329–43.

Feuer, Jane (1993, second edition). *The Hollywood Musical*. Bloomington: Indiana University Press.

Filene, Benjamin (2000). *Romancing the Folk: Public Memory and American Roots Music*. Chapel Hill: University of North Carolina Press.

Fitzgerald, William (2001). "Oppositions, Anxieties, and Ambiguities in the Toga Movie," in Sandra Joshel, Martha Malamud, and Don McGuire, Jr. (eds), *Imperial Projections: Ancient Rome in Modern Popular Culture*. Baltimore: Johns Hopkins University Press, 23–49.

Flensted-Jenson, Pernille (2002). "Something Old, Something New, Something Borrowed: The *Odyssey* and *O Brother, Where Art Thou?*" *Classica et Mediaevalia* 53: 13–30.

Fletcher, Judith (2014). "The Catabasis of Mattie Ross in the Coens' *True Grit*." *Classical World* 107.2: 237–54.

Fontana, Benedetto (1993). "Tacitus on Empire and Republic." *History of Political Thought* 14.1: 27–40.

Foster, B. O. (trans.) (1922). *Livy: History of Rome, Volume II: Books 3–4*. Loeb Classical Library. Cambridge, MA: Harvard University Press.

Fowler, Harold N. (trans.) (1921). *Plato: Theaetetus. Sophist*. Loeb Classical Library. Cambridge, MA: Harvard University Press.

Frankel, Glenn (2013). *The Searchers: The Making of an American Legend*. New York: Bloomsbury.

Frankel, Valerie Estelle (2014). *Women in Game of Thrones: Power, Conformity, and Resistance*. Jefferson, NC: McFarland.

Franzoni, David (2000). Transcript of *Gladiator* Screenplay. <https://sfy.ru/transcript/gladiator_ts> (last accessed December 26, 2017).

Fratantuono, Lee (2007). *Madness Unchained: A Reading of Vergil's Aeneid*. Lanham, MD: Lexington Books.

French, Peter A. (1997). *Cowboy Metaphysics: Ethics and Death in Westerns*. Lanham, MD: Rowman and Littlefield.

Galinsky, Karl (1988). "The Anger of Aeneas." *The American Journal of Philology* 109.3: 321–48.

Galinsky, Karl (1996). *Augustan Culture: An Interpretive Introduction*. Princeton: Princeton University Press.

Galinsky, Karl (ed.) (2005). *The Cambridge Companion to the Age of Augustus*. Cambridge: Cambridge University Press.

Gantz, Timothy (1993). *Early Greek Myth*. Baltimore: Johns Hopkins University Press.

Garza, Randal P. (2008). *Understanding Plague: The Medical and Imaginative Texts of Medieval Spain*. New York: Peter Lang.

Gatz, Bodo (1967). *Weltalter, goldene Zeit und sinnverwandte Vorstellungen*. Hildesheim: Olms.

Geers, Jeff (2012). "'The Great Machine Doesn't Wear a Cape!': American Cultural Anxiety and the Post-9/11 Superhero," in Matthew Pustz (ed.), *Comic Books and American Cultural History: An Anthology*. New York: Bloomsbury Academic, 250–62.

Gelbart, Matthew (2007). *The Invention of "Folk Music" and "Art Music": Emerging Categories from Ossian to Wagner*. Cambridge: Cambridge University Press.

Gerstenzang, Peter (2016). "Richard Barone Breathes New Life into the Golden Age of Village Folk." *Observer*. August 4, <http://observer.com/2016/08/richard-barone-breathes-new-life-into-the-golden-age-of-village-folk/> (last accessed December 26, 2017).

Ginsburg, Judith (2006). *Representing Agrippina: Constructions of Female Power in the Early Roman Empire*. Oxford: Oxford University Press.

Glei, Reinhold F. (1998). "The Show Must Go On: The Death of Marcellus and the Future of the Augustan Principate," in H.-P. Stahl (ed.), *Vergil's Aeneid*. London: Duckworth, 119–34.

Goldhill, Simon (2007). "*Naked* and *O Brother, Where Art Thou*: The Politics and Poetics of Epic Cinema," in Barbara Graziosi and Emily Greenwood (eds), *Homer in the Twentieth Century: Between World Literature and Western Canon*. Oxford: Oxford University Press, 245–67.

Goldman, Eric (2012). "*The Walking Dead*: 'Beside the Dying Fire' Review." March 18, <http://www.ign.com/articles/2012/03/19/the-walking-dead-beside-the-dying-fire-review> (last accessed December 26, 2017).

Goldstone, Jack A. (2002). "Efflorescences and Economic Growth in World History: Rethinking the 'Rise of the West' and the Industrial Revolution." *Journal of World History* 13.2: 323–89.

Goold, G. P. (rev. trans.) (1986; rev. 1999). *Eclogues. Georgics. Aeneid: Books 1–6*, trans. H. Rushton Fairclough. Loeb Classical Library. Cambridge, MA: Harvard University Press.

Goold, G. P. (rev. trans.) (rev. 2000). *Aeneid: Books 7–12*, trans. H. Rushton Fairclough. Loeb Classical Library. Cambridge, MA: Harvard University Press.

Grebe, Sabine (2004). "Augustus' Divine Authority and Vergil's *Aeneid*." *Vergilius* 50: 35–62.

Green, Archie (1965). "Hillbilly Music: Source and Symbol." *The Journal of American Folklore* 78: 204–28.

Green, Steven J. (2004). "Playing with Marble: The Monuments of the Caesars in Ovid's *Fasti*." *Classical Quarterly* 54.1: 224–39.

Greenberg, Amy S. (2012). *Manifest Destiny and American Territorial Expansion: A Brief History with Documents*. Boston: Bedford/St. Martin's.

Griffin, Sean (2018). *Free and Easy? A Defining History of the American Film Musical Genre*. Hoboken, NJ: Wiley-Blackwell.

Griffith, R. Drew (2001). "Sailing to Elysium: Menelaus' Afterlife (*Odyssey* 4.561–569) and Egyptian Religion." *Phoenix* 55.3/4: 231–43.

Gross, Nicolas P. (2003–4). "Mantles Woven with Gold: Pallas's Shroud and the End of the Aeneid." *Classical Journal* 99: 135–56.

Grossman, Dave (2009). *On Killing: The Psychological Cost of Learning to Kill in War and Society*. New York: Back Bay Books.

Gruen, Erich (2005). "Augustus and the Making of the Principate," in Karl Galinsky (ed.), *The Cambridge Companion to the Age of Augustus*. Cambridge: Cambridge University Press, 33–52.

Günsberg, Maggie (2005). *Italian Cinema: Gender and Genre*. New York: Palgrave Macmillan.

Gutzwiller, Kathryn J. (1991). *Theocritus' Pastoral Analogies: The Formation of a Genre*. Madison: University of Wisconsin Press.

Hake, Sabine (2002). *German National Cinema*. New York and London: Routledge.

Hamilton, Edith (1942). *Mythology*. Boston: Little, Brown.

Hanesworth, Pauline (2015). "Monuments, Men and Metaphors: Recreating Ancient Athens in Film," in Marta García Morcillo, Pauline Hanesworth, and Óscar Lapeña Marchena (eds), *Imagining Ancient Cities in Film: From Babylon to Cinecittà*. New York: Routledge, 91–112.

Hansen, Mogens Herman (ed.) (2005). *The Imaginary Polis. Acts of the Copenhagen Polis Centre vol. 7*. Copenhagen: Royal Danish Academy of Arts and Letters.

Hanson, Victor Davis and John Heath (1998). *Who Killed Homer? The Demise of Classical Education and the Recovery of Greek Wisdom*. New York: Free Press.

Hardie, Philip (1983). "Some Themes from Gigantomachy in the *Aeneid*." *Hermes* 111: 311–26.

Hardie, Philip (2014). *The Last Trojan Hero: A Cultural History of Virgil's Aeneid*. New York: I. B. Tauris.

Hark, Ina Rae (1993). "Animals or Romans: Looking at Masculinity in *Spartacus*," in Steven Cohan and Ina Rae Hark (eds), *Screening the Male: Exploring Masculinities in Contemporary Hollywood Cinema*. New York: Routledge, 151–72.

Hark, Ina Rae (2012). *Deadwood*. Detroit: Wayne State University Press.

Harmon, D. P. (1973). "Nostalgia for the Age of Heroes in Catullus 64." *Latomus* 32.2: 311–31.

Harries, Martin (2001). "In the Coen Brothers' New Film, the Dark Utopian Music of the American South." *The Chronicle of Higher Education*. February 2, <http://chronicle.com/article/In-the-Coen-Brothers-New/35196> (last accessed December 26, 2017).

Harrison, Juliette (2015). "Antony and Atia: Tragic Romance in *Rome*," in Monica S. Cyrino (ed.), *Rome, Season Two: Trial and Triumph*. Edinburgh: Edinburgh University Press, 155–68.

Harryhausen, Ray and Tom Dalton (2004). *Ray Harryhausen: An Animated Life*. New York: Billboard Books.

Hassler-Forest, Dan (2010). "The *300* Controversy: A Case Study in the Politics of Adaptation," in Joyce Goggin and Dan Hassler-Forest (eds), *The Rise and Reason of Comics and Graphic Literature*. Jefferson, NC: MacFarland, 119–29.

Helford, Elyce Rae (2000). "Feminism, Queer Studies, and the Sexual Politics of *Xena: Warrior Princess*," in Elyce Rae Helford (ed.), *Fantasy Girls: Gender in the New Universe of Science Fiction and Fantasy*. Lanham, MD: Rowman and Littlefield, 135–62.

Henderson, A. A. R. (1969). "Tibullus, Elysium and Tartarus." *Latomus* 28.3: 649–53.

Henney, Eric (2010). Interview with Neil Marshall. *City Paper*. August 27, <http://www.michaelfassbender.org/citypaper.html> (last accessed December 26, 2017).

Henry, Elisabeth (1992). *Orpheus with His Lute: Poetry and the Renewal of Life*. Carbondale: Southern Illinois University Press.

Herzfeld, Michael (1982). *Ours Once More: Folklore, Ideology, and the Making of Modern Greece*. Austin: University of Texas Press.

Hesiod (1914; repr. 1982). *Hesiod: The Homeric Hymns and Homerica*, trans. Hugh G. Evelyn-White. Loeb Classical Library. Cambridge, MA: Harvard University Press.

Hesiod (1970). *Hesiodi Opera*, ed. Friedrich Solmsen. Oxford: Clarendon Press.

Higgins, Charlotte (2010). "*Centurion* Kicks Off British Sword and Sandals Film Wave." *The Guardian*. April 22, <https://www.theguardian.com/film/2010/apr/22/eagle-of-the-ninth-centurion> (last accessed December 26, 2017).

Hirschhorn, Clive (1984). *Gene Kelly*. New York: St. Martin's Press.

Hitchens, Christopher (1987). *The Elgin Marbles: Should They Be Returned to Greece?* London: Chatto & Windus.

Holt, Frank (2005). *Into the Land of Bones: Alexander the Great in Afghanistan*. Berkeley: University of California Press.

Holtsmark, Earling B. (2001). "The Katabasis Theme in Modern Cinema," in Martin M. Winkler (ed.), *Classical Myth and Culture in the Cinema*. Oxford: Oxford University Press, 23–50.

Homer (1919; second edition 1995). *Odyssey, Volume I: Books 1–12*, trans. Augustus Taber Murray, rev. George E. Dimock. Loeb Classical Library. Cambridge, MA: Harvard University Press.

Homer (1920). *Homeri Opera*, ed. Thomas W. Allen and David B. Munro. Oxford: Oxford University Press.

Homer (1924). *Iliad, Volume I: Books 1–12*, ed. Augustus Taber Murray. Loeb Classical Library. Cambridge, MA: Harvard University Press.

Homer (1995, second edition). *The Odyssey, Volume II: Books 13–24*, trans. Augustus Taber Murray, rev. George E. Dimock. Loeb Classical Library. Cambridge, MA: Harvard University Press.

Hooper, W. D. and Harrison Boyd Ash (trans.) (1934). *Cato and Varro: On Agriculture*. Loeb Classical Library. Cambridge, MA: Harvard University Press.

Horsley, G. H. R. (2000). "Homer in Pisidia: Aspects of the History of Greek Education in a Remote Roman Province." *Antichthon* 34: 46–81.

Horton, Andrew (1984). "Jules Dassin: A Multi-National Filmmaker Considered." *Film Criticism* 8.3: 21–35.

Houghton, L. B. T. (2007). "Tibullus' Elegiac Underworld." *The Classical Quarterly* n.s. 57.1: 153–65.

Hunter, Richard (1993). *The Argonautica of Apollonius*. Literary Studies. Cambridge: Cambridge University Press.

Hunter, Richard (2004). "Homer in Greek Literature," in Robert Fowler (ed.), *The Cambridge Companion to Homer*. Cambridge: Cambridge University Press, 235–53.

Hurwit, Jeffrey (2004). *The Acropolis in the Age of Pericles*. Cambridge: Cambridge University Press.

Hutcheon, Linda (2000). "Irony, Nostalgia and the Postmodern," in Raymond Vervliet and Annemarie Estor (eds), *Methods for the Study of Cultural Memory*. Amsterdam and Atlanta: Rodopi, 189–207.

IMDB (n.d.) "Top-US-Grossing Musical Titles." <http://www.imdb.com/search/title?genres=musical&sort=boxoffice_gross_us,desc> (last accessed December 26, 2017).

Ipsen, Guido (2012). "Conan the Blueprint: The Construction of Masculine Prototypes in Genre Films," in Karen Ross (ed.), *The Handbook of Gender, Sex, and Media*. Malden, MA: Wiley-Blackwell, 135–56.

Jackson, Steven (1997). "Argo: The First Ship?" *Rheinisches Museum für Philologie* n.s. 140.3/4: 249–57.

James, Paula (2009). "Crossing Classical Thresholds: Gods, Monsters and Hell Dimensions in the Whedon Universe," in Dunstan Lowe and Kim

Shahabudin (eds), *Classics for All: Reworking Antiquity in Mass Culture*. Newcastle upon Tyne: Cambridge Scholars, 237–60.

Jameson, Fredric (1981). *The Political Unconscious: Narrative as a Socially Symbolic Act*. London: Methuen.

Jameson, Fredric (1991). *Postmodernism or, the Cultural Logic of Late Capitalism*. Durham, NC: Duke University Press.

Jameson, Fredric (2005). *Archaeologies of the Future: The Desire Called Utopia and Other Science Fictions*. New York: Verso.

Johnston, Patricia A. (1980). *Vergil's Agricultural Golden Age: A Study of the Georgics*. Leiden: Brill.

Johnston, Patricia and Sophia Papaioannou (2013). "Introduction: Idyllic Landscapes in Antiquity: The Golden Age, Arcadia, and the *locus amoenus*." *Acta Antiqua* 53.2–3: 133–44.

Jones, H. Stuart and J. E. Powell (eds) (1942, second edition). *Thucydides: Historiae, Vol. I (Books I–IV)*. Oxford: Clarendon Press.

Jost, Madeline (2007). "The Religious System in Arcadia," in Daniel Ogden (ed.), *A Companion to Greek Religion*. Malden, MA: Wiley, 264–79.

Kahane, David (2007). "*300* Shocker." *National Review Online*. March 12, <http://www.nationalreview.com/article/220264/300-shocker-david-kahane> (last accessed December 26, 2017).

Kahn, Ed (1996). "The Carter Family on Border Radio." *American Music* 14.2: 205–17.

Karalis, Vrasidas (2012). *A History of Greek Cinema*. New York: Continuum.

Kassimeris, George and John Buckley (eds) (2010). *The Ashgate Research Companion to Modern Warfare*. Oxford: Routledge.

Keen, Tony (2014). "A Wild West Hero: Motifs of the Hollywood Western in the Four Hadrian's Wall Movies." Classical Association Presentation.

Keetley, Dawn (2014). "Introduction: We're All Infected," in Dawn Keetley (ed.), *"We're All Infected": Essays on AMC's The Walking Dead and the Fate of the Human*. Jefferson, NC: McFarland, 3–25.

Keith, Alison (2000). *Engendering Rome: Women in Latin Epic*. Cambridge: Cambridge University Press.

Kelly, Rachael (2015). "Problematic Masculinity: Antony and the Political Sphere," in Monica S. Cyrino (ed.), *Rome, Season Two: Trial and Triumph*. Edinburgh: Edinburgh University Press, 169–81.

Keppie, Lawrence (1989). "The Fate of the Ninth Legion: A Problem for the Eastern Provinces?" in David H. French and Chris S. Lightfoot (eds), *The Eastern Frontier of the Roman Empire*. London: BAR, 247–55.

King, Helen and Jo Brown (2015). "Thucydides and the Plague," in Christine Lee and Neville Morley (eds), *Handbook to the Reception of Thucydides*. Malden, MA: Wiley-Blackwell, 451–73.

Kirkman, Robert (2003–). *The Walking Dead*. Portland: Image Comics.

Kirkman, Robert, Charlie Adlard, and Cliff Rathburn (2013). *The Walking Dead Compendium 2*. Berkeley: Image Comics.

Koliopoulos, John (2008). "'Modern Greece': An Old Debate," in Mark Mazower (ed.), *Networks of Power in Modern Greece: Essays on Honor of John Campbell*. New York: Columbia University Press, 129–35.

Konstan, David (1997). "The Greek Polis and Its Negations. Versions of Utopia in Aristophanes' *Birds*," in Gregory W. Dobrov (ed.), *The City as Comedy: Society and Representation in Athenian Comedy*. Chapel Hill: University of North Carolina Press, 3–22.

Kooijman, Jaap (2005). "Turn the beat around: Richard Dyer's 'In Defence of Disco' revisited." *European Journal of Cultural Studies* 8.2: 257–66.

Kopff, E. Christian (1999). *The Devil Knows Latin: Why America Needs the Classical Tradition*. Wilmington, DE: Intercollegiate Studies Institute Books.

Kovacs, George and C. W. Marshall (2011). *Classics and Comics*. Oxford: Oxford University Press.

Kovacs, George and C. W. Marshall (2015). *Son of Classics and Comics*. Oxford: Oxford University Press.

Kutulas, Judy (2003). "'You Probably Think This Song Is About You': 1970s Women's Music from Carole King to Disco Divas," in Sherrie A. Innes (ed.), *Disco Divas: Women and Popular Culture in the 1970s*. Philadelphia: University of Pennsylvania Press, 172–93.

Lacy, Tim (2013). *The Dream of a Democratic Culture: Mortimer J. Adler and the Great Books Idea*. New York: Palgrave Macmillan.

Lagny, Michèle (1992). "Popular Taste: The Peplum," in Richard Dyer and Ginette Vincendeau (eds), *Popular European Cinema*. London and New York: Routledge, 163–180.

Lamberton, Robert (2005). "Ancient Reception," in John Miles Foley (ed.), *A Companion to Ancient Epic*. Malden, MA: Blackwell, 164–73.

Langford, Barry (2005). *Film Genre: Hollywood and Beyond*. Edinburgh: Edinburgh University Press.

Lattimore, Steven (trans.) (1998). *Thucydides: The Peloponnesian War*. Indianapolis: Hackett.

Lauwers, Jeroen, Marieke Dhont, and Xanne Huybrecht (2012). "'This is Sparta!': Discourse, Gender, and the Orient in Zack Snyder's *300*," in Almut-Barbara Renger and Jon Solomon (eds), *Ancient Worlds in Film and Television: Gender and Politics*. Leiden: Brill, 79–94.

Lawrence, Tim (2003). *Love Saves the Day: A History of American Dance Music Culture, 1970–1979*. Durham, NC: Duke University Press.

Leonard, Miriam (2006). "The Uses of Reception: Derrida and the Historical Imperative," in Charles Martindale and Richard F. Thomas (eds), *Classics and the Uses of Reception*. Malden, MA: Blackwell, 116–26.

Leonard, Miriam (2015). *Tragic Modernities*. Oxford: Oxford University Press.

Leontis, Artemis (1995). *Topographies of Hellenism*. Ithaca: Cornell University Press.

Levick, Barbara (1982). "Morals, Politics, and the Fall of the Roman Republic." *Greece & Rome* 29.1: 53–62.

Levick, Barbara (2010). *Augustus: Image and Substance.* New York: Routledge.

Levin, Harry (1969). *The Myth of the Golden Age in the Renaissance.* Bloomington: Indiana University Press.

Levitas, Ruth (1990). *The Concept of Utopia.* Syracuse, NY: Syracuse University Press.

Levitas, Ruth (2013). *Utopia as Method: The Imaginary Reconstitution of Society.* New York: Palgrave Macmillan.

Lewis, Tyson and Daniel Cho (2006). "Home is Where the Neurosis Is: A Topography of the Spatial Unconscious." *Cultural Critique* 64: 69–91.

L'Hoir, Francesca Santoro (1994). "Tacitus and Women's Usurpation of Power." *Classical World* 88.1: 5–25.

Liehm, Mira (1984). *Passion and Defiance: Film in Italy from 1942 to the Present.* Berkeley: University of California Press.

Liu, Narayan (2016). "The 15 Highest-Grossing Superhero Films Ever." *CBR*. October 25, <http://www.cbr.com/the-15-highest-grossing-superhero-films-ever/> (last accessed December 26, 2017).

Livy (1922). *History of Rome, Volume II: Books 3–4*, trans. B. O. Foster. Loeb Classical Library. Cambridge, MA: Harvard University Press.

Llewellyn-Jones, Lloyd (2009). "Hollywood's Ancient World," in Andrew Erskine (ed.), *A Companion to Ancient History*. Oxford: Blackwell, 564–79.

Lloyd, Alan (2005). *Marathon: The Crucial Battle that Created Western Democracy*. London: Souvenir Press.

Lloyd-Jones, Hugh (trans.) (1950). *Sophocles: Ajax. Electra. Oedipus Tyrannus*. Loeb Classical Library. Cambridge, MA: Harvard University Press.

Lockett, Christopher (2010). "Accidental History: Mass Culture and HBO's *Rome*." *Journal of Popular Film and Television* 38: 102–12.

Lomax, Alan (1959). "Bluegrass Background: Folk Music with Overdrive." *Esquire* 52: 108.

Lonsdale, Stephen H. (2000). *Dance and Ritual Play in Greek Religion.* Baltimore: Johns Hopkins University Press.

Loraux, Nicole (1993). "Éloge de l'anachronisme en histoire." *Le Genre Humain* 27: 23–40.

Lotan, Yael (1962). *Phaedra*. New York: Bantam.

Lovatt, Helen (2009). "Gutting the *Argonautica*? How to Make Jason and the Argonauts Suitable for Children," in Dunstan Lowe and Kim Shahabudin (eds), *Classics for All: Reworking Antiquity in Mass Culture.* Newcastle upon Tyne: Cambridge Scholars, 17–38.

Low, Polly (ed.) (2008). *The Athenian Empire*. Edinburgh: Edinburgh University Press.

Lowrie, Michèle (2005). "Vergil and Founding Violence." *Cardozo Law Review* 27.2: 945–76.

Luciano, Patrick (1994). *With Fire and Sword: Italian Spectacles on American Screens, 1958–1968*. Metuchen, NJ: Scarecrow Press.

Lucretius (1924). *On the Nature of Things*, trans. W. H. D. Rouse. Loeb Classical Library. Cambridge, MA: Harvard University Press.

Lyne, R. O. A. M. (1987). *Further Voices in Vergil's Aeneid*. Oxford: Clarendon Press.

Mackenzie, Compton and William Stobbs (1974). *Golden Tales of Greece: The Stories of Perseus, Jason, Achilles, and Theseus*. London: Aldus Books.

MacKinnon, Kenneth (1986). *Greek Tragedy into Film*. London: Croom Helm.

Mann, Thomas (2001). *Death in Venice and A Man and His Dog: A Dual Language Book*, trans. Stanley Appelbaum. Mineola, NY: Dover.

Marchand, Suzanne (1996). *Down from Olympus: Archaeology and Philhellenism in Germany, 1750–1970*. Princeton: Princeton University Press.

Marincola, John (2006). "Herodotus and the History of the Past," in Carolyn Dewald and John Marincola (eds), *The Cambridge Companion to Herodotus*. Cambridge: Cambridge University Press, 13–28.

Marinelli, Peter V. (1971). *Pastoral*. London: Routledge

Marshall, C. W. (2003). "Aeneas the Vampire Slayer: A Roman Model for Why Giles Kills Ben." *Slayage: The Online International Journal of Buffy Studies* 3.1: 34–9. <http://www.whedonstudies.tv/uploads/2/6/2/8/26288593/marshall_slayage_3.1.pdf> (last accessed December 26, 2017).

Martin, George R. R. (2005). "What I'm Watching." October 7, <http://www.georgerrmartin.com/rome/> (last accessed December 26, 2017).

Martin, George R. R. (2011). *A Song of Ice and Fire*. New York: Bantam.

Marx, Leo (1964). *The Machine in the Garden: Technology and the Pastoral Ideal in America*. Oxford: Oxford University Press.

Maslon, Laurence (2013). *Superheroes! Capes, Cowls, and the Creation of Comic Book Culture*. New York: Crown Archetype.

Mast, Gerald (1982). *Howard Hawks: Storyteller*. New York: Oxford University Press.

Mattson, Kevin (2009). *"What the Heck Are You Up To, Mr. President?" Jimmy Carter, America's "Malaise" and the Speech That Should Have Changed America*. New York: Bloomsbury.

Maurice, Lisa (2015). "Children, Greece and Rome: Heroes and Eagles," in Lisa Maurice (ed.), *The Reception of Ancient Greece and Rome in Children's Literature*. Leiden: Brill, 1–14.

Mayer, Roland (2002), *Seneca: Phaedra*. London: Duckworth.

Maynard, John Arthur (1991). *Venice West: The Beat Generation in Southern California*. New Brunswick, NJ: Rutgers University Press.

McBride, Joseph (2011). *Searching for John Ford: A Life*. Jackson: University Press of Mississippi.

McCullough, Anna (2015). "Livia, Sadomasochism, and the Anti-Augustan Tradition," in Monica S. Cyrino (ed.), *Rome, Season Two: Trial and Triumph*. Edinburgh: Edinburgh University Press, 128–40.

McDonald, Marianne (1983). "Dassin's *Phaedra*: Fireworks and Death among the Jet Set," in Marianne McDonald, *Euripides in Cinema: The Heart Made Visible*. Philadelphia: Centrum.

McDonough, Christopher M. (2013). "Ancient Allusions and Modern Anxieties in *Seven Brides for Seven Brothers* (1954)," in Monica S. Cyrino (ed.), *Screening Love and Sex in the Ancient World*. New York: Palgrave Macmillan, 99–110.

McGilligan, Patrick (2012). "Jules Dassin," in Patrick McGilligan and Paul Buhle (eds), *Tender Comrades: A Backstory of the Hollywood Blacklist*. Minneapolis: University of Minnesota Press, 199–224.

McInnes, Colin (2005). "A Different Kind of War? September 11 and the United States' Afghan War," in Isabelle Duyvesteyn and Jan Angstrom (eds), *Rethinking the Nature of War*. London: Frank Cass, 109–34.

McInnis, Maurie (2011). "George Washington: Cincinnatus or Marcus Aurelius?" in Peter S. Onuf and Nicholas P. Cole (eds), *Thomas Jefferson, the Classical World, and Early America*. Charlottesville and London: University of Virginia Press, 128–68.

McLean, Adrienne (2004). *Being Rita Hayworth: Labor, Identity, and Hollywood Stardom*. New Brunswick, NJ: Rutgers University Press.

Melchior, Aislinn (2011). "Caesar in Vietnam: Did Roman Soldiers Suffer from Post-Traumatic Stress Disorder?" *Greece & Rome* 58: 209–23.

Mercouri, Melina (1971). *I Was Born Greek*. New York: Doubleday.

Michelakis, Pantelis (2013). *Greek Tragedy on Screen*. Oxford: Oxford University Press.

Miles, Gary (1999). "The Aeneid as Foundation Story," in Christine Perkell (ed.), *Reading Vergil's Aeneid: An Interpretive Guide*. Norman: University of Oklahoma Press, 231–50.

Miles, Richard (2011). "Hannibal and Propaganda," in Dexter Hoyos (ed.), *A Companion to the Punic Wars*. Hoboken, NJ: Wiley, 260–79.

Miller, Frank Justus (trans.) (1946a, second edition). *Ovid: Metamorphoses, Volume I: Books 1–8*. Loeb Classical Library. Cambridge, MA: Harvard University Press.

Miller, Frank Justus (trans.) (1946b, second edition). *Ovid: Metamorphoses, Volume II: Books 9–15*. Loeb Classical Library. Cambridge, MA: Harvard University Press.

Miller, Frank and Lynn Varley (1998). *300*. Milwaukee: Dark Horse Books.

Mitchell-Boyask, Robin (2008). *Plague and the Athenian Imagination: Drama, History and the Cult of Asclepius*. Cambridge: Cambridge University Press.

Molyviati-Toptsis, Urania (1994). "Vergil's Elysium and the Orphic-Pythagorean Ideas of After-Life." *Mnemosyne* ser. 4, 47.1: 33–46.

Morcillo, Marta García (2015). "The East in the West: The Rise and Fall of Ancient Carthage in Modern Imagery and Film," in Marta García Morcillo, Pauline Hanesworth, and Óscar Lapeña Marchena (eds),

Imagining Ancient Cities in Film: From Babylon to Cinecittà. New York: Routledge, 135–62.

More, Thomas (2003). *Utopia*, trans. Paul Turner. New York: Penguin.

Morgan, Llewelyn (1998). "Assimilation and Civil War: Hercules and Cacus (Aen. 8.185–267)," in H.-P. Stahl (ed.), *Vergil's Aeneid*. London: Duckworth, 175–97.

Morgan, Theresa (1998). *Literate Education in the Hellenistic and Roman Worlds*. Cambridge: Cambridge University Press.

Morris, Ian Macgregor (2004). "The Paradigm of Democracy: Sparta in Enlightenment Thought," in Thomas J. Figueira (ed.), *Spartan Society*. Swansea: Classical Press of Wales, 339–62.

Morrison, James V. (2006). "Interaction of Speech and Narrative in Thucydides," in Antonios Rengakos and Antonios Tsakmakis (eds), *Brill's Companion to Thucydides*. Leiden and Boston, MA: Brill, 251–77.

Movieweb (2007). "Zack Snyder on Directing *300*." March 5, <http://movieweb.com/zack-snyder-on-directing-300/> (last accessed January 4, 2018).

Muller, Herbert J. (1952). "The Romantic Glory of Classical Greece," in Herbert J. Muller, *The Uses of the Past*. New York: Oxford University Press, 99–143.

Mulvey, Laura (1975). "Visual Pleasure and Narrative Cinema." *Screen* 16.3: 6–18.

Murnaghan, Sheila (2011). "Classics for Cool Kids: Popular and Unpopular Versions of Antiquity for Children." *Classical World* 104.3: 339–53.

Murphy, Shaunna (2013). "Robert Kirkman and Greg Nicotero on *The Walking Dead*'s Season 4 Premiere." *Vulture*. October 14, <http://www.vulture.com/2013/10/robert-kirkman-and-greg-nicotero-the-walking-dead-premiere-interview.html> (last accessed December 26, 2017).

Murray, Augustus Taber (trans.), George E. Dimock (rev.) (1919; second edition 1995). *Homer: Odyssey, Volume I: Books 1–12*. Loeb Classical Library. Cambridge, MA: Harvard University Press.

Murray, Augustus Taber (trans.), George E. Dimock (rev.) (1995). *Homer: Odyssey, Volume II: Books 13–24*. Loeb Classical Library. Cambridge, MA: Harvard University Press.

Mynors, R. A. B. (ed.) (1990). *P. Vergili Maronis Opera*. Oxford: Oxford University Press.

Myrsiades, Kostas (2007). "The Gunfighter as Homeric Epic." *Reading Homer in the 21st Century* (= *College Literature* 34.2): 279–300.

Nagy, Gregory (1979). *The Best of the Achaeans: Concepts of the Hero in Archaic Greek Poetry*. Baltimore: Johns Hopkins University Press.

Nagy, Gregory (1996). *Homeric Questions*. Austin: University of Texas Press.

Nappa, Christopher (2005). *Reading After Actium: Vergil's Georgics, Octavian and Rome*. Ann Arbor: University of Michigan Press.

Neils, Jenifer (2005). *The Parthenon: From Antiquity to the Present*. Cambridge: Cambridge University Press.

Nelsestuen, Grant A. (2014). "Overseeing *Res Publica*: The *Rector* as *Vilicus* in *De Re Publica*." *Classical Antiquity* 33: 130–73.

Nelsestuen, Grant A. (2015). *Varro the Agronomist: Political Philosophy, Satire, and Agriculture in the Late Republic*. Columbus: Ohio State University Press.

Nelson, Stephanie A. (1998). *God and the Land: The Metaphysics of Farming in Hesiod and Vergil*. New York and Oxford: Oxford University Press.

New York Times (2012). "Arnold Schwarzenegger: By the Book." *New York Times Sunday Book Review*. December 27, <http://www.nytimes.com/2012/12/30/books/review/arnold-schwarzenegger-by-the-book.html> (last accessed January 18, 2018).

Nikoloutsos, Konstantinos (2013). "Between Family and the Nation: Gorgo in Cinema," in Konstantinos Nikoloutsos (ed.), *Ancient Greek Women in Film*. Oxford: Oxford University Press, 255–78.

Nilges, Mathias (2010). "The Aesthetics of Destruction: Contemporary US Cinema and TV Culture," in Jeff Birkenstein, Anna Froula, and Karen Randell (eds), *Reframing 9/11: Popular Culture and the "War on Terror."* New York: Continuum, 23–34.

Nisbet, Gideon (2008). *Ancient Greece in Film and Popular Culture*. Liverpool: Bristol Phoenix Press.

Nowell, Richard (2013). "Hollywood Don't Skate: US Production Trends, Industry Analysis, and the Roller Disco Movie." *New Review of Film and Television Studies* 11.1: 73–91.

Nurse, Angus (2014). "Asserting Law and Order Over the Mindless," in Dawn Keetley (ed.), *"We're All Infected": Essays on AMC's The Walking Dead and the Fate of the Human*. Jefferson, NC: McFarland, 68–79.

O'Brien, Daniel (2014). *Classical Masculinity and the Spectacular Body on Film: The Mighty Sons of Hercules*. New York: Palgrave Macmillan.

O'Hara, James J. (1990; repr. 2014). *Death and the Optimistic Prophecy in Vergil's Aeneid*. Princeton: Princeton University Press.

Ormand, Kirk (2014). "Medea's Erotic Text in *Jason and the Argonauts* (1963)," in Konstantinos P. Nikoloutsos (ed.), *Ancient Greek Women in Film*. New York: Oxford University Press, 75–94.

Osgood, Josiah (2006). *Caesar's Legacy: Civil War and the Emergence of the Roman Empire*. Cambridge: Cambridge University Press.

Ovid (1946a, second edition). *Metamorphoses, Volume I: Books 1–8*, trans. Frank Justus Miller. Loeb Classical Library. Cambridge, MA: Harvard University Press.

Ovid (1946b, second edition). *Metamorphoses, Volume II: Books 9–15*, trans. Frank Justus Miller. Loeb Classical Library. Cambridge, MA: Harvard University Press.

Panofsky, Erwin (1955). "*Et in Arcadia ego*: Poussin and the Elegiac Tradition," in Erwin Panofsky, *Meaning and the Visual Arts*. Garden City, NY: Doubleday, 295–320.

Papaioannou, Sophia (2003). "Founder, Leader, and Civilizer: Vergil's Evander and His Role in the Origins of Rome." *Mnemosyne* 56.6: 680–702.

Parks, Rita (1982). *The Western Hero in Film and Television: Mass Media Mythology*. Ann Arbor: UMI Research Press.

Parry, Adam (1963). "The Two Voices of Virgil's *Aeneid*." *Arion* 2.4: 66–80.

Patay-Horváth, András (2015). "The Contest Between Athena and Poseidon: Myth, History and Art." *Historika V*: 353–62. <http://www.ojs.unito.it/index.php/historika/article/view/1924> (last accessed December 26, 2017).

Pate, Stephen (2015). "Joan Baez Was the Pinnacle of Golden Age of Folk Says Dylan." *NJN Network*. April 8, <http://njnnetwork.com/2015/04/joan-baez-was-the-pinnacle-of-golden-age-of-folk-says-dylan/> (last accessed December 26, 2017).

Patterson, Annabel M. (1987). *Pastoral and Ideology: From Virgil to Valéry*. Berkeley: University of California Press.

Paul, Joanna (2007). "Working with Film: Theories and Methodologies," in Lorna Hardwick and Christopher Stray (eds), *A Companion to Classical Receptions*. Oxford: Blackwell, 303–14.

Paul, Joanna (2013). *Film and the Classical Epic Tradition*. Oxford: Oxford University Press.

Payne, Mark (2007). *Theocritus and the Invention of Fiction*. Cambridge: Cambridge University Press.

Pelling, Christopher (2006). "Homer and Herodotus," in M. J. Clarke, B. G. F. Currie, and R. O. A. M. Lyne (eds), *Epic Interactions*. Oxford: Oxford University Press, 75–104.

Perkell, Christine G. (1981). "On Creusa, Dido, and the Quality of Victory in Virgil's Aeneid," in Helene P. Foley (ed.), *Reflections of Women in Antiquity*. New York: Gordon and Breach, 355–77.

Perkell, Christine (1999). "Editor's Introduction," in Christine Perkell (ed.), *Reading Vergil's Aeneid: An Interpretive Guide*. Norman: University of Oklahoma Press, 3–28.

Perkell, Christine (2002). "The Golden Age and its Contradictions in the Poetry of Vergil." *Vergilius* 48: 3–39.

Pierce, Jerry (2011). "'To Do or Die Manfully': Performing Heternormativity in Recent Epic Films," in Michael G. Cornelius (ed.), *Of Muscles and Men: Essays on the Sword and Sandal Film*. Jefferson, NC: McFarland, 26–44.

Pippin, Robert B. (2010). *Hollywood Westerns and American Myth: The Importance of Howard Hawks and John Ford for Political Philosophy*. New Haven, CT: Yale University Press.

Pittas-Herschbach, Mary (1990). *Time and Space in Euripides and Racine: The Hippolytus of Euripides and Racine's Phaedra*. New York: Peter Lang.

Plato (1921). *Theaetetus. Sophist*, trans. Harold N. Fowler. Loeb Classical Library. Cambridge, MA: Harvard University Press.

Platte, Ryan C. (2015). "Scholarly Feedback: Homeric Studies and American Song Culture in Coen Brothers Films," presented at the 111th meeting of the Classical Association of the Middle West and South, Boulder, CO, March 27.

Pliny (1994). *Natural History, Volume V: Books 17–19*, trans. H. Rackham. Loeb Classical Library. Cambridge, MA: Harvard University Press.

Plutarch (1931). "The Sayings of Spartan women," in *Plutarch: Moralia, Volume III*, trans. Frank Cole Babbitt. Loeb Classical Library. Cambridge, MA: Harvard University Press, 454–69.

Plutarch (1998). *Plutarch: Greek Lives*, trans. Robin Waterfield. Oxford: Oxford University Press.

Poe, Edgar Allen (1984). "To Helen," in Edgar Allen Poe, *Poetry and Tales*. Library of America. New York: Literary Classics of the United States, 62.

Pollitt, J. J. (1972). "The World Under Control: The Classical Moment, c. 450–430 B.C.," in J. J. Pollitt, *Art and Experience in Classical Greece*. Cambridge: Cambridge University Press, 64–97.

Pomeroy, Sarah B. (1975). *Goddesses, Whores, Wives, and Slaves: Women in Classical Antiquity*. New York: Schocken Books.

Postgate, J. P. (trans.) (1962). *Catullus, Tibullus, and Pervigilium Veneris*. Loeb Classical Library. Cambridge, MA: Harvard University Press.

Pressfield, Steven (1998). *Gates of Fire*. New York: Doubleday.

Prime, Rebecca (2007). "Cloaked in Compromise: Jules Dassin's 'Naked' City," in Frank Krutnik, Steve Neale, Brian Neve, and Peter Stanfield (eds), *"Un-American" Hollywood: Politics and Film in the Blacklist Era*. New Brunswick, NJ: Rutgers University Press, 142–51.

Prince, Stephen (2009). *Firestorm: American Film in the Age of Terrorism*. New York: Columbia University Press.

Prince, Stephen (2012). *Digital Visual Effects Cinema: The Seduction of Reality*. New Brunswick, NJ: Rutgers University Press.

Procopius (1914). *History of the Wars, Volume I: Books 1–2 (Persian Wars)*, trans. H. B. Dewing. Loeb Classical Library. Cambridge, MA: Harvard University Press.

Pustz, Matthew (ed.) (2012). *Comic Books and American Cultural History: An Anthology*. New York: Bloomsbury Academic.

Putnam, Hilary (1981). *Reason, Truth and History*. Cambridge: Cambridge University Press.

Putnam, Michael C. J. (1966). *The Poetry of the Aeneid*. Cambridge, MA: Harvard University Press.

Putnam, Michael C. J. (1999). "*Aeneid* 12: Unity in Closure," in Christine Perkell (ed.), *Reading Vergil's Aeneid: An Interpretive Guide*. Norman: University of Oklahoma Press, 210–30.

Pye, Douglas (1996). "Genre and History: *Fort Apache* and *The Man Who Shot Liberty Valance*," in Ian Cameron and Douglas Pye (eds), *The Book of Westerns*. New York: Continuum, 111–22.

Quint, David (1993). *Epic and Empire: Politics and Generic Form from Vergil to Milton*. Princeton: Princeton University Press.

Quintus Smyrnaeus (1962). *The Fall of Troy*, trans. A. S. Way. Loeb Classical Library. Cambridge, MA: Harvard University Press.

Rackham, H. (trans.) (1994). *Pliny: Natural History, Volume V: Books 17–19*. Loeb Classical Library. Cambridge, MA: Harvard University Press.

Rammel, Hal (1990). *Nowhere in America: The Big Rock Candy Mountain and Other Comic Utopias*. Urbana and Chicago: University of Illinois Press.

Rath, Arun (host) (2014). "The Secret Behind Romero's Scary Zombies: 'I Made Them the Neighbors'." *NPR Weekend Edition*. July 20, <http://www.npr.org/2014/07/20/332644099> (last accessed December 26, 2017).

Rawson, Elizabeth (1969). *The Spartan Tradition in European Thought*. Oxford: Oxford University Press.

Rea, Jennifer A. (2008). *Legendary Rome: Myths, Monuments and Memory on the Palatine and Capitoline*. London: Duckworth Academic.

Reay, Brendan (2005). "Agriculture, Writing, and Cato's Aristocratic Self-Fashioning." *Classical Antiquity* 24: 331–61.

Reckford, Kenneth (1958). "Some Appearances of the Golden Age." *The Classical Journal* 54.2: 79–87.

Reeder, Roberta (1980). "The Mythic Mode: Archetypal Criticism and *Red River*." *Ciné-tracts* 3.2: 58–67.

Reid, Craig (1996). "Hercules and Xena: The Legends Continue . . ." *Sci-Fi Channel Magazine*, April: 54–8; 70.

Reid, Gary B. (2015). *The Music of the Stanley Brothers*. Urbana, Chicago, and Springfield: University of Illinois Press.

Reinhold, Meyer (1980). "Augustus' Conception of Himself." *Thought* 55: 36–50.

Renault, Mary (1964). *The Lion in the Gateway*. New York: Harper & Row.

Rich, Ruby (2004). "After the Fall: Cinema Studies Post-9/11." *Cinema Journal* 43: 109–15.

Richards, Dean (2007). "Film Gives Stars 'Rippling Abs'." *Chicago Tribune*. March 9, <http://articles.chicagotribune.com/2007-03-09/news/0703100025_1_digital-effects-special-effects-sin-city> (last accessed December 26, 2017).

Richardson, J. S. (2012). *Augustan Rome 44 BC to AD 14: The Restoration of Republic and the Establishment of Empire*. Edinburgh: Edinburgh University Press.

Ridley, Jim (2006). "Brothers in Arms," in William Rodney Allen (ed.), *The Coen Brother Interviews*. Jackson: University Press of Mississippi, 133–6.

Riefenstahl, Leni (1993). *Leni Riefentstahl: A Memoir*. New York: St. Martin's Press.

Riggsby, Andrew (2006). *Caesar in Gaul and Rome: War in Words*. Austin: University of Texas Press.

Rives, James (trans.) (2010). *Tacitus: Agricola*. New York: Penguin.

Roberts, Jennifer T. (2011). *Herodotus: A Very Short Introduction*. Oxford: Oxford University Press.

Rogers, Elizabeth, Jeffrey W. Smith, and Chris Murray (eds) (2016). *The Golden Age: Nostalgia in Word and Image*. Newcastle upon Tyne: Cambridge Scholars.

Romney, Jonathan (2006). "Double Vision," in William Rodney Allen (ed.), *The Coen Brother Interviews*. Jackson: University Press of Mississippi, 127–32.

Rose, Peter W. (2004). "The Politics of *Gladiator*," in Martin M. Winkler (ed.), *Gladiator: Film and History*. Malden, MA: Blackwell, 150–72.

Rosenberg, Neil (1985). *Bluegrass: A History*. Urbana: University of Illinois Press.

Rosenstone, Robert (2006). *History on Film/Film on History*. Harlow: Pearson.

Ross, Dalton (2013). "*Walking Dead* Boss on Rick vs. Carol." *Entertainment Weekly*. November 8, <http://www.ew.com/article/2013/11/08/walking-dead-scott-gimple-rick-carol> (last accessed December 26, 2017).

Rouse, W. H. D. (trans.) (1924). *Lucretius: On the Nature of Things*. Loeb Classical Library. Cambridge, MA: Harvard University Press.

Rubino, Carl A. (2014). "Wounds That Will Not Heal: Heroism and Innocence in *Shane* and the *Iliad*." *Dialogue: The Interdisciplinary Journal of Popular Culture and Pedagogy* 1.1. <http://journaldialogue.org/issues/issue-1/wounds-that-will-not-heal-heroism-and-innocence-in-shane-and-the-iliad/> (last accessed December 26, 2017).

Ruffell, Ian (2002). "The World Turned Upside Down: Utopia and Utopianism in the Fragments of Old Comedy," in David Harvey and John Wilkins (eds), *The Rivals of Aristophanes: Studies in Athenian Old Comedy*. London: Duckworth, and Swansea: Classical Press of Wales, 473–506.

Ruiz, Teofilo F. (2011). *The Terror of History: On the Uncertainties of Life in Western Civilization*. Princeton: Princeton University Press.

Rushing, Robert A. (2016). *Descended from Hercules: Biopolitics and the Muscled Male Body on Screen*. Bloomington: Indiana University Press.

Rushton, Richard (2001). "Narrative and Spectacle in *Gladiator*." *Cineaction* 51: 35–43.

Russo, Joseph (1988). *A Commentary on Homer's Odyssey III*. Oxford: Oxford University Press.

Rusten, Jeffrey S. (ed.) (1989). *Thucydides: The Peloponnesian War Book II*. Cambridge: Cambridge University Press.

Safran, Meredith E. and Monica S. Cyrino. (2015). "Introduction: Cinemyths," in Monica S. Cyrino and Meredith E. Safran (eds), *Classical Myth on Screen*. New York, NY: Palgrave Macmillan, 1–13.

Salzman-Mitchell, Patricia and Jean Alvares (2017). *Classical Myth and Film in the New Millennium*. New York: Oxford University Press.

Sammons, Loren J., II (ed.) (2007). *The Cambridge Companion to Athens in the Age of Pericles*. Cambridge: Cambridge University Press.
Sanders, Julie (2006). *Adaptation and Appropriation*. New York: Routledge.
Sargent (2010). *Utopianism: A Very Short Introduction*. Oxford: Oxford University Press.
Schaefer, Jack (1984 [1949]). *Shane: The Critical Edition*, ed. James C. Work. Lincoln: University of Nebraska Press.
Schein, Seth L. (2008). "'Our Debt to Greece and Rome': Canon, Class and Ideology," in Lorna Hardwick and Christopher Stray (eds), *A Companion to Classical Receptions*. Hoboken, NJ: Wiley, 75–85.
Schenk, Irmbert (2006). "The Cinematic Support to National(istic) Mythology: The Italian Peplum 1910–1930," in Natascha Gentz and Stefan Kramer (eds), *Globalization, Cultural Identities, and Media Representations*. Albany: State University of New York Press, 153–68.
Scherer, Burkhard (2006). *Mythos, Katalog, und Prophezeiung: Studien zu den Argonautika des Apollonios Rhodios*. Stuttgart: Franz Steiner.
Schilling, William R. (ed.) (2002). *Nontraditional Warfare: Twenty-First Century Threats and Responses*. Washington, DC: Potomac Books.
Schopp, Andrew and Matthew B. Hill (eds) (2009). *The War on Terror and American Popular Culture*. Madison: Farleigh Dickinson University Press.
Schrank, Sarah (2009). *Art and the City: Civic Imagination and Cultural Authority in Los Angeles*. Philadelphia: University of Pennsylvania Press.
Sciretta, Peter (2015). "Superhero Movie Release Dates: A Complete Look at the Future of Comic Book Movies." *Slash Film*. February 11, <http://www.slashfilm.com/superhero-movie-release-dates> (last accessed December 26, 2017).
Scott, A. O. (2007). "Battle of the Manly Men: Blood Bath with a Message." *New York Times Movie Review*. March 9, <http://query.nytimes.com/gst/fullpage.html?res=9400E2DA1231F93AA35750C0A9619C8B63> (last accessed December 26, 2017).
Scott, A. O. (2010). "Blockbuster 4: The Same, but Worse." *New York Times*. June 6, <http://www.nytimes.com/2010/06/13/movies/13scott.html> (last accessed December 26, 2017).
Segal, Charles (1981). *Poetry and Myth in Ancient Pastoral*. Princeton: Princeton University Press.
Segal, Charles (1989). *Orpheus: The Myth of the Poet*. Baltimore: Johns Hopkins University Press.
Severy, Beth (2003). *Augustus and the Family at the Birth of the Roman Empire*. New York: Routledge.
Shalev, Eran (2009). *Rome Reborn on Western Shores: Historical Imagination and the Creation of the American Republic*. Charlottesville and London: University of Virginia Press.
Shapiro, Peter (2005). *Turn the Beat Around: The Secret History of Disco*. New York: Faber & Faber.

Shapiro, Susan O. (2014). "Pasolini's *Medea*: A Twentieth-Century Tragedy," in Konstantinos P. Nikoloutsos (ed.), *Ancient Greek Women in Film*. New York: Oxford University Press, 95–116.

Shelley, Peter (2011). *Jules Dassin: The Life and Films*. Jefferson, NC: McFarland.

Sherrard, Philip (1978). *The Wound of Greece: Studies in Neo-Hellenism*. London: Rex Collings.

Shields, John C. (2001). *The American Aeneas*. Knoxville: University of Tennessee Press.

Shotter, David (2008). *Nero Caesar Augustus: Emperor of Rome*. London: Pearson Longman.

Sijpestijn, P. J. (1996). "Die Legio Nona Hispana in Nimwegen." *ZPE* 111: 281–2.

Skoie, Mathilde and Sonia Bjørnstad Velázquez (eds) (2006). *Pastoral and the Humanities: Arcadia Re-inscribed*. Exeter: Bristol Phoenix Press.

Smith, Mayne L. (1965). "An Introduction to Bluegrass." *The Journal of American Folklore* 78: 245–56.

Smith, R. Alden (2003). "Dido as Vatic Diva: A New Voice for the Persona of the Lost Lover." *Classical Journal* 98.4: 433–6.

Smith, Riggs Alden (2005). *The Primacy of Vision in Vergil's Aeneid*. Austin: University of Texas Press.

Snyder, Zack (2007a). Interview with Jonah Weiland. "*300* Post Game: One-on-One with Zack Snyder." *Comic Book Resources*. March 14, <http://www.comicbookresources.com/?page=article&id=9647> (last accessed December 26, 2017).

Snyder, Zack (2007b). Audio Commentary. *300* DVD. Warner Bros/Legendary Pictures.

Solmsen, Friedrich (ed.) (1970). *Hesiodi Opera*. Oxford: Clarendon Press.

Solomon, Jon (1978; rev. 2001). *The Ancient World in the Cinema*. New Haven, CT: Yale University Press.

Solomon, Jon (2004). "*Gladiator* from Screenplay to Screen," in Martin M. Winkler (ed.), *Gladiator: Film and History*. Malden, MA: Blackwell, 1–15.

Sophocles (1950). *Ajax. Electra. Oedipus Tyrannus*, trans. Hugh Lloyd-Jones. Loeb Classical Library. Cambridge, MA: Harvard University Press.

Spence, Sarah (2002). "*Pietas* and *Furor*: Motivational Forces in the Aeneid," in William S. Anderson and Lorina N. Quartarone (eds), *Approaches to the Teaching of Vergil's Aeneid*. New York: MLA Press, 46–52.

Stanford, W. B. (1952). "The Homeric Etymology of the Name Odysseus." *Classical Philology* 4: 209–13.

Stanley, Ralph (2009). "Dr. Ralph Stanley: 'Man of Constant Sorrow'." Interview with Diane Rehm. *The Diane Rehm Show*, National Public Radio. October 14, <https://dianerehm.org/shows/2009-10-14/dr-ralph-stanley-man-constant-sorrow-gotham-books> (last accessed December 26, 2017).

Steiner, George (1961). *The Death of Tragedy*. London: Faber & Faber.

Stevens, Dana (2007). "A Movie Only a Spartan Could Love: The Battle Epic *300*." *Slate*. March 8, <http://www.slate.com/articles/arts/movies/2007/03/a_movie_only_a_spartan_could_love.html> (last accessed December 26, 2017).

Strain, Ellen (1997). "Snapshots of Greece: *Never on Sunday* and the East/West Politics of the 'Vacation Film'." *Journal of Film and Video* 49.1/2: 80–93.

Strong, Anise K. (2008). "Vice is Nice: Rome and Deviant Sexuality," in Monica S. Cyrino (ed.), *Rome, Season One: History Makes Television*. Oxford: Blackwell, 219–31.

Strong, Anise K. (2014). "A Christian Concubine in Commodus' Court." *EuGeStA* 4.

Suetonius (n.d.). *De Vitis Caesarum*. <http://www.thelatinlibrary.com/suet.html> (last accessed December 26, 2017).

Sutcliff, Rosemary (1954). *The Eagle of the Ninth*. Oxford: Oxford University Press.

Swift, Jonathan (2005). *Gulliver's Travels*, ed. Claude Rawson and Ian Higgins. Oxford: Oxford University Press.

Tacitus (2010). *Agricola*, trans. James Rives. New York: Penguin.

Tacitus (n.d.). *Annales*. <http://www.thelatinlibrary.com/tac.html> (last accessed December 26, 2017).

Taft, Michael (2006). *The Blues Lyric Formula*. New York: Routledge.

Tandy, David W. and Walter C. Neale (1996). *Hesiod's Works and Days: A Translation and Commentary for the Social Sciences*. Berkeley: University of California Press.

Taplin, Oliver (1990). "The Closing of Democracy," in Oliver Taplin, *Greek Fire*. New York: Atheneum, 194–215.

Tharoor, Ishaan (2014). "Zack Snyder and the West Should Stop Killing Ancient Persians." *Time*. March 10, <http://time.com/17578/300-greece-persians-xerxes/> (last accessed December 26, 2017).

Thibodeau, Philip (2011). *Playing the Farmer: Representation of Rural Life in Vergil's Georgics*. Berkeley: University of California Press.

Thomas, Rosalind (2000). *Herodotus in Context: Ethnography, Science, and the Art of Persuasion*. Cambridge: Cambridge University Press.

Thompson, Kristin (1999). *Storytelling in the New Hollywood: Understanding Classical Narrative Technique*. Cambridge, MA: Harvard University Press.

Thucydides (1942, second edition). *Thucydides: Historiae, Volume I (Books I–IV)*, ed. H. Stuart Jones and J. E. Powell. Oxford: Clarendon Press.

Thucydides (1989). *Thucydides: The Peloponnesian War Book II*, ed. Jeffrey S. Rusten. Cambridge: Cambridge University Press.

Thucydides (1998). *Thucydides: The Peloponnesian War*, trans. Steven Lattimore. Indianapolis: Hackett.

Tibullus (1962). *Catullus, Tibullus, and Pervigilium Veneris*, trans. J. P. Postgate. Loeb Classical Library. Cambridge, MA: Harvard University Press.

Tobin, Ronald W. (1971). *Racine and Seneca*. Chapel Hill: University of North Carolina Press.

Toffoletti, Kim and Victoria Grace (2010). "Terminal Indifference: The Hollywood War Film Post-September 11." *Film-Philosophy* 14.2: 62–83.

Toher, Mark (2015). "Characterizing Augustus," in Rhiannon Ash, Judith Mossman, and Francis B. Titchener (eds), *Fame and Infamy: Essays for Christopher Pelling on Characterization in Greek and Roman Biography and Historiography*. Oxford: Oxford University Press, 225–37.

Tomasso, Vincent (2013). "Gorgo at the Limits of Liberation in Zack Snyder's *300* (2007)," in Monica S. Cyrino (ed.), *Screening Love and Sex in the Ancient World*. New York: Palgrave Macmillan, 113–26.

Tompkins, Jane (1992). *West of Everything: The Inner Life of Westerns*. New York: Oxford University Press.

Toscano, Margaret M. (2009). "Homer Meets the Coen Brothers: Memory as Artistic Pastiche in *O Brother, Where Art Thou?*" *Film and History* 39.2: 49–62.

Trollope, Anthony (1875). *The Way We Live Now*. London: Chapman & Hall.

Trundle, Matthew (2013). "The Glorious Defeat," in Christopher Matthew and Matthew Trundle (eds), *Beyond the Gates of Fire: New Perspectives on the Battle of Thermopylae*. Barnsley: Pen & Sword Military, 150–63.

Tsitsopoulou, Vassiliki (2000). "Greekness, Gender Stereotypes, and the Hollywood Musical in Jules Dassin's *Never on Sunday*." *Journal of Modern Greek Studies* 18.1: 79–93.

Turner, Susanne (2008). "'Only Spartan Women Give Birth to Real Men': Zack Snyder's *300* and the Male Nude," in Dunstan Lowe and Kim Shahabudin (eds), *Classics for All: Reworking Antiquity in Mass Culture*. Cambridge: Cambridge University Press, 128–49.

TVTropes.com (n.d.) "Arcadia." <http://tvtropes.org/pmwiki/pmwiki.php/Main/Arcadia> (last accessed January 4, 2018).

Tziovas, Dimitris (ed.) (2014). *Re-imagining the Past: Antiquity and Modern Greek Culture*. Oxford: Oxford University Press.

United States Department of the Army (2010). *Special Forces Unconventional Warfare Training Manual*. Training Circular No. 18–01. Fort Bragg, NC, and Washington, DC: Department of the Army.

Van Noorden, Helen (2015). *Playing Hesiod: The "Myth of the Races" in Classical Antiquity*. Cambridge: Cambridge University Press.

Vergil (1990). *P. Vergili Maronis Opera*, ed. R. A. B. Mynors. Oxford: Oxford University Press.

Vernant, Jean-Pierre (1996). "The Myth of Prometheus in Hesiod," in Jean-Pierre Vernant, *Myth and Society in Ancient Greece*, trans. Janet Lloyd. New York: Zone, 183–201.

Vernant, Jean-Pierre (2006). "Myth Structures," in Jean-Pierre Vernant, *Myth and Thought Among the Greeks*, trans. Janet Lloyd with Jeff Fort. New York: Zone, 25–113.

Vidal-Naquet, Pierre (1978). "Plato's Myth of the Statesman, the Ambiguities of the Golden Age and of History." *Journal of Hellenic Studies* 98: 132–41.

Virgil (1986; rev. 1999). *Eclogues. Georgics. Aeneid: Books 1–6*, trans. H. Rushton Fairclough (rev. G. P. Goold). Loeb Classical Library. Cambridge, MA: Harvard University Press.

Virgil (2000). *Aeneid: Books 7–12*, trans. H. Rushton Fairclough (rev. G. P. Goold). Loeb Classical Library. Cambridge, MA: Harvard University Press.

Volk, Katharina (ed.) (2008). *Vergil's Eclogues*. Oxford: Oxford University Press.

Vrettos, Theodore (1997). *The Elgin Affair: The Abduction of Antiquity's Greatest Treasures and the Passions It Aroused*. New York: Arcade.

Wallace-Hadrill, Andrew (1982). "The Golden Age and Sin in Augustan Ideology." *Past and Present* 95: 19–36.

Walters, Jonathan (1997). "Invading the Roman Body: Manliness and Impenetrability in Roman Thought," in Judith P. Hallett and Marilyn B. Skinner (eds), *Roman Sexualities*. Princeton: Princeton University Press, 29–44.

Wandtke, Terrence R. (2012). *The Meaning of Superhero Comic Books*. Jefferson, NC: McFarland.

Ward, Allen M. (2004). "*Gladiator* in Historical Perspective," in Martin M. Winkler (ed.), *Gladiator: Film and History*. Malden, MA: Blackwell, 31–44.

Ward, Allen M. (2009). "History, Ancient and Modern, in *The Fall of the Roman Empire*," in Martin M. Winkler (ed.), *The Fall of the Roman Empire: Film and History*, 51–88.

Warfield, Nancy (1975). "*The Man Who Shot Liberty Valance*: A Study of John Ford's Film." *The Little Film Gazette of N. D. W.* 6.1.

Warshow, Robert (1954). "Movie Chronicle: *The Westerner*." *Partisan Review* 21.2: 190–203.

Waterfield, Robin (trans.) (1998). *Plutarch: Greek Lives*. Oxford: Oxford University Press.

Watt, Roderick H. (1985). "'Wanderer, Kommst Du nach Sparta': History Through Propaganda into Literary Commonplace." *Modern Language Review* 80.4: 871–83.

Way, A. S. (trans.) (1962). *Quintus Smyrnaeus: The Fall of Troy*. Loeb Classical Library. Cambridge, MA: Harvard University Press.

Webb, Timothy (1993). "Romantic Hellenism," in Stuart Curran (ed.), *The Cambridge Companion to British Romanticism*. Cambridge: Cambridge University Press, 148–76.

Weems, Mason (1927). *A History of the Life and Death, Virtues and Exploits, of General George Washington*. New York: Grosset & Dunlap.

Weinlich, Barbara P. (2005). "Odyssey, Where Art Thou?: Myth and Mythmaking in the Twenty-First Century." *Classical and Modern Literature* 25.2: 89–108.

Weisbrot, Robert (2004). *Hercules: The Legendary Journeys. An Insider's Guide to the Continuing Adventures*. Lanham, MD: Taylor Trade.

Weiss, M. Jerry (1961). *Reading in the Secondary Schools*. New York: Odyssey Press.

West, M. L. (1997). *The East Face of Helicon*. Oxford: Clarendon Press, 312–19.

Wifstrand Schiebe, Marianne (1986). "The Saturn of the *Aeneid*: Tradition or Innovation?" *Vergilius* 32: 43–60.

Williams, Raymond (1966). *Modern Tragedy*. London: Chatto & Windus.

Wills, Garry (1984). *Cincinnatus: George Washington and the Enlightenment*. Garden City, NY: Doubleday.

Wilson-Okamura, David (trans.) (1996, rev. 2014). *Aelius Donatus: Life of Virgil*. <virgil.org/vitae> (last accessed December 10, 2017).

Winkler, Martin M. (1985). "Classical Mythology and the Western Film." *Comparative Literature Studies* 22.4: 516–40.

Winkler, Martin M. (1995). "Cinema and the Fall of Rome." *Transactions of the American Philological Association* 125: 135–54.

Winkler, Martin M. (1996). "Homeric *Kleos* in Western Film." *Syllecta Classica* 7: 43–54.

Winkler, Martin M. (2001a). "Tragic Features in John Ford's *The Searchers*," in Martin M. Winkler (ed.), *Classical Myth and Culture in the Cinema*. Oxford: Oxford University Press, 118–47.

Winkler, Martin M. (2001b). "The Roman Empire in American Cinema after 1945," in Sandra R. Joshel, Martha Malamud, and Donald T. McGuire, Jr. (eds), *Imperial Projections: Ancient Rome in Modern Popular Culture*. Baltimore: Johns Hopkins University Press, 50–76.

Winkler, Martin M. (2004a). "Homer's *Iliad* and John Ford's *The Searchers*," in Arthur M. Eckstein and Peter Lehman (eds), *The Searchers: Essays and Reflections on John Ford's Classic Western*. Detroit: Wayne State University Press, 145–70.

Winkler, Martin M. (2004b). "*Gladiator* and the Colosseum: Ambiguities of Spectacle," in Martin M. Winkler (ed.), *Gladiator: Film and History*. Malden, MA: Blackwell, 87–110.

Winkler, Martin M. (2005). "Neo-Mythologism: Apollo and the Muses on the Screen." *International Journal of the Classical Tradition* 11.3: 383–423.

Winkler, Martin M. (2008). "*Arma Virosque Canit*: John Ford, America's Virgil." The Classical Association of the Middle West and South annual meeting, Tucson, AZ, April.

Winkler, Martin M. (2009a). *Cinema and Classical Texts: Apollo's New Light*. Cambridge: Cambridge University Press.

Winkler, Martin M. (ed.) (2009b). *The Fall of the Roman Empire: Film and History*. Hoboken, NJ: Wiley.

Winkler, Martin M. (2015). "The Course of Empire in Virgil and John Ford." Film & History conference, Madison, WI, November.

Winterer, Caroline (2004). *The Culture of Classicism*. Baltimore: Johns Hopkins University Press.

Wiseman, T. P. (1974). "Legendary Genealogies in Late-Republican Rome." *Greece & Rome* 21.2: 153–64.

Woll, Allen L. (1983). *The Hollywood Musical Goes to War*. Chicago: Nelson-Hall.

Woodford, Susan (2003). *Images of Myths in Classical Antiquity*. Cambridge: Cambridge University Press.

Wright, Bradford W. (2003). *Comic Book Nation: The Transformation of Youth Culture in America*. Baltimore: Johns Hopkins University Press.

Wyke, Maria (1997; repr. 2013). *Projecting the Past: Ancient Rome, Cinema, and History*. Abingdon: Routledge.

Wyke, Maria (1999). "Screening Ancient Rome in the New Italy," in Catherine Edwards (ed.), *Roman Presences: Receptions of Rome in European Culture, 1789–1945*. Cambridge: Cambridge University Press.

Xanadu Preservation Society (n.d.). "The Xanadu Story." <http://www.donosdump.com/TheXanaduStory/index.html> (last accessed December 26, 2017).

Zanker, Andreas T. (2010). "Late Horatian Lyric and the Vergilian Golden Age." *American Journal of Philology* 131.3: 495–516.

Zanker, Andreas T. (2013). "Decline and *Parainesis* in Hesiod's Race of Iron." *Rheinisches Museum für Philologie* 1.56: 1–19.

Zanker, Andreas T. (2017). "The Golden Age," in Vanda Zajko and Helena Hoyle (eds), *A Handbook to the Reception of Classical Mythology*. Hoboken, NJ: Wiley.

Zanker, Paul (1988). *The Power of Images in the Age of Augustus*, trans. Alan Shapiro. Ann Arbor: University of Michigan Press.

Zeiler, Xenia (2013). "'Universal's Religious Bigotry Against Hinduism': Gender Norms and Hindu Authority in the Global Media Debate on Representing the Hindu God Krishna in *Xena: Warrior Princess*," in Almut-Barbara Renger and Jon Solomon (eds), *Ancient Worlds in Film and Television: Gender and Politics*. Leiden: Brill, 229–45.

Zeitlin, Froma I. (1996). "Signifying Difference: The Case of Hesiod's Pandora," in Froma I. Zeitlin, *Playing the Other: Gender and Society in Classical Greek Literature*. Chicago: University of Chicago Press, 53–86.

Zeitlin, Froma I. (1999). "Aristophanes: The Performance of Utopia in the *Ecclesiazousae*," in Simon Goldhill and Robin Osborne (eds), *Performance Culture and Athenian Democracy*. Cambridge: Cambridge University Press, 167–97.

Index

Page numbers in *italics* refer to illustrations.

CPSIA information can be obtained
at www.ICGtesting.com
Printed in the USA
JSHW050740090920
7725JS00001B/16